Wet Techniques

THE CUMULATIVE CLOTH

A Guide to Fabric Color, Pattern, Construction, and Embellishment

Susan Brandeis

SCHIFFER CRAFT
4880 Lower Valley Road • Atglen, PA 19310

Other Schiffer Craft Books by the Author:

The Intentional Thread: A Guide to Drawing, Gesture, and Color in Stitch, ISBN 978-0-7643-5743-5

Other Schiffer Craft Books on Related Subjects:

Threads Around the World: From Arabian Weaving to Batik in Zimbabwe, Deb Brandon, ISBN 978-0-7643-5650-6

Organic Embroidery, Meredith Woolnough, 978-0-7643-5613-1

The Studio Formulas Set for The Art and Science of Natural Dyes: 84 Cards with Recipes and Color Swatches, Joy Boutrup and Catharine Ellis, ISBN 978-0-7643-6618-5

Drawings and diagrams by Susan Brandeis.

Photographs by Marc Brandeis: 01-01, 01-05, 01-13, 01-14, 01-25, 01-33, 01-34, 04-01, 04-24, 04-27, 04-28, 04-30, 04-31, 04-32, 04-37, 04-39, 05-01, 05-56, 06-02, 06-09, 06-12, author portrait.

Photographs by Susan Brandeis: 01-06, 01-07, 01-41, 02-02, 03-10, 04-05, 04-42, 04-43, 04-44, 04-45, 05-02, 05-12, 05-13, 05-14, 05-15, 05-16, 05-17, 05-18, 05-19, 05-20, 05-21, 05-22, 05-23, 05-24, 05-25, 05-26, 05-27, 05-28, 05-30, 05-31, 05-33, 05-34, 05-51, A-01.

Library of Congress Control Number: 2023931255

Cover and interior design by Ashley Millhouse
Type set in Colonna/Times New Roman

ISBN: 978-0-7643-6690-1

Printed in China

Published by Schiffer Craft
An imprint of Schiffer Publishing, Ltd.
4880 Lower Valley Road
Atglen, PA 19310
Phone: (610) 593-1777; Fax: (610) 593-2002
Email: Info@schifferbooks.com
Web: www.schifferbooks.com

FSC
www.fsc.org
MIX
Paper | Supporting responsible forestry
FSC® C104723

for Marc,
again,
of course

CONTENTS

ACKNOWLEDGMENTS

As with *The Intentional Thread*, the development of this book drew nourishment from the help of many kind and talented people, and therefore my debts are also many.

I hadn't intended to write a new book so soon after the first, or perhaps at all. This book exists because my supportive husband, Marc Brandeis, repeatedly said to me that "you wrote a book about expressive stitchery, but you also have decades of experience with surface design, a wealth of knowledge that could be helpful to other people—and there doesn't seem to be any other book quite like the one you've imagined for so long."

Without his enthusiasm, brainstorming, photographic assistance, and management of our domestic life, I wouldn't have undertaken, or successfully completed, this enormous and challenging project. His journalism and paralegal experiences also make him a vigilant editor, and he greatly improved the content, organization, and writing style of the final manuscript.

Perhaps the single most difficult task in the preparation of this book was the creation of photographs that not only depict the textiles clearly and beautifully but also fully convey their tactile qualities. I again owe enormous thanks to Sally Van Gorder, who was also the main photographer for *The Intentional Thread*, for accomplishing this with finesse, dedication, imagination, enthusiasm, hard work, and good humor.

During the process of writing, I highly valued the commentary from my three superb readers: Mary Beth Yates (practicing stitcher and textile artist), Stephanie Witchger (painter, stitcher, book artist, art librarian), and Christine Zoller (my occasional teaching collaborator, and professor emerita of textile art at East Carolina University). These generous women provided continuous and insightful chapter-by-chapter reviews and superb advice over the two years I spent working on the manuscript. I am deeply thankful for their time, perception, suggestions, and belief in the desirability of this book.

I received the gift of professional encouragement from a core group of members of the Southeast Fibers Educators Association, including, in particular, Edwina Bringle, Katherine Diuguid, Gabrielle Duggan, Catharine Ellis, Susan Iverson, Jeana Klein, Kate Kretz, Precious Lovell, and Pat Mink—several of whom shared their professional expertise on various details of the text—and Georgia Springer, retired instructor of color and surface design at Meredith College in Raleigh, who generously read through the chapters on dyes and pigments.

The seeds from which this book sprouted were collected in the black-and-white, spiral-bound studio guides I developed during my years in the classroom, because I could not find existing textbooks that addressed the full range of what I wanted to teach. The "real time" response to those guides, across the decades, by engaged and dedicated students, both at North Carolina State University's College of Design and in many summer craft school workshops, sharpened and clarified the book manuscript eventually born.

I was once again fortunate to receive the support and guidance of a fine publishing team at Schiffer: an enthusiastic editor, Sandra Korinchak, who got me moving on this idea and provided a calm voice, good commonsense advice, and tactfully phrased suggestions; Pete Schiffer, for responding with enthusiasm to this second proposal; and the talented design staff and marketing staff, who guided the book over many hurdles.

Finally, I am forever indebted to three people who live on in beloved memory: My mother, Ellen Dowman, and grandmother Fern Rhodes, who treasured textiles of all kinds, guided my first attempts, and sparked a passion that has enriched and gladdened my life. And my father, Harry Dowman, who first taught me the use of basic shop tools and the value of good craftsmanship, personally made my first loom-warping board (of lovely Indiana cherry wood), and believed there need be no limits on his daughter's possibilities in life.

PREFACE

When I first began teaching surface design 40 years ago, I had to compress a world of technical knowledge into a one-semester class. I needed a broad but detailed and reliable but easily understood textbook but couldn't find anything in print that covered everything I wanted to include. Thus, I began to gather, test, and sequence my own collection of technical instructions from the wide range of books, booklets, articles, and journals then available, as supplements to my own hands-on studio experiences. I collected my resources in three-ring binders, a format that freed me to insert, discard, describe, distill, reorganize, rewrite, and update repeatedly. From these, I condensed and synthesized technical information into a "studio manual" to support students' work outside the classroom.

The first version was a simple black-and-white photocopied and spiral-bound volume. Students' enthusiastic responses to the manual encouraged me to update, retest, and share new information with each new semester or workshop teaching opportunity. Therefore, many "editions" of that manual are still out there in the world, and students from decades ago tell me that they still use it.

When I retired from university teaching and simultaneously reduced my workshop engagements, former students began nudging me, gently but persistently, to "turn those manuals into a real book" that would include color photos of my samples, discussions and tidbits from the slide presentations, working tips, design approaches, and project challenges—in effect re-creating the experience of classroom or workshop learning. Since I myself also continued to lament the absence of a good, complete, and inclusive text on surface design, addressing the range of wet and dry techniques and usable by fiber craftspeople at many levels of experience, I parked the idea in the back of my mind for "someday."

Eventually, "someday" became "now."

As my first book, *The Intentional Thread*, set out to share what I had learned and taught over many years about the expressive use of stitch, so this new two-part work now shares what I have learned and taught about the building of rich fabric surfaces through color, pattern, constructed layers, and embellishment.

Welcome.

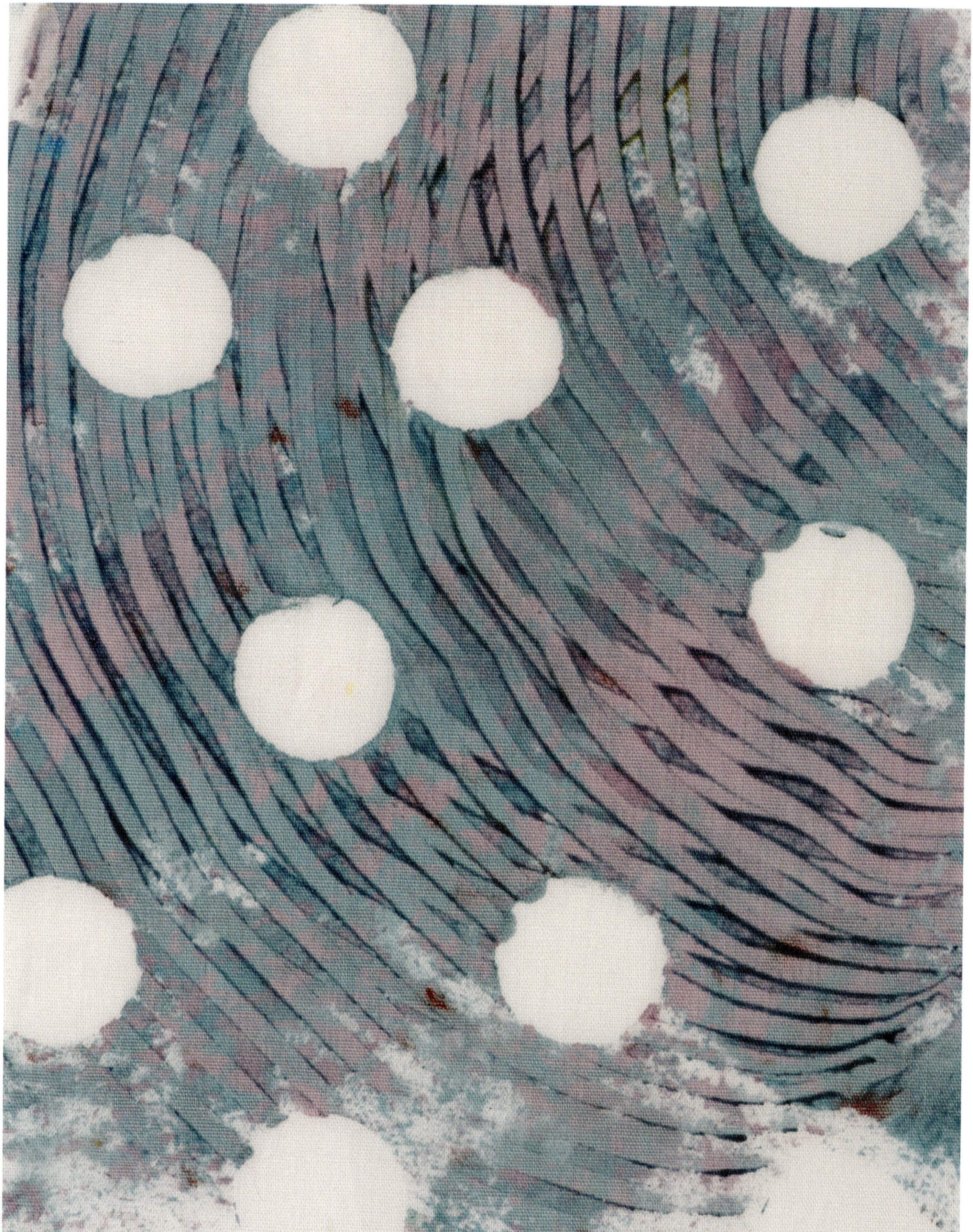

ABOUT THIS BOOK

You hold in your hands a reference library and guided tour of the major wet surface design techniques for applying color, texture, pattern, and image to cloth, and for building rich textile surfaces and forms. These pages combine technical and design information ("how to"), inspiration for expressive application ("why to"), and encouragement for invention and experimentation in your own projects ("What if?").

Those words—invention, experimentation, building, and expression—are the keys to the book's purpose. Whatever your particular interest, you can "say" almost anything and depict almost anything with cloth.

This book is intended to offer valuable information to anyone from the enthusiastic beginner to the accomplished surface designer, from the person working quietly at home, to a group of friends in an artists' circle, to students in a workshop or college classroom.

As a longtime teacher, I'll be doing a lot of friendly explaining along the way. I'll be "talking" to you through the text, as if I was standing next to you in a workshop. My goal as a teacher is always to help individual learners find *their* way, regardless of whether it would be *my* way. While the book provides many examples drawn from my own work and classroom demonstrations, they're not meant to be copied but, rather, to spark your brainstorming, and to help and encourage you toward finding your own approach to creating.

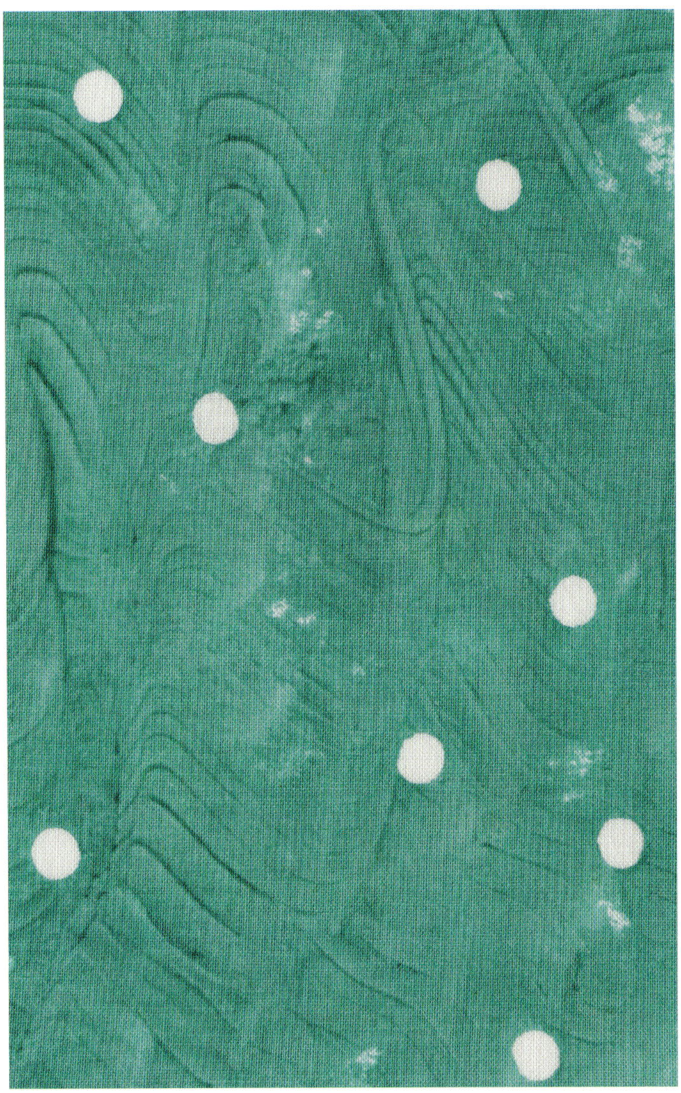

How This Book Is Organized

Each chapter is devoted to a specific surface design technique and its methods of use and application. This book focuses on expression with wet techniques; a separate companion book focuses on dry techniques. You'll learn about each technique through definitions, vocabulary, a bit of technical history, photo examples, and instructions for studio setup, supplies and equipment, safety guidelines, and processes. You'll also find "technical tips" in an array of sidebars and text boxes.

Each chapter offers some open-ended projects ("Try this!"), inviting you to experiment with materials and ideas, to test combinations, and to invent your own effects. You can repeat many of these, in differing ways, as often as you like.

Each chapter's list of "Try this!" suggestions ends with an optional "Cumulative Cloth Challenge," in which techniques from previous chapters can be combined with the techniques being discussed in the current chapter. You will carry the pieces of cloth you dye in the Challenge projects through this entire book, adding and layering techniques as they are introduced, and recombining them into a single textile at the end.

The appendixes cover finishing completed work, materials and tools, and using samples to experiment and save as references.

No book, of course, can be all things to all people, nor can any single book encompass everything there is to know about its subject. (If that were the case, we wouldn't need libraries!) So you need to know about this book's focus, which means that I need to mention some things you *won't* find in this book.

- While there may indeed be "wrong" ways to do certain kinds of work with textiles, often there is not a single unambiguously "right" way to accomplish a particular outcome. In many cases, the approaches discussed in this book are not the "only" way to do something. Instead, they are the methods that I myself have found most successful in my own work and in several decades of teaching textile makers ranging from freshman college students to retirees.

- I've made the assumption that a professional screen printer or a "volume" textile production operation has already achieved a level of advancement and knowledge far beyond anyone's book. I have therefore focused *The Cumulative Cloth* on the interests and needs of the single craftsperson, or small group working together, or participants in a workshop or college classroom, and ranging from beginner to relatively experienced.

- With that in mind, the chapters on "wet" techniques do not go into advanced production processes, techniques requiring particularly hazardous chemicals that I consider ill-advised for the home or small-group studio, or procedures requiring specialized equipment or facilities (photo darkrooms, professional-grade workspace air exhaust systems, or wide-format industrial printers for large runs of yardage, etc.).

- The book does contain a chapter on small-scale fabric printing from digital image files. However, among all the subjects in the book, digital techniques are the ones most continually in a state of change, update, or technological obsolescence. Any comments about specific hardware or software would soon be outdated. Therefore, I discuss a *general* approach to digital printing, to preparing image files, and to doing small-scale printing on a color printer in a home or group studio.

- Some types of textile color work—ikat, batik, silk painting, precision use of natural dye formulas, etc.—are so specialized that they deserve entire books devoted to their technique alone. Fortunately, such books already exist, and you will find a selection in this book's Bibliography, but I have sought to meet the potential needs of many generalists of widely varying interests, rather than to address single-technique specialists.

How to Use This Book

Although the chapters focus on the *separate* effects of various techniques, of course, in the process of making compositions, these characteristics will combine and overlap.

I've called the book *The Cumulative Cloth* because you can, if you choose, start at the beginning of the book with undyed yardage and then proceed, chapter by chapter, to dye it, print on it, hand-paint it with pigments, and remove bits of color with "discharge" techniques. The companion book on dry techniques enables you to "build" it into a rich multilayered surface with piecing, appliqué, reverse appliqué, and assorted embellishments: a truly cumulative cloth based on an accrual of skills and surface design processes.

But, of course, you needn't follow the topics in the exact order they're presented, and you should feel free to leaf back and forth for multiple ideas and inspiration, to "dip in" anywhere to explore something that especially interests you, and to choose whichever techniques "speak" to your own ideas about creating "cumulative cloth." You don't have to try everything here at the same time, and you don't have to enjoy all the techniques equally, or even use all of them in your work. Think of the topics in this book as a collection of present and future *possibilities*.

In short, use this book in any way that helps you. I'm inviting you to discover through creative play. Let's get started . . .

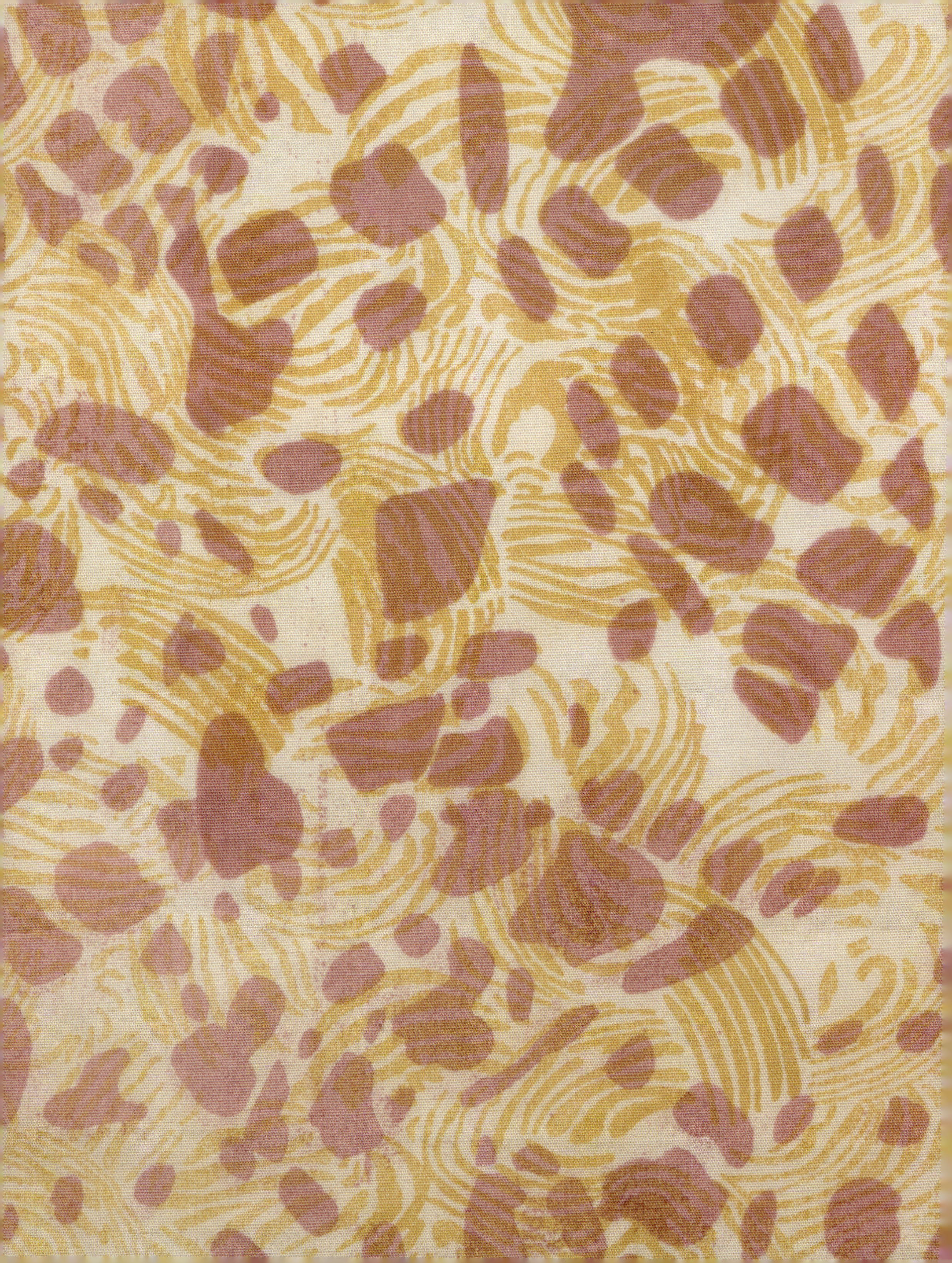

INTRODUCTION

The most logical, practical, and expressive foundation for creating a custom-designed fabric is dyed, printed, or painted *color*, forming a ground against which all the other techniques can play. This opens the door to the richly expressive, if "messy," world of dyes and pigments—colorants specifically formulated for textiles—and auxiliary chemicals. Their use requires an easy-to-clean studio equipped with forgiving table and floor surfaces, and immediate access to hot and cold running water. Some of the products and techniques are hard to accommodate safely in a home environment; the chapters in this book will outline the hazards as well as the rewards of this "wet work."

Dyes physically penetrate the fibers of the fabric and become locked into them by mechanical or chemical means. In a dyed fabric, the color appears to reside deeply within the fabric, and the reverse side of the fabric will usually look the same color as the front. The "hand" or the feel of the fabric doesn't change, leaving the fabric surface available for the addition of pigments. Dyes are most useful to impart overall color to larger pieces of fabric.

Pigments lie *on top of* the fabric, held to the surface by a binder. The back of a fabric printed with pigments ranges from blank to a "ghost" of the pattern from the front, because the pigment has not completely penetrated the structure of the fabric itself. Because they reside on the surface of the fabric—and can also be overlaid on fabric that has already been dyed—pigments are most easily applied by paintbrush, screen, or stamps. However, depending on the thickness of their application, pigments can change the hand of the fabric by making it stiffer and less pliable.

Chemical fabric treatments are used mainly for the intentional *reduction* of color already imparted to the fabric, even after dyes and pigments have been applied.

Each of these categories of fabric treatments possesses a range of jobs it does best. None is superior for *all* situations. Your choice among these products and techniques will depend on the specific needs of your projects. But *combining* them can also open paths to richer textile surfaces and invention.

In the following chapters we'll learn about the use of colorants for immersion dyeing (solid and uneven), resist dyeing (manipulated and bound), direct application and printing (with both dyes and pigments), and digital printing (with pigment-based inks). At the end, we'll round out the color options by addressing chemical techniques useful for *subtracting* color.

The "Try this!" exercises, presented from simple to complex in each chapter, help you practice and explore. The final exercise, "The Cumulative Cloth Challenge," invites you to combine what you've learned in all the chapters so far.

1 / DYES AND DYEING: CHOOSING EXPRESSIVE FOUNDATION COLOR

Dyeing or choosing the specific ground color of a piece of cloth (or the thread or yarn used to create the cloth) is a natural first step in building a custom color surface. Choosing an overall color sets the tone, the context, and the guiding atmosphere of the work to come. Dyeing is the "messiest" of the wet processes but, if done before other wet or dry techniques, allows progressively "cleaner" techniques to continue to layer the color surface in logical steps. Dyeing leaves the quality of the fabric surface unchanged and receptive to subsequent resist dye or pigment application in successive layers.

Humans have a "love affair" with color and began dyeing cloth and thread at least eight millennia ago, a time that even predates, by about 2,500 years, origins of the first written languages. With preindustrial natural fibers usually limited to the tan, beige, brown, black, gray, and white of their original sources, native dyestuffs dramatically expanded the range of possibilities. Potential dyes and mordants existed (and still do) in almost every human-inhabited place: plant roots, stems, leaves, and seeds; colorful insects; mollusk shells; minerals; and soil itself.

In the 21st century, the use of natural dyestuffs by textile makers remains very much alive around the world (see the Bibliography), but no color palette limitations need restrict present-day textile makers who wish to expand beyond the natural. Synthetic chemical dyes—a description that includes both "acid" and "fiber reactive" types—are very much the "youngsters" in dye history, the first acid dyes having been developed in the 19th century and the first fiber reactive dyes only in the 1950s.

Although the final portions of this chapter will include abbreviated discussions of acid dyes, tea "dyeing" (or staining), and rusting, **this chapter focuses mainly on the dyeing of cloth and yarns made from natural (i.e., nonsynthetic) fibers, using fiber reactive dyes, whose strengths include ease of use in a home studio and an enormous range of possible colors.**

The human eye is uniquely capable of perceiving millions of individual colors, stimulated by light reflections off the

01-01 White commercial yardage transformed by fiber reactive dyes and screen printing with pigments, then pieced, appliquéd, and stitched. Cotton fabric. Scale: 8" × 11". Collection: School of Law, University of North Carolina, Chapel Hill.

surface qualities of objects. The characteristics of the light sources (time of day, season, weather conditions, nature of indoor lighting) and the surface characteristics of the materials (rough, smooth, bumpy, slick) combine to change our perceptions of color. In addition to all these variables, each individual person carries varied capacities for perceiving colors and their subtle variations, while interpreting them through the filter of personal experience and color associations.

Responses to color are often based on our emotions, rooted in cultural norms (uses, associations, practices, and choices), and tempered by our own individual perceptions, boosting their expressive power by allowing us to "read" psychological and emotional messages in the colors of objects in our environment.

In practical terms, differences in color allow us to distinguish shapes and objects from each other and from their surroundings. In subjective terms, color can trigger emotions, associations, and memories by providing visual "cues" we associate with safety or warning, pleasure or discomfort, agitation or peace of mind. More universally, this human capacity to perceive color transforms our world into a richly "decorated" and lively place.

Regardless of dyestuff source, the ability to use color precisely and with expressive intent is a powerful—and essential—tool.

01-02 High- and low-intensity colors. Fiber reactive dyes. Low immersion dyed, arashi-resisted, discharge-printed, pieced, appliquéd, hand- and machine-stitched. Cotton and silk organza. Scale: 8" × 11".

Dyeing Cloth at Home

You might ask: *Why bother to use dyes today?* After all, today's market offers an astonishing range of specialty dyed fabrics and threads. With sufficient resources, you can purchase most kinds of dyed cloth or thread you may want, avoiding the hassle, time, mess, and technical requirements of setting up a dye space. But if you go to retail fabric stores, you may be disappointed with the range of color in commercially available fabrics. Most are of fairly high intensity and medium value, therefore lacking in nuance. To equip yourself with a full range of expressive possibilities, you'll want more diversity—for example, a great variety of hues, in high, medium, and low intensities and values. There are, for example, hundreds of colors you could describe as "pink" or "green" or "red-orange." But which one do *you* want for *your* purposes? Searches for the "right" color in store-bought fabrics are apt to be time-consuming and even fruitless.

Dyeing cloth oneself, by hand and in small quantities, physically transforms white cloth into colored cloth. This transformation changes our perception of the cloth itself. Therein lies a certain amount of magic, what the ancients might have called "alchemy." In fact, a certain degree of stigma actually attached to dyers of antiquity precisely because of such associations with the magical. People who could inexplicably transform natural fibers into brightly colored ones were believed to possess supernatural or mystical powers, skills from "the other world," which were sometimes thought slightly suspicious, even dangerous—although simultaneously in demand.

We understand dye transformations more scientifically today, of course, but there is indeed still an element of wonder, of "magic," in seeing fabric transformed before our eyes.

When controlling color as precisely as you envision it, you have greater command over the aesthetics, design, and meaning of the resulting cloth. The challenge of learning to control color can be fraught with failures and frustrations. In searching for the right color relationship to express an idea, you won't always be able to match the color vision in your mind. Sometimes you will miss it, sometimes you will hit it precisely, and every so often you will surpass your original vision (an exciting and inspiring outcome). The more skilled and practiced you are at measuring, controlling, and reproducing the color you want, the more control you will have over its expressive possibilities in your work. Dyeing your own cloth or threads places a powerful artistic tool in your hands.

With some practice, you can get exactly the colors you want. Dyeing your own fabrics puts you in control of the *exact* result. When you apply the dyes yourself, you can also

HELPFUL HINTS IF YOU JUST DON'T WANT TO DYE YOUR OWN FABRICS

- Skip the rest of this chapter (sorry to see you go!) but still check out chapter 3, and those after it, because the "wet" techniques discussed there may still appeal to you and can be used on some types of store-bought pre-dyed fabrics.
- Even if you choose not to dye your own fabrics, you can still begin the *color story* of your projects with a full and varied color palette, all purchased from commercial sources. But this does require that you think very carefully about your specific color choices, and that you purchase with forethought about exactly how they'll be used.
- Although dyeing educates your eye to the many nuances of color and its potential with specific applications to cloth, you can also learn these by mixing paint (oil, watercolor, or acrylic) or working with colored pencils. Any color medium will teach you to distinguish among a proliferation of hues, and to detect the slight differences between their closely related values and intensities.
- If you want to find diverse and unusual colors in pre-dyed commercial fabrics, you are most likely to find success with companies, or individual dyers, who market to quilters.

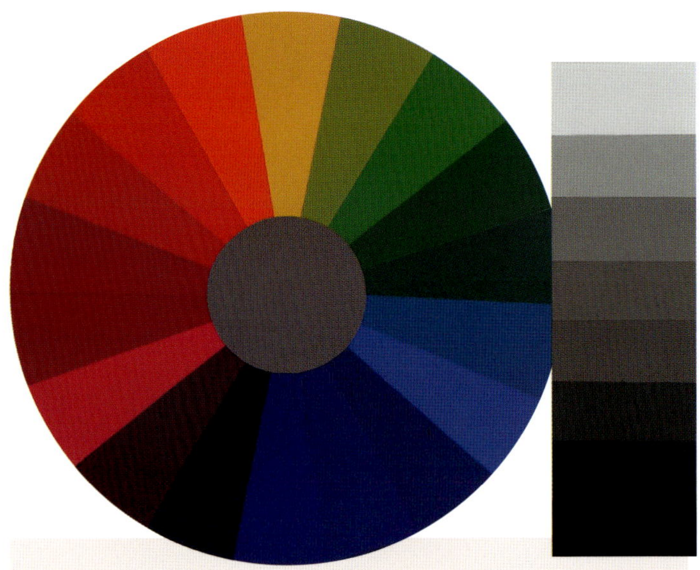

IDENTIFYING VALUES

If you don't have a value scale, or a color wheel that incorporates one, and you're having trouble identifying the values present in a color palette or a drawing, make a black-and-white photocopy of it. This will immediately reduce the colors to a gray scale, revealing the values present. This may also help you visually separate the effects of value and intensity in any color palette.

experiment with unusual and unique color (not readily available in commercial pre-dyed products), such as intentionally uneven color, watercolor blending of colors, and painted images. But one of the best reasons to dye your own fabric, even occasionally, is the reward of witnessing that "magical" transformation that you yourself have created.

As you choose colors for your projects, you may also find it helpful to use a *color wheel* and a *value scale*. Commercial color wheels usually contain color chips in the basic hues, and some may bear additional internal wheels showing values or the results of color mixing. A good color wheel will also be helpfully imprinted with concise synopses of color theory, terminology, and classic color relationships. The value scale, which displays even steps of gray between white and black, can help you determine the relative value (low, medium, or high) of your colors, a factor that is sometimes masked by the hue. Either tool can be consulted as a general reference or held directly against fabrics for closer comparison and decision-making. Together, these tools can help you choose individual colors or entire color palettes; construct effective color combinations, contrasts, and relationships; and compose the expressive color story of your work.

TIPS ON COMBINING VALUE AND INTENSITY

Confused? Not to worry. Because the concepts of value and intensity operate *simultaneously* in all colors, many people have trouble visually separating the two concepts. But try to think of them as two *cooperating* attributes that lend each color its unique personality, making it distinguishable from all other colors.

Some confusion arises with the terms themselves. To describe the lightness or darkness of hues, we use only the word "value," in order to describe how nearly white or black it is. "Value" says it all. But for intensity, multiple words are used interchangeably although having exactly the same meaning: "saturation," "chroma," "intensity," "purity." This attribute is the amount of pure color present, without the interference of other colors mixed with it in the dye pot, paint palette, or printing press.

The best way to work your way through these issues is to practice the following exercise to analyze a single color, using a gray scale and a graded color wheel as aids. This will help train your eye to visually separate these linked characteristics.

First: Identify the color's value. Hold a value scale next to the color you are analyzing and slide it along until you find the step in the scale that matches the color in relative lightness or darkness. Which step in the scale does it match? Is it near white (high value), black (low value), or somewhere in the middle (medium value)?

Second: Identify the color's intensity or saturation. Hold a graded color wheel near the color. Rotate and slide to find the correct hue first, then find its degree of purity. Where is it on the color wheel? Near full strength (high intensity), near a color that you can't quite describe or name (low intensity), or somewhere in between (medium intensity)?

Third: Combine them. Use the value and intensity modifiers together in a phrase to describe the color's characteristics fully. It may help if you remember that a color may be dull (*low* intensity) even though light (*high* value), or bright (*high* intensity) even though dark (*low* value). This may be the most confusing part, but once you wrap your mind around the idea of two attributes working together to form a color, it will make sense and will allow you to "read" the formative characteristics of any color.

Practice in identifying value and intensity of single colors will expand your ability to move beyond notions that certain colors "go" only with other colors, and will allow more adventurous color palettes in your cloth work.

LEFT: Example of a CMY (cyan-magenta-yellow) color wheel and value scale, made from Color-aid papers with a foam core base. Match colors to a commercial or online version or make your own in any size or materials.

PRACTICAL ASPECTS OF WORKING WITH COLOR CONTRAST

Color contrasts call attention to certain places in a composition. Depending on the context, even small amounts of certain colors, in certain places, can generate dramatic impact. For example, in a composition composed mainly of pastel washes (high values), a small amount of dark blue instantly calls attention to itself, and the viewer's eye immediately gravitates toward it.

Proportion: The proportion of colors in a composition places emphasis on one color or another and conveys the sense of one mood or another. For example, if you use 80% grays and 20% reds in your composition, it will "read" as relatively subdued, but with spots of bright color. If, on the other hand, the composition is 80% reds and 20% grays, it will "read" as relatively more dynamic, but with some tempering. The colors are the same in either case, but proportion affects the visual result.

Reducing color intensity but *not* value: To reduce the saturation/intensity of a color (make it duller) without changing its value (lightness/darkness), *add its complementary color to it*. Example: If you have a green fabric you want to make a bit more dull, overdye it with magenta or place a magenta fabric of similar value next to it in your composition.

Reducing color intensity *and* increasing *or* decreasing value: To reduce the saturation/intensity of a color (make it duller) *and* change its value, *add black or white* (the "value changers") *before you also add the complementary color*.

The importance of your surroundings: Color matching should be done in a working environment that is neutral. If, for example, you work in a blue room, this will affect your color perception of everything you make (or photograph) there. Try to minimize color and pattern around you. White is the ideal wall color for your workspace, because it least influences color perception of objects and materials in the room. Ideally, the room's floor should also be a neutral color without strong patterning.

"Managing" your eyes and color perception: When your eyes feel tired and you begin to see color afterimages, you should probably "take the hint" and stop working for a while! But as an alternative, stare at a neutral gray for three to five minutes. A gray card (available from camera sellers) is useful for this purpose. If, on the other hand, you leave the work for long periods of time, allow your eyes to adapt to the environment again for about 10 minutes before resuming.

01-03 Dyed foundation using lighter- and higher-intensity "pinks" to produce a softer, more delicate impression. Low-immersion Procion MX fiber reactive dyes, screen-printed with pigments. Cotton fabric. Scale: 9" × 12".

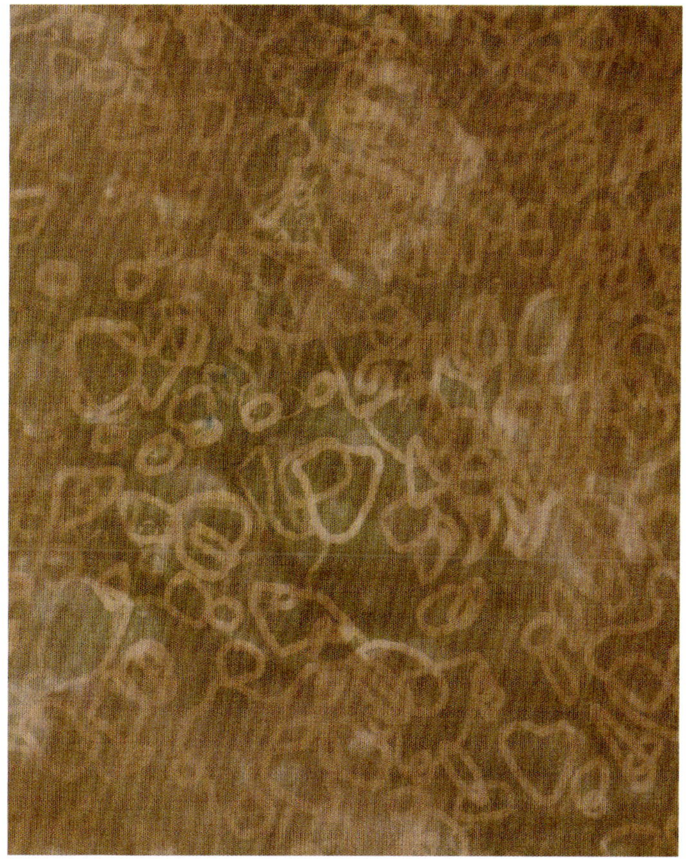

01-04 Darker, heavier, and lower-intensity mixed brown/olive-green foundation, a more earthy (even "mysterious" or "gloomy") impression. Low-immersion Procion MX fiber reactive dyes, screen-printed with discharge chemicals. Cotton fabric. Scale: 9" × 12".

Colors are perceived only in *relationship* to the colors around them—that is, in context. And because dyes are transparent, this principle of color in context means that each layer of color will both affect and be affected by any additional colors used before or after it, so that the "perceived" overall color becomes a composite. Because of the interaction of context and transparency, adding brown on top of a pink, for example, will produce a completely different result from adding the very same brown on top of an olive green. And the same applies to combinations of dyes more alike than different. (See also 01-03 and 01-04.)

For a more detailed discussion of color theory and the expressive use of color, see chapter 9 of my book *The Intentional Thread.*

USING "EXTERNAL" COLOR SOURCES TO INSPIRE YOUR PALETTE

To guide or spark your imagination and intent, it's often useful to start your color selection with a defined and easily "read" source: a photograph, a drawing or painting, a color sketch, a stack of color chips, threads you'll use to make or embellish the cloth, or even your own clothing. In other words, something concrete and tangible to choose and match dye colors, in order to build "atmosphere" from the very beginning.

Choose sources with complex color palettes including a variety of hues, values, and intensities, or those in which color has been blended and built up on the surface.

If using a photograph, for example, ignore its actual subject but concentrate on the proportions and interaction of its specific colors. Consider photos of landscapes, textured nature scenes, travel destinations, food, plants, close-up images of animals (fur, feathers, scales), or the paintings of the impressionists or abstract expressionists.

To control the number of separate colors in your dyed cloth, analyze the color source to understand which colors *predominate* (i.e., which are essential and which are expendable). Work directly from the source, holding it up against fabric or dye samples to refine your color story.

Here (01-05) is a detail of one of my own pieces, set beside my photographic color sources (01-06 and 01-07), which were close-up views although surrounded by tall ferns, of plant roots, lichen, and moss on rocks along the coast of Oregon.

01-05 Detail.

01-06 Color source.

01-07 Color source.

The characteristics of the base cloth color will either invite or obscure the addition of subsequent layers of colors, images, patterns, or marks. For instance, let's go back to that light pink cloth (01-03). Because the color is light (high value), and warm (temperature), the fabric could, if desired, still accept a substantial amount of dye in several forms: you could "overdye" it (with a second round of immersion dyeing), resist-dye it (with marks in a contrasting darker color), or directly apply pigments or screen printing to add pattern or images. The dark olive green in 01-04, on the other hand, would be difficult to alter unless the added colors were much *darker* (lower value) than the green, or you resorted to *removing* color with discharge chemicals (as was also done in 01-04). (See chapter 6 for discharge techniques.)

Matching Dyes and Fibers

All dye techniques require the assistance of water, chemicals, time, and a required sequence of steps to achieve a permanent color change. However, dyes are fiber specific; that is, fully effective only on a certain type of fiber, under a particular set of conditions (such as acidity, alkalinity, or salinity), and in the presence of appropriate chemical assistants. Almost any coloring agent can simply "stain" a fabric, as we know (all too well!) from food stains on tablecloths and clothing. But it is the *controlled* use of chemistry that makes the difference between mere staining (indiscriminately throwing a piece of cloth into some kind of colorant) and the full expressive potential and permanence of matching the "right" dye to the "right" cloth. In each of your dye sessions, you therefore need to know the fiber content of what you're about to dye, and then the fiber itself will dictate—will "want"—the most appropriate dyestuff and conditions.

Introduction to the Fibers

Let's start with a few words about the types of fibers you might want to dye. For the purpose of choosing dye—and keeping in mind that here we're focused on cloth, rather than fiber materials derived (for example) from wood or metal—there are two major fiber types: synthetic and natural, each of which is further subdivided among specific fibers. Synthetics, whether or not pre-colored, are chemically manufactured in the laboratory and factory. Examples include polyester, acetate, spandex, modal, olefin, acrylic, many others, and countless hybrids of these. **Generally speaking, synthetic fibers require the use of chemicals and processes that raise serious health safety concerns when used at home, and therefore this book focuses on dyes, chemistry, and processes considered safe if properly handled, for natural fibers.**

As their name suggests, natural fibers come from living or naturally occurring organisms (i.e., plants or animals). Natural *cellulose fibers* come from the stems (bast), leaves, seeds, or flowers of plants. Examples are cotton, linen, hemp, ramie, reed, rayon, and bamboo. Natural *protein fibers* come from the hair or fur of animals. Examples include wool, camelid fibers (camel, llama, alpaca), and silk. (Nylon, although technically a synthetic, is nevertheless also receptive to the acid dyes used on natural protein fiber—which is yet another example of the need to match dyestuffs to the object being dyed.)

01-08 Cellulose fabrics. *Left to right*: handwoven cotton twill, cotton damask, cotton velveteen, cotton gauze, cotton cheesecloth, heavyweight linen, lightweight linen, heirloom linen napkin.

When you buy fabrics, yarns, or threads, keep a record of their fiber content so you can choose the best dye to use on each. For easy identification, keep the original fiber content tags, attach your own handwritten tags, or sort and store fabrics and yarns in bins according to fiber type. This ready information will remove the element of guesswork when the time comes to dye them, and will eliminate a possible mismatch between fiber and dye. (For a discussion of the relationship between images and fabric types, see the section on "Choosing Fabrics for Digital Printing" in chapter 5.)

As you can see in illustration 01-08 on the previous page, each fabric varies in thread count, fiber type, weave structure, and weight. These variations cause each fabric to accept dye differently and, in turn, yield variations in color. If you are new to dyeing, you can demonstrate this to yourself with a simple test: cut 8" square samples from an assortment of different cottons, linens, rayons, and silks; put them all in the same dyebath; then compare the results. The differences may surprise you. This simple exercise should encourage you to test fabrics before embarking on large projects and will help you choose fabrics appropriate to your needs.

01-09 Cellulose threads and tapes. *Clockwise from upper left*: 1. combed knitting cotton, 2. rayon sewing thread, 3. rayon chenille, 4. cotton twine, 5. rayon embroidery floss, 6. blue linen embroidery thread, 7. cotton embroidery floss, 8. cotton shoestring tape, 9. unbleached linen thread, 10. heavyweight combed knitting cotton.

01-10 Silk and nylon fabrics and threads. *Left to right*: Silk noil, silk dupioni, torpedo silk, silk organza, silk organza netting, nylon netting. *On top*: heavy silk floss (on bobbin), lightweight six-strand silk floss (in ball).

01-11 Wool fabric, yarns, and threads. *Underneath*: wool flannel. *On top, left to right*: wool embroidery thread and three weights of wool tapestry yarn.

Introduction to the Dyes

Dyes are a class of substances that *penetrate* the fibers of fabric, imparting color. Some dyes (e.g., fiber reactive dyes and vat dyes) actually bond chemically with and become part of the fabric. Other dyes (e.g., acid dyes and household dyes) penetrate the fiber pores and are trapped by the action of an assistant such as acid (for protein fibers) or salt (for cellulose fibers). Dyes usually leave the surface qualities and hand of the fabric unchanged.

All dyes have varying qualities of brilliance, washfastness, and colorfastness. It takes time and practice to become familiar and comfortable with the various kinds of dyes and the processes for using them. To avoid rushing or becoming flustered, allow extra time for dyeing sessions.

Fiber Reactive Dyes (the main focus of this chapter)

These dyes chemically bond with the fibers, using salt and soda ash (sodium carbonate) as the catalyst or activator on cellulose fibers (such as cotton, linen, ramie, rayon), and citric acid crystals on protein fibers (such as silk and wool). Because of their brilliant color results, ease of use, and permanence (washfastness and lightfastness), fiber reactive dyes have, for decades, been the popular choice in private textile studios and small businesses. Furthermore, fiber reactive dyes need only "cold-water processing" (i.e., the dyebaths do *not* require a heat source or simmering). Fiber reactive dyeing can be done with hot tap water in simple plastic tubs or buckets. For all-round flexibility, access, cost, and simplicity of process, these dyes meet most needs in the home studio. For these reasons, the most detailed information in this chapter focuses on fiber reactive dyes. Keep in mind that many of the color ideas and application methods presented for fiber reactive dyes are also useful with other types of dyes.

Acid Dyes

Specifically used for silk, wool, or nylon (although it is a synthetic), acid dyes yield strong, brilliant, jewel-like colors. They are superb for bound or stitched resist dyeing (see chapter 2), where the goal is to attain clear and precise resist markings. Acid dyes require a more complex and exacting process than fiber reactive dyes, the use of dedicated stainless-steel dye pots, access to a dedicated heat source (stovetop or burners that are not also used for food preparation), and a temperature high enough to bring and hold the dyebaths at a simmer to complete the chemical reaction and dye take-up. The particular acids and their chemical assistants vary depending on the dye chosen. Lanaset dyes (a specific type, for which basic instructions appear later in this chapter) are lightfast and washfast, can be mixed for custom colors (many other acid dyes cannot), and require

HOUSEHOLD DYES

Commercially popular "household dyes," typically sold prepackaged and inexpensively in "big box" retail stores or "hobby" stores, sometimes even in grocery stores or drugstores, are combinations of several different kinds of dyestuffs, only some of which (or even only one of which) may actually be best for the specific fabric type (cellulose, protein, synthetic, etc.) being dyed. Their "selling point," which is true within its limits, is that they'll quickly dye *anything*—regardless of the type of fabric immersed in them—and "just get the job done." But their multiple-dyestuff formulation means that dyestuffs unsuited to the specific fabric type are essentially wasted and then washed down the drain.

I believe that fast-acting household dyes are useful "in a pinch" (for example, dyeing a garment or theater costume that is needed soon and may be used only once or twice), and they do have the slight advantage of producing reasonably good color on *synthetic* fabrics. However, household dyes prove less satisfactory on more durable items, especially objects of heirloom, artistic, or archival quality, and their dye colors are usually less intense, and often less lightfast or washfast, than the dyestuffs discussed in this book. For this reason, I don't consider household dyes to be high-quality products for the serious textile maker. I rarely use them, and this book focuses on matching good dyestuffs *appropriate* to what is being dyed.

The broad and easy availability of household dyes may also imply that they are safer to use, which is definitely *not* the case. If you decide to use household dyes, (1) treat them with the same respect and safety guidelines as you would any other type of dye (multiple safety precautions for dyeing are discussed in this chapter); (2) don't use home cooking pots or food storage containers as dye buckets; (3) don't use your kitchen or bathroom as a dye studio; (4) buy only those products that supply detailed process and safety instructions; and (5) buy only from manufacturers who provide an online link, or other easy access, to the appropriate Materials Safety Data Sheets (MSDS).

only sodium sulphate (Glauber salts) and white vinegar to fix the color. (See the Bibliography for further reading on acid dyes other than Lanaset.)

Natural Dyes

Unlike fiber reactive and acid dyes, both of which are synthetic (manufactured), natural dyes and mordants are derived directly from plant, animal, insect, shell, earth, and mineral sources, often processed by drying, grinding, measuring, or cooking the original material. They work well on both natural cellulose and protein fibers. Most (except indigo) require hot-water processing and mordants (metal salts) for setting the color. Mordants can be simple substances such as alum, or more complex compounds such as potassium aluminum sulfate, sodium acetate, or ferrous sulfate. The colors produced are very beautiful, but somewhat more sensitive than chemical dyes to daylight and washing, and therefore also more prone to fading over time. European tapestries found in museum collections are good examples of how natural dye colors fade: once-brilliant colors have become low-intensity soft pastels. Effective and reliable natural dye processes are well beyond the scope of this book, although two easy "natural" techniques, tea dyeing and rusting, are briefly outlined later in this chapter. (See the Bibliography for more-thorough information focused on a variety of natural dyes.)

Safety Issues with Dyes

I'm going to talk to you about multiple dangers of using dyestuffs on fabric. When you're done reading what I have to say, you may find yourself asking, "Why in the world would anyone ever want to use these substances?" But don't be discouraged. These are *potential* dangers that arise mainly when dyestuffs are handled *incorrectly*. My intention is not to frighten you away, but I do want to emphasize that satisfying and creative color results, regardless of dyestuff, are nevertheless also accompanied by (preventable) hazards. Follow safety protocols "to the letter."

01-12 Protective safety equipment. *Clockwise from left*: denim work shirt, elbow-length rubber gloves, rags, work apron (here fashioned from an old pair of men's overalls), organic-filtering mask, plastic goggles. (To complete the personal protection kit, add a tube of hand cleaner and a roll of paper towels.)

Three main ingredients are required to dye cloth: the *dyestuff* (the specific dye itself); enough *water* to submerge the goods; and the appropriate *fixative* (chemicals for synthetic dyes—i.e., fiber reactive and acid—and mordants for natural dyes). Therefore, dyeing has always been a messy business, generating vats of coloring agents and spent dyebath ingredients that then require proper disposal or reconstitution. In addition, dyeing—especially with natural dyes—can be quite "aromatic." As natural dyestuffs decompose, ferment, boil, or cook, they produce quite pungent smells that many people find unpleasant. (This is why, over the centuries, discrete "dyers' quarters" were usually situated at the edge of town to spare the rest of a village this olfactory "experience.") Even today, for similar reasons, commercial-scale dyeing operations are rarely located in "prime" neighborhoods.

While modern chemical dyes may ameliorate some of the smells, their use remains potentially toxic. This includes everything from the initial handling and mixing of the dye powders, to exposure to the chemical fixatives, to the disposal of spent dyebaths into individual septic tanks or community sewer systems. Everyone who dyes fabric and thread, whether a large commercial dyer or the individual practitioner, must treat dyes as potentially hazardous substances, handle them with care, and dispose of them in a way that minimizes contamination of drinking-water sources.

Dyes are, of course, in no way unique in the requirement that they be used with care. The same can be said about the explicit need for care in taking medicines, or using knives and cooking equipment in a kitchen or power tools in a garden or workshop, or operating and repairing a car. And so on. Almost every technology involves a mix of benefits and risks; the goal is to maximize the former but minimize the latter.

Chemical dyes are most dangerous to the individual dyer when they are in powdered—as opposed to pre-mixed liquid—form. The dry particles are tiny (too small to see with "the naked eye"), lightweight, and easily airborne and can therefore be inhaled directly into the lungs without your even sensing their presence in the air around you. Exposure to the powder can occur at several points in the dyeing process, but you should exercise the most vigilant caution in these two situations: First, unless handled properly, the powder can become airborne when you open the original container and remove any quantity of dye, and can then settle on countertops, your clothing, your hair or skin, and anything else in the immediate area. Second, splashed or spilled liquid from a dyebath, if left to dry, will return to powder, with the same potential for inhalation.

Exposure to dye in liquid form presents other potential hazards: First, if a dyebath spills or splashes onto your skin, the dye enters directly into your body. Second, improperly disposed dyebaths pollute your local water supply. Thus, even once the dye is dissolved in a stock solution (see definition and instructions below) or a dyebath, its risks still need to be addressed.

Although they come from plants, insects, or other "natural" sources, natural dyes are not automatically safer than manufactured chemical dyes. While the dyestuff itself may be relatively safe, some hazards are nevertheless associated with the heavy-metal mordants (fixatives) best suited for coaxing bright colors from natural dyes on certain fibers. Because each natural dyestuff responds differently to different mordants, you must choose your dyestuffs and mordants carefully, understand their basic chemistry, and handle them safely. Therefore, all the general guidelines listed below should still be followed even when using natural dyes. (As already stated above, this book focuses on specific chemical dyes, because the complex subject of natural dyes merits entire books of its own. See the Bibliography, in particular for authors Ellis and Boutrup.)

Another reason that vigilant and continuous care is imperative: *dye toxicity increases with repeated exposure over time (i.e., it is cumulative, not acute).*

This book outlines safety procedures for every dye technique discussed. Read and follow the general dye safety guidelines below. Acquire and read Materials Safety Data Sheets (MSDS) for the products you use (these sheets are required by law to be made available to you from each product manufacturer or vendor). Be responsible; inform yourself fully; work safely; and protect yourself, your family, and your community when using these products for the marvelous fabric colors they can produce.

Dye Safety Practices

Control Who Comes in Contact with Dyes

- *Never use dyes or harsh chemicals if you are pregnant.* For the duration of the pregnancy, switch to pigments or another kind of nonchemical creative work altogether.

- *Never use dyes around small children* or allow them to help you dye without special precautions and *close* supervision. There are methods and starter kits for dyeing with children that isolate them from touching the dyes, but use even those only with older children and with great care. When children are present, whatever *can* go wrong *will* eventually go wrong. If you want to dye fabric with kids, look into simple home methods for dyeing with food coloring or Kool-Aid.

- *Follow the same precautions when working around other family members or unknowledgeable adults.* Whenever possible, exclude people from an active dyeing area unless they are actually helping with the dye project—in which case they also need to follow the same safety precautions as you.

01-13 Custom gradations of color with high-intensity contrasting accents. Fiber reactive dyes, then pieced, appliquéd, and machine-stitched. Cotton fabrics. Scale: 48" × 48". Collection: David and Jane Schumann, Cary, North Carolina.

Establish a Safe Dye Workspace

- *Never use dyes (in any form) in or near food preparation areas.* Your kitchen is *not* a dye studio. Work outdoors or in a basement, carport, or garage with an open door, or—better yet—in a separate isolated room, especially when mixing powdered dyes into solution. (Local arts organizations sometimes have group dye studios for use or rent.)

- *Do not store dyes (or, for that matter, any other chemicals) in a place (e.g., cabinet, refrigerator) or in a type of container in which you also store foods.*

- *Use a nonabsorbent, easy-to-clean worktable and work in a space with a nonabsorbent, easy-to-clean floor.* No rugs or carpets, which can absorb dyes but then can't be completely washed out.

- *Select and use dedicated utensils, pots, and equipment in the dye space.* Never "borrow" utensils from the kitchen for use with dyes, unless you will *never* again use those utensils in the kitchen.

- *Do not consume food or drink in or near your dye space.* Airborne powdered dye can settle on food, bowls, plates, cups, and utensils and then be (yes, really) accidentally eaten. Keep your refreshments in another room and remove your work apron, rubber gloves, goggles, and other safety "kit" *before* leaving the dye space to touch, prepare, or consume any food.

- *Mix and store your dyes in stock solutions (dissolved in water) to minimize unnecessary exposure to dye powders.* Plastic squeeze bottles with tight-fitting caps are useful to dispense a small stream of dye. These allow good control of the mixture and help prevent accidents and spills.

- *Choose a deep sink with a good drainage system.* Ideally, add a filtration system to clean up the spent dyebath contents.

- *Provide a work surface that is both near the sink and at a convenient height, so that you can pick up, carry, and empty tubs or pots without splashing.*

Handle Dyes Carefully

- *Keep dye manufacturers' MSDS in a notebook readily available in your dye space.* The commonly used dyes and chemicals discussed in this chapter are all potentially hazardous materials. When you purchase any specific dye or chemical, always ask for the accompanying MSDS.

- *Protect your skin, clothing, and the work area itself from dye spills.* Use long rubber gloves, even if you will stir your dyes with a stick or other implement. Wear a large shirt with sleeves that completely cover your arms, other clothing that completely covers your legs and feet, and an apron to provide additional protective cover over the clothing. Avoid overagitating or splashing the dyebath, especially when emptying it into the sink. *Dye-stained hands or skin are not "badges of honor" for having done intense studio work. On the contrary, they are evidence of carelessness.*

- *Immediately remove any dye from your skin,* using only a specially formulated dye-removing hand cleaner (available from all dye suppliers). Never, *never* use bleach to remove dye from your skin; the combination of dye and bleach should be considered potentially hazardous.

- *After handling powdered dyes, promptly wash all clothing, both "personal" and safety related, to remove any powder residue.* Never wear unwashed dye clothing around your home, in the kitchen, or for sleeping. Store the washed work clothing in the dye space itself.

- *When handling powdered dyes, work in a well-ventilated (but not drafty) space.* Close windows and turn off room fans to minimize air circulation during dye powder mixing. If your home has "forced air" heat or air conditioning, do the same.

- *When handling powdered dyes and mixing them into solution, always wear, at a minimum, an N-95 (US classification) particulate-filtering mask—although a dual-canister painter's mask, such as shown in 01-12, is even better.* These capture smaller particulates than "garden variety" particle masks. They are adjustable to fit different sizes and shapes of faces.

- *Wear goggles to prevent dye particles from lodging on your eyes or contact lenses.* (And this rule applies even if you wear eyeglasses, because the open spaces around them would still permit particle intrusion.)

- *When handling powders, don't rush.* Move slowly and smoothly to minimize disturbance of the invisible particles.

- *When handling boiling or simmering dye pots, use large padded oven mitts* of the type you might use in the kitchen—but *not* the *same* set of gloves you use in the kitchen—to protect your hands and lower arms from burns. Choose a style that covers your lower arm at least halfway up to the elbow.

- *Never leave simmering dye pots unattended.* If you can't remain in the space until hot dyeing is completed, wait until you can.

- *Protect your body from strain.* Depending on the amount of their contents, dye pots can be heavy. If so, lift with your legs to prevent back strain. Or keep dyebaths relatively small so they weigh less. Or get assistance (from helpers *in suitable safety gear*). Arrange your working situation to manage your dye pots at a convenient working height. *All these precautions also minimize the likelihood of spills.*

- *If you regularly dye large amounts of fabric, consider buying an inexpensive top-loading (deep fill) washing machine dedicated only to studio use.* If you monitor the timing and manually control the machine settings, you can dye, agitate, and rinse a larger quantity of fabric than you could physically manage by hand.

Clean Up after Each Dye Session

- *Clean up any dye spills on countertops, tables, floors, and cabinets immediately and thoroughly after each dye session.* Spilled dye dries and becomes powder again, which will become airborne and potentially inhaled.

- *Immediately remove any dye from your skin if you neglected to do so during the dye session itself.* As noted above, use a specially formulated dye-removing hand cleaner. *Never* use bleach.

- *If spent dyes will be discarded into a plumbing drain, test them with pH paper and, if necessary, neutralize them to pH 7 to prevent undue wear and tear on sewer pipes and residential plumbing.* Use white vinegar to neutralize alkaline dyebaths (left over from dyeing cellulose fibers), or soda ash to neutralize acid dyebaths (left over from dyeing protein fibers).

- *To discard leftover stock solutions, gather them into a disposal container with a tight-fitting lid and dispose of the collected fluid as you would any other hazardous waste at your local collection site.*

- *Before permanently vacating a space where you have used dyes or other chemicals (whether that be an apartment, a rented studio, or your own house), thoroughly clean the space*, in consideration of the residents who follow you.

If you believe that you can't establish a fully safe dye space in your home, seek another way to dye fabric in a safe and quality-controlled setting, such as classes at local community art centers or colleges, workshops at established art and craft schools or textile conferences, short-term rentable studios, or one-on-one study with a friend or colleague who has an appropriately outfitted dye space.

Fiber Reactive Dyes

The characteristics of fiber reactive dyes make them the most versatile and relatively safe of the dyestuffs available to the small home studio. They provide brilliant, washfast, and lightfast colors, using a simple and relatively safe dye process and easy-to-obtain chemicals. The colors mix together easily for extensive variety and nuance. (If you are new to dyeing fabric, you'll be delighted with the range of the colors achievable with fiber reactive dyes, from very bright to very muted and very light to very dark.)

Among the different dye types, fiber reactive dyes are very "forgiving" and even allow you to "tinker" with dyebaths already in progress. **This section of the book will provide many recipes, with relatively precise measurements, for achieving certain effects, and, of course, if you intend to reproduce previous results, you'll also want to adhere to**

01-14 Brilliant and muted varied colors achieved with Procion MX fiber reactive dyes. Pieced. Cotton fabrics. Scale: 8" × 11".

the same recipe (whether from this book or a recipe you developed for yourself). But don't be intimidated by all the recipes. Imparting color to cloth is exciting—and fun. Think of the instructions in this section as tools for achieving particular results. **As you become more practiced in using fiber reactive dyes, you will increasingly come (almost instinctively) to "know" what to do, know how a particular kind of fabric is likely to accept dye, know whether an in-progress dyebath needs more color added, and so on.** With practice, accurate measurements, and good recordkeeping, you can learn to match color sources, color chip samples, or fabrics you previously dyed; create harmonious color palettes for a specific project; or dye diverse natural-fiber types (such as cotton, linen, wool, and silk) in the same color.

These dyes are the best *all-around* choice for use on both cellulose *and* (with different chemistry) protein fibers (i.e., cotton, linen, viscose, rayon, hemp, bamboo, ramie, silk, wool, alpaca, and other camelid fibers).

Cellulose fibers require the assistance of salt and soda ash (sodium carbonate, *not* baking soda, which is sodium *bi*carbonate) in hot tap water.

Protein fibers, on the other hand, require acetic or citric acid and work best when simmered.

A Core Inventory of Dyes

Fiber reactive dyes (I've often used the Procion MX brand) are available in a wide number of colors and from a variety of local and online vendors. Chemically speaking, they are essentially the same, so you can shop your favorite vendor or choose a source for best color ranges or customer service.

Fiber reactive dye manufacturers and vendors offer an amazing array of colors, which can lead to a temptation to "buy the whole lot" and collect dozens of luscious colors to keep on hand. But the truth is that you won't use most of them. If you simply maintain a core inventory of about 12 colors, you can mix almost any *composite color* (a color created by combining two or more different commercial dye colors). The core inventory is also more cost effective in the long run, and it hones your color mixing skills through hands-on practice. Wait to indulge in buying unusual or one-off colors until you have a specific project that really requires them.

By maintaining a basic inventory, you can achieve a broad range of colors through mixing. For example, using the Procion MX color names, mixing "Golden Yellow" with "Scarlet" will produce a different "orange" than mixing "Lemon Yellow" with "Scarlet" or "Golden Yellow" with "Magenta." Through precise color control, you can develop greater nuances of color, a personally expressive "color signature," to enliven your work and make it uniquely yours.

CHOOSING YOUR CORE INVENTORY

This will typically include a black; a gray; a tan or beige; "warm" and "cool" versions of yellow, red, blue, and brown; and a dark blue. This example uses color names from the Procion MX product line:

1. Golden Yellow
2. Lemon Yellow
3. Scarlet
4. Mixing Red/Magenta
5. Turquoise
6. Basic Blue
7. Navy
8. Chino
9. Basic Brown
10. Chocolate Brown
11. Pearl Grey
12. Cotton Black or Black

Preparing the Goods for Dyeing

Fabric

Most local fabric stores don't carry ready-to-dye fabric yardage. More important than the issue of availability, their products may contain chemicals that resist, or interfere with, the easy acceptance of dyes. (These include chemical substances within the manufactured structure of the woven cloth itself, which cannot be washed out, and chemical finishes on the surface of the cloth, which may or may not.) If you want to dye fabric in your home studio, it's best to purchase it from a company that specializes in *uncoated*, ready-to-dye fabrics.

If fabric from a ready-to-dye specialty company is slightly soiled, wash it *thoroughly* in an automatic washing machine with hot water and detergent (for which I recommend Synthrapol, an unscented, mild, and widely available liquid soap intended specifically for cloth). Then rinse the fabric *thoroughly* to remove all traces of the detergent. You can then transfer the wet fabric directly into a dyebath or dry it for later use.

Recycled fabrics will probably have received past launderings sufficient to ensure that no original factory finishes remain intact. Use them as you would ready-to-dye, finish-free fabrics.

Fibers, Threads, Yarns, and Cords

Before placing them in a dyebath, loose fibers should be secured in a nylon mesh bag and handled gently in the dyebath to prevent tangling.

Yarns, threads, or cords are best wound into skeins and then secured for dyeing. Using a skein winder, the back of a chair, or (as in 01-15) a wooden or cardboard measuring stick, wind the desired length of thread/yarn into a loose skein. When you complete the winding, tie the first end of the skein to the last end, leaving at least 2" ends hanging from the joining knot so you can easily find the knot again. With small lengths of a contrasting thread, secure the skein by adding at least three equally spaced ties around its length, threaded through with a figure-eight motion, to hold the skein threads in place. Leave the ties loosely tied around the skein so the individual yarns can slide and contact the dye. Secure the ends of the ties with firm knots. Avoid pulling the ties tightly against the skein itself, which will create resist spots on the yarns.

Wash prepared skeins *by hand* in hot water and detergent such as Synthrapol. To avoid tangling the threads, minimize the agitation during washing. Do *not* use an automatic washer as a "shortcut" to washing skeins or other bagged loose fibers; that's an invitation to disaster. Skeined materials should be dyed using the same chemicals and processes you use for fabric yardage, but agitated very gently to prevent nightmarish tangles or (in the case of wool) unwanted felting.

Calculate Dye Amounts

Your first task is to imagine each hue you want to use in your project, then select its relative value and intensity (also called *depth of dye*). To measure or calculate the amount of dye you need to produce these specific colors, dye manufacturers provide *approximate* measurement charts to achieve light, medium, and dark color values. A chart like the one on the next page may accompany your dye package or instruction sheets:

However, these instructions assume that you will be throwing powdered dye directly into a pot of water, which I consider both unsafe and a completely "hit or miss" approach. I recommend the use of *stock solutions* (dye mixed with water) and a basic understanding of the concept of *depth of dye* (relative value or intensity of the color). You will find the details on each of these terms below. (See also the revised chart with amounts of dye stock solution below.)

You can achieve fairly uniform, accurate, and reliable colors if you weigh fabrics and measure dyes by using *the same equipment, tools, ratios, and procedures each time.*

01-15 How to tie a skein for dyeing (front view). Cotton thread wound lengthwise around a 6.5" wooden measuring stick and then (*at left*) loose ends tied with a tight overhand knot. Contrasting black string then threaded through the skein, in figure-eight motions (in and out of the skein), at equally spaced locations, then also tied with tight overhand knots. Although the knots are firm, the black string *around* the skein should be left loose to prevent unintended resist-dye outcomes.

Procion MX Fiber Reactive Dyes (if directly using powder): for *each pound* of goods to be dyed (for fabric, about 2–4 yards of medium-weight fabric, 36 inches wide), add the following to **2.5 gallons** of water:		
Pale or Light color	¼ tsp. powdered dye	3 T. salt
Medium color	½ tsp. powdered dye	6 T. salt
Dark color	1 tsp. powdered dye	9 T. salt

01-16 Example of depth of dye sequence (and also a value gradation) with the amount of dye doubled in each successive dyebath. Procion MX fiber reactive dye. Color: Green 700 at .25%, .5%, 1%, and 2%. Cotton print cloth. Scale: 4" × 2".

Depth of Dye

The more dye particles in the dye pot, the more color will be imparted to the fabric, and the greater the depth of dye. Compare the four identically weighted fabrics in 01-16, each dyed with the same manufacturer's green, but in dyebaths containing different amounts of the green dye. The dye pot with the least amount of the color will be lightest (and the resulting fabric airy, lighthearted, and soft); the one with the largest amount of dyestuff will be the darkest (and, depending on the specific color, richer, or more serious, or more dense); and all other concentrations will lie in between these in value.

Stock Solutions

A *stock solution* is simply powdered dye dissolved in water to create a concentrated liquid. Mixing a stock solution simultaneously transforms a hazardous powder that is easily inhaled into a safer-to-handle liquid. The solutions are more convenient, easier to store, more quickly and readily mixed with the larger volume of water in a dyebath, and easier to measure in the very small amounts necessary for dyeing light colors or small quantities of goods, and they eliminate much of the time otherwise spent to measure, weigh, and paste powdered dye every time you prepare a dyebath.

Note: Although metric measuring equipment is recommended for the most precise work, it is perfectly possible to measure weight in ounces or pounds and to measure volume in teaspoons, tablespoons, cups, pint, and quarts, or to mix metric and US standard kitchen measures. The key is to *be careful and consistent* with whatever weighing and measuring method you choose and to *keep records* of what you do, so that you can repeat it.

Once the powder is mixed into solution, using standard kitchen measures (USA) to add dye to each dyebath (teaspoons [tsp.], tablespoons [T.], cups [c.], pints [pt.], quarts [qt.], and gallons [gal.]) yields nearly exact color reproduction if you want to dye a color again in the future.

I recommend that you mix your stock solutions in one-pint squeeze bottles that can be capped, in a ratio of about 2 T. powdered dye per pint of water (or 1 T. powdered dye per cup of water). Then use the chart below to measure out the amounts of dye you need for each dyebath.

To minimize confusion, mix all your stock solutions for a project or for storage at one consistent ratio and label each bottle with the color name, ratio, and date. Stock solutions will begin to lose their potency after some time, and different colors degrade at different rates. If you rely on their freshness for reproducible color results, use your stock solutions within a month. Keep the stock solutions cold to increase their shelf life. I have often kept my stock solutions for four to six weeks and continued to use them despite noticeable lessening of color intensity.

How to Mix and Use Stock Solutions

1. *For safety reasons, set up the mixing area outdoors, or in a carport, open garage, or open studio shed, rather than an individual room (unless it has excellent exhaust ventilation).*

    - Line the work surface with wet paper towels or wet rags to catch and dissolve any falling dye powder (because some "fallout" will occur no matter how carefully you handle the powder).
    - Have the dyes, measuring implements, and some distilled or tap water close at hand.
    - Put on your rubber gloves, particle-filtering face mask, goggles, and work apron.
    - Turn off any active fans running in the workspace.

STANDARD KITCHEN MEASURES (USA)

3 tsp. = 1 T.
16 T. = 1 c.
2 c. = 1 pt.
2 pt. = 1 qt.
4 qt. = 1 gal.

SUPPLY CHECKLIST FOR MIXING STOCK SOLUTIONS

1. access to hot and cold running water
2. Procion MX fiber reactive dyes, in powdered form
3. calculator (to calculate precise dye amounts)
4. measuring implements: spoons and cups
5. plastic storage bottles (pt. or qt.) with graduated measurements marked on the outside
6. goggles and organic-filtering face mask
7. work smock or apron
8. rubber gloves: long enough to cover the hand and lower arm
9. hand cleaner / dye remover
10. paper towels and rags

2. *Measure the dye powder.*

    - Place the open squeeze bottle (or other plastic container) on the wet paper towels.
    - Measure and add the dye powder into the empty plastic container, in the ratio of 2 T. per intended pint of water (or 1 T. per cup).

3. *Add water to make the stock solution.*

    - Add warm tap water to the dye powder in the bottle or container.
    - Replace the bottle lid and close tightly.
    - Shake vigorously for 60 seconds to mix well. Let the solution sit a few minutes and then shake again. Repeat until all visible lumps of dye have dissolved.

4. *Clean up the dye-mixing area.*

- After each dye-mixing session, clean the work surface thoroughly and discard the dye-soaked paper towels into a plastic garbage bag.

5. *Label the stock solution bottles.*

- Label the storage bottles of stock solution with:

  type of dye (fiber reactive, acid)
  color name or code number
  strength of the stock solution (ratio of dye powder to water)
  date the solution was mixed

- If multiple people are mixing and sharing stock solutions, add your name and contact information only to the labels of the dyes you personally mixed.

- If, for ventilation reasons, you've been mixing powder in an outdoor setting or garage, you can now move indoors when done handling the powders, their cleanup, and the labeling of the stock solutions.

6. *Storage and disposal of stock solutions*

- Store stock solutions in airtight plastic containers or squeeze bottles, with the lids firmly closed, and out of direct sunlight. The shelf life of a stock solution varies with the type of dye, the color, the water, and the storage conditions.

- Be sure to stir or shake stock solutions carefully and thoroughly *before each use*, since some dye may precipitate out and settle to the bottom during storage.

- Most stock solutions can be stored in a dark, cool place for at least a month.

- However, over time, all stock solutions will hydrolyze and lose their strength and permanence, which means that the dye may still impart some color but will be weaker and will become unreliable for color matching, reproducing past colors, and permanence. Check the dates on the bottles regularly and frequently.

- To responsibly dispose of concentrated stock solutions, neutralize them to pH7 (if necessary), collect them in a single container, and take them to your local hazardous waste disposal site. (See page 24 text box about pH.)

7. *How to* ***use*** *a stock solution*

- Once you have a set of dyes mixed into stock solutions, you can begin to combine them in various proportions to create custom colors in dyebaths. Use standard kitchen measuring spoons to add stock solution colors directly to the dyebaths (see chart at top of page 23). Or, for a more spontaneous approach, squeeze the dye directly from the bottle into the dyebath.

Your main uses for fiber reactive dyes will fall into one of the following categories: immersion dyeing in uneven and even colors; dyeing gradations of colors; overdyeing; and dye solutions and pastes for direct application and screen printing. Each of these will be discussed separately in the following major sections, further subdivided into discussions of differing methods and/or color effects.

Procion MX Fiber Reactive Dyes for *each pound* of goods to be dyed (for fabric, about 2–4 yards of medium-weight fabric, 36 inches wide), add the following amounts of stock solution to **2.5 gallons** of water:			
Depth of Dye	**Stock Solution**	**Salt**	**Soda Ash (*for cellulose*)** *or* **Citric Acid Crystals (*for silk*)**
Light color	1.25 T.	8 T.	4 T.
Medium color	2.5 T.	8 T.	4 T.
Dark color	5 T.	9 T.	4 T.

SETUP FOR DYEING

- nonabsorbent, easy-to-clean countertops or tables at a convenient height for you to move and lift heavy dye pots
- smooth-surfaced, nonabsorbent, easy-to-clean floors (no rugs or carpet to absorb dye powder or spills)
- for dyeing *wool*, hot plates or a stovetop to accommodate stainless-steel dye pots
- high-quality overhead light (full-spectrum daylight bulbs ideal)
- laundry machines used *only* for studio purposes: top-loading deep-fill washer to dye and agitate large pieces of cloth, and an efficient dryer.

Supply Checklist for Immersion Dyeing

- deep sink with hot and cold running water with filtered drains to the water system
- fiber reactive dyes
- chemicals for cellulose fibers (use *both* of the following): salt (table variety, *noniodized*, which facilitates penetration of dye molecules into the fabric) and sodium carbonate (soda ash, which permanently fixes dye to fabric)
- chemicals for silk (use only *one* of the following): citric acid crystals (simplest and safest), or acetic acid, or ammonia
- measuring spoons and cups
- goggles and particulate-filtering face mask
- plastic, enamel, or stainless-steel buckets, one for each color, large enough to contain the goods and enough water to cover them
- sticks: plastic or wooden, to stir the dyebaths
- kitchen timer
- candy thermometer (to monitor hot-water *wool* dyebath temperatures)
- work smock or apron
- rubber gloves: long enough to cover the hand and lower arm
- hand cleaner / dye remover
- laundry lines (and clothespins), or an automatic dryer, for drying dyed goods
- paper towels or rags for clean up
- Synthrapol detergent or dishwashing liquid to wash goods after dyeing

UNIVERSAL RINSE-OUT INSTRUCTIONS FOR FIBER REACTIVE DYES

Use these instructions at the conclusion of all the methods of immersion dyeing discussed in the sections below, and for the resist-dye processes in chapter 2. (I have not repeated these rinse-out instructions with each set of immersion dyeing instructions below, because they are the same for each.)

1. Remove goods from dyebath and set aside.

2. Discard the dyebath: Before emptying spent dyebaths into residential plumbing, test the solution with pH paper and add white vinegar (to reduce pH toward 7) or soda ash (to increase pH toward 7). This saves wear on sewer pipes. (See also the pH info below.)

3. Return the goods to the dye bucket and rinse under continually refreshed running *cold* water for two minutes, then drain while leaving the goods in the bucket.

4. Fill the bucket (once) with *very hot* water (e.g., 140°F), then add ½ ounce Calgon water softener or metaphos (sodium hexametaphosphate) per gallon of water. (No detergent at this stage.) Agitate the goods by hand for two minutes, then drain.

5. Refill the bucket (once) with *very hot* water (e.g., 140°F), then add 1 ounce detergent (Synthrapol or a mild dishwashing liquid per gallon. Let the goods soak for five minutes (further hand agitation is probably unnecessary during this step). Discard the soapy water, then rinse the goods with *warm* water (105°F), then drain.

6. Refill the bucket with *warm* water and rinse under continually refreshed running *warm* water for two minutes, then drain.

7. Refill the bucket with *cold* tap water, rinse for one minute, then drain. Repeat this step until the discard water is clear.

8. Hang the fabric to air-dry, or use your usual clothes-drying machine. (If you have thoroughly rinsed the goods, they should be safe to place in your household dryer. However, in case of any residual traces of unrinsed dye, I still recommend against drying the goods in the same dryer "load" as personal clothing items.)

pH (POTENTIAL OF HYDROGEN OR POWER OF HYDROGEN)

In chemistry, a scale numbered from 1 to 14 that defines the relative acidity or alkalinity of a liquid, solution, or (in our case) a dyebath. In the center of the scale, pH 7 is neutral and is the natural pH of (pure) water. pH above 7 is more alkaline, pH below 7 more acid.

How to check pH of a dyebath

To check pH, tear off a length of commercially produced pH paper (it comes on a roll in a dispenser, available from dye vendors), then dip it in the solution. The paper will change color. To determine the pH, compare the dipped strip of paper to the color guide on the dispenser. The color in a dyebath may obscure the color change on the paper and hinder an accurate reading. If this happens, consider buying a digital pH meter from one of the dye companies to take more clearly accurate readings.

How to change pH

To increase the pH of an acid solution to neutral 7, add soda ash (sodium carbonate). You can also add "baking soda" (sodium bicarbonate), but a larger amount of it will be required to shift the pH to neutral, and you cannot actually use baking soda to make dyebaths themselves.

To reduce the pH of an alkaline solution to neutral 7, add citric acid crystals or white vinegar.

As you add soda ash (or, as the case may be, citric acid or white vinegar), keep testing with the pH paper until you've achieved a pH of 7.

Recipes and Procedures for Fiber Reactive Dyes: Immersion Dyeing in Uneven and Even Colors

Immersion Dyeing: *Uneven* Colors

Dyeing fabric in any quantity requires considerable physical work, so you need good reasons to undertake it. The following techniques allow you to dye your own materials, not only in custom color palettes but with intentionally uneven colors, variegations, combinations, and unusual results on the *same* cloth. And here's some good news: uneven dyeing is actually *less* work, and the procedures less exacting! Here are some alternatives that might persuade you to experiment.

Uneven Color: "Cold Water" Super-Short and Easy *Full*-Immersion Method

Note that "cold water," although common parlance among dyers, is an imprecise nickname, because dyeing cellulose fibers with fiber reactive dyes actually requires *warm* tap water. The term "cold water" distinguishes this process only from other dyeing methods that require a direct heat source and *boiling*.

This quick-dye method (which, in classrooms and workshops over the years, I humorously called "the slapdash method") is intended for cellulose fibers and some lightweight silks (but *not* for wool).

It is a useful time-saver if you have several simultaneous tasks in the workspace. You can combine all the dyebath ingredients together, then go off to do something else while the goods soak and your unattended fabric continues to dye. Because you dispense with precise measurements and just estimate approximate amounts of dye and chemicals, this method is delightfully easy and the color just as permanent as the long method outlined below.

The process requires *no agitation* of the dyebath and produces *very uneven* and *unpredictable* color distribution, a rather "marbled" appearance (01-17) that captures the folds and water flow of the dyebath in the fabric itself. In addition, pure dye colors mixed into a composite color often separate in the dyebath, because of their differing speeds of reaction and penetration, to create halos of the individual components.

1. Keeping the goods set aside and dry for now, fill a plastic bucket with the amount of warm tap water (about 105°F) that you estimate will barely cover them.

2. Put on your rubber gloves and work apron.

3. Add the desired amount of dye in stock solution to the water. Check the approximate hue and depth of dye by dipping in pieces of white paper towel.

4. *All at once*, add the *entire* necessary amounts of salt and soda ash (for cellulose fibers) or citric acid crystals (for silks). Use about ¼–½ cup salt and 1–2 T. soda ash for every ½ yard of medium-weight fabric such as cotton broadcloth. Use 1–2 T. citric acid crystals for every ½ yard of light-to-medium-weight silk. (I know these are a bit more than the ratios I laid out in the typical chart above, but with this uneven color technique, in which the goods will sit unattended for a while, the extra assistants help.)

5. Add the dry goods. (If you underestimated the amount of water necessary to completely cover them, add more *hot* tap water now.) Let the bath stand, *without* agitating, for one to two hours, or even overnight.

6. Rinse out. (See the "Universal Rinse-Out" text box, page 24.)

01-17 Attractive uneven mottling of color with the "Super-Short and Easy *Full*-Immersion Method." Procion MX fiber reactive dyes. Composite color: sage 715 and strong orange 202, mixed together thoroughly in equal amounts before adding to dyebath. Cotton print cloth and knitted cotton shoestring tape.

01-18 Dramatic color separations and value contrasts, using the Uneven Color: Low-Immersion Method, "cold water." Procion MX fiber reactive dyes. Composite color: sage 715 and strong orange 202 (the *same* colors as 01-17), added to dyebath separately in equal amounts, mixed while arranging fabric. Cotton print cloth.

Uneven Color: "Cold Water" *Low*-Immersion Method

This quick-dye method is similar to the Uneven Color "Cold Water" Super-Short and Easy *Full*-Immersion Method, above, but intentionally deprives the goods of the full amount of water and thereby increases the intensity and amount of *unevenness* of the dye distribution. Use it to achieve *very* textured and serendipitous dye results (01-18).

1. Place a small amount of water in a bucket, *but not enough to cover the goods*. Typically, at least half of the goods should be in water, with the remainder extending upward into the air in folds. But the amount of water will vary with the amount and type of goods and may require some differently shaped and sized dye containers for small batches.

2. Put on your rubber gloves and work apron.

3. Add the necessary amount of dye in stock solution to the water. (Check the approximate hue and depth of dye by dipping in pieces of white paper towel.) When you've achieved your desired color, add salt and soda ash (for cellulose goods) or citric acid crystals (for protein goods). Use about ¼–½ cup salt and 1–2 T. soda ash for every ½ yard of medium-weight fabric such as cotton broadcloth. Use 1–2 T. citric acid crystals for every ½ yard of light-to-medium-weight silk.

4. Add the dry (unsoaked) goods, pushing them down into the water, intentionally folding, wadding, wrinkling, or crumpling them so that some of the goods are immersed in the dyebath but some are not. Move the goods around just enough so that all of them come in contact with the dye *at first* (but *not* necessarily repeatedly), even though some of them will extend out of the dye for the remainder of the process.

5. Allow the goods to sit in the dyebath for one to two hours, or longer, depending on the thickness and amount of the goods. (For example, a silk organza might need to sit in the bath for only an hour or two, while a heavy cotton twill might require 24 hours or more.) If there are multiple dye colors in the combined color you add to the dyebath, some of them will separate out and provide a surprise as they wick, arrange, and combine on the goods.

6. Rinse out. (See the "Universal Rinse-Out" text box, page 24.)

Uneven Color: "Cold Water" Rainbow Dye Method for *Cellulose* Fibers or Silk

Rainbow dyeing (01-19) is a version of low-immersion dyeing that allows you to spontaneously pour or squirt a variety of colors (in solution) directly onto sections of the partially immersed fabric. The results can be dramatic (high color contrast) or subtle (low color contrast), depending on the color palette, the dye concentrations, and the methods or tools used to pour.

1. Keeping the goods set aside and dry for now, place a small amount of warm (about 105°F) tap water in a bucket, *but not enough to cover the goods*.

2. Put on your rubber gloves and work apron.

3. For cellulose fibers, add the salt to the hot water. But omit this step if you are dyeing silk.

4. Add the goods, pushing them down into the water while intentionally folding, wadding, wrinkling, or crumpling them so that some of the goods are in the water and some are extending above it. Move them enough so that all the goods come in contact with the water *at first* (but *not* necessarily repeatedly), even though some of them will extend out of the dyebath for the remainder of the process.

5. For this technique, your stock solution is too concentrated to squirt or pour directly onto the goods in the dye pot, and you will not be agitating the goods in the water after you apply the color to them. You therefore need to create a weaker (more watered-down) version of each color you want to squirt or pour. In a separate plastic squeeze bottle for each color, mix its stock solution with warm water (the amount depending on your desired depth of dye) and then add soda ash (for cellulose fibers) or citric acid crystals (for protein fibers) to each squeeze bottle to create a more dilute but still-activated version of the original stock solution. (You might, for example, create a diluted red solution in one squeeze bottle and a diluted blue solution in another. But if you want to combine them for a customized purple *before* squirting or pouring it on the fabric, you can also combine two or more stock solutions in the same squeeze bottle and then dilute and activate them.)

6. *One at a time,* introduce the activated liquid dyes (however many you made) into the goods and water by dribbling or pouring the liquid dye directly onto the goods, or by squirting the goods with a syringe or plastic squeeze bottle, but *do not* agitate the goods. (For a more focused application, you can even aim the liquid dye at specific parts of the goods.) Add all the colors you chose, side by side or overlapping. Don't be shy about adding enough dye; this is a dramatic color exercise!

7. Allow the goods to sit in the dyebath (it's OK if some of the goods still protrude into the air) for one to two hours, or longer, depending on the thickness and amount of the goods. Or allow the goods to sit for 30 minutes or so (some still immersed in the dyebath, and perhaps some not), then remove the goods and seal them in a plastic bag for 24 hours. (Sealing them in a bag for much more than 24 hours won't make a large difference in the color but may invite mildew or mold.)

8. Rinse out. (See the "Universal Rinse-Out" text box, page 24.)

01-19 Strong and dramatic outcome, using the Uneven Color: Rainbow Dye Method, "cold water." Procion MX fiber reactive dyes. Composite color: sage 715 and strong orange 202 (the *same* colors as 01-17 and 01-18) but poured separately and directly on the partially submerged goods. Cotton print cloth.

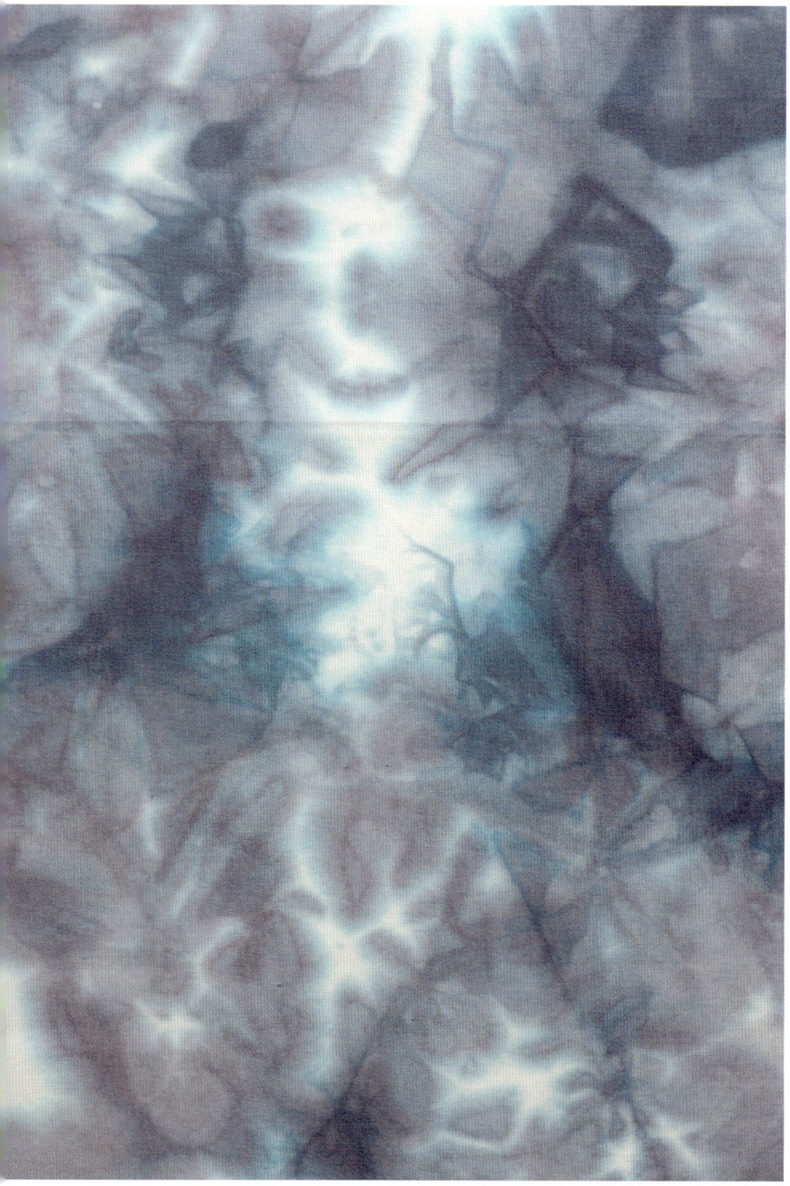

1. Weigh the goods while they are still dry. Then soak the goods in warm tap water (the exact temperature isn't important) for 10–15 minutes.

2. Fill a separate plastic bucket with the amount of warm tap water (about 105ºF) that you estimate will cover the goods. Then add the desired amount of dye and the necessary amount of salt. Stir thoroughly.

3. Put on your rubber gloves and work apron.

4. Transfer the wet goods to the dyebath, stirring occasionally for 15 minutes.

5. Based on the original dry amount of goods, calculate the correct amount of soda ash (for cellulose fibers) or citric acid crystals (for silk) and add it to the dyebath. Stir thoroughly to mix, then continue stirring occasionally for another 15 minutes.

6. Press excess dye from the goods (but don't strenuously wring them, which might remove too much dye and moisture), then seal the *very wet* goods in a plastic bag for 24 hours. (Batching for more than 24 hours won't make a large difference in the color but may invite mildew or mold.)

7. Rinse out. (See the "Universal Rinse-Out" text box, page 24.)

Uneven Color: "Cold Water" Short-Immersion Method Plus Batching, for *Cellulose* Fibers or Silk

This method, a middle ground between the shorter and longer methods, requires less agitation of the dyebath but still creates uneven color. It combines a short period of immersion with *batching* (closing up the wet goods in plastic to sit and "marinate"). This method still exposes the goods to dye and water for a long period (essential for the chemical reaction), but in the meantime you can leave the goods substantially unattended. If you don't want dyebaths left unattended in the workspace, this method allows you to simply package up the goods in a plastic bag, set them safely aside, and return later to complete the rinse-out.

Immersion Dyeing: *Even* Colors

Because of the wealth of solid-colored fabrics and threads on the commercial market, you may regard dyeing your own *solid, even-colored* fabric as unnecessary or even a waste of time. However, it's a valuable skill to match color chips for a commissioned work; to maintain a textile product line (such as scarves or yardage) in specific colorways; or to create those precise custom colors you imagine for your work. To achieve accurate, smooth, and reliable results, use one of the long methods of immersion dyeing detailed below. Although the long method takes more time, it delivers solid, even color and the best washfastness and lightfastness possible. Dye solid-custom-colored fabrics to piece or appliqué, or to provide smooth, uncluttered backgrounds for resist dyeing, screen printing, and direct application.

01-20 Low immersion and batching. Procion MX fiber reactive dyes. Cotton fabric.

Even Color: "Cold Water" Long Method, for *Cellulose* Fibers (e.g., cotton, linen, rayon, ramie)

1. Begin with clean, prepared, fully rinsed and then completely *dried* goods. Weigh the goods and make note of the weight.

2. Wet out (soak) the goods thoroughly for 15–20 minutes (set a kitchen timer) in plain warm tap water (about 100°F). This helps ensure that the dye will go into the fabric evenly.

3. Put on your rubber gloves and work apron.

4. Consult the chart at top of page 23 to calculate amounts of dye stock solution. Based on the weight of the goods, and the desired depth of dye, calculate the amount of stock dye solution you need for your dyebath. Measure out that amount of stock dye solution and set it aside to add to the dyebath later.

5. Calculate the amount of warm water needed for the weight of the goods at a rate of approximately 2.5 gallons per pound (or 20–30 times the total weight of the goods). Place that amount of *warm* tap water (about 105°F) in a plastic, enamel, or stainless-steel bucket or tub.

6. Calculate the amount of salt needed for the dyebath. Use 2–3 T. of salt per yard of goods. Measure out the salt and divide it into three approximately equal parts onto pieces of dry paper towel or in dry small cups. (Alternatively, dissolve the salt in hot water in equal amounts in three small cups.)

7. Calculate the amount of soda ash (sodium carbonate) needed for the dyebath. Use 1 T. of soda ash per yard of goods. Measure out the soda ash and dissolve it in a bit of boiling water (a larger amount of water for large dyebaths, and smaller for smaller, whatever is a sufficient amount of water to dissolve the soda ash). This step prevents spots and helps ensure even dye distribution.

8. Set aside the prepared salt and soda to be ready for use in later steps.

9. Add the dye stock solution to the warm water in the tub and stir to mix well.

10. Add the soaked and *still-wet* goods to the warm water.

11. Agitate the fabric in the dyebath continuously for 10–15 minutes (use a timer). Agitation is the single most important step to achieve solid, smooth, and evenly distributed color. *From this point and continuing through the steps below, continuously move the goods within the dyebath* to prevent folds, wads, tangles, wrinkles, or layers of cloth pressed against each other—any of which can produce uneven color or unwanted resists. Move the fabric however you wish: roll it, lift it, rearrange it, swirl it around, or do some of each. Just keep it moving (but don't make it slosh out of the pot).

12. At five-minute intervals (use a timer), add one of the three equal portions of salt. Keep the goods within the dye bucket but push them aside. Add the salt to the nongoods side of the dyebath (i.e., do *not* put the salt directly onto the goods, where it will cause spots) and agitate the bath thoroughly to dissolve the salt. Then push the goods back into the main bath and immediately begin agitating the bath *thoroughly and continuously*. Repeat for each addition of salt.

13. After all the salt is added, continue to agitate the goods for 20 minutes (use a timer).

14. The addition of the soda ash mixture is the step that creates the most dramatic visible change in the color of the goods. Keep the goods within the dye bucket, but push them aside. Add the soda ash solution to the nongoods side of the dyebath (i.e., do *not* put the soda ash mixture directly onto the goods), then push the goods back into the main bath and (using a timer) immediately begin agitating the bath *thoroughly and continuously* for 10 minutes, then agitate again at least every five minutes for a total of 60 minutes. (Yes, it's tedious, but it gets good results.)

15. Rinse out. (See the "Universal Rinse-Out" text box, page 24.)

01-21 Solid, even dye color with Procion MX fiber reactive dyes, using the Even Color: Long Method, "cold water." Color: strong orange 202. Cotton print cloth and 5/2 pearl cotton yarn.

SODA ASH VS. CITRIC ACID ON MIXED CELLULOSE AND PROTEIN FIBERS

Dyers work with many natural-fiber types, primarily cellulose and protein. As we discussed, each fiber type requires a different dye chemistry: acidic baths (approximately pH 3 from citric acid crystals) work best for protein fibers (silk and wool), and alkaline baths (approximately pH 11 from soda ash) work best for cellulose fibers (cotton, linen, rayon, ramie).

If you want to *combine* cellulose and protein fibers in the *same* dyebath, use soda ash as the catalyst. It works best on cotton and linen but will still produce reasonably good dye penetration and permanent coloration on silk.

If, to save time, you want to dye both fiber types *simultaneously* but in *separate* dyebaths, plan to physically separate the acid baths from the alkaline baths. Place them in different parts of the room and label them clearly to prevent confusion and accidental combination of citric acid and soda ash in the same bath. (If combined—something you'll typically want to prevent—citric acid and soda ash can cause an acid-base chemical reaction in which they essentially offset each other, bring pH close to neutral 7, and thereby defeat their individual usefulness as catalysts to attach dye to fiber. Such an acid-base chemical reaction also produces a nondangerous but dramatic small "eruption" as carbon dioxide is released, with attendant fizzing, hissing, and bubbling.)

Even Color: "Cold Water" Long Method, for *Silk*

Some silk goods will respond to the "cold water" method outlined in detail above, in particular the lighter-weight silks and silk organza. However, they require hotter tap water (at least 140ºF) to ensure success. Silk processed by this method may not take the dye as deeply and will, in any case, require *citric acid crystals in place of both the salt and soda ash.*

Follow the Even Color: "Cold Water" Long Method, for *cellulose fibers,* detailed above, *except* instead of adding salt and soda ash (as in steps 12, 13, and 14), pull the goods out of the way and add the correct amount of citric acid crystals to the dyebath, stirring well to mix. Use 1 T. of citric acid crystals per yard of goods. Mix the bath thoroughly after the addition.

Fiber reactive dyes usually don't "exhaust" as a result of the dye process (i.e., they don't just completely penetrate the goods and then leave only clear water behind). However, in my experience, silk organza often *does* exhaust with this long method, so don't be surprised.

Even Color: "Hot Water" Long Method, for *Protein Fibers,* such as wool and silks

For the most permanent and deepest depth of dye color results with fiber reactive dyes on protein fibers, a "hot water" process is best. This requires a temperature-controlled heat source (stovetop or hot plate), metal or enamel dye pots (not plastic), and simmering of the dyebath for the duration. When moving or handling the hot dye pots, use padded oven mitts over your rubber gloves to prevent burns on your arms and hands. Consult the chart at top of page 23 to calculate amounts of dye stock solution.

1. Put on your rubber gloves and work apron.

2. Wash the goods thoroughly in warm water, soap, and ammonia (¼ c. ammonia per 1 gallon of water). Rinse the goods *thoroughly* and let them soak in a separate bucket of plain tap water for 10 minutes.

3. Using 3.5 gallons of water per pound of goods (yes, plenty of water to let the goods "swim"), fill an enamel or stainless-steel dye pot with warm tap water, about 105ºF (check with a candy thermometer). Place the pot on the burner. Add a sufficient amount of ammonium acetate, acetic acid, white vinegar, or citric acid crystals (but only *one* of those, not all!) to produce a pH of 7.0. (I usually prefer white vinegar or citric acid, because I consider them safer.) Check with pH paper. (See page 24 text box about pH.)

4. Place the wet goods in the pot. Let the goods soak in this solution for 15 minutes (set a timer) with the burner turned on a low setting but sufficient to maintain the temperature close to 105ºF (monitor with a candy thermometer).

5. Lift the goods out of the bath momentarily, add the dye in stock solution (consult the chart at top of page 23 to calculate amounts of dye stock solution), and stir thoroughly. Reintroduce the goods and continue to stir while *slowly* bringing the temperature of the dyebath to a simmer, as close as possible to 185ºF for silk or 200ºF for wool, but *not* exceeding these temperatures, because hotter temperatures will destroy silk and may felt wool. Hold the temperature steady and simmer the dyebath for 60 minutes, stirring occasionally (with a stick or large spoon, *not* your gloved hand) and gently (because too much agitation and too-rapid changes in temperature will also cause wool to felt).

6. Leaving the goods in the dyebath, remove the dyebath from the heat source and allow it to cool naturally to room temperature.

7. Choose the appropriate rinsing instructions for your fabric:

   • *For silk*: Rinse out. (See the "Universal Rinse-Out" text box, page 24.)

   • *For wool*: After the goods reach room temperature, rinse the goods with *tepid* water until the water runs clear. Then wash in *tepid* water with Synthrapol. Move the goods around *gently* in the Synthrapol solution or just allow them to soak. Rinse thoroughly in *cool* water to remove any excess dye and soap. Press excess water out of the goods by hand (but *don't* wring them). Spread paper or plastic on the floor to catch drips as you hang the goods to dry. (Note: You *never* want to put dyed wool in a heated clothes dryer, because doing so will reduce your lovely, loose batch of dyed wool to a dense, shrunken "hair ball" of felted wool.) When the goods have dried, discard the paper (or wash off the plastic) you placed under them.

01-22 Dyed wool yarns.

Recipes and Procedures for Fiber Reactive Dyes: Overdyeing

Until now, we have focused on dyeing white fabric with dyes mixed to create *composite* colors for each individual dyebath. Now we'll look at *overdye*, a way to mix fiber reactive dye colors sequentially in two or more separate and successive dyebaths. Each subsequent dyebath lays another color over the previous one to alter the color incrementally. The *visual* result subtly suggests the *physical* layers of color on the cloth, since they combine optically to create a custom color with depth and a slight visual vibration (01-23).

One of the advantages of fiber reactive dyes is their ability to overdye, and you can take advantage of this characteristic in several ways. Most simply, if you dye a color that is "just not right," you can overdye it with any other color to change, tone, enrich, or shift the original hue to match your imagination. With each successive dyebath, the color of the fabric will continue to change, shift hues, or darken (or a combination of these). For example:

- If you dye a cloth blue but then find it is too light, you can darken it with a subsequent dyebath.

- If the blue seems to lean too much toward the violet, you can correct it with a subsequent dyebath that leans toward the green.

- If colors are too bright (high intensity), you can *tone them down* by overdyeing with their complements, or with gray, or with a custom toner. (See the text box about toners.)

- If colors are too light (high value), you can *darken* them by overdyeing with more of the same dye or any other darker color.

Caveats:

- Because there is no such thing as a white dye, overdyeing cannot lighten or raise the value of a color. To accomplish that goal with fabric you've already dyed, you'll need to use a discharge process (discussed in chapter 6).

- After a certain number of overdye attempts with fiber reactive dyes, cellulose fibers will reach saturation (i.e., the fibers just won't physically accept any more dye). Beyond that point, *no* amount of continued overdyeing will produce a change in the color. Each fabric or yarn will have its own different and particular threshold for this capacity.

- When fiber reactive dyes cease to overdye on *silk*, you can still switch to acid dyes (discussed later in this chapter) for additional color changes.

01-23 Overdye sequence with multiple colors (three variables). Procion MX fiber reactive dyes. Colors: fuchsia + yellow gold + a composite color mixed from turquoise and sky blue. Cotton broadcloth.

TONING OR ALTERING COLORS *WITHOUT OVERDYEING*

You can change the *perceived* color of a custom hand-dyed fabric or commercially dyed/printed fabric, without actually resorting to more dye work, by *overlaying* it with transparent fabrics, such as netting, mesh, illusion, organza, or organdy. (For more ideas, see chapter 8 in the *Dry Techniques* book.)

01-24 Overdyeing. Original fabrics dyed/printed in blues, greens, browns, pinks, and golds, and *all* those fabrics were then overdyed in the *same* brown/medium-value dyebath. Procion MX fiber reactive dyes. Cottons, silk, velveteen.

The chance to re-dye, adjust, and fine-tune color allows you to create harmonious color palettes with leftover fabrics. For example, if you have a group of dyed fabrics that you consider weak, ugly, or visually unconnected, overdye them *all in the same dyebath* to create a group of more harmonious fabrics. The common dyebath introduces a continuous color link among the fabrics, and although subtle, it connects them visually. A light-color (high value) overdye (as in 01-24) will tone and harmonize them. A medium-color (medium value) overdye will offset the original hues more thoroughly and bring them much closer together visually (as in a dark-blue overdye, which results in all the fabrics appearing as various types of "blue"). Overdyeing with very dark colors (very low value from a strong depth of dye) will "swamp" the original colors and result in only very slight variations of that single hue (which is not a "bad" thing, if it's what you actually want). Any of these results could be quite useful as you prepare a palette of colors for piecing, appliqué, or other fabric construction work.

For overdyeing, use any of the immersion techniques discussed in the preceding major section.

WHAT IS A TONER?

A *toner* is stock solution of black combined with several other hues. The additions to black usually include a pair of complementary colors, or a pair of split complements, or a pair of "near" complements, in differing ratios (within the pair, or between the pair and the black, or both). Practically speaking, the toner is a complex dark gray with chromatic undertones. It can tilt toward warm or cool gray, depending the other colors mixed with the black.

Mixing a toner

Because you yourself "design" the toner, there is no set recipe for making it. Start with all component dye colors mixed into stock solutions. As you concoct the toner mix, keep track of the percentage relationships of the various components (for example: 50% black, 25% magenta, 25% green; or one-third each; or other). As desired, shift the color of the toner by changing the relative amounts of other hues added to the black. To make the toner warmer, add larger amounts of red, orange, and/or yellow to the black. To make the toner cooler, add larger amounts of blue, green, and/or violet to the black. To make the toner more "earthy," add more brown to the black.

Uses for toners

Whether used alone or in combination with other dye colors, toners can be useful both in overdyeing (see pages 32–33) and gradation dyeing (see pages 35–45).

Although they contain black, toners provide more complex, sophisticated, and mysterious color nuances than using black alone. They can be used to decrease the intensity of overly intense hues with overdyeing, to create darker moods and contexts in color palettes, or to work with constant and/or variable hues in a gradation sequence.

The depth of dye resulting from toner, used alone, depends on the amount added, just as the depth of dye resulting from using a color stock solution alone depends on the amount of dye added. If you use a combination of both toner *and* a color dye in the same bath, the resulting depth of dye will be a composite of the two. The principle for each is the same: the less (or more) you add, the less (or greater) the impact on the resulting dyed cloth. If only a small amount of toner is used, its effect on the dyebath is likewise reduced, but the more toner you add to a dyebath, the darker the depth of dye, the more muted (de-intensified) the color (because of the black introduced by the toner), and the more the toner will dominate the dyebath color.

Recipes and Procedures for Fiber Reactive Dyes: Dyeing Gradation Sequences of Color

In essence, a *gradation* is a gradual and orderly change. In drawing, artists use gradations of marks or colors to shade objects and create the illusion of three-dimensional space on a flat surface. Similarly, sculptors might gradate the size, proportions, or position of three-dimensional objects to lead the eye through space. Gradations serve the same purposes in fabric compositions and constructions such as pieced quilts. *Color gradations* in textiles are of two basic types: those created by a set of *separately dyed* skeins of yarn or pieces of fabric (which I'll discuss here) and those created across the surface of a *single* piece of fabric (as discussed in chapter 3).

Use any of the immersion techniques (even or uneven) discussed in the preceding sections to create the gradating colors. Choose the specific type of gradation you want to produce from the basic list below and follow its guidelines to calculate the amounts of dye you'll need for each successive dyebath in the gradation.

Generally speaking, you will build the color gradation by increasing or decreasing the amount of dye *from dyebath to dyebath* in regular, plotted, incremental steps. Thus, the amount and type of change from one piece of fabric to the next in the sequence are orderly and measured. Gradated fabric colors work together harmoniously in pieced textiles, quilts, wall hangings, garments, or accessories.

A color gradation may vary in *speed*; that is, the number of steps required to move from one clearly discernible hue to the next in the sequence. The speed is controlled by the size of the unit of measure you use. For example, a very large unit might be a ¼ c. of dye stock solution, which would create dramatic visual jumps from step to step in the sequence. On the other hand, a small unit might be 2 tsp. of dye stock solution, which would yield smooth, fluid transitions in which colors seem to "melt" or blend together from step to step.

By their nature, gradations share at least one hue (i.e., that hue is present, in some amount, in each dyebath), which creates an "internal harmony" that links the fabrics visually (even when the link is subtle). When used together in the same composition or construction, these gradating colors will lead the eye along the path of the color change or will create the illusion of depth or space.

OPPOSITE: 01-25 Complementary gradation, warm to cool. Pieced and appliquéd. Procion MX fiber reactive dyes and print pigments. Cotton broadcloth. Scale: 72" × 54". Collection: Embassy Suites Hotel, East Syracuse, New York.

01-26 Short, four-step gradation, cool to warm, using Procion MX fiber reactive dyes in four separate dyebaths. Cotton print cloth.

Constants and Variables: The Essential Concepts of Dyeing Gradations

All gradations rely on the relationships between *constant* colors and *varying* colors in a sequence of dyebaths. Understanding these two basic concepts will help you understand the instructions for gradation dyeing.

A *constant* is a given hue (which may be a mixture of several pure "out of the bottle" hues, what we will call a "composite color"), at a given depth of dye or strength, that remains a consistent ingredient throughout a progression. Therefore, the constant can be mixed up ahead of time and added *in the same amount* to each dyebath.

A *variable* is a given hue or composite color, which *changes* in strength as it moves along a specified depth of dye range, throughout the sequence of dyebaths. The variable can move from a smaller depth of dye to a larger one, or vice versa.

All gradations contain variables (that's what produces the change in colors). But some gradations contain both constants and variables working together. We will discuss both types in the specific examples below. If you like setting up systems, you can devise your own variations on the basic ones, including the use of more than two hues.

Gradations are fun and exciting to dye. The color mixing involved will produce unusual and unexpected composite colors that you might not ordinarily have tried to achieve, which will dramatically enrich your "color vocabulary" and provide wonderful ranges of color for the techniques we'll discuss in the companion book *Dry Techniques*.

Specific Types of Gradations

The types of gradations outlined in this section are based on the basic color relationships you will find outlined in any book about design fundamentals. With each specific gradation, you'll find an explanation of the constant or variable hues, or both, along with guidelines for calculating the amounts of stock solution for each dyebath in the series (measured with simple kitchen-type implements, such as measuring spoons and cups). You will find the step-by-step instructions for dyeing all types of gradations at the conclusion of this section.

This simple, relaxed approach to gradation dyeing maintains the distinct color changes from dyebath to dyebath but allows you to play with the color changes instead of worrying about precise measurements. This will produce one-time unique outcomes that introduce you to the possibilities of gradation dyeing. Later, you can learn to use more precise methods of measurement if you want exact reproductions of gradated colors.

TO ACHIEVE EQUAL *VISUAL* STEPS IN A DYED GRADATION

If, for example, you want to dye five equal *visual* steps (i.e., a gradation on five pieces of fabric), *double* the amount of dye in each sequential dyebath (a *geometric* progression). I used this approach to concoct the example sequences in this section (i.e., ½ T., 1 T., 2 T., 4 T., 8 T.). Or, if you wanted to dye eight equal visual steps (i.e., a gradation on eight pieces of fabric), you would continue the doubling of stock solution accordingly.

A note: If you increase the amount of dye by the *same unit or increment* (an *arithmetical* progression) in each of five dyebaths (e.g., 1 T., 2 T., 3 T., 4 T., 5 T.), you will produce a gradation of sorts, but the amount of color change *will not appear to be equal* from one fabric to the next.

01-27 Gradation with one variable (value or depth of dye gradation) but no constant. Procion MX fiber reactive dyes. Color: brown 510 doubled in each successive dyebath. Cotton print cloth.

01-28 Gradation with one constant and one variable (shade gradation) with change in depth of dye across three pieces of fabric. Procion MX fiber reactive dyes. Colors: constant fuchsia amount in each dyebath but black (the variable) doubled from one dyebath to the next. Cotton broadcloth.

Let's talk first about how to figure the *amount* of color for a certain sequence. Then, in the next section, we'll talk about how to actually *do* the gradated dyeing.

1. Calculating Colors: Gradation Sequence with *One Variable* but No Constant

This is essentially a depth-of-dye sequence and is the simplest of all gradations to calculate and process.

Add *one* single hue or composite color in regularly increasing (or decreasing) amounts to each dyebath in the sequence. Choose a simple but consistent unit of measure to vary the size of color change steps in the sequence as you wish, also consistent with the amount of fabric to be dyed. To achieve equal visual steps, use the same amount of *fabric* in each dyebath but double the amount of *stock solution* from dyebath to dyebath in succession. (For example, in a five-step gradation you might use ½ T., 1 T., 2 T., 4 T., 8 T. of stock solution.)

Result: A sequence of fabrics that range from lighter or less intense to darker or more intense applications of a single hue. For example, light to dark brown (01-27).

01-29 Gradation with one constant and one variable (analogous gradation) with change in depth of dye across six pieces of fabric. Procion MX fiber reactive dyes. Colors: constant turquoise amount in each dyebath but magenta doubled from one dyebath to the next. Cotton print cloth.

01-30 Gradation with one constant and two variables (analogous gradation) with hues of differing values and change in depth of dye. Procion MX fiber reactive dyes. Colors: red (constant amount), yellow added in *decreasing* amounts in each successive dyebath, and scarlet added in *increasing* amounts in each successive dyebath. Cotton broadcloth.

01-31 Gradation with two combined constants and one variable (toner gradation) with change (increase) in depth of dye. Procion MX fiber reactive dyes. Colors: scarlet and red mixed together to make a single constant, then a cool toner (composed of black, sea blue, navy, avocado, turquoise) doubled in each successive dyebath. Cotton broadcloth.

01-32 Complementary gradation with a constant depth of dye. Procion MX fiber reactive dyes. Colors: decreasing amounts of scarlet with increasing amounts of avocado green. Cotton broadcloth.

2. Calculating Colors: Gradation Sequence with *One Constant* Color and *One Variable*

In this gradation an *equal* amount of one color is added to all the dyebaths. Then a *varying* amount of a second color is added to each in succession, which produces a sequence with varying depths of dye.

Constant: One single hue or composite color at a single depth of dye. Add the same *amount* (for example, 3 T.) of the constant hue to each dyebath.

Variable: Add your chosen hue in regularly increasing (or decreasing) amounts to each dyebath in the sequence. You can vary the size of color change steps in the sequence as you wish, but to achieve equal visual steps, use the same amount of *fabric* in each dyebath but double the amount of stock solution from dyebath to dyebath in succession. (For example, in a five-step gradation you might use ½ T., 1 T., 2 T., 4 T., 8 T. of stock solution.)

Results: The *color relationship* between the constant and variable colors will govern the result of their mixture. Some possible sequences among many:

- Black will create a *shade sequence* in which the constant color is increasingly dulled (lower intensity) and darkened (lower value), and the sequence moves toward black (01-28).

- Analogous colors (those next to each other on the color wheel; for example, yellows and oranges) will create a harmonious gradation in even steps around the color wheel (01-29 and 01-30). With two hues of approximately the same value (for example, red and orange), the color change will be more equally weighted; if one hue is lighter (higher value) than the other (for example, yellow and orange), then the darker hue will dominate the color progression faster.

- Custom-mixed toner (discussed in the text box above) will create a sequence of colors that become increasingly de-intensified or duller (01-31). Most toners contain black and a pair of complementary hues.

- Complementary colors (directly across from each other on the color wheel, such as green and magenta) will produce a sequence of fabrics with pure colors at each end and a series of de-intensified colors (that are hard to name) in the middle. This is perhaps the most visually interesting of the gradation sequences and generates a large number of rich and unusual colors in the process.

3. Calculating Colors: Gradation Sequence with *Two Variables* and Constant Depth of Dye

In this gradational sequence (such as 01-32), the total depth of dye remains *constant* across the gradation (i.e., the total amount of dye in each dyebath is the same, but the *ratio* of the two hues changes. (See the chart below for an example.)

Variables: Add two hues to each successive dyebath, the first in regularly *increasing* amounts, the second in correspondingly *decreasing* amounts. The two hues could be *complementary* (those directly across from each other on the color wheel), *analogous* (those next to each other on the color wheel), or *one hue plus a custom-mixed* toner (see the text box on mixing toners).

Select a single depth of dye and unit of measure (which equals the "part" in the chart below) for the sequence. For example, a sequence of six dyebaths would be set up as in the following chart.

In this example, each dyebath will contain a total of seven "parts" (that is, one part equals 1/7 of the total amount

Calculation Chart for One-Constant, One-Variable Gradation Sequence

Parts	Dyebath 1	Dyebath 2	Dyebath 3	Dyebath 4	Dyebath 5	Dyebath 6
Variable #1	1 part	2 parts	3 parts	4 parts	5 parts	6 parts
Variable #2	6 parts	5 parts	4 parts	3 parts	2 parts	1 part
Total parts	7	7	7	7	7	7

01-33 Unevenly dyed custom color palette with analogous gradations. Procion MX fiber reactive dyes. Cotton fabrics.

of stock solution in each dyebath). Decide on the amount that constitutes *one part*. (In the sample chart above, if one part equals 1 T., then dyebath #1 will contain 1 T. of variable #1 and 6 T. of variable #2, and so on down the line.) You will add the two variable hues to each dyebath in the correct number of parts.

If *your* sequence has fewer than six steps, then you will have fewer total parts in each dyebath (for example, four parts for three dyebaths). If it has *more* than six steps, then you will have more total parts in each dyebath (for example, nine parts for eight dyebaths).

Select the two hues to vary throughout the sequence. Assign the amount of dye stock solution that equals "one part," using any standard unit of measure you wish. (For example: one part could be equal to 1 T.) Make a chart similar to the one above (but with the correct number of dyebaths for your sequence) to add the correct number of parts of each hue to each dyebath. To avoid confusion, measure and add variable #1 to each dyebath first. Then measure and add variable #2 to complete each dyebath's components.

SUPPLIES CHECKLIST FOR DYEING GRADATIONS WITH FIBER REACTIVE DYES

- fiber reactive dyes, in stock solution form, in the hues you wish to combine
- chemicals for cellulose fibers (salt and soda ash) or for silk (citric acid crystals)
- access to hot and cold running water
- plastic, enamel, or stainless-steel buckets, one for each color in the gradation sequence
- several short wooden sticks, to slightly tip the buckets forward
- masking tape and a permanent black marker
- longer sticks (plastic or wooden) to stir the dyebaths
- kitchen timer
- rubber gloves to cover the hand and lower arm
- work smock or apron
- hand cleaner / dye remover
- paper towels and rags for cleanup
- Synthrapol detergent for washing out dyed goods

Instructions for dyeing gradation sequences ("cold water" method):

The following sets of instructions describe dyeing a sequence of fabrics or skeins, each differently colored, in separate dyebaths. Gradations of color are most easily dyed in a series of dyebaths *in progress simultaneously*, where the steps in the sequence are visible and all the dye stock solutions are the same age and percentage of concentration. Although the process of tending multiple simultaneous dyebaths raises some logistical issues, this approach compresses the dyeing time necessary for an *entire sequence* into only slightly more time than a *single* dyebath. (It's a wonderful time-saver.)

1. Choose the *type* of gradation you desire from the alternatives above: one variable, one constant / one variable, or two variables.

2. Choose the *hues* you want to combine in the gradation. For ease of handling and measuring, prepare stock solutions of these component hues.

3. Choose the number of *steps* intended for your color sequence. At least four steps are needed to reveal the color gradation (01-26), but more than 12 make the dyeing task unwieldy.

4. Prepare and weigh the goods: Divide the goods into equally sized or weighted units, then cut fabric into equal-sized pieces and wind yarn or threads in equal-sized skeins. Separate the fabric pieces or skeins into the number of steps in your sequence; that is, one pile of goods for each dyebath. Weigh or measure the goods for each dyebath while they are still dry.

5. Choose your consistent *unit of measure* to be used for putting your stock solutions into the dyebath water, based on the amount of fabric. This will determine the amount of change from one step to the next in your gradation. Larger units (for example, 2 T. or ¼ c.) create larger visual steps that are more noticeable; smaller units (for example, ½ or 1 tsp.) create smaller steps that seem to melt into each other visually. Once you choose a unit of measure, use it consistently across the entire sequence of dyebaths.

6. Assemble the correct *number* of dye pots, one for each of the steps in your gradation. To help reduce confusion about the correct order of the dyebaths in each dyeing session, line the dye pots up *in order* (step 1, step 2, step 3, etc.) on your table or working surface. Number each of them temporarily with a short piece of masking tape and use a permanent black marker to write the step number on it. Keep the dye pots in this order as you work.

7. Calculate the *amount of warm water* needed for the weight of the goods in each dye pot at a rate of approximately 2.5 gallons per pound (or 20–30 times the total weight of the goods). Place that amount of *warm* tap water (about 105°F) in each plastic, enamel, or stainless-steel bucket or tub. Since you cannot be in more than one place at one time (it's a law of physics!), you cannot fully attend simultaneously to all the dyebaths in a sequence. Thus, you will have to devise a way to keep the fabrics or skeins submerged sufficiently in the dye while you move from pot to pot down the line, adding chemicals and agitating the goods. Try placing a wooden stick *under* the back edge of each dye pot to tip it slightly toward you. This effectively deepens the bath level and better submerges the goods.

8. Calculate the correct amount of *dye stock solution* needed for each dyebath, using the consistent unit of measure you established in step 5. (Consult the instructions for the specific gradation method you've chosen.)

9. Calculate the amount of *salt* needed for the dyebath (but omit this step for silk). Use 8 T. of salt per pound of goods (see chart above). Measure out the salt for each dyebath onto pieces of dry paper towel or in small cups that you place in front of each dyebath.

10. Calculate the amount of *soda ash* (for cellulose fibers) or *citric acid crystals* (for silk) needed per dyebath. Use 3 T. of soda ash or citric acid per pound of goods (see chart above). Measure out the soda ash or citric acid crystals for each dyebath in the sequence and dissolve the correct amount in a bit of boiling water (a larger amount of water for large dyebaths, and smaller for smaller, whatever is a sufficient amount of water to dissolve the soda ash). This step prevents spots and helps ensure even dye distribution. Place each dissolved soda or citric acid solution in a separate small cup in front of each dye pot.

11. Measure and add the correct amount of dye stock solution to the warm water in each of the dye pots and stir to mix well. (Consult the specifications for the specific type of gradation you want to produce.)

12. Add the *salt* to *each* dyebath and stir *each* to mix well.

13. Add the same amount of *fabric* to *each* dyebath and stir

each dyebath well, moving down the line of dye pots steadily and without interruption. (You'll need to work fairly quickly to get all of the dyebaths engaged with their respective pieces of fabric.)

14. Agitate the fabric in the dyebath continuously for 20 minutes (use a timer). To avoid contamination of colors from one dyebath to the next, use a *separate* stick to stir each dyebath, moving slowly along the line of pots, stirring each in succession, so that no dyebath goes unattended for very long. (The exact recipes and procedures for various depths of dye, addition of fixatives, and achieving even or uneven color are discussed above in the section on immersion dyeing.) If you have a studio assistant or a friend willing to help, four hands can do this better than two. You may be able to improvise other methods based on the size and shape of your dye pots or your willingness to accept (or even welcome) uneven dye results on the goods.

15. The addition of the soda ash mixture is the step that creates the most dramatic visible change in the color of the goods. Add the soda ash to *each* dyebath, in sequence, as follows: Keep the goods within the dye bucket but push them aside with your gloved hand. Add the soda ash solution to the nongoods side of the dyebath (i.e., do *not* put the soda ash mixture directly onto the goods), then push the goods back into the main bath and immediately begin agitating the bath *thoroughly*.

16. Dye the goods for an additional 60 minutes (use a timer), agitating each dye pot with its stick at least every five minutes for the rest of this hour-long cycle.

17. Rinse out. (See the "Universal Rinse-Out" text box, page 24.)

18. Dry the goods. Hang to dry or use a dryer (in the case of skeins of yarn or thread, use only air drying, to prevent tangling).

01-34 Thickened fiber reactive dyes used for screen printing. Cotton broadcloth, thread, polyester batting.

SUPPLY CHECKLIST FOR DIRECT APPLICATION SOLUTIONS AND PASTES

- hot and cold water
- sodium alginate (a natural thickener made from seaweed, available from most sellers of fiber reactive dyes)
- metaphos (sodium hexametaphosphate, available from most sellers of fiber reactive dyes, essentially a water softener that makes a smoother paste when combined with the sodium alginate)
- urea crystals (a humectant, also available from dye sellers, in odorless pearlized form)
- salt, soda ash, or citric acid crystals
- dye in stock solution form
- cups, spoons
- electric mixer and large bowl (for thick pastes only)

Recipes and Procedures for Fiber Reactive Dyes: Dye Solutions and Pastes for Direct Application and Screen Printing

In addition to the wide range of immersion dye possibilities, fiber reactive dyes can be directly applied to cloth with painted washes, stamped patterns, and screen-printed images. Dyes create *transparent* colors, images, and patterns that "sink into the fibers" visually, as they optically mix or create new composite colors where the dyes overlap. Dyes also leave the fabric surface *unchanged* and ready to accept later applications of dye or pigment.

This section will discuss formulas to prepare dye intended for direct application. See chapters 3 and 4 for ways to *use* these dye preparations in direct application and screen printing.

To prepare fiber reactive dyes for direct application, you must mix them into a chemical solution or a thickener (as outlined on pages 43 to 45), or both, in one of two basic concentrations, and add the activating chemicals just before use. You can test and decide on the specific relative thickness of the solution to produce the results you want.

I'll discuss a "thin solutions" method of direct application and a "thick paste" method, and the most appropriate uses of each. However, before starting either of these methods, you need to make *chemical water*. This is easily prepared by combining three ingredients: metaphos, urea, and water.

Instructions for mixing chemical water:

1. In a plastic quart jar, stir together 2 tsp. metaphos, 4 T. granulated urea, and 2 c. of hot (140°F) tap water.

2. After these are well dissolved, add 2 c. of cold tap water, cover the jar tightly, and shake well. This makes 1 quart of chemical water, which can be stored indefinitely but lasts longer when refrigerated.

Thin Solutions

Thinned dye solutions are particularly good for watercolor painting, spraying, brushing, sprinkling, spattering, sponging, or painting on wet or dry fabric to create soft, blended, or indefinite edges and layered composite colors. For these applications, simply mix the dye stock solution into chemical water. There is no hard-and-fast rule or recipe for the amount of dye; instead, it will just depend on the depth of dye you want to achieve. Then you'll activate the dye solution as usual, by adding soda ash (for cellulose fibers) or citric acid crystals (for silk).

Instructions for making a thin dye solution:

1. Put the desired amount of chemical water in a cup or bowl.

2. Put on rubber gloves and apron. Follow appropriate dye safety precautions as described earlier in this chapter.

3. Add the desired amount of dye, in stock solution form, to the chemical water. Mix thoroughly. An approximate rule of thumb:

   1 c. chemical water + 1 tsp. stock solution = light value

   1 c. chemical water + 4 tsp. stock solution = medium value

   1 c. chemical water + 8 tsp. stock solution = dark value

   Note: This rule of thumb assumes a stock solution prepared with 1 T. of powdered dye per cup of water. But if you made your stock solution stronger, you'll need less stock solution per cup of chemical water than the formulas above to achieve the respective values. If you made your stock solution weaker, you'll need more of it.

4. Just before you start to apply the dye, *activate the solution* by adding soda ash (for cellulose fibers) or citric acid crystals (for protein fibers) in the ratio of 1 tsp. of activator per cup of the *combined* chemical water and stock solution. *The activator is essential but will remain effective for about an hour, so after activation, plan to work steadily and relatively quickly.*

5. Apply the activated dye solution to the fabric in whatever way you desire. See chapter 3 (direct application) for ideas.

6. *Before* rinsing out, use *one* of the methods under "Setting the Dyes" on page 45.

Thick Pastes

You can apply thick dye pastes by using almost any object or tool you can imagine: *drawing* with a ruling pen, quill, squeeze bottle, or syringe; *painting* with brushes, feathers, or found objects; *sponging* on color; *stamping* with rubber stamps, spatulas, knives, rollers, found objects, or carved vegetables (yes, really—but only with *firm* vegetables!); and *screen printing* (01-34). See chapters 3 and 4 for details.

To apply colored dye in specific areas and keep it in place (so it won't spread, wick, or blur edges), thicken it into a paste form. Mix the paste to any desired consistency, testing it as you might a sauce when cooking (e.g., thin enough to easily run off of a spoon, or thick enough to cling completely to the spoon, even when turned upside down). The thicker the paste, the harder the edge it will hold when applied to the fabric, and the more precise you can be in making marks with the dye color. Once you have mixed a dye paste, you can still thin it, but you must do so with *chemical water*, because plain tap water will dilute the fixative chemistry.

Instructions for making a thick dye solution or paste:

Note: Many dye vendors sell very effective print paste mixtures in which the components of my following recipe are already present in the correct proportions and require only the addition of water, then stirring. These products cost more than "doing your own" but may prove convenient, since they eliminate the need to stock the metaphos and urea separately.

1. To make the basic thickener, sprinkle 3–10 tsp. of sodium alginate (a seaweed derivative) into 1 qt. of *chemical water* (see recipe above) in a large bowl. Stir with a dedicated electric mixer on low speed until the mixture is thickened and free from lumps, then continue stirring for another five minutes, slightly increasing the mixer's speed each minute (you'll see the mixture actually thickening as you work).

2. Let the mixture sit until the air bubbles have popped and all sodium alginate particles have dissolved and fully swelled. Best practice: allow the thickener to stand overnight, but even if you are in a rush, allow *at least one hour*. (Note: If, as I recommend, you intend to add your dye in stock solution form, prepare your paste a little thicker, because the water in the stock solution will thin the paste.)

3. Put the desired amount of paste in a small cup or bowl, then thoroughly stir the desired amount of dye stock solution into it.

4. Just *before* you begin to apply the dye paste to the fabric, add the activator (soda ash for cellulose fibers, citric acid crystals for protein fibers) and stir thoroughly until it's completely dissolved. Add the soda ash or citric acid crystals in the ratio of 1 T. per 1 c. of paste. (If you want to achieve more even, solid color, then dissolve the activator in a bit of hot water *before* adding it.) Once activated, the paste deteriorates rapidly. *Use the paste within one hour.*

5. Apply the dye paste to the fabric in whatever way, and with whatever implements, you desire. See chapter 3 (direct application) and chapter 4 (screen printing) for ideas.

6. *Before* rinsing out, use *one* of the methods under "Setting the Dyes" on page 45.

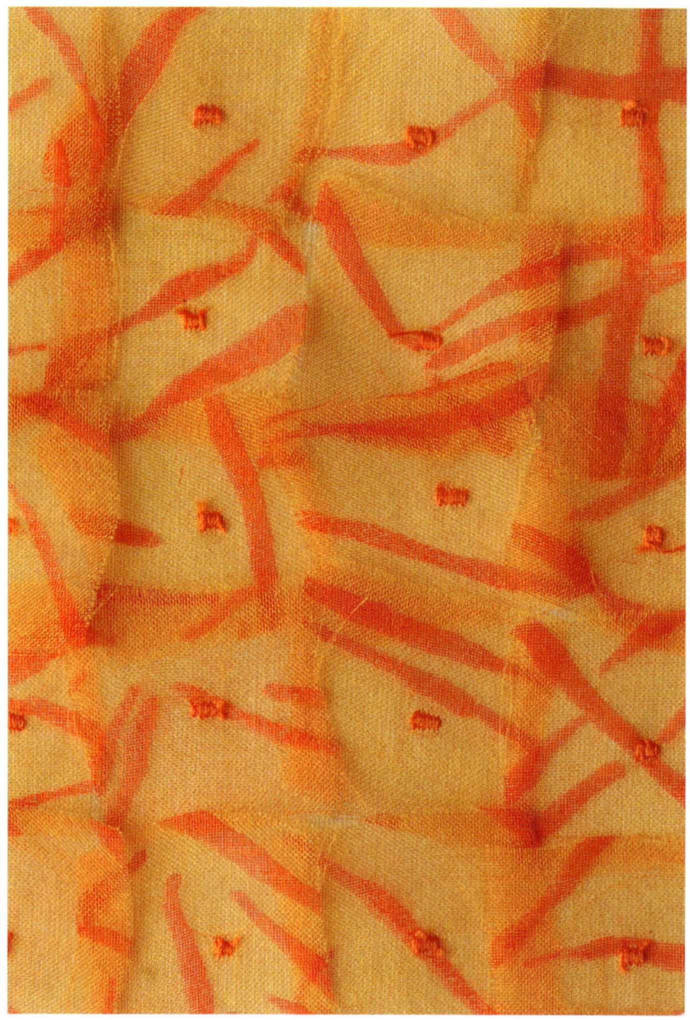

> ### FABRIC PRETREATMENT FOR DIRECT APPLICATION OF DYE
>
> Have you ever forgotten to add the activator (soda ash or citric acid) to your dye paste? I have, and the result is weak colors, accompanied by gnashing of teeth. Here is another option: add the activator to the fabric beforehand! This has two distinct advantages:
>
> - Better color results. You will retain better color intensity through the process. This removes a lot of the color guesswork in directly applied dye.
> - Longer "shelf life" for dye paste or dye solution. A paste with activator added is useful for about an hour, but a dye paste *without* activator will last for several days, allowing your process to be more relaxed, thoughtful, and reflective and reducing the amount of "expired" paste you'll need to discard. (Note that expired paste will cause plumbing problems if washed down a drain and therefore must be placed in your outgoing household waste.)
>
> Pretreatment solution and procedure: Make a solution composed of 3 T. soda ash (or 3 T. citric acid crystals for silks) per 1 gallon of water. Soak the fabric in this solution for at least 15 minutes. Remove the fabric from the solution. Gently press out the water with your gloved hands. Don't wring the fabric, and don't rinse it. Hang the fabric on a line to dry (don't put it in the dryer). When it is dry, proceed with your direct-application techniques.

Setting the Dyes

Unlike immersion dyeing, directly applied dye doesn't stay wet as long and must be "fixed" or "set" for permanence. There are several methods, arranged here from simple to complex.

Electric blanket (yes, the kind used on your bed, but* not *the same one that you use when sleeping):
Wrap your fabric in plastic, then roll it inside an electric blanket. Turn the setting to high and let it sit for eight hours. Unroll. Rinse out. (See the "Universal Rinse-Out" text box, page 24.)

Batching:
If the fabric is still *quite wet* from the dye application, work quickly to cover it tightly with plastic. Small pieces can be encased in a zippered plastic bag, larger pieces rolled in plastic sheets. Let the fabric sit for 24–48 hours. (The color may be less intense, but the process is easy. You can compensate for projected color loss by making your initial color application more intense.) Rinse out. (See the "Universal Rinse-Out" text box, page 24.)

Steam iron:
To prevent scorching, place the fabric between two press cloths or papers, then move the iron around slowly for about five minutes. Make sure the iron contacts the entire fabric surface out to all of the edges. Rinse out. (See the "Universal Rinse-Out" text box, page 24.)

Setting with steam heat:
Commercially manufactured steamers, each accompanied by its own instructions for use, offer a direct and easy way to steam heat set. However, they are expensive and bulky to store and are cost-effective *only* if you'll be regularly steaming large quantities of fabric. Commercial steamers come in two basic varieties: upright or horizontal. The former is a tall bullet-like cylindrical contraption in which the fabric is suspended around a vertical internal tube and the steam is produced by a self-contained heating element and receptacle at the contraption's base. The latter is a long, low, stainless-steel box, also containing a tubular center to be wrapped in the fabric, but lacking its own internal heating element, and the box itself is then placed across two stove burners to heat the water inside it. Both work reasonably well, but the process is tedious and the correct length of steam time often hard to gauge. (Over-steaming will actually lead to a *loss* of color.) Not to mention that you may be burned by the steam if you're even slightly careless, and a potential fire hazard (and ruined fabric) will result if the water receptacle is accidentally allowed to boil dry.

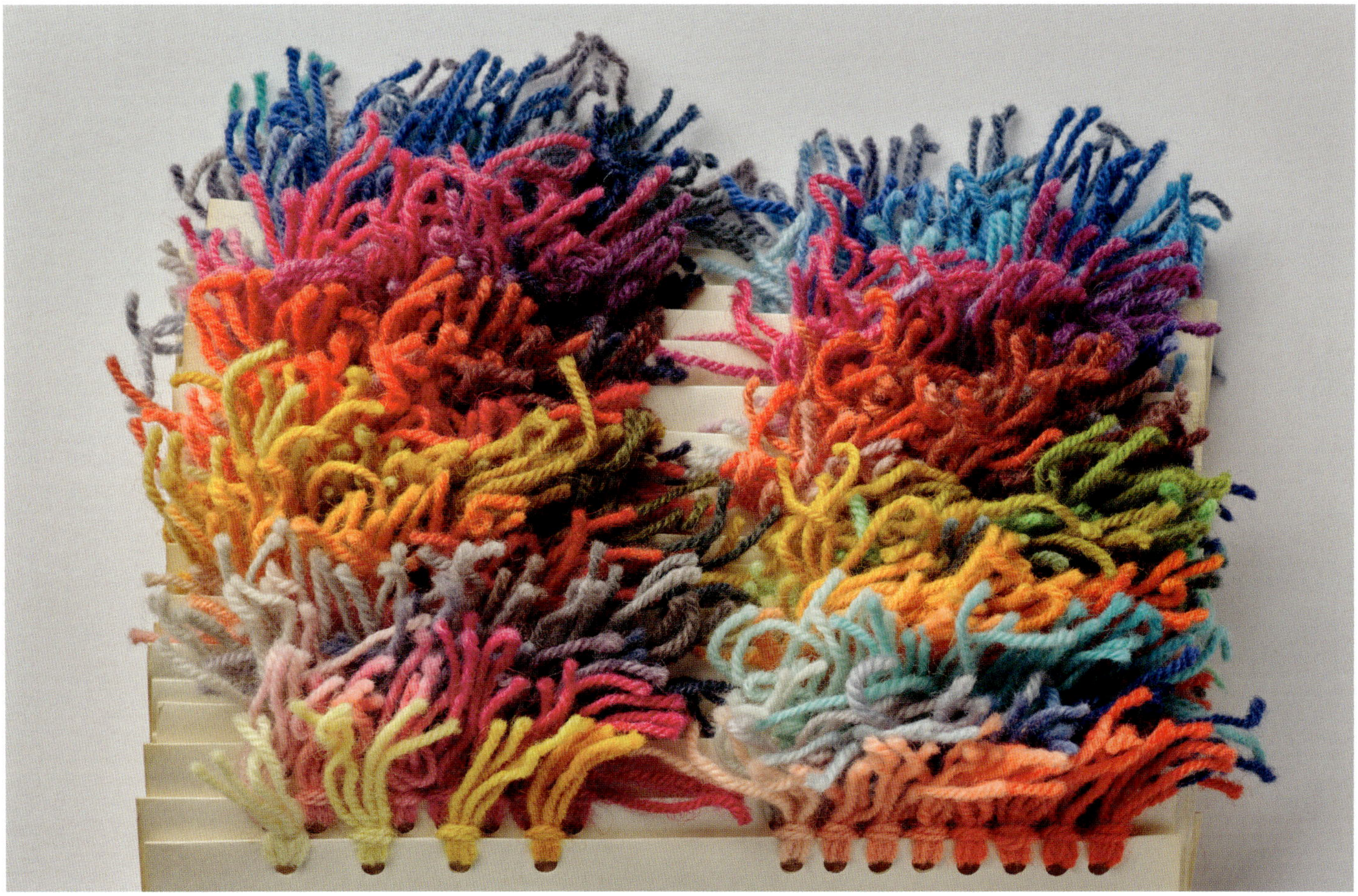

Acid Dyes

Although they're slightly more complex to process, and a bit "touchy" about correct pH, acid dyes produce brilliant, sparkling pure colors on silk, wool, and nylon, visually jewel-like, and not usually achievable with any other dye types (01-35). *Unlike* fiber reactive dyes, which wick and spread easily, *acid dyes* have long been the mainstay for resist dyeing on silk because they leave crisply defined resist marks (01-36). (We'll return to that in chapter 2.)

Acid dyes involve a "hot water" process and attach to the fibers only in an acid (low pH) environment, so they require stovetop burners or hot plates and large stainless-steel or enamel pots. The general dye safety and handling guidelines at the beginning of this chapter apply equally to acid dyes, with the *added risk* of skin burns from handling hot pots and simmering dyebaths.

If you are accustomed to working with fiber reactive dyes, you may be surprised at the greater amount of water recommended for acid dyebaths. Because of the mechanisms at work with acid dyeing, the extra water *does not dilute* the intensity of the dye colors. In fact, the dye is completely "taken up" into the goods (the dyebath is said to "exhaust"), leaving behind nearly clear water and a few unspent chemicals. It looks like a bit of magic.

With most acid dyes, the dyeing process is lengthy (allow two to three hours) and involves slowly and carefully raising the dyebath temperature to a simmer (185°F for silk, up to 200°F for wool), then maintaining that temperature for the duration of the dye time. Further adjustment of the chemistry with more acid, added while the bath is already in progress, is often necessary to complete the dye take-up.

There are several varieties of acid dyes on the market. Each requires slightly different processes and chemicals. Most will come with alternative instructions, simpler ones for doing just a bit of dyeing, and very technical ones for those who want to reproduce exact colors time after time. For simple and forgiving processing, safer chemical assistants, enhanced

01-35 Wide range of light to dark, dull to intense colors. Acid dyes. Wool yarns.

mixing possibilities, greater permanence on the fabric, and beautiful results, I recommend the Lanaset acid dyes, which are usually available in powdered form and mix readily into composite colors.

Note that you *cannot* overdye any acid dyes. That is, once you have acid-dyed a cloth or fiber, you *cannot* put it into a subsequent acid dyebath and dye it *again* to add other colors or to tone the original color. With acid dyes, *unlike* fiber reactive dyes, you must do *all* of your color mixing in the initial dyebath, *before* you ever immerse the goods.

Because Lanaset acid dye instructions vary somewhat from vendor to vendor and don't allow much deviation, the best way to proceed is to follow the directions provided by the manufacturer or vendor for the specific acid dye product you purchase. But here are the basic instructions for using most Lanaset dyes.

Basic instructions for Lanaset acid dyes:

1. Prepare yourself and the goods: Put on your protective clothing, apron, mask, and rubber gloves. Weigh the goods while they are still dry, and make note of the weight. Then wet out (completely soak) the goods in tepid water for 10 to 20 minutes.

2. Because powdered acid dye powders require the same safety and inhalation precautions as fiber reactive dye powders, I recommend that you mix them outdoors or in a carport, open garage, or open studio shed, rather than an individual room (unless it has excellent exhaust ventilation).

3. Dissolve the dye: In a small heatproof container or mortar, dissolve the powdered dye in a small amount of hot water (at least 140ºF), stirring with a spoon or pestle, just enough to turn the clumping powder into a thin paste. After making the paste, add about one more cup of hot water and stir.

4. Set up the dyebath: Fill a large stainless-steel or enamel pot with tepid tap water (whether you measure in liters or US gallons, make note of the amount) sufficient to hold the goods without crowding them. Add the correct amount of *Glauber salts* (about 20% of the *dry* weight of the fabric) and stir until they are dissolved. Add white distilled vinegar (at the rate of 40 grams per quart of water) and sodium acetate (at the rate of 1 to 2 grams per liter of water). If you measured your water in US gallons, a gallon is 3.78 liters, so multiply the amount of vinegar and sodium acetate accordingly. Then stir well. *After* you've completed this dyebath setup, add the dye itself and stir just enough to dissolve it completely into the bath.

SUPPLIES NEEDED FOR ACID DYES

- Lanaset colors
- heat-resistant bowl or mortar sufficient to hold at least a cup of liquid
- stainless-steel or enamel dye pot appropriate for use on a stove
- stovetop burners or hot plates
- candy thermometer to monitor dyebath temperatures
- oven mitts (for insulation from heat)
- Glauber salts (sodium sulfate)
- sodium acetate (a pH buffer to help hold the pH of the dyebath to 4.5)
- white distilled vinegar or citric acid crystals
- ammonia
- washing soda, sodium carbonate (*not* bicarbonate), or soda ash (all the same chemical)
- wool or silk goods
- face mask with organic-compounds filter
- rubber gloves
- work apron
- sticks for stirring the dyebaths
- laundry line and clothespins

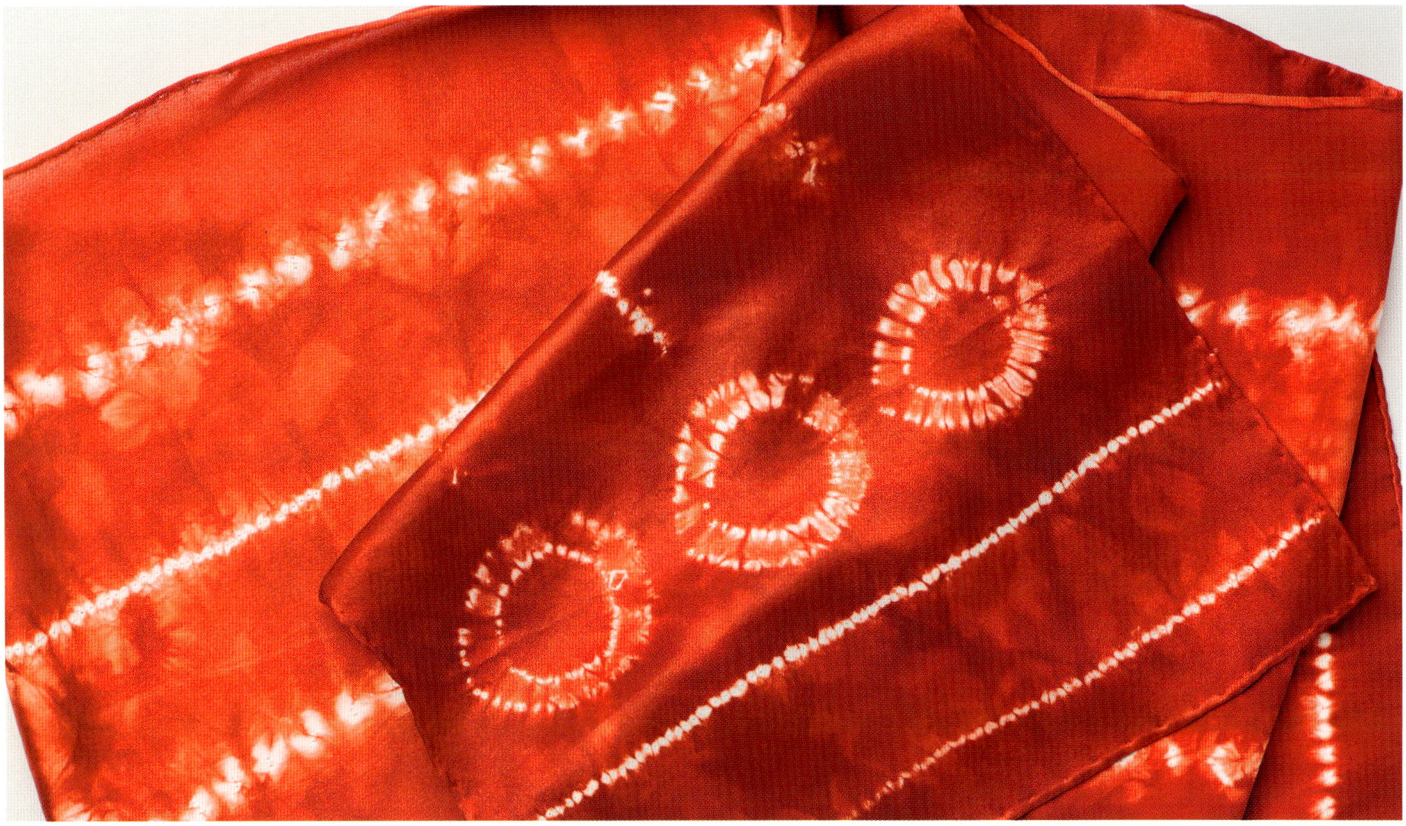

5. Add the goods to the dyebath and stir.

6. Dyeing sequence: Turn the stove or hot-plate burner on low, leaving the pot uncovered, but over the next 40–45 minutes, *slowly* raise the temperature of the dyebath to a simmer (185°F for silk; 200°F for wool), stirring the goods gently every five minutes. (Remember that *sudden* temperature changes and vigorous agitation will cause wool to felt.)

7. When the dyebath reaches the target temperature, hold it there steadily for another 45–60 minutes. *Do not let the dyebath rise to a full boil or cool off.* Occasionally, briefly and gently stir the dyebath while it simmers, moving the goods from top to bottom and side to side to rearrange their places and prevent heat from being trapped at the bottom of the pot. If the dye stops taking up (i.e., if the dye water is not becoming steadily lighter), temporarily remove the goods from the bath, stir in 2 T. more vinegar, then reintroduce the goods. At the end of the cycle, the dye should be fully taken up by the goods, and the bath should be nearly clear (exhausted).

8. Stopping the dye process: At the end of the dye cycle, turn off the heat and remove the dye pot from the burner but *don't* pour off the bath water. Instead, leave the goods in it and allow the entire pot to cool gradually (about 30–45 minutes) to room temperature.

9. Wash out and dry: Transfer the goods to a plastic wash tub (probably less heavy to manage than the dye pot itself) and wash out the goods with *slightly* warm or tepid soapy water. Synthrapol is ideal. (If the dyebath was exhausted, not much color will wash out.) Rinse out the soap with clear tepid water. Hang the goods to air-dry.

10. Dispose of the dyebath: Neutralize your acid dyebath remains to pH7 before discarding, by adding ½ cup of soda ash for every 2 to 3 gallons of leftover water.

01-36 Clearly defined and crisply outlined stitch resist marks. Lanaset acid dyes. Color: red. Silk habotai.

Natural Dyes

For many thousands of years, *all dyes were natural dyes*. Local materials made up the bulk of color-imparting substances, and the color of cloth was tied both geographically and botanically to local settlements, thus functionally producing "cultural color palettes." In ancient eras, cloth dyed in bright, luscious, and appealing colors was startling, exciting, rare, and quite expensive, since it usually came from particular and unique locations or from difficult-to-gather raw materials. In most cultures, exotic colors and imported dyestuffs were reserved for the rich and elite. Only in recent times have chemical dyes given nearly everyone access to wonderfully colored textiles (a kind of "color democracy") and thus, in most places around the globe, largely ended sumptuary laws (which restrict certain colors, fibers, or clothing styles to royalty or other elites).

It was not until the middle of the 19th century that humans discovered, invented, and developed synthetic chemical means of dyeing textiles. Today, most of us are accustomed to owning clothing and household textiles in a prodigious range of colors (with no color forbidden to us), all chemically dyed by industrial processes. Nevertheless, we still harbor deeply embedded cultural associations for certain colors. We voluntarily, and often quite subconsciously, self-censor the colors we wear in public or use in our homes, to "compose" a pleasing, enviable, or socially acceptable image of ourselves. We enjoy unlimited varieties of colored fabrics, without thinking much about the sources, processes, or ecological repercussions of the dyeing itself.

01-37 Rich colors from natural dyes. Dye sources: in first column, weld (*top*) and lac (*bottom*); in second column, osage; in third column, indigo (*top*) and indigo overdyed with pomegranate and weld (*bottom*); in fourth column, cutch (*top*) and madder (*bottom*). Cotton embroidery floss and tapes.

Over the last century, interest in natural dyestuffs has gone in cycles among artisans, textile artists, hand dyers, and craftspeople. I first tried natural dyeing as a student in the 1970s. Curious about its possible nontoxic and earth-friendly potential, I experimented with such locally available sources as walnut hulls (01-38) and onion skins. But what I found in the instructional literature of the time was either romantic, folksy, vague, or disappointingly unreliable for repeated studio use. The color I achieved was usually lackluster at best and faded quickly in the light or with washing. Some of the practices advocated in the old books were not only incompletely described or ill informed, but in some cases slightly dangerous. I quickly abandoned the approach in favor of chemical dyes, which I have used in a highly controlled and safety-conscious manner over the years, as the more reliable choice in both my teaching and studio practice. But today, at last, we have access to the right combination of good science and good craft in reliable and detailed texts. Because of intensive research by a handful of dedicated natural-dye experts around the world, you can now pursue this approach to color and dye practice with reliable chemical support.

Because of this natural-dyeing renaissance, many small businesses now offer a range of beautiful naturally dyed threads, yarns, and fabrics at reasonable prices. However, you may still want to establish your own natural-dye practice for aesthetic, conceptual, or ecological reasons (for example, if your home studio water empties into a septic system, natural dyes are your safest choice). Natural dyeing has four wonderful advantages: First, from a very long history of use worldwide, we know it works. Second, the dried plant materials and minerals are readily available, and many can be homegrown. Third, the processes are relatively safe if used carefully with respect to the toxicity of mordants (the metal salts used to fix natural dyes). And fourth, they yield beautifully luminous, mysterious, and softer, more "natural feeling" color ranges than chemical dyes (01-37).

The main challenge with natural dyes is the complexity of the dyeing process itself. To be effectively and safely controlled, natural dyes require more steps to produce the color and depend on a certain level of knowledge about the various plant and animal sources, which might extend to growing, gathering, or harvesting them yourself. Each source will need to be processed appropriately to make the dyestuff and prepare the dyebath; the correct mordants must be selected for different fiber types, dyestuffs, and color goals; and fibers may need to be pretreated or mordanted in a separate operation before the dyeing itself. The final dyeing process requires practice, correct timing, and careful control for successful results. Embracing a dye practice based on natural dyes requires a significant time commitment to achieve a full color palette. Those fascinated with and dedicated to a blend of ancient dyeing processes and modern chemical understanding will enjoy the results.

Because natural dyes are a coloring "world" justifying entire books on that subject alone, my own discussion here will necessarily be brief and will cover only two easy, safe, and accessible natural techniques: tea dyeing and rusting. If you are interested in exploring natural dyes, see the Bibliography, in particular authors Ellis and Boutrup.

01-38 Delicate browns on a variety of wool yarns. Natural dye source: walnut hulls.

01-39 Tea staining without pretreating fabric. Twenty black tea bags were steeped in 8 cups of hot water, with all fabrics then added simultaneously to the same pot. Steeping times before removal were (*top to bottom*) 5, 10, 15, 20, 25, and 30 minutes, but the resulting color gradations were very subtle. *Left to right*: softened linen, silk noil, cotton print cloth.

Tea "Dyeing" or Staining

Perhaps one of the simplest and safest ways to change the color of white fabric is by staining it with tea. Yes, the same kinds of tea we drink. Each kind of tea (black, green, ginger, hibiscus, etc.) will stain cloth a slightly different color, so try several, perhaps starting with whatever happens to be on your pantry shelf. Tea will soften industrial white fabric (which is often made "too" white by the manufacturing process itself or by the inclusion of whitening chemicals) into shades of soft beige, greens, and pinks. The depth of color, from light to dark, depends on the type and *quantity* of the tea used, the type of *fibers* in the fabric, and, to some extent, the amount of *time* you leave the fabric in the tea (see 01-39).

My tests indicate that silks stain darker and more readily than cellulose fabrics such as cotton and linen. The color will get darker on silk with increased time in contact with the tea, allowing you to easily produce subtle gradations of color. However, on cotton and linen, increasing the *strength* of the tea (more tea in the same amount of water) rather than the time is more effective in producing darker colors.

If your ideas call for old fabrics (used, recycled, heirloom) but you're unable to find them, this method will help you manufacture "faux" aged cloth! The action of tea softens or decreases the intensity of a fabric's color or makes it acquire an "aged" or faded look, whether it starts out as white or another high-value dyed color (see text box on aging fabric prematurely).

Safety

The source plant material (tea) is obviously not toxic to ingest, so is it safe to use around children and is something you may already have on hand. Nevertheless, you may want to use dedicated pots and utensils to stain with tea, and protect your hands from the tannins in the tea by wearing latex or rubber gloves when you process the fabric. (See Bibliography for Sussman.)

Basic Instructions for Tea Dyeing

1. Optional (may improve the permanence and depth of color results on some fabrics): Pretreat the fabric by soaking it in a mixture of 1 cup of alum in 1 gallon of water, with a few teaspoons of water softener. Soak for about 20 minutes, then squeeze out the alum mixture, but *don't* rinse the fabric. Allow the fabric to air-dry.

2. Boil water as you would for tea.

3. Place 2 to 4 cups of boiling water in a heat-resistant bowl or stainless-steel stock pot.

4. Add 10 to 50 tea bags (the more tea, the darker the staining) and allow them to steep for 15 minutes.

5. Remove the tea bags and add approximately 3 to 6 cups of cool water. If necessary, move the diluted tea to a larger or deeper pot, tub, or bowl of sufficient size to submerge the amount of fabric.

6. Add the fabric to the tea and stir. Allow the fabric to remain in the tea anywhere from 5 to 30 minutes, stirring from time to time, checking on how dark it is getting. (But remember that the fabric will look darker while wet and lighter after it dries.) Extra time in the tea will darken the results on silk; cellulose fabrics will usually not darken with time.

7. When the fabric is stained to your satisfaction, remove it from the tea.

8. Wash in mild soap (e.g., Synthrapol) and rinse the fabric well in cool water to remove the excess tea and tannins.

9. Dry and press to remove wrinkles.

PREMATURELY "AGING" FABRIC WITH COLORANTS

As household linens age, white cloth naturally goes to yellow or tan. As clothing is worn and used, dyed colors naturally fade and become mottled. To create such appearances without waiting years, even decades, for fabrics to "do it on their own," try the following methods.

Natural substances

- *Real used cloth*: Use cut-up pieces of worn clothing and household linens as fabrics for your work. They come "pre-aged" and provide a natural way to recycle textiles and to demonstrate that the materials in your work have their own history—*your* history. If textiles from your family's life are not available, search for discarded used textiles in secondhand stores, antique shops, yard sales, and flea markets, or directly from your friends. (What they view as "decluttering" may represent "treasure" to you!) As you construct compositions, cut, piece, add, and subtract to highlight rather than hide worn areas.

- *Real dirt*: If you want the fabric to look dirty, rub dirt into it! Soil, itself a mix of many kinds of minerals and decayed plant materials, varies widely from place to place. Try collecting dirt from different locations to discover the different colors they produce, or bury a fabric in your garden for a couple of rainy months (yes, really). Of course, burying fabric in the ground may cause deterioration in the fibers, but that's the whole point of intentionally trying to create "old" fabric. Some direct encounters with soil will produce permanent results on cloth. Otherwise, to protect them from washing out, brush or paint transparent screen-printing base (discussed in chapter 4) on top of the dirt and let it air-cure for a week or more. You don't need to wash out the fabric again after doing this.

- *Real stains*: To intentionally generate stains, rub the fabric with the same foodstuffs you already find so annoyingly difficult to remove from your clothing or table linens: tomatoes, tomato sauce, berries, coffee, tea, oils, or wine. And, although it's not a foodstuff (well, one hopes not), blood is another option. Try using a pristine white cloth to clean up in the kitchen (gathering food stains naturally over time) or in the garage (gathering all sorts of organic matter from gardening, car grease and dirt, or spider debris), or to dab away blood from a superficial wound (preferably your own, because it's usually not nice to accost other people for some "real stain" colorant while they're bleeding). From experience, we know that contact with these substances will certainly leave at least a ghost of discoloration behind, even after repeated washings.

Please don't confuse any of the above with the permanent results you could achieve through skilled and controlled natural-dye procedures. This is simple staining, which is different, and also tends to fade with washing, but is nevertheless useful for certain purposes.

Studio-Based Techniques

- *Aging with tea*: see the section above.

- *Aging with fiber reactive dyes*: If you prefer to use fiber reactive dyes, use weak dye concentrations and low-immersion dyeing. That combination will dampen down the industrial white of new cloth and will apply the faint dye color unevenly.

- *Faded*: To make dyed colors look "faded," overdye with gray toners that lean toward the complement of the color on the cloth. You may have to do this several times to get the level of de-intensified color you want. With darker colors, use bleach or discharge paste (see chapter 6) to lighten or reduce the color overall or selectively.

- *Dirty*: For a "dirty" appearance with more control of the results than the natural dirt method discussed above, (1) Substitute textile *pigments* (see chapter 3) for actual dirt. Mix some light-value and dull colors that resemble dirt, such as beiges, tans, rusts, and ochers. Rub the color into the cloth with a rag (wear gloves!), aiming for the kind of dirt smears you might get if you were working in the garden on your knees, or you were a baseball player sliding into home plate. (2) Try similarly "earthy" colors of fiber reactive *dye*, such as very light beige, ocher, khaki, chino, or tan. To produce uneven color across the surface, use low-immersion dyeing or apply thin washes of color with wide foam brushes, but without leaving visible brush marks (because real dirt isn't known for its use of brushes).

- *Stained*: You can also produce the *appearance* of old stains through chemical means. Directly dab on light color washes with a soft foam brush to apply "faded" color, or drop thinned pigment or dye from a loaded eyedropper in specific locations and allow it to wick naturally (see chapter 3). Keep the colors "muddy" and low intensity. (Study some old work clothing or dish towels for inspiration!)
- *Tormented*: Rips, holes, broken threads, fraying, and abrasion will add to a sense of age and wear, because they are indeed among the many misfortunes that can befall the life of a cloth. For suggestions, see the information in chapter 10 in the *Dry Techniques* book about how to distress fabric.

Rusting

When pressed against damp fabric, rusty metal objects leave behind interesting, slightly ghostly, and evocative imprints (01-40, 01-41). Rusting is an easy, overnight process that requires little or no supervision. To start the process, find some interesting metal pieces *that will rust* (must contain *iron*). Any object with *some* existing rust is already a likely candidate: old washers, screws, nails, metal bars, gears, rods, or other items you might find in your basement, attic, or garage, or along the road when you take a walk. Test a metal for "rusting potential" by wetting it and letting it sit in a plastic bag overnight to see if some rust has formed. In the rusting process, the *shapes* of your metal pieces will be transferred to the fabric entirely or in part, depending on how you turn, orient, position, and arrange their contact points with the fabric.

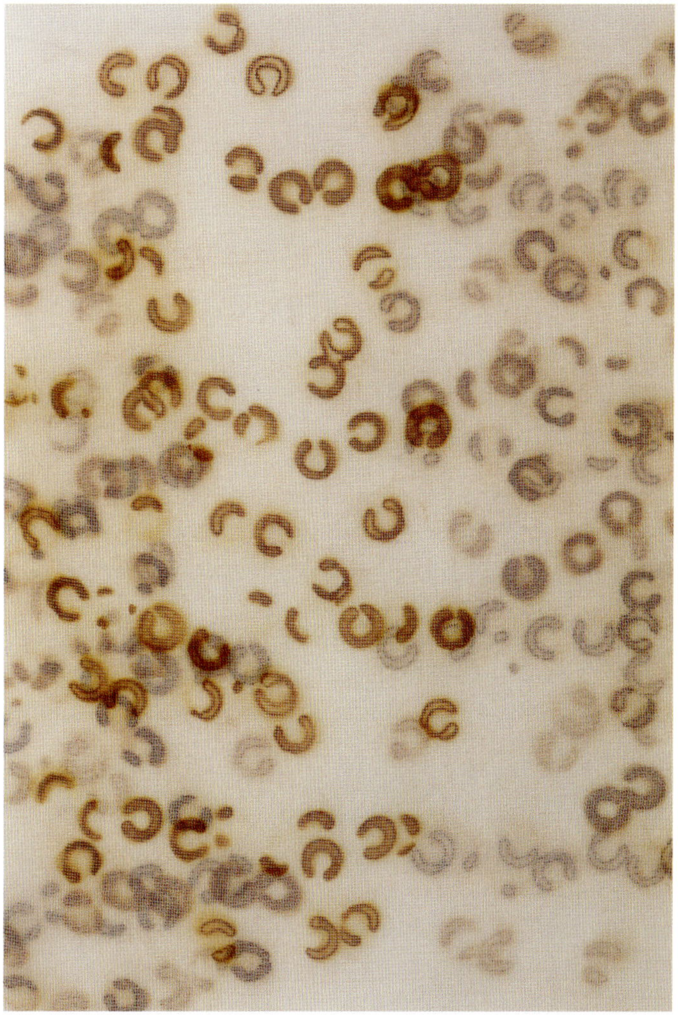

01-40 Three layers of transparent silk organza mesh, each rusted with metal washers.

Basic Instructions for Rusting Fabric

1. Select the metal pieces you want to rust, but don't place them on the fabric yet.
2. Lay the fabric on your worktable over a piece of protective plastic.
3. Spray the fabric with white vinegar (or a strong vinegar-water mixture) until it is quite damp but not soaking wet.
4. Position the metal pieces on the damp fabric as you wish the shapes to be arranged, and leave the fabric flat on the plastic. Or, if desired, you can manipulate or fold the fabric, which will create multiple contact points with the metal but may also cause many of the metal pieces to fall to the "bottom" of the three-dimensional fabric. Or, to minimize dislocation of the metal pieces, just roll up the dampened fabric, with or without first folding its edges.

5. To seal in the moisture: If you rolled the fabric or left it flat, cover the fabric with more plastic, then tape the plastic in place. Or, if you manipulated the fabric, place it in a shallow plastic container (perhaps the kind you would use in the kitchen for leftover food storage) and cover it with the lid.

6. Let the fabric sit overnight, or longer, then periodically check the progress of the rusting until you are satisfied with its extent. Note that small metal pieces usually rust fast, while larger pieces (or any size of piece with a lower amount of iron) will take longer.

7. Remove the metal pieces and wash out the fabric in a baking soda (sodium *bi*carbonate) and water solution (1 oz. of soda per 1 gallon of water). Then rinse some more with clear tap water.

8. Hang to dry, then press (dry heat or steam, depending on the fabric) to remove wrinkles. Because rusted fabric can transfer its stains and damage your usual "good" iron, use only a *separate dedicated iron* for this purpose.

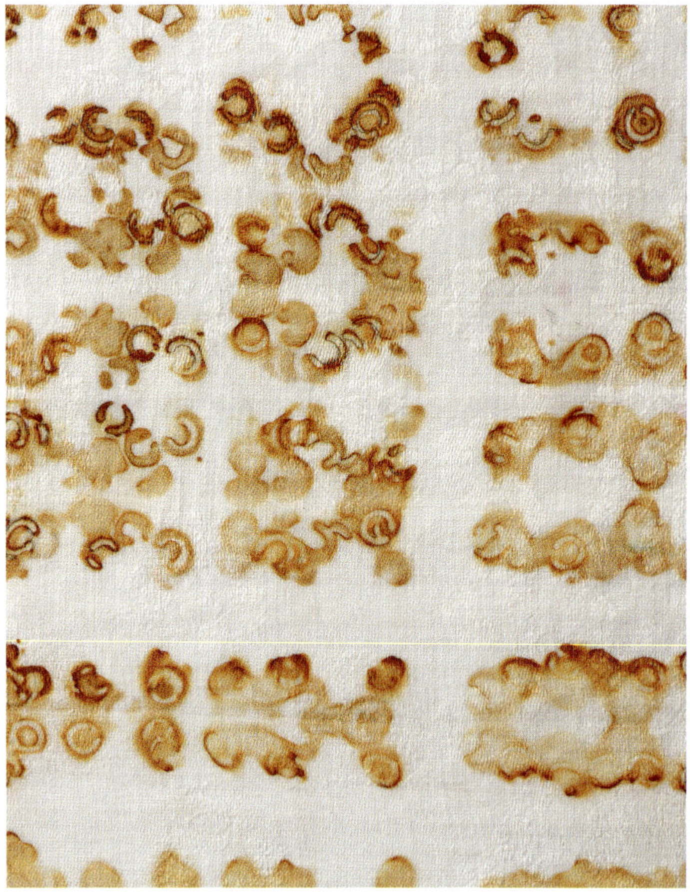

01-41 Folded heirloom linen fabric with rust marks from metal washers.

Note: Rust marks on fabric will continue to grow rust (even if you counteract the vinegar with a baking-soda bath at the end of the process) and, over long periods of time, will begin to "eat" the fabric. Therefore, rusted fabrics are definitely not "archival." The rusted contact points on the fabric will degrade more quickly than other parts of the fabric surface. Thus, while rusted fabrics are quite beautiful and mysterious, hopes of preserving their original appearance are likely to be frustrated.

Some people like the slow degradation of naturally rusted fabrics. Others would prefer a more enduring outcome. For that group, I have found a method that produces the characteristic colors and marks of rusting but also creates a more archivally sound fabric: digital manipulation and printing. My approach is to rust the fabric; process, rinse, and dry it; scan the fabric into the computer; and then *print* the *scanned* image onto a fresh piece of fabric. This is a longer process and requires computer hardware and software, and a printer suitable for fabric, but accomplishes those twin goals of rusting and preservation.

Try this!

1.1 Practice dyebaths with fiber reactive dyes

Set up two practice dyebaths with sufficient water to dye ¼ to ½ yard of cotton fabric in each. Mix a composite color by combining at least three different "pure" colors from your core inventory in dye stock solution. Use the composite color in both dyebaths, in roughly the same amounts or depths of dye.

- In the first dyebath, process the goods by the Even Color: "Cold Water" Long Method, with constant agitation to achieve even application of the color.

- In the second dyebath, use either the Uneven Color: "Cold Water" Super-Short and Easy *Full*-Immersion Method, or the Uneven Color: "Cold Water" *Low*-Immersion Method to allow uneven dispersal of color. Rinse, dry, and press.

Rainbow dyebath: See the Uneven Color: "Cold Water" Rainbow Dye Method for cellulose fibers or silk. Start with ¼ to ½ yard of cotton fabric. Choose the same dye color stock solutions you mixed in the practice dyebaths above, but this time *separately* pour each of the three colors onto the fabric (which is the nature of rainbow dyeing) in the very low-immersion bath. Process, rinse, dry, and press.

1.2 Practice dyebath with acid dyes

Set up a dyebath for a collection of several different weights and types of silk (perhaps include a silk scarf) *and* wool fabrics *and* yarns. Use a single color of Lanaset dye and prepare the dyebath according to the directions. Weigh and place *all* the several goods into the same dyebath and keep the bath no hotter than 185ºF (to preserve the silk). Process and rinse. Compare the color results on each type of protein fiber. Clip and save swatches of all the dyed goods to mount in your Dye Sample Notebook along with notes on the dye colors, depth of dye, and other distinguishing features of the experience (see Appendix C).

1.3 Colors in gradation with fiber reactive dyes

Using instructions from the "Dyeing Gradation Sequences" section of this chapter, dye a gradating sequence of at least five to seven colors (each color on a separate ¼-yard fabric sample) or five to seven skeins of yarn or thread (each color on a separate 10 to 30 yard per skein). Choose *one* type of gradation from the options discussed in that section, then choose the required constant or variable colors (or both) for it. Set up and run all of the dyebaths simultaneously, using any of the immersion-dyeing methods discussed in this chapter. (It is normal for the setup to dye a sequence to take a considerable amount of time. Allow yourself an hour for set up.) Once you have dyed your gradation sequence, rinse and dry the goods. Save the fabrics for "Try this!" projects in chapters 7, 8, or 9 in the *Dry Techniques* book.

1.4 Overdye experiment for three different purposes

- Gather five or six assorted fabrics or skeins of yarn or thread that you consider weak, ugly, or incompatible to combine in the same design or composition. Overdye all of them with the same color *in the same dyebath*. Choose the overdye color carefully to tweak (but not overpower) their original colors so they'll work in harmony. Set them aside for a "Try this!" project in the *Dry Techniques* book.

- Gather some "overbright" colored fabrics, ones you consider garish or "loud." Overdye each with its complementary color, or with a warm or cool gray, or your own custom-mixed toner. The objective is to *tone down* the intensity of each fabric, so consider and overdye each fabric separately. Set them aside for a "Try this!" project in the *Dry Techniques* book.

- Gather some fabrics whose colors you consider weak, washed out, or simply too light to register as a "color." Overdye each fabric with the same dye color (or a different color) to *lower* its value (i.e., darken it) or raise its intensity (i.e., brighten it). Set them aside for a "Try this!" project in the *Dry Techniques* book.

1.5 Gradation sequence comparison

Using the same set of *complementary* colors in each of seven dye pots, ¼ yard of fabric per dye pot, and the instructions in the "Dyeing Gradation Sequences" of this chapter:

- Dye a gradation sequence with these colors in which you allow the depth of dye to *change* (use one constant, one variable).

- Then, using the same color set and seven dye pots, dye another gradation sequence in which you keep the depth of dye *constant* (use two variables, no constant).

- Compare the results in the two sequences. Save the dyed fabrics for "Try this!" projects in chapters 7, 8, and 9 in the *Dry Techniques* book.

1.6 Advanced gradation dyeing

Dye ¼ yard pieces of fabric in separate dyebaths for each type of gradation outlined in the "Dyeing Gradation Sequences" section of this chapter, using a different set of colors for each gradation type (for example, don't make all the samples in blues). This will give you a lot of practice in dyeing gradations. Save the dyed fabrics for "Try this!" projects in chapters 7, 8, and 9 in the *Dry Techniques* book.

1.7 Rust a fabric

Armed with a plastic bag, take a walk in places likely to produce bits of metal litter: a sidewalk by a busy urban road, a construction site, or the perimeter of an appliance or car repair shop. Or you may live in a town with a business that sells small pieces of scrap. Or you can search through that bin of miscellaneous hardware "stuff" that you keep in your home because you think you'll have a use for it "someday," but you know you're just fooling yourself. Don't try to be overly ambitious: if the metal piece is much larger than a baby's hand, or not very suitable for laying flat on a piece of fabric, leave it behind. Use the pieces and follow the instructions (pages 53–54) to rust a piece of silk, linen, wool, or cotton, arranging the contact points to suit your ideas or aesthetics. Set aside the rusted fabric for "Try this!" project 7.6 in the *Dry Techniques* book.

1.8 "Age" a new fabric

Choose a piece of natural-fiber white or pastel fabric; old scraps will do. Try to make the fabric look "old" by using any one of, or a combination of, the techniques in the text box (pages 52–53) about "Prematurely 'Aging' Fabric with Colorants" or the separate section about "Tea 'Dyeing' or Staining." Repeat by playing with as many of the "aging" techniques as interest you. Set aside the pieces of fabric for a project in chapter 10 in the *Dry Techniques* book.

1.9 "Freshen" an old fabric

Your goal is to give old textiles a new life. Gather at least six different old or used cotton or linen fabrics. If possible, don't spend money on them; acquire them through bargaining, scavenging for old clothing, household textiles, and so on. Choose materials from different sources, whether similar or not in weight or texture. If you use old clothes, disassemble them.

Choose a color palette of six harmonious dye colors and overdye each of the six fabrics a different one of those colors to create a palette of freshened materials. Set them aside for "Try This!" project 7.9 in the *Dry Techniques* book.

1.10 THE CUMULATIVE CLOTH CHALLENGE

You will carry the pieces of cloth you dye in this challenge project through this entire book, adding and layering techniques as they are introduced, and recombining them into a single textile at the end.

The goal in this first layer: establish a color story that sets the tone for the textile you want to produce. Start by choosing a color source (such as a photograph). Look through some nature, cooking, travel, or gardening magazines to locate some inspirational images printed on paper, particularly those with beautiful, appealing, or unusual color combinations. Choose an image that you particularly like, one that contains a wide range of hues, values, *and* intensities: light and dark, bright and dull, in addition to neutrals, black, and white. From that source, select a color palette of four light- or medium-value colors (they can be as bright or dull as you wish). Avoid dark (low value) colors, because they'll preclude further additions of dye in later steps.

Begin with a minimum of 1 yard (and up to 4 yards) of cotton, rayon, linen, or cellulose blend fabric. Split the fabric into four equal-sized pieces. Using any of the immersion dye techniques (even or uneven) in this chapter, dye each piece of fabric in one of the colors from your palette. These four colored fabrics now form the foundation layer and color context for the additions you'll make in later chapters. Make a note about the dye colors and methods you used, and make a photograph of the four fabrics as they appear now. Set the fabrics aside for the Cumulative Cloth Challenge of chapter 2.

2 / RESIST DYEING (*SHIBORI*): ADDING PATTERN WITH DYES

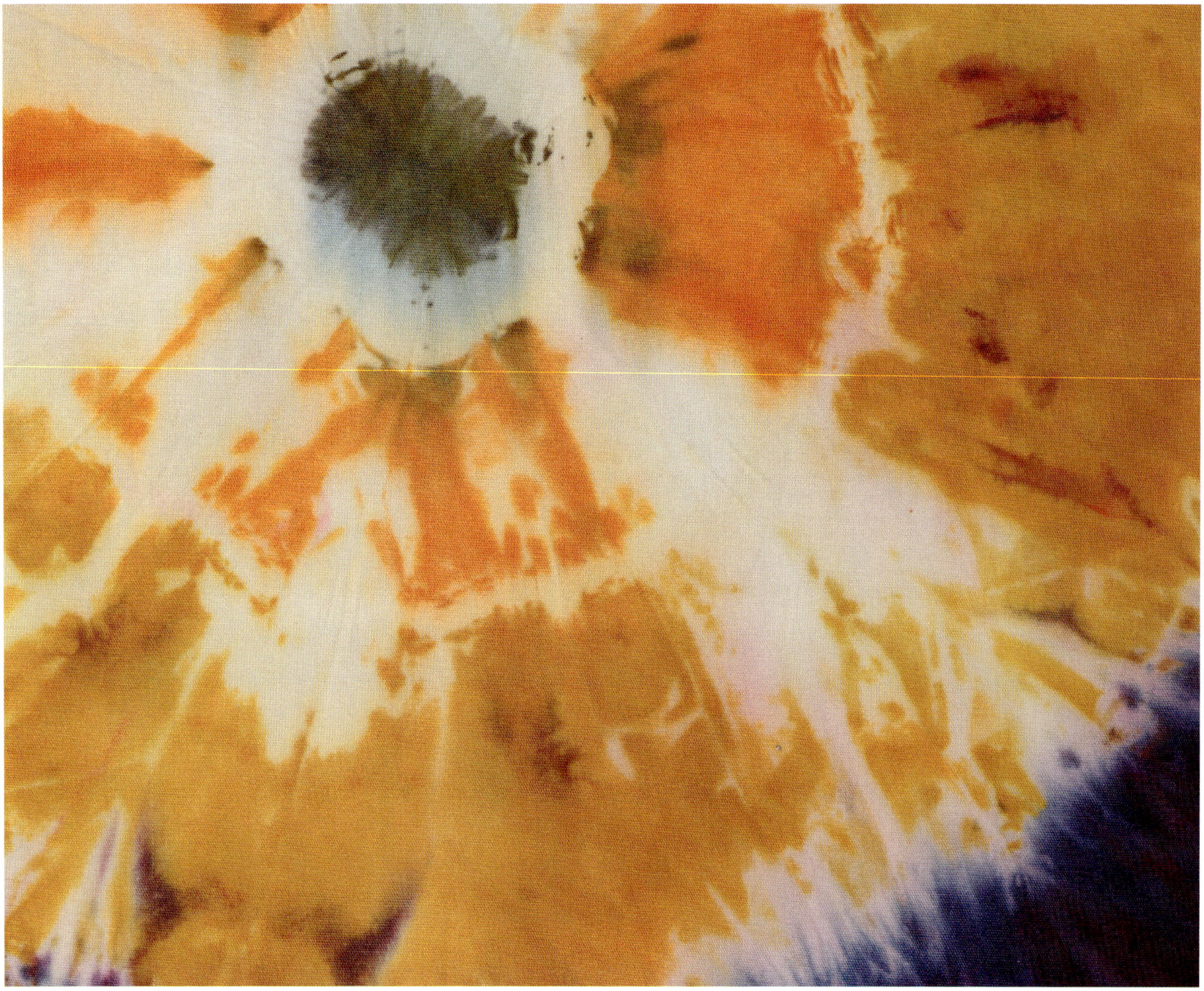

Resist dyeing is the selective application of dye to create *intentional*, but controlled, patterns, textures, or colored marks on cloth. All resist techniques use either *pressure* or *blocking agents*—folding, binding with cords, stitching and gathering, clamping, or applying starch, paste, or wax—to *prevent* dye penetration in protected areas of a fabric while leaving other areas free to accept the dye. Resist dyeing leaves characteristic marks or shapes that reflect the specific kinds of bindings or pastes applied as *selective* dye *barriers*. The marks themselves (the parts of the fabric *protected* from this application of dye) retain the background color of the fabric. Dyes don't change the fabric's surface quality, and, useful for purposes of a *cumulative cloth*, the surface therefore remains receptive to the future addition of directly applied or screen-printed *pigments* and other nondye methods of introducing color, pattern, or physical embellishment.

Resist-dye techniques developed in diverse world cultures, most notably in Japan, Malaysia, Thailand, Indonesia, India,

02-01 Tie-dye (also called *ne-maki shibori*) bound in concentric rings (diagram 02-46). Multiple colors of painted, thickened, fiber reactive dye. Cotton broadcloth. Scale: 9.5" × 8".

and Central and South America. Each region had its own set of terms for the tools and methods employed. Therefore, books on resist dyeing often use a confusing array of terms from various places. In this chapter, I use English terms to describe the techniques, sometimes accompanied by the terms from the country of origin. (For wonderful expertise in *shibori* methods, see the Bibliography for titles by Yoshiko Wada. For a broad, historically informed perspective, see Jack Lenor Larsen.) In general, be less concerned about the "right" terminology and more about learning the techniques and developing your own approach to resist-dye work.

This chapter focuses solely on the collection of pressure and binding techniques that the Japanese call "shibori" (for which we have no comparable English word), meaning "shaped resist dyeing." (See the Bibliography for resources about other forms of resist dyeing such as ikat and batik.)

In general, *shibori* techniques yield organic patterns, textures, or images composed of informally repeated and slightly varying shapes or marks. Each of the four individual *shibori* techniques also produces its own highly specific and identifiable visual characteristics. However, *unlike* the identical repetition of a screen-printed image or mark, resist-dyed "patterns" are never completely exact repeats. Variations, reflecting the action of the human hand, the manipulated form of the fabric, the type of binding, and the movement of dye in water, are appealingly recorded in the resulting textile. Think of these as their *signature markings*, a beautifully patterned trace of the binding or pressure used to create them. The techniques are versatile, equally successful at small scale to make delicate marks and patterns and at large scale to create energetic sweeps of color.

Resist dyeing may be practiced at many levels of expertise. Basic methods are easy to learn and produce interesting patterns, even on the first try. Acquiring fine control of techniques, mark placement and modulation, or color combinations requires practice over time, and thus even experienced practitioners continue to find interesting challenges. The few necessary tools and equipment are simple, inexpensive, and easily obtained. You may already have them on hand.

Most resist methods require *time*: to manipulate the cloth, bind and dye, remove bindings, and wash, rinse, and dry. Depending on the complexity of the binding, the amount of fabric, and the weather conditions (humidity or dryness in your work area), the process can take several days to several weeks. Be patient, and don't rush any of the steps. Allow the process and the results to unfold naturally as you tend to other tasks or prepare the next round of fabrics for resist dyeing.

This chapter presents techniques from four major *shibori* categories in general order of increasing difficulty:

- folding and fold-and-clamp, including instructions for the fabric manipulation and the dye methods applicable to this method alone
- bound resist (including random bound resist, twisting, knotting, and tie-dye), including instructions for the predye manipulation and binding on each type, followed by the single set of dyeing instructions common to all of them
- pole wrapping, including instructions for the fabric manipulation and the dye methods applicable to this method alone
- stitch-and-gather, including instructions for the fabric manipulation and the dye methods applicable to this method alone

BUYING FABRICS ALREADY RESIST-DYED

If you don't want to use dyes or pigments at home, or you just aren't interested enough in resist dye to do it yourself, you can buy resist-dyed fabrics of all types (not just *shibori*) at quilt stores and from online fabric vendors. Produced by large textile-manufacturing companies or hand-dyed by individual artisans or small cooperatives, these may come from domestic US sources or from around the world, especially Japan, India, South America, and Southeast Asia. The patterns and colors range widely (e.g., geometrics, florals, animals, birds, leaves, textures) and offer many options to aid expression in your fabric work. However, unlike doing your own custom resist dye, you'll need to settle for what is commercially available. You can use these fabrics in lieu of your own resist-dyed cloth in the Cumulative Cloth Challenges in the coming chapters.

SUPPLY CHECKLIST FOR RESIST DYEING

- Supplies listed in chapter 1 for mixing fiber reactive dye stock solutions, immersion dyebaths, and direct-application pastes. But if you're working on protein fibers (silk, wool), you'll need the supplies for Lanaset acid dyeing.

Technique-specific supplies are listed in the following sections, but supplies useful in all resist-dye work include:

- twine, thread, or cord, strong enough to withstand intense pulling and binding tension
- needles: sized to accommodate the twine, thread, or cord
- leather gloves or "first aid" tape to protect your hands from blistering while tightly pulling bindings
- steam iron (buy a high-quality professional model with an automatic on/off switch)
- drop cloth
- brushes or sponges
- scissors: small sharp-pointed ones for clipping threads, larger shears for cutting fabric
- fabric-marking tools that will wash out or disappear easily in water
- Synthrapol to prevent unwanted redeposit of dyestuffs on resist areas during final washout
- fabric such as cotton or silk. I recommend purchasing from a vendor that specializes in ready-to-dye goods without finishes. But if you're unable to do so, see the separate text box on steps you may need to take in preparing the fabric.

PREPARING THE FABRIC FOR RESIST DYEING

If you bought ready-to-dye fabric, you're already set to go.

- With all other fabrics, machine-wash with Synthrapol to remove soil or sizing chemicals. (To test for sizing, put a drop of water on the fabric. If it beads up on the surface rather than instantly sinking in, sizing is present.) Rinse the fabric very thoroughly to remove all traces of soap and chemicals, then dry it thoroughly (by air or by clothes dryer). You can, if you wish, now proceed directly to binding and resist dyeing.

- But if you'll be using fiber reactive dyes for your resist projects, *pretreating* your fabric, *after* the washing above but *before* binding and dyeing, will improve the likelihood of attaining good depth of dye and color retention *without heat setting.* Plan to pretreat fabrics the day *before* you plan to dye them, because soaking and drying usually requires at least 24 hours. For *cellulose* fibers, soak the cloth in a soda water solution ratio of 1 T. of soda ash per 1 gallon of water. Or, for *protein* fibers, substitute the same amount of citric acid crystals in the soaking solution. Then soak the fabric in the solution for one hour. Gently squeeze out the soaking solution *without rinsing.* Hang the fabric over a line to *air-dry* completely before manipulating and binding it. (Because soda ash is combustible, *never* put soda-ash-soaked fabric in a home or commercial dryer to rush the drying.)

Note: If you'll be using acid dyes, preliminary soaking in water is recommended, especially if you allowed the fabric to dry after its Synthrapol washing, but no other specific pretreatment is needed, because wool and silk fabrics rarely bear any manufacturing chemicals that would interfere with dye uptake.

UNIVERSAL RINSE-OUT INSTRUCTIONS FOR RESIST DYEING WITH FIBER REACTIVE DYES

Use these instructions at the *conclusion* of all four of the *shibori* resist-dye techniques discussed in the sections below.

1. Fill a bucket (once) with *very hot* water (at least 140°F) and add ½ oz. of water softener or metaphos (sodium hexametaphosphate) per gallon of water. (*No* detergent at this stage.) Agitate the goods by hand for two minutes, then drain.

2. To *protect the undyed areas* of your fabric from being contaminated with excess dye, use a soap specifically formulated to prevent dye redeposit, such as Synthrapol. Refill the bucket (once) with *very hot* water (at least 140°F), then add 1 oz. of Synthrapol per gallon. Let the goods soak for five minutes (further hand agitation is probably unnecessary during this step). Discard the soapy water, then rinse the goods with *warm* water (105°F), then drain.

3. Refill the bucket with *warm* water and rinse under continually refreshed running *warm* water for two minutes, then drain.

4. Refill the bucket with *cold tap* water, rinse for one minute, then drain. *Repeat* this step until the discard water is clear.

5. Hang the fabric to air-dry, or use your usual clothes-drying machine. (If you've thoroughly rinsed the goods, they should be safe to place in your household dryer. However, in case of any residual traces of unrinsed dye, I still recommend against drying the goods in the same dryer "load" as personal clothing items.)

Shibori Method: Folding and Fold-and-Clamp

Fold-and-dip dyeing is the simplest, fastest, and most immediate of all shaped-resist processes. (It's also fun.) It consists of pleating fabric in single or multiple directions, then dipping or immersing the folded fabric into dyes along the folds, the edges, the corners, or a combination of these. The folds create appealing repeat patterns, from delicate single-color lines or stripes, to radiating patterns reminiscent of a kaleidoscope, to large-scale grids or geometric networks. The dyes "capture" the folding patterns and lock them into the cloth.

SUPPLY CHECKLIST FOR FOLD DYE

- iron and ironing board
- lightweight white fabric (cotton or silk)
- clamps
- binding cord
- rubber gloves
- small containers for dye solutions
- fiber reactive dyes for cotton, acid dyes for silk
- appropriate chemical assistants for the dyes
- plastic bags with zip closure

02-02 Large-scale (blue and gold) fold dye on cotton, used as a background for other printed and dyed fabrics in composition. Dyed, discharge-screen-printed, digitally printed, stamped, pieced, hand-appliquéd, free-motion-machine-stitched, hand-embroidered and hand-quilted. Cotton and bamboo. Scale: 26.5" × 70".

02-03 Fold-and-dip dye. Rectangular fold followed by multiple triangular (diagonal) folds radiating from the fabric center. Dipped in fiber reactive dye. Cotton print cloth. Scale: 7.5" × 8".

The characteristic marks and patterns reveal the underlying geometric networks of fold lines, with soft, fuzzy edges between colors. The patterns resulting from fold dye can be nearly infinite in variety, though predominantly *geometric* in character, and depend on three interdependent factors: the weight or thickness of the fabric; the sequence, type, and shape of the folds; and the sequence or combination of dye colors used. On certain tightly woven fabrics, increased pressure or painting with dye paste (see chapter 1 for recipe) can also produce crisp and defined edges. With fold dye you can experiment quickly and widely to test combinations of folds, sequences of colors, and angles of tilting the fabric edges into the dye, with lots of room for creative invention.

02-04 View of the folds and dips that produced 02-03.

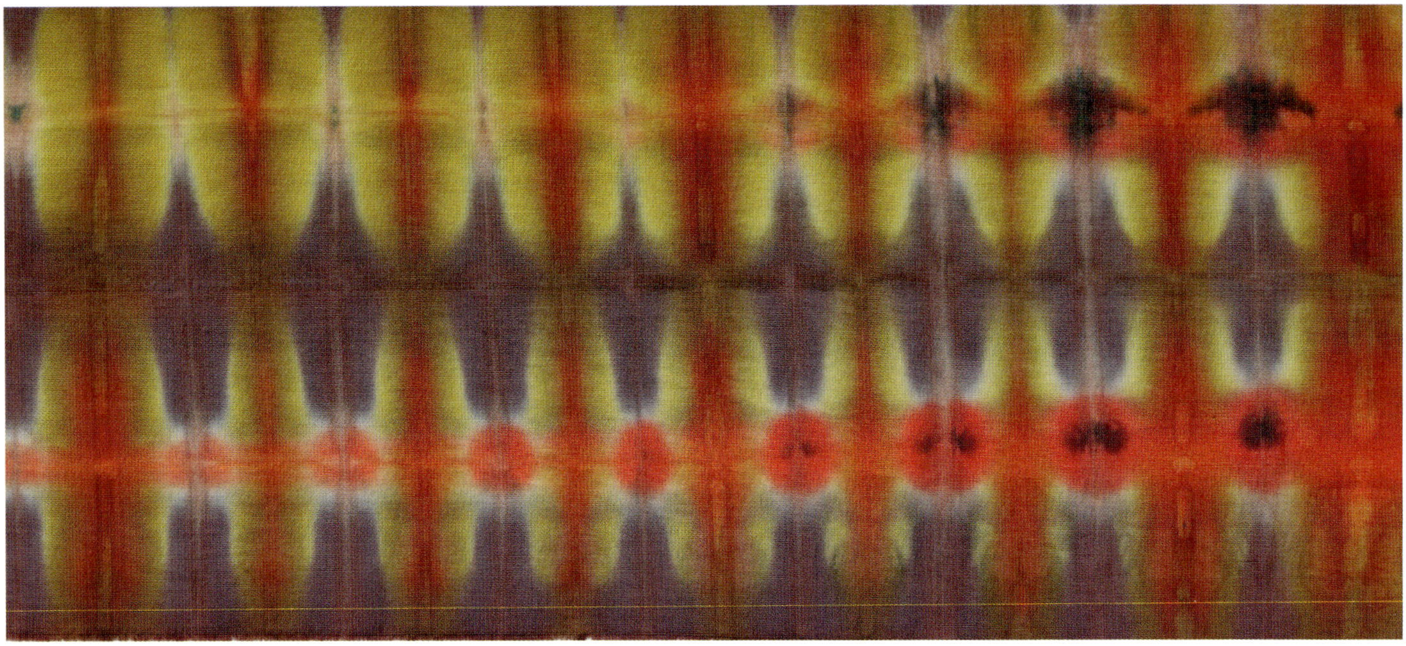

02-05 Fold-and-dip dye. Smaller accordion folds (no binding) produce a fine-scaled pattern, enlivened by strong color contrasts. Dipped in Procion MX fiber reactive dyes. Cotton print cloth. Scale: 5.5" × 12.25".

02-06 View of the folds and dips that produced 02-05.

Specific Folds and Manipulations before Dyeing

Thinner, lightweight fabrics are the easiest to fold, control, and dye. The thinness minimizes the bulk of the repeated and overlapping folds and allows the dye to penetrate through all layers quickly.

Before actual dyeing with any of the following fold dye techniques, see also "Color Factors in Fold Dyeing" and "Dip-Dyeing Folded Fabrics" on pages 75–76.

02-07 Fold-and-dip dye. Rectangular and triangular folds on thin cotton gauze allows easy folding and creates soft colors. Dipped in Procion MX fiber reactive dyes. Scale: 9.5" × 10".

Accordion folds alternate in direction: one fold up, one fold down, one up, one down, and so on, running across the width of the fabric (02-05, 02-09). The accordion-folded fabric package will be long, narrow, and somewhat thick. Dip the long folded *edges* directly into the dye solution to produce parallel stripes of color, as in 02-11. Dip the *ends* of the package to produce striped bands that lie perpendicular to the fold direction, shown in 02-34. Or do some of each, edges and ends. As an alternative to dipping, dye paste can be painted on the edges or ends but, unlike liquid dye, will sit primarily on the outer folds of the cloth rather than penetrate (02-31). Turning the long, narrow accordion-folded package and then folding it a second time along its length yields patterns with mirror images across the cloth (02-10, 02-13, 02-21).

02-08 View of the folds and dips that produced 02-07.

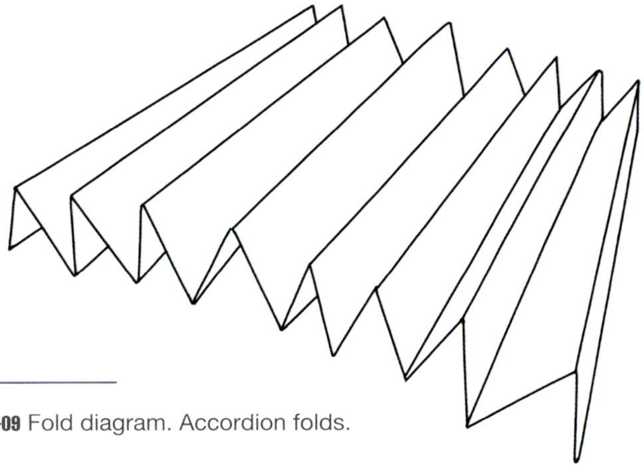

02-09 Fold diagram. Accordion folds.

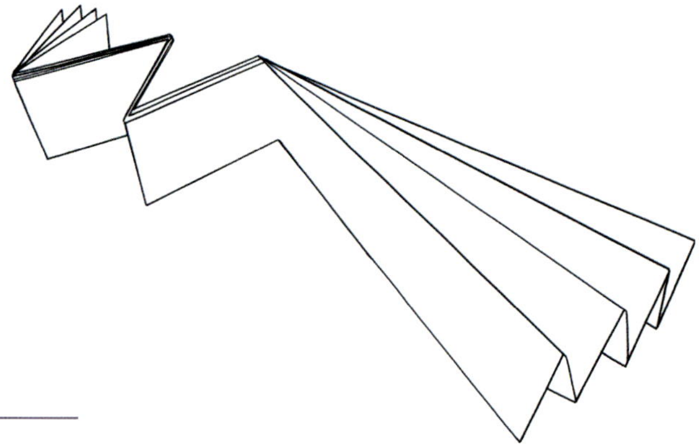

02-10 Accordion folds (as in 02-09), folded again in the perpendicular direction.

02-12 View of the folds and dips that produced 02-11.

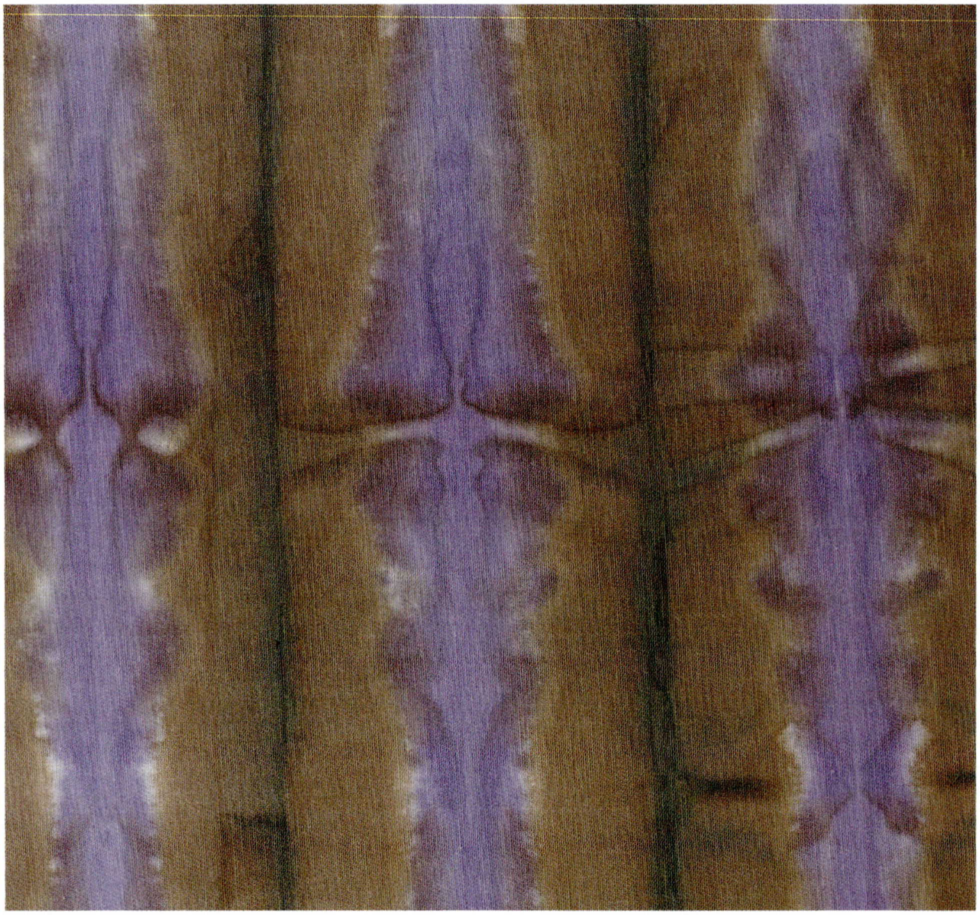

02-11 Fold-and-dip dye. Larger accordion folds (1.5") create a bolder effect. Dipped in Procion MX fiber reactive dyes. Heavy cotton twill. Scale: 8.75" × 9".

02-13 Fold-and-dip dye. Horizontal accordion folds, subsequently folded in the perpendicular direction to achieve mirrored color spots. Dipped in Procion MX fiber reactive dyes. Cotton print cloth. Scale: 7.5" × 8".

Rectangular or Square Folds

Multiple rectangular or square folds, overlapped in multiple directions, create a compact stacked fabric package (02-15). Rectangular folds produce distinctly geometric patterns that align both vertically and horizontally with the grain of the fabric (see 02-18). The larger the folds and the thicker the package, the more time it takes for dye to penetrate to the interior. To better control color placement on the folded package, paint on the dye (thin or pasted) with a sponge brush.

02-14 View of the folds and dips that produced 02-13.

02-16 Fold-and-dip dye. Rectangular folds: folded in half, turned, and folded in half again. Then folded into a triangle to dip in Procion MX fiber reactive dyes. Silk organza mesh. Scale: 3" × 3.5".

02-15 Multiple rectangular folds in sequence.

02-17 View of the folds and dips that produced 02-16.

02-18 Fold-and-dip dye. Rectangular folds in two directions, followed by one triangular fold. Corners and one edge dipped in Procion MX fiber reactive dyes. Cotton print cloth. Scale: 7.5" × 8.25".

02-19 View of the folds and dips that produced 02-18.

Triangular Folds

Triangular folds add diagonal lines to underlying rectangular folds (see folding diagram 02-20). When triangular folds radiate out from the center, the resulting imagery resembles the view through a kaleidoscope (02-03, 02-18).

02-21 Fold-and-dip dye. Uneven accordion folds in two directions, and a triangular fold. Dipped in Procion MX fiber reactive dyes. Cotton print cloth. Scale: 9.25" × 6.25".

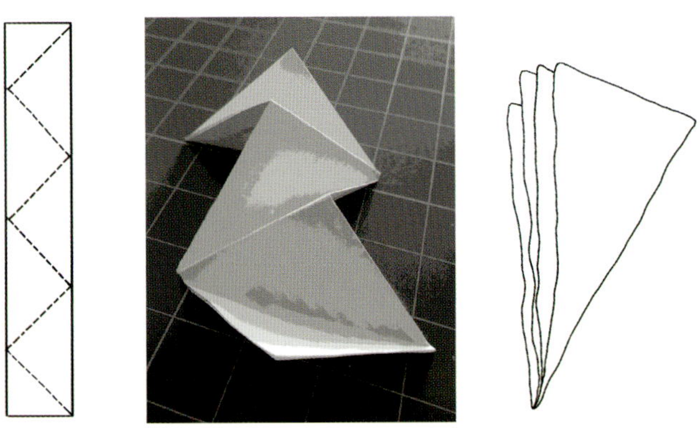

02-20 Multiple triangular folds in sequence.

02-22 View of the folds and dips that produced 02-21.

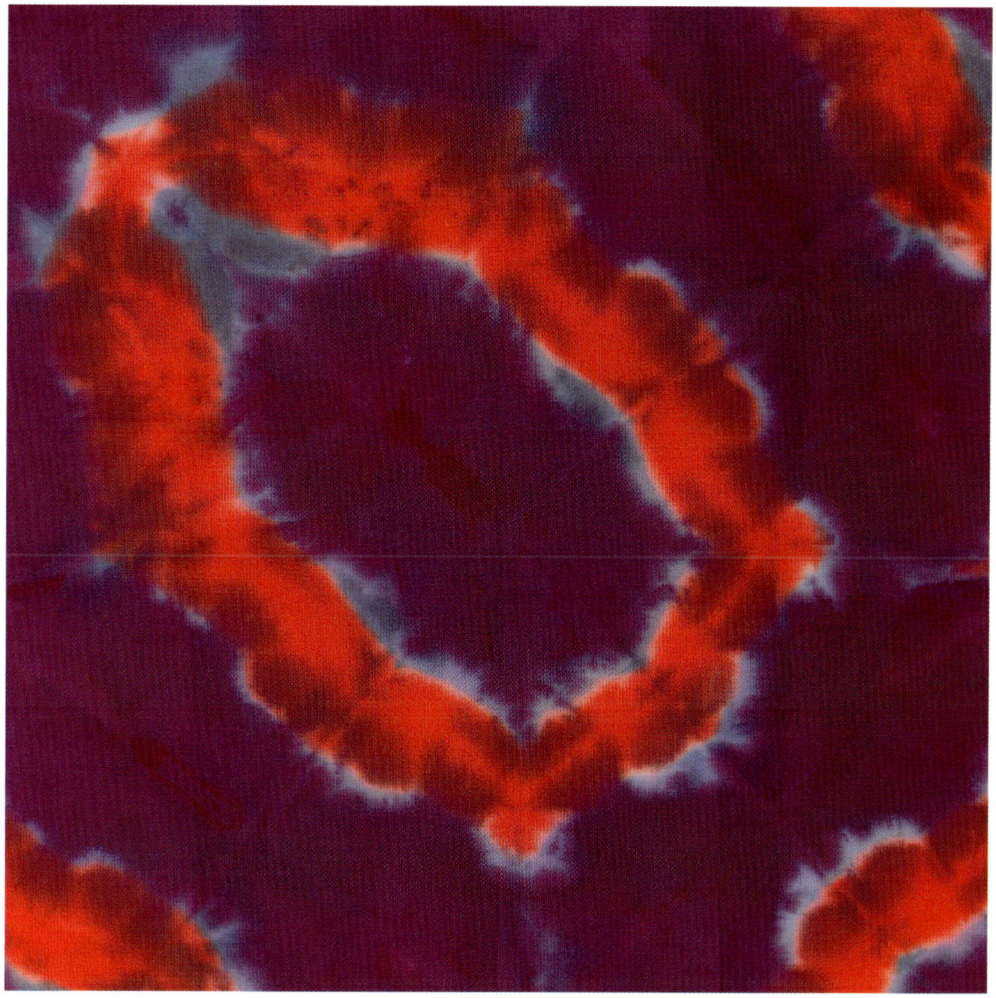

02-23 Fold-and-dip dye. Triangular folds in multiple directions. Dipped in Procion MX fiber reactive dyes. Cotton print cloth. Scale: 10" × 10".

Free-Form ("Eccentric") Folding

In addition to the basic folds described above, try to adapt origami folds (usually made on paper) or sew darts or pleats into fabric (usually made on clothing parts) at odd angles for quasi-geometric images. (See also chapter 10 in the *Dry Techniques* book for instructions on darts and pleats.) Or, throw caution to the wind and experiment with folding the fabric in any crazy way you like. Once dyed, these more eccentric folds create more unexpected, dynamic, and irregular results.

02-24 View of the folds and dips that produced 02-23.

02-25 Fold and clamp resist (*itajime*). C-clamped accordion folds; yellow dots indicate the rounded points of contact of the circular C-clamp. Dipped in Procion MX fiber reactive dyes. Cotton print cloth. Scale: 8" × 8".

02-26 View of the folds, clamped circle shape, and dips that produced 02-25.

Folding Combined with Clamping (*Itajime*)

To add more definition to fold dye resist, you can clamp the cloth bundle. The clamp itself also becomes a "handle" for dipping the folded-fabric package into the dye and adds the imprint of its "gripping teeth" to the resist mark. Because clamping applies very tight pressure, it effectively prevents the wicking of fiber reactive dyes, even when immersed in a dyebath for the duration of its usual length of time (see chapter 1).

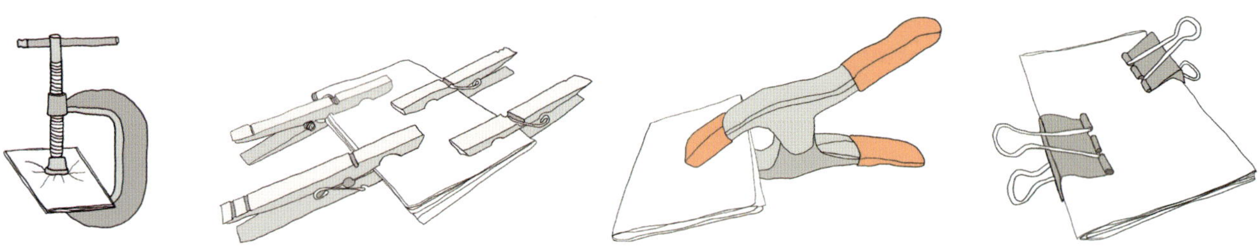

02-27 Various methods of clamping folded fabrics: C-clamp, clothespins, large spring clamps, office paper spring clamps.

Use manufactured spring clamps, C-clamps, clothespins, or any other kind of device that firmly presses and holds tension on the folded cloth (02-27, 02-28). In 02-25, the pressure points from a small C-clamp preserve the original yellow color, punctuate the squares in the design with circles, and emphasize the repeating fold patterns and high-intensity colors in eye-catching contrast.

You can also introduce specific resisted shapes onto the folded cloth by placing a *pair* of *identical* custom-made shapes, one per side of the cloth bundle, *between* the clamp and the bundle. These shapes can be geometric, organic, or recognizable (a circle, a triangle, a tree leaf, your hand, your dog, Santa Claus). The resulting resisted shape will be more clearly delineated on the outside layers of the fabric package and more soft and indistinct on the inside. Cut specific shapes from a rigid material that's unlikely to stain, rust, or bend (I prefer hard sheet acrylic). Place the two shapes on opposite sides of the package and aligned with each other, then C-clamp them into place with tight pressure (see 02-28, 02-29, and 02-30).

Still more unconventionally, try using common objects—coins, washers, miscellaneous flat hardware items—as shapes to be clamped.

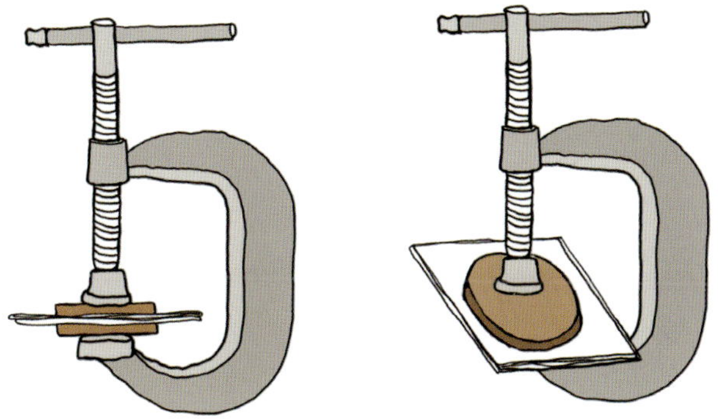

02-28 C-clamp used to press fabric between identical cut shapes.

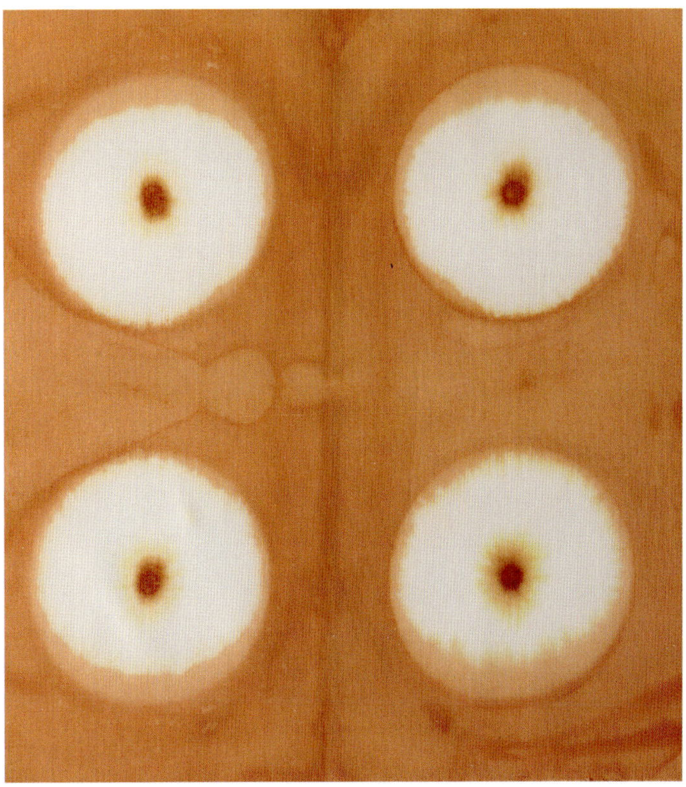

02-29 Fold and clamp resist (*itajime*). Multiple rectangular folds with clamp resist circles cut from Plexiglas (see 02-28 clamping diagram). Procion MX fiber reactive dyes. Cotton print cloth. Scale: 7.25" × 8.25".

02-30 View of the folds, clamped plastic circle shape, and dips that produced 02-29.

02-31 Fold dye using ordinary paper clips as clamps. Small accordion folds or alternating pleats (0.5") create a more delicate pattern. The paper clips left fine resist lines on the cloth, but also spots of quick rusting from the moisture. Thickened Procion MX fiber reactive dyes. Cotton print cloth. Scale: 6" × 5.25".

02-32 View of the folds, paper clip placements, and dips that produced 02-31.

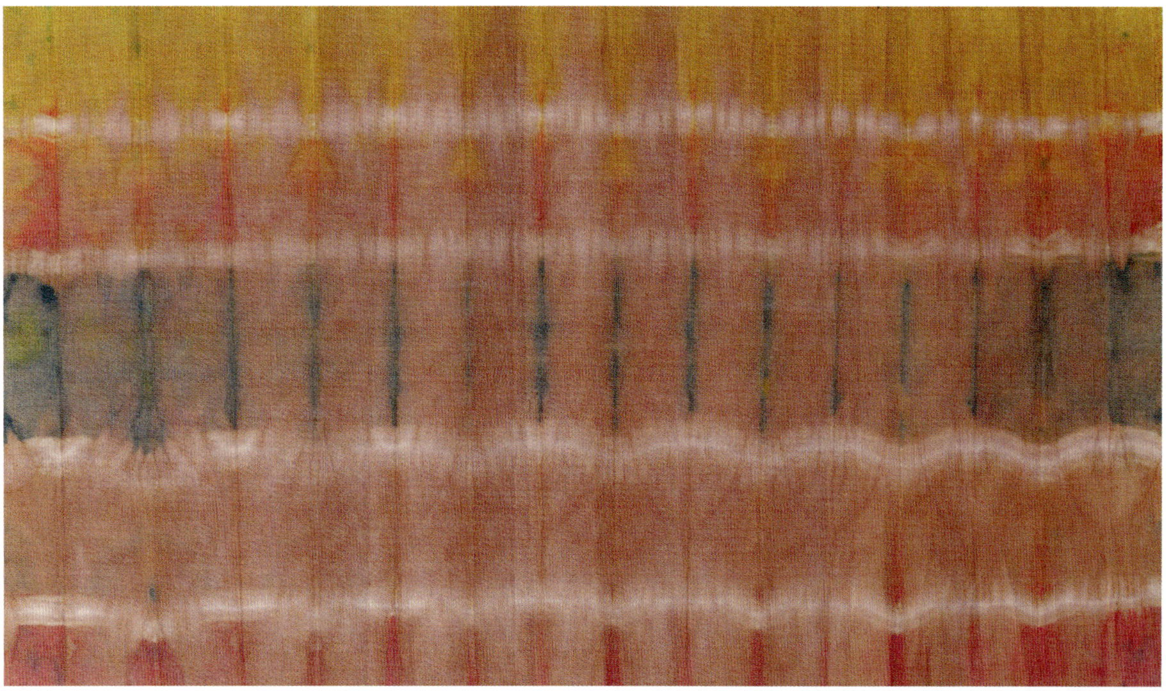

02-33 Accordion folds, bound with cord, producing white resist marks (see binding diagram 02-35). Painted thickened Procion MX fiber reactive dyes. Cotton print cloth. Scale: 6" × 10".

02-34 Folded, bound, and dipped view for 02-33.

Folding Combined with Binding

Binding the folded fabric introduces finely scaled resist lines *across* the larger color areas (02-33, 02-34, and binding diagram 02-35). For differing patterns, use thread or cord to bind at regular or irregular intervals, and in horizontal, vertical, or diagonal directions. The tighter the bindings, the stronger the impression of lines will be; looser bindings create a softer impression.

02-35 Pleated or folded fabric bound at intervals (see 02-34 for dyed example).

Color Factors in Fold Dyeing

Color effects and patterns achieved by dipped fold dye will depend not only on the type and sequence of the folds, but also on these interacting dyeing factors:

1. *Physical depth of the dip:* The shallower the dip, the more narrow or delicate the color lines. The deeper the dip, the larger the blocks of color.

2. *Angle of contact*: Most simply, hold the *edges* of the folded fabric *parallel* to the surface of the dye solution, then dip them straight downward in single or successive colors. Because the dyes naturally wick and run to some extent, this results in roughly repeating geometric lines or shapes with soft, fuzzy edges. However, inserting the fabric package into the dye *at an angle* to the edges, or across the corners, produces a slightly different result and introduces diagonal lines into the resulting pattern.

3. *Amount of time*: Naturally, the longer you dip and hold the fabric in the dye, the more the dye and chemicals have time to wick, react, intensify, and lock into the cloth. In any case, the amount of time is small (e.g., dipping for one second to several seconds).

4. *Sequence of separate and distinct color dips*: Generally, dip the lighter colors first and proceed to the darker ones. Use what you know about color mixing to create composite colors as you dip.

5. *Amount of pressure*: Some amount of pressure is necessary to secure the folded package so it can be dipped into the dye. The least pressure results in the softest edges and the most color blending. Firmer pressure results in crisper and clearer edges on patterns, shapes, or marks where they meet the original color of the fabric. The most direct method of applying pressure is with your (gloved) fingers, simply holding the package together with either light, medium, or intense pressure. To increase the pressure (especially for dips of longer duration) and simultaneously extend the range of outcomes with fold dye, use the clamping methods discussed on pages 72–73.

6. *Single or multiple colors:* You can dip folded edges and corners in separate colors or dip the entire package, squeeze out the excess, then dip edges or corners to overdye the colors. Apply your knowledge of color theory and test unusual color combinations and overdyes (see chapter 1).

7. *Overdyed fold dyeing:* To layer fold-dye effects, completely process the fabric: fold, dye, batch, rinse out, dry, and press. Then *re-fold* the fabric, this time placing the folds in different locations or orientations, and dip-dye the package again. The overdyed color mixtures will be interesting and unusual, the overlay of patterns mysterious and intriguing.

8. *Wet vs. dry fabrics:* Fold dye on *dry* manipulated fabrics creates more distinct patterns; wet or damp fabric mutes dye color and blurs color edges. To experiment with soft, blended color in fold dye, simply re-wet the *folded* dry fabric package, just before dipping it in the dye, then squeeze out the excess water and proceed to dip.

Dip-Dyeing Folded Fabrics

Folded dip dyeing, whether for cellulose fibers or protein fibers (in this case, usually silk, *not* wool), is best done with fiber reactive dyes.

For fold dyeing, large-size immersion dyebaths and lengthy soaking are unnecessary. Instead, we'll use very small, *concentrated* "dip dyebaths" and *briefly* (one second to several seconds) immerse the folded fabric, then remove it. The short time in the dyebath capitalizes on fiber reactive dyes' strong color and ease of use but prevents the excessive wicking that would result from longer dips. *Batching* (described below) ensures that the dye and chemistry stay wet long enough to set the colors into the fabric.

Safety guidelines:

Dip dyeing requires some safety precautions. When dipping folded fabric packages into dye solutions, your fingers often dip into the dyes. Always wear rubber gloves to protect your hands, and a work shirt or apron (or both) to protect your clothing from accidental spills or splashes. Follow all the dye safety rules discussed in chapter 1.

1. While the fabric is still dry, plan for the results you want to achieve. Use a "disappearing ink" pen to mark, along the edges of the fabric, the specific points where you intend to fold. Use your *steam iron* to press each individual fold accurately and compactly in place. Prepare and press *all* of your folded-fabric packages for the dye session *before* you mix or activate the dyes and start to dip.

2. Put on rubber gloves and a work apron.

3. Use fiber reactive dyes mixed as stock solutions. (See chapter 1 for instructions.)

4, Make a quart of chemical water (see chapter 1) and distribute at least 1 cup of it into each of several small containers (imagine an empty, clean container that formerly held cottage cheese), one container for each dye color you plan to use. Or, for folded-fabric packets of larger size, use a larger container and make proportionally more chemical water to allow room to dip the folds into a few inches of dyebath.

5. Add dye, in stock solution form, to the containers of chemical water. (For folded-fabric packets of larger size, add proportionally more stock solution.) Because the contact time between the fabric and dyebath is brief, a rule of thumb is to add about twice as much dye as you need for the desired depth of dye color (i.e., just make it more concentrated).

6. Immediately *before* using the now-combined dye / chemical water solutions, mix in soda ash (for cellulose fibers) or citric acid crystals (for silk) to activate the dye (in a ratio of 1 T. per cup of chemical water). Mix well. After the activator is added, the dye is *also* activated and will quickly deteriorate and lose its potency (typically in about an hour), so use it promptly.

7. To prevent dye contamination from one dipping container to the next, set up a *separate* empty container or bucket (just one) into which you can squeeze excess dye after each dipping.

8. To prevent contamination of lighter colors in the dipping sequence, dip the *lighter colors first*, before proceeding to the darker colors. Dip the folded fabric in the dyes, choosing the folds and edges you wish to color. Hold the bundle steadily in place and contact the dye straight or at an angle. (Remember that because the fabric is wet, the color will look darker and more intense now than after it is later processed and dried.) Let the cloth absorb color until it looks (to your eye) a bit more intense or darker than you actually want. Vertically lift the fabric out of the dyebath. Hold the dipped package over your separate wastewater bucket and squeeze the colored edge carefully to remove excess dye and water.

9. Proceed to the next color in your dipping sequence. Remove excess water and dye by squeezing it into the wastewater bucket after each dip in a new color.

10. When you have completed all the different color dippings on a folded package, press it between layers of paper toweling or rags to remove the rest of the excess moisture and dye. (You want it to stay wet but not drip.)

11. Use either a batching method or heat-setting method to set the color.

- **Batching** (shorter and easier): While the fabric is still wet, tightly seal small pieces in plastic bags. Cover larger pieces with sheets of plastic, roll them up, and seal with tape. Let the sealed package sit undisturbed for 24 hours. Open the plastic bag, unfold the fabric, and go to step 12 below.

- **Heat setting** (longer and more complicated): While the fabric is still wet, immediately unfold it and spread it flat or hang it to dry. To avoid transferring dyes to unwanted (preserved) areas or contaminating the colors while unfolding, take care not to touch the fabric to itself or to touch undyed fabric areas with your dye-covered fingers. Air-dry first and then heat-set by one of the methods outlined in the "Setting the Dyes" section of chapter 1. Then go to step 12.

12. Rinse out. (See the "Universal Rinse-Out for Resist Dyeing" text box, page 61.)

Shibori Method: Bound Resist (*Plangi*)

Plangi (a Malay-Indonesian word) and *banda* (an Indian word) both describe types of *bound resist* cloth, which many English-speaking people call "tie-dye." In this section we'll look at four types of *bound resist*, presented in increasing order of difficulty—*random bound resist, twisted bound resist, knotted bound resist, and tie-dye*.

For each type, you will manipulate the fabric into a three-dimensional form—crumple, fold, gather, twist, wrap, roll, knot, pull into points or cones—and then *bind* it with cord or thread. When dipped in a dyebath or painted with a thickened dye paste, pressure from the cords prevents dye penetration on the "sealed off" fabric portions, while parts of the fabric left free or only loosely bound accept the dye. The *proportion* of cloth protected from the dye determines whether the color in the preserved areas or the open areas predominates in the finished cloth.

Bound-resist fabric is also characterized by color areas *crossed* by delicate lines left behind by the protective pressure of the binding cords that "captured" the manipulated form.

Nor does bound resist of a single fabric need to be a one-time event. You can repeatedly bind and dye the same fabric in a sequence of colors, scales, or contrasting patterns, to produce even more complex patterns.

I'll first give instructions for the pre-dye manipulation and binding on *each* type of bound resist, followed by the *single* set of dyeing instructions common to all of them.

02-36 Tie-dye (also called *ne-maki shibori*) bound in concentric rings (diagram 02-46). Dipped and painted, thickened, fiber reactive dye. Cotton kettle cloth. Scale: 6" × 10".

SUPPLY CHECKLIST FOR BOUND-RESIST PROCESSES

- lightweight white fabric (cotton or silk)
- Twine, thread, or cord: strong enough to withstand intense pulling and binding tension. Larger-diameter cord binds large areas faster and creates larger-scale resist marks. Smaller threads produce more-delicate resist lines. You can use several layers of thinner cord to provide extra protection in the resist and strengthen the cord.
- scissors: small and sharp pointed, for clipping threads; larger shears for cutting fabric
- washable fabric-marking tools
- *shibori* device (optional): for making tiny tie-dye dots (see images 02-55, 02-56)

Specific Manipulations and Bindings before Dyeing

The following types of bound resist form the heart of *shibori* and produce some of its most recognizable and appealing marks and patterns. Each bound-resist variation can be worked at small or large scale and dyed in subtle or dynamic colors for a range of outcomes and end uses.

Random Bound Resist

Random bound resist essentially consists of wadding/crumpling the fabric, binding it with cord (02-39), then dyeing it. The method produces a characteristic wide and random scattering of small colored patches, crisscrossed with delicate lines, all floating in a nearly open field, more space than marks (see 02-37 and 02-38). In design terms, random bound resist preserves large expanses of the original cloth color (whether white or previously dyed) while adding delicate touches of a contrasting color and inviting further additions of pattern, marks, or embellishments.

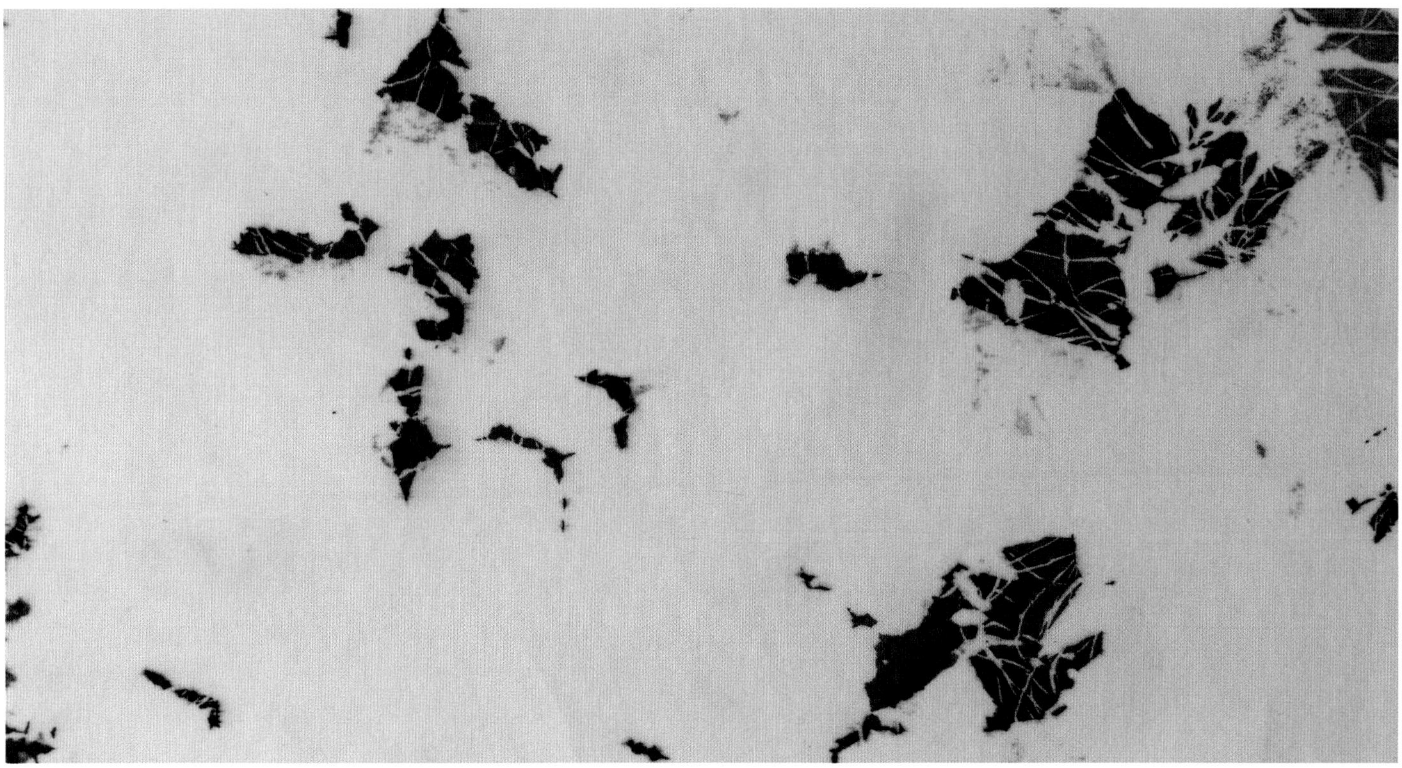

02-37 Random bound resist (see 02-39 for binding diagram). Painted thickened Procion MX fiber reactive dyes on dry fabric; single dye color. Cotton broadcloth. Scale: 8" × 11".

02-38 Random bound resist (see 02-39 for binding diagram). Painted thickened dye on wet fabric; composite dye color. Cotton print cloth. Scale: 8" × 7.5".

Random bound-resist outcomes will differ, depending on whether the fabric is wet (softer, blurry marks) or dry (more distinct, crisp marks) when bound and dyed. With fiber reactive dyes on cotton, you might, for example, use an immersion dyebath to achieve soft and subtle effects, or paint on thickened dye paste to produce sharper edges on the naturally occurring marks. With acid dyes, just drop the bound ball into the dyebath for clear markings. Regardless of the application method (immersion or painting), the dye will leave widely distributed and irregularly shaped spots of color across the surface. The marks achieve full intensity only on the bits of fabric *on the outside* of the wadded ball. On most fabric types, the dye will not penetrate to the center of the wad, but test your specific cloth, particularly if it's thin or delicate.

Random bound resist can be applied in multiple layers on the same cloth, with different patterns of crumpling and binding between layers, or used to create a light foundation for other resist, direct-application, or embellishment techniques.

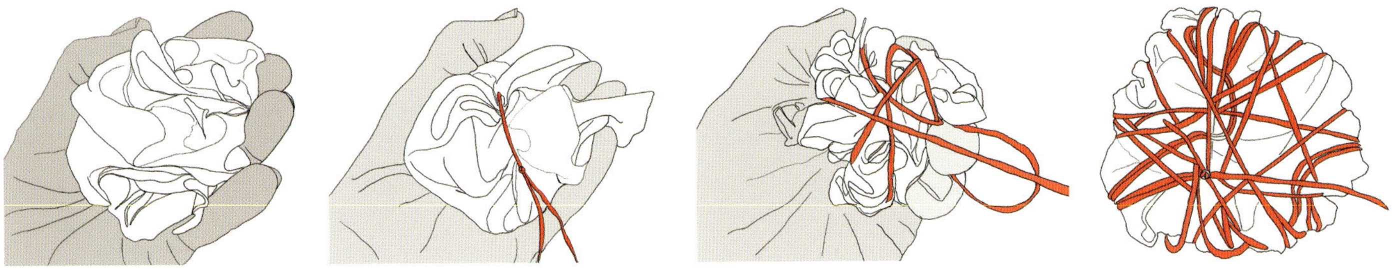

02-39 Wadding and binding random resist in sequence. Cord shown in red for clarity.

Instructions for wadding and binding (as shown in 02-39):

In random resist dyeing, as in all the other techniques in this chapter, the binding determines the results. Here are the general guidelines:

1. Before you start to wad, have strong, easy-to-handle cord of any size, with a slipknot tied (with a long tail) at one end. (A contrasting *color* of cord for binding is easier to see after the dyeing.) Cotton twine or pearl cotton thread is a good, inexpensive choice in this binding variation. The length of the cord will depend on how much fabric wrapping you'll want to do, but in any case you'll want several extra inches of cord beyond the wrapping itself.

2. Crumple and wad the fabric in your hand. Arrange the wrinkles and folds as you wish.

3. Hold the wadded fabric ball in place in your hand as you put the slipknot end of the cord around the entire wad, and pull the knot tight to secure the cord around the wadded shape. Hold the wadded ball in one hand, while with the other hand you begin to *tightly* wind the cord around the ball, overlapping back and forth while rotating the ball. Bindings can be close together or far apart, evenly or unevenly spaced.

4. Stop wrapping when the wad is secure. Tie off the cord with another knot but leave a long tail, so your final knot will be easier to locate when the time comes to clip the cords. (The initial slipknot should already be easy to loosen when you unwind the cord.)

5. For a quick alternative that generates a slightly different kind of resist mark and is easily removed at the end of the dye process (no cords, no knots), wrap the wadded fabric ball in rubber bands instead of fiber cords.

Placement of dyed marks in random bound resist:

The unplanned and impromptu nature of the wadding and binding directly translates into spontaneous and informal marks and shapes. This can be an advantage if you want to achieve a "natural" look in your projects. But that same ease of manipulation and binding raises difficulties for *controlling* the resulting pattern. You might, for example, want the spontaneous-looking results of random resist dyeing but want the marks only to show up on the center of the fabric, or at the edges, or to appear "layered." Here are a few approaches to place the resulting dyed shapes approximately where you want them—to achieve "random" without going all the way to "chaotic."

- *To scatter random dyed shapes across the surface*: Pick up the fabric with its front side (the nap or woven pattern side) facing outward as you *randomly* wad the fabric. Keep the front side of the fabric consistently on the outside of the ball as you bind.

- *To concentrate dyed shapes in the center of the fabric*: Wad the fabric with the *center* sections of the front side on the *outside* of the ball, and the edges tucked *inside* as you bind.

- *To scatter dyed shapes around the edges of the fabric*: Wad the fabric, front side facing outward, and keeping the *edges* of the fabric on the *outside* of the ball and the center tucked *inside,* then bind.

- *To place dyed shapes in predetermined clusters or at specific points*: Spread the fabric flat and then, using a temporary marking tool, make a circle or point where you want dyed shapes to occur. As you wad the fabric, intentionally place the *marked points on the outside* of the wadded ball and keep everything else tucked inside.

Twisted Bound Resist

Unlike more classic bound-resist techniques in this section, *twisted bound resist* is not a "named technique" with strong historical precedents. But *twisting* a cloth (or parts of it), and binding that twist in place, creates long, broken, dyed shapes that resemble ropes, tree branches, or wood bark (02-40). Like the classic bound-resist methods, these markings are recognizable as the spirals that formed from the twisting. Twisting is quick, immediate, and random and leaves large undyed areas suited to combination with other dye processes.

02-40 Twisted bound fabric resist (see diagram 02-41). Painted, thickened, fiber reactive dye. Pre-dyed cotton broadcloth. Scale: 5.5" × 8.5".

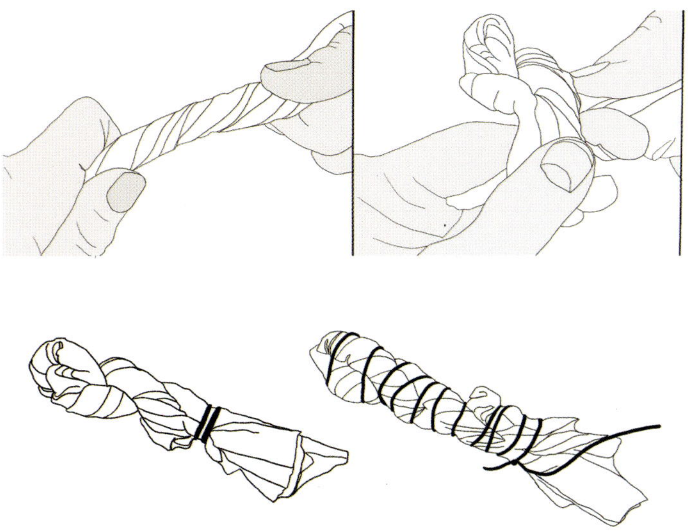

02-41 Twisted bound resist in sequence.

Instructions for twisting and binding (as shown in 02-41):

1. Grasp two ends or two corners of fabric, one in each hand, and twist them in *opposite* directions (one hand twists away from your body and one hand twists toward your body, *as if* you were wringing out a wet cloth).

2. Keep twisting until the fabric tightens and finally *overtwists* and folds back onto itself. (To apply even greater force or pressure to the twist, tie one end of the fabric to a stationary object, such as a doorknob or hook, and twist against its solidity.) When you have sufficient twist in the fabric, you can proceed to the binding. (Variations: make *multiple* twists in different parts of the same piece of fabric, each bound separately; *fold* the fabric before twisting and binding; or *braid* several pieces of fabric together, then twist them.)

3. While the tightness of the twist will create a resist by itself, you must bind the fabric with cord to hold the twist in place. To place resist lines only at the ends of the twist, bind the two ends of the twisted fabric together and tie a knot in the cord. To add extra resist lines, bind a cord around the entire length of the twist. Start the binding with a knot at one end, wrap around in a spiral to the other end, and secure with a knot, but leave a long tail.

Knotted Bound Resist

Another spontaneous technique that is both "unnamed" and "without pedigree," knotted bound resist involves simply tying the cloth itself into a knot. Knotting works best on long, narrow pieces of fabric (such as strips or scarves), or on the pointed corners of rectangular or triangular fabric pieces. Knotting usually leaves large resist areas in the center of the knot's location, with most of the color in elongated dyed shapes clustered at the corners or edges (02-42).

02-42 Knotted bound resist (see diagram 02-43) on dry fabric, leaving open space in the center and color at the edges of the cloth. Single color of fiber reactive dye. Cotton print cloth. Scale: 7.5" × 8".

Instructions for knotting and binding (as shown in 02-43):

1. Grasp two places on the cloth (such as the two ends of a long strip or the twisted corner of a rectangle) and tie an *overhand* knot. The tighter the knot, the more complete the resist. (Variations: a single large knot in the center or at a corner; a sequence of small knots along the entire length of a scarf; small, individually knotted fabric "points" distributed in a pattern across a very lightweight fabric.)

2. A tight knot creates a large resist area from its own pressure. But binding the knot will introduce small-scale lines that cross and break up the dyed areas. Choose the direction and spacing of the binding cords based on the shape of the cloth and the size of the knot(s).

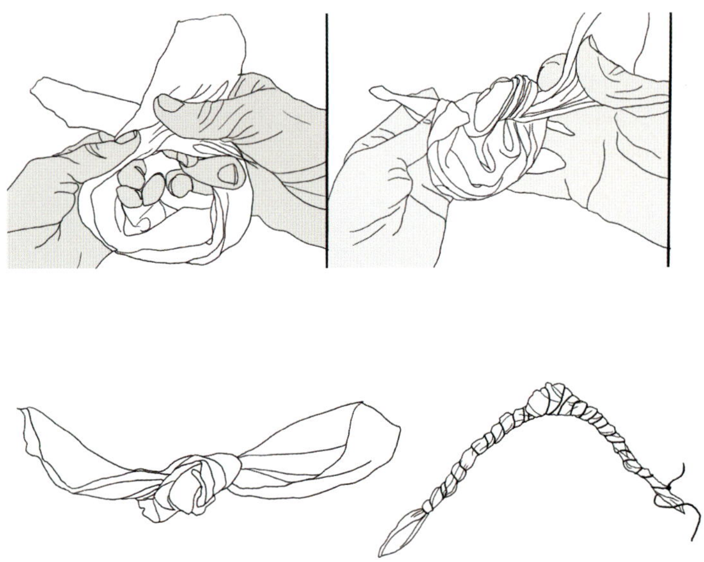

02-43 Knotted bound resist in sequence.

02-44 Tie-dye (also called *ne-maki shibori*) bound in concentric rings (diagram 02-60). Multiple colors of Procion MX fiber reactive dyes, dipped and painted. Cotton broadcloth. Scale: 8" × 8".

Tie-Dye Bound Resist (*Plangi*)

In tie-dye (also called *plangi* from the Malay-Indonesian word *pelangi*, meaning "many colored" or "reserved dot"), parts of the fabric are raised into a cone shape and bound with strong thread or cord. Tie-dye has many variations, with corresponding styles of binding and characteristic resist lines from the cords.

The variations in marks, patterns, and visual effects with tie-dye depend on a combination of the size, spacing, and placement of the fabric cones and the binding cords, all of which will eventually be captured by the way you apply the dye. For example: thick cords produce wider resist lines, while thin threads yield more-delicate ones; sparsely spaced bindings become distinct and separate, while closely spaced bindings blend to create larger more-solid areas of resist.

In this section we'll look at three tie-dye variations and discuss their bindings—*ne-maki shibori* (closely-tied bindings that create rings of resist), varieties of *rasen shibori* (more-open spiral bindings that create spiral or spiderweb markings), and *kanoko shibori* (closely-tied single-thread bindings to create tiny rings or dots), followed by the dyeing instructions common to all bound resist.

02-45 Tie-dye (also called *ne-maki shibori*) bound in concentric rings (diagram 02-46). Multiple colors of painted, thickened, fiber reactive dye. Cotton print cloth. Scale 7.5" × 7".

Ne-maki shibori

This is the Japanese name for the classic form of bound resist that creates *rings* of resist on the dyed cloth (as in 02-44 and 02-45). The binding is done on large cones of fabric, pulled up and then bound with a single cord wrapped around the cone, or with multiple separate cords tied at intervals along the cone, to form concentric rings radiating out from a center point as in 02-46. The bound fabric can be painted all one color to unify the cloth, or with different colors to dramatically emphasize the separations created by the binding cords (02-01). Your own interpretations can range from subtle and elegant to intensely colorful and energetic and can be applied to decorate or to create images or designs.

To vary the shape and appearance of the rings, you can insert small objects (such as marbles, pebbles, plastic, glass, beads, rice kernels, seeds, or beans) into the *tip* of the cone and then tie closely to encase them (02-47). The shape and texture of each different type of object will produce a slightly different resist.

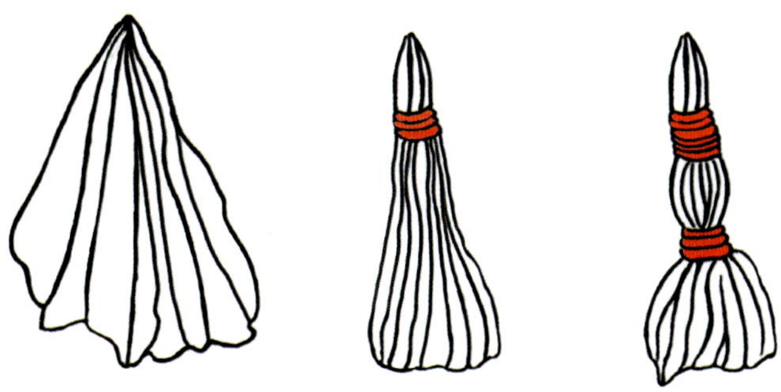

02-46 Binding diagram for *ne-maki shibori.*

Instructions for manipulating and binding ne-maki shibori*:*

1. Choose a size of thread or cord that will make the size of resist line you want. (If you use a contrasting color of thread for the binding, it will be easier to see and remove after the dyeing.)

2. *Pinch* the fabric between your thumb and first finger, allowing the rest of the fabric to drop down and fall in gathers on all sides from the pinched point. Arrange the gathers and folds to suit your idea, large or small, and even or uneven in placement and size.

3. To begin the binding on each pinched cone, you can either tie a slipknot at the tip around the cone or thread a needle with the thread and anchor it in the cloth with a knot.

4. Proceed to wrap the thread around the manipulated fabric several times, then pull the cords very tight. (To help pull the cord tighter without hurting your hands, try wrapping the end of the cord around scissors or a metal rod to use as a handle for pulling the cords. This will improve your grip and reduce the labor while simultaneously setting the cords firmly into the manipulated fabric.) After the ring is bound, knot off the thread but leave a long tail.

   To create separate (multiple) concentric rings of resist, use separate pieces of cord placed at intervals from top to bottom of the cone (02-46 right). You can space the bindings sparsely or densely.

5. The steps above assume that you're binding from a cone pinched from a single point, as in 02-46. But you can also choose to pull up cones at *multiple* points on the *same* piece of cloth (as in 02-51). To do this, mark the fabric with dots *before* beginning to bind, using a temporary marking tool to indicate *each* of the places where you will then pinch the fabric to raise a cone for binding. (Without marking, the gradual bunching of the cloth in the binding processes can disorient your ability to plot and control their placement.)

Rasen shibori

This is the Japanese name for more openly bound (spaces between the wraps of the cord) tie-dye involving *spiral* bindings (as in 02-48 and 02-49), first made popular in America in the 1960s on tie-dyed T-shirts. The binding is done on large cones of fabric, pulled up and then bound with a single cord wrapped around the cone in a spiral radiating out from a center point as in diagram 02-50. The fabric can be painted all one color to unify the cloth (02-49), or with different colors to dramatically emphasize the separations created by the binding cords (02-48). Your own interpretations can range from subtle and elegant to intensely colorful and energetic and can be applied to decorate or to create images or designs.

02-47 Tie-dye (also called *ne-maki shibori*) bound in concentric rings (diagram 02-60) with small stones also bound inside the cone tips. Contrasting colors painted with thickened Procion MX fiber reactive dyes. Cotton broadcloth. Scale: 9.5" × 9.5".

02-48 Tie-dye with spiral binding on cones of fabric (*rasen shibori* in spiderweb pattern). Procion MX fiber reactive dyes on silk noil. Scale: 5" × 8.5".

02-49 Tie-dye with spiral binding on cones of fabric (*rasen shibori* in spiderweb pattern). Sewing-thread spiral binding yields delicate lines (see binding diagram 02-50). Painted, thickened, Procion MX fiber reactive dyes prevent wicking. Cotton broadcloth. Scale: 3" × 6".

Instructions for manipulating and binding rasen shibori*:*

1. Choose a size of thread or cord that will make the size of resist line you want. If you use a contrasting color of thread for the binding, it will be easier to see and remove after the dyeing.

2. *Pinch* the fabric between your thumb and first finger, allowing the rest of the fabric to drop down and fall in gathers on all sides from the pinched point. Arrange the gathers and folds to suit your idea, large or small, and even or uneven in placement and size.

3. To begin the spiral-wrapped bindings on each pinched cone, you can either tie a slipknot at the tip or base of the cone or thread a needle with the thread and anchor it in the cloth with a knot.

4. Proceed to wrap the thread around the manipulated fabric *in a spiral*, then pull the cords very tight. (To help pull the cord tighter without hurting your hands, try wrapping the end of the cord around scissors or a metal rod to use as a handle for pulling the cords. This will improve your grip and reduce the labor while simultaneously setting the cords firmly into the manipulated fabric.) At the end of binding each cone, knot off the thread but leave a long tail. (To create a more complex design or resist marks, try binding from the *base* of the cone *up* to the tip, then reverse directions and work your way back down the cone to the base, crossing the threads along the way.)

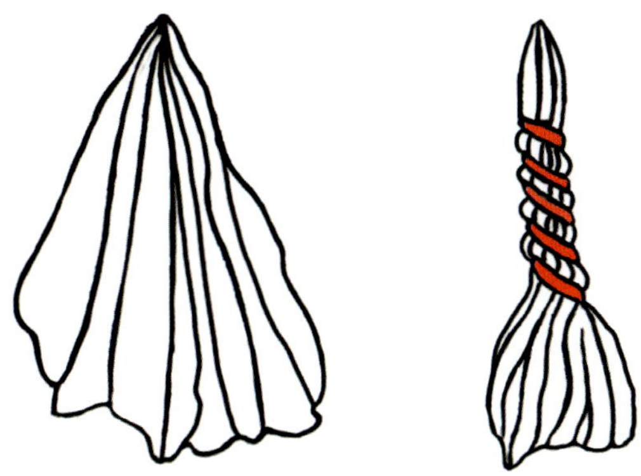

02-50 Binding diagram for *rasen shibori.*

5. The steps above assume that you're binding from a cone at a single point, as in 02-50. But you can also choose to pull up cones at *multiple* points on the *same* piece of cloth (as in 02-51). To do this, mark the fabric with dots *before* beginning to bind, using a temporary marking tool to indicate *each* of the places where you will then pinch the fabric to raise a cone for binding. (Without marking, the gradual bunching of the cloth in the binding processes can disorient your ability to plot and control their placement.)

02-52 Tie-dye with spiral binding on cones of fabric (*rasen shibori* in spiderweb pattern). Multiple colors of painted, thickened, fiber reactive dye (see binding diagram 02-50). Cotton broadcloth. Scale: 4" × 5".

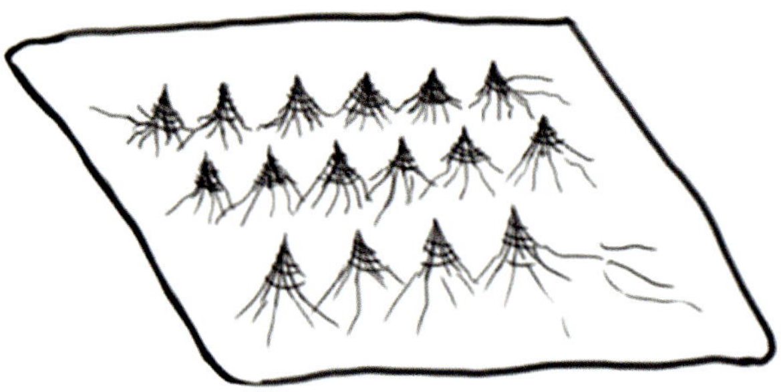

02-51 Fabric pinched and tightly spiral bound at multiple points (*rasen shibori* in spiderweb pattern).

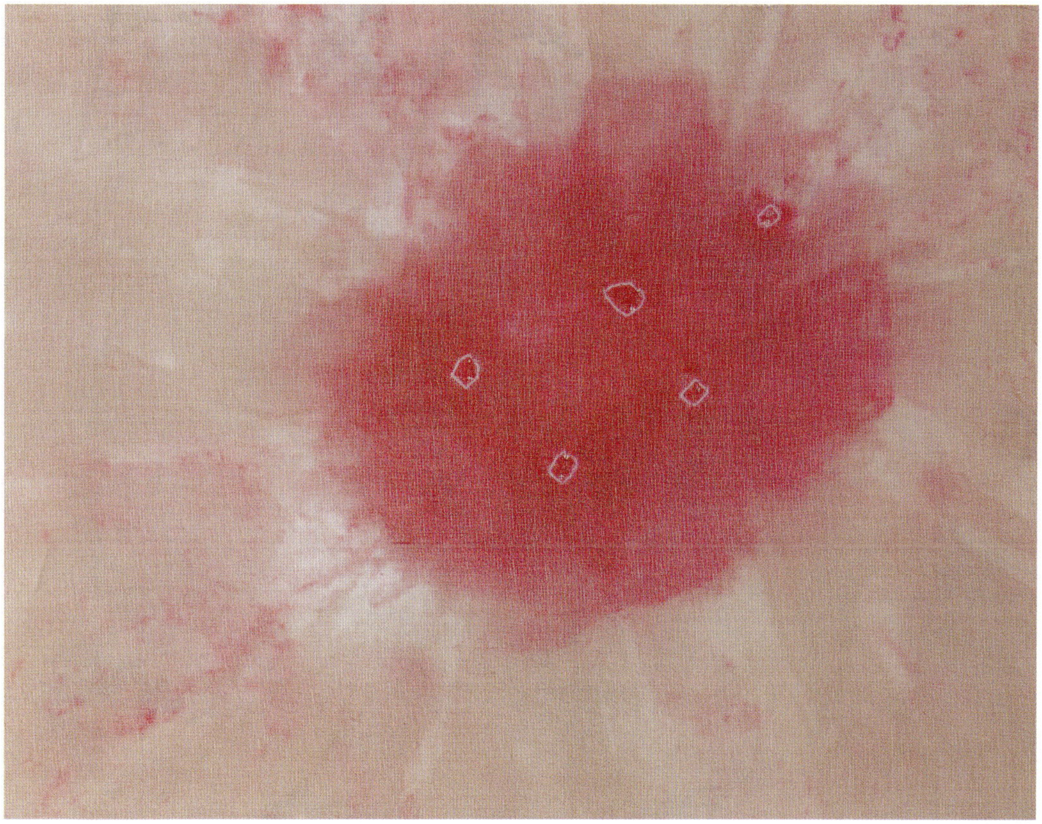

02-53 *Kanoko* dots made with a *shibori* device. Procion MX fiber reactive dyes. Silk organza. Scale: 6.5" × 8".

Kanoko shibori

This technique uses a *single* tie at the *tip* of each tiny pinched cone to create small resisted rings on the fabric (in Japan called *kanoko dots*), as in 02-53 and 02-56. Historically in Japan, these tiny precise "dots" of resist were eloquently executed in *clusters* to form intricate shapes or images on kimonos. Tying the threads on these small-scale cones presents challenges to even the smallest hands and sharpest eyes. You may be able to tie small rings with relative ease and no assistance, but when closely spaced, these *very tiny dots* require the use of a *shibori* hook or device, such as the one shown in 02-55.

Because *kanoko* dots are so tiny, and it is difficult to pull their bindings really tight, they are best done on silk (because of its light weight and flexibility) and dyed in acid dyes (not only because acid dyes are the best match for silk itself, but because the goal of making *kanoko* dots is the clarity of the resulting marks, and acid dyes, unlike fiber reactive dyes, won't wick).

Instructions for manipulating and binding* kanoko shibori*:

1. *Mark the fabric:* Using a washable marking tool, directly mark the fabric with the locations of individual dots, or the outline of shapes you intend to fill with clusters of dots. (Without marking, the gradual bunching of the cloth in the binding processes can disorient your ability to plot and control the dot placement.)

2. Choose one of the following:

   - *To pinch and bind the fabric dots by unaided hand* (02-54): Start in the center of the cloth. Pinch and hold each tiny fabric cone as you tightly wrap a single loop of thread around it and tie a knot. Move to the next dot, pinch up a cone of fabric, then bind and knot off. Work your way systematically outward from the center of the cloth to pinch and bind at each marking point until you have either covered the whole cloth or filled the specific shape you outlined. As you gain experience, you may find that you can use a single length of thread to bind several cones in a row or cluster.

   - *To pinch and bind the fabric by using a shibori device for truly small dots:* To more easily place and tie small dots, use a *shibori device* (pictured in 02-55). These simple devices provide a small hook or needle to hold the tip of the pinched cone. That hook becomes a kind of "third hand," which leaves both your hands free to move the fabric along and bind. The device allows finer-scaled work than your fingers alone can easily achieve.

     Choose a marked dot in the center of the fabric as a starting point. Hook a few intersections of the threads of your cloth (at that dot) on the needle of the *shibori* device. Wrap and loop a thread around the cone near the needle insertion. This simple loop, pulled tight, should be sufficient to bind and hold each dot. Using continuous lengths of the binding thread (from one small cone to the next, *without* cutting the thread), proceed to hook and bind each marked dot across the cloth until you have covered either a manageable area, the whole cloth, or a specific configuration of dots according to your design (02-53, 02-56). The device will feel awkward at first, but with practice you will be able to tie many small rings smoothly and quickly.

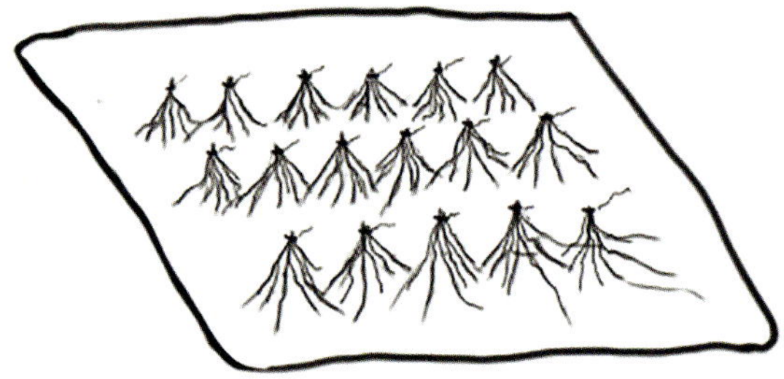

02-54 Fabric pinched and bound with a single thread to create rings (*kanoko shibori*).

02-55 *Shibori* device. Adjustable table clamp model with screw-in needle armature for creating very small cones of fabric. Stainless steel. Scale: clamp 1" × 2"; needle armature 5".

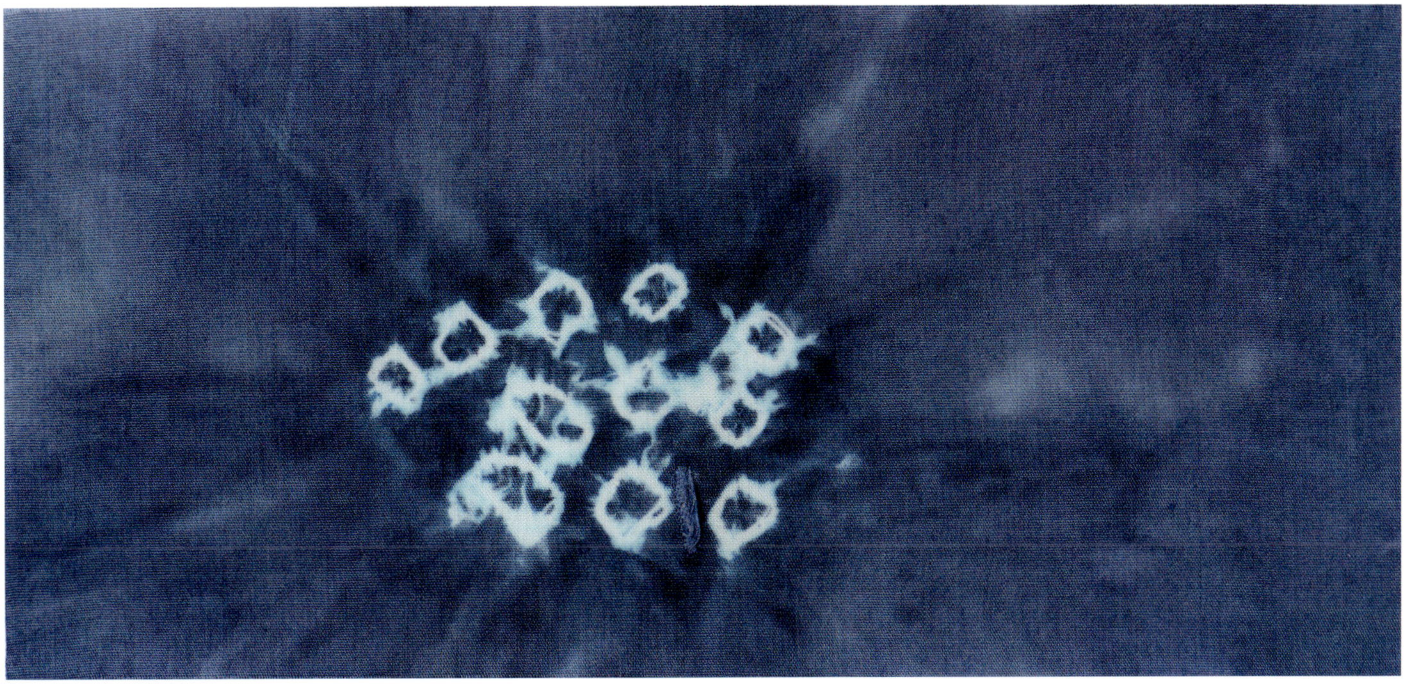

Dyeing Bound Fabrics (Applicable to All Binding Methods Above)

Safety guidelines: Always wear rubber gloves to protect your hands and a work shirt or apron (or both) to protect your clothing from accidental spills while painting on the dye paste, removing the bindings, and washing out the fabric. Follow all the dye safety rules discussed in chapter 1.

1. Choose and prepare the best dyestuff for your fabric and project. Keep these tips in mind:

   - *Fiber reactive dyes* (for cellulose fibers and silk) work best in paste form for bound resist. However, if your cords are pulled *very tight,* you can put them in an immersion dyebath (see chapter 1), which will create soft, blended resists and even color on the cloth. One advantage of these dyes for bound resist is that each different color penetrates and reacts at a different rate or speed. When you mix a composite dye color for the resist dyeing, this rate-of-reaction difference shows up in the form of unexpected and interesting multicolored halos at the edges of the resist marks where the colors *physically* separate. I view this as a delightful advantage.

   - *Acid dyes* are easy to use for resist dyeing, provide clear pure colors on silks and wools, and work best to preserve clean and distinct resist marks. Lanaset acid dyes also allow you to mix custom colors. Prepare the dyebath according to instructions for Lanaset dyes in chapter 1 and insert bound fabrics.

2. Dye the bound cloth. Choose any *one* of the following methods for dyeing, depending on the fiber type and project. (Refer to the dyeing information in chapter 1.)

Method 1: Painting fiber reactive dye paste on bound cloth

   - This painted approach produces an appealingly mottled or uneven color on bound cloth, reflecting the brush or sponge marks and the inevitable inconsistencies in color application. Single dye colors emphasize the marks; multiple combined colors shift attention to the overall color palette. I prefer this method because it's easier and produces clearer resist marks.

   - If you pretreated the fabric, mix and apply dye paste without adding any further activator. If you did *not* pretreat the fabric, add the dye activator to the thickened dye paste *before* applying it to the cloth with a brush. In either case, experiment to find which thickness of dye paste behaves the best on the specific cloth you are dyeing. Aim for the "sweet spot" between fluidity (the color flows on smoothly) and stability (the dye stays where you put it).

02-56 *Kanoko* dots made with a *shibori* device. Fiber reactive dye. Cotton broadcloth. Scale: 2.5" × 3.5".

• Insert the dyed and still-bound cloth into a sealed plastic bag. After 24 hours, open the bag, remove the still-bound cloth, and allow it to air-dry. (Dye paste has a slippery consistency, so the drier the cloth, the easier to remove the bindings without smearing dye in places where it wasn't wanted, and the less likely you'll accidentally cut the fabric itself while using scissors to remove the bindings.)

Method 2: Immersion dyeing with fiber reactive dyes

• If you pretreated the fabric, you don't need to add dye activator to the dyebath, because the activator is already in the treated and now-dried cloth. If you did *not* pretreat, make sure to add the appropriate dye activator (soda ash for cellulose fibers, citric acid crystals for silk) to the dyebath *before* immersing the bound cloth.

• Use any of the immersion dye recipes and drying methods in chapter 1.

Method 3: Immersion dyeing with acid dyes

• For protein fibers (both silk and wool can be bound resist), acid dyes provide the clearest and cleanest resist marks.

• Because of the way that acid dyes bond chemically to the fibers, they don't require the special care described above concerning fiber reactive dyes, and, if you wish, bindings prepared for acid dyes need only be moderately tight.

• Drop the wetted-bound fabric into the prepared acid dyebath (see chapter 1) and complete the Lanaset dyeing procedure discussed there.

3. For best results, allow the still-bound fabric to dry thoroughly *after* the dyeing process but *before* untying the cords.

4. Remove the bindings *before* rinsing out the fabric: Excess dye will rub off on your fingers *regardless* of whether the bound cloth is completely dry or still damp. To minimize this (by maximizing the dexterity of your own finger movements while handling the bundles or clipping the cords), substitute very thin medical gloves for the thicker rubber gloves you wore during dyeing.

02-57 Scissors for clipping cords, *from left to right*: curved-tip decoupage/nail, 4" classic embroidery, 4" plastic-handled embroidery, suture with dip cut in one blade, featherweight thread clippers. Scale: 3.5"–4" in length.

• To more easily catch individual threads when clipping the cords, *but without catching and clipping the fabric itself*, you'll need a tool with a single pointed tip to wiggle under the cords. Use a small pair of very sharp, pointed scissors: nail, embroidery, decoupage, or suture scissors; a carefully wielded seam ripper; or specialty weaver's scissors with a dip cut out from one scissor tip (02-57).

• Moving slowly and carefully, insert the tip of the scissors or cutter beneath key cords before clipping. If possible, find your knots and clip them first. In all cases avoid pointing the tip of the cutting tools directly toward the cloth. Move from section to section, removing the cords in approximately the *reverse order* in which they were originally applied. When all the cords are removed, open out the cloth and proceed to rinsing.

5. Rinse out. (See the "Universal Rinse-Out for Resist Dyeing" text box, page 61.)

REUSING DYED CORDS FOR ADDED COLORS

If you used *cotton* cords to bind your resist-dyed fabrics, the cords carry residues from their time in a dyebath and can be reused to *intentionally transfer* colored lines onto your next bound-resist project. The random bits of contrasting color lines provide a counterpoint to the larger dyed areas of the cloth. While especially effective on larger-scale tie-dye and pole-wrapped resisted fabrics, try it with any bound resist.

1. After using *new* cotton cord for its *first* binding and dyeing, carefully *unwind* the binding cords to "harvest" them *in long pieces instead of clipping them*.

2. Because this transfer of color depends on *leaving* dye residues in the cords, *do not* wash or rinse them. Instead, just press out any excess water and dye and then set the cords aside while you finish processing the resist-bound fabric on which they were just used for the first time.

3. If you will reuse the cords immediately, leave them damp. Or, to save for future use, let them dry out undisturbed, then store them in a plastic bag.

4. Use the cords to bind a new piece of fabric. Wear rubber gloves to protect your hands from dye rub-off as you bind. When you dye the newly bound fabric (immersed or painted), the dye residue already present on the previously used cords will moisten simultaneously and transfer its color onto the fabric at the binding contact points. Vary the type of cords for differing line characters.

02-58 Pole wrapping (*arashi*) to create a wood grain (*mokume*) pattern. Fabric placed flat and square on the pole, then scrunched into gathers while binding (see binding diagrams 02-66 through 02-70). Single color of painted, thickened, fiber reactive dye. Cotton print cloth. Scale: 7.5" × 10".

Shibori Method: Pole Wrapping (*Arashi*)

In *pole wrapping*, the resist pattern transfers to cloth wrapped around and bound with *a single continuous cord* to a cylinder, pole, tube, or dowel. In Japan, the technique is called *arashi* (which is also what it's called almost everywhere, because saying "arashi" is not only shorter but also more melodious than "pole wrapping"). The poles traditionally used in Japan were wooden logs or tree trunks (stripped of bark), mounted on a rotating axle for greater ease in feeding the binding cord into a spiral around the cloth placed on the pole. The binding cords hold the fabric in place and create pressure against the cloth along their lengths. These contact lines then create the resists. Each different fabric or cord used, and each physical binding variation, changes the quality of resist marks on the fabric. For example, a sequence of separate bindings and color applications creates a more complex pattern (02-61), the transparent dyes combine in "composite" colors when overlaid, especially on sheer fabrics (02-64), and several layers of pole-wrapped sheer fabrics create a subtle and mysterious image (02-65).

Variations in patterning depend on the interaction of the orientation of the fabric on the tube (squarely aligned or at a diagonal); the form of the fabric as it is placed on the pole (flat, folded, pleated, twisted); the size of the binding cord; the density of gathers if the fabric is scrunched along the tube; the presence of any pleats or folds that interrupt the binding lines; the number, character, and relationships of the colors used; and the way the colors are applied (dipped, painted, batched, immersed). Although hundreds of variations exist, *arashi* patterns nearly always create graceful, organic stripes (02-58), often reminiscent of wood grain (02-59). In the Japanese tradition, the classic patterns are easily recognizable and possess separate formal names.

Laying the fabric *flat* against the pole and binding evenly produces slender regular undulating stripes (02-60). The space between revolutions of binding cord can be regular or irregular, overlapped or wound back on themselves in the opposite direction. First folding or pleating the fabric introduces interruptions in the stripes, occasional diagonals (02-62), or fountain shapes. Scrunching or compressing the fabric along the tube yields repeating long marks (02-58 and 02-59). The cloth will "remember" each unique variation in the form of identifiable markings (see also page 6).

02-59 Pole wrapping (*arashi*) to create a wood grain (*mokume*) pattern with scrunched fabric. Single color painted with thickened fiber reactive dye. Cotton broadcloth. Scale: 8" × 11".

02-60 Pole wrapping (*arashi*) to create stripes. Fabric placed flat and square on the pole and kept flat during binding (no scrunching). This approach reveals the simple but elegant and delicate marks of the individual binding cords across the fabric. Single color of painted, thickened, fiber reactive dye. Cotton broadcloth. Scale: 6" × 10".

02-61 Pole wrapping (*arashi*) to create a wood grain (*mokume*) pattern. Multiple colors of painted, thickened, Procion MX fiber reactive dyes. Cotton broadcloth. Scale: 8" × 9".

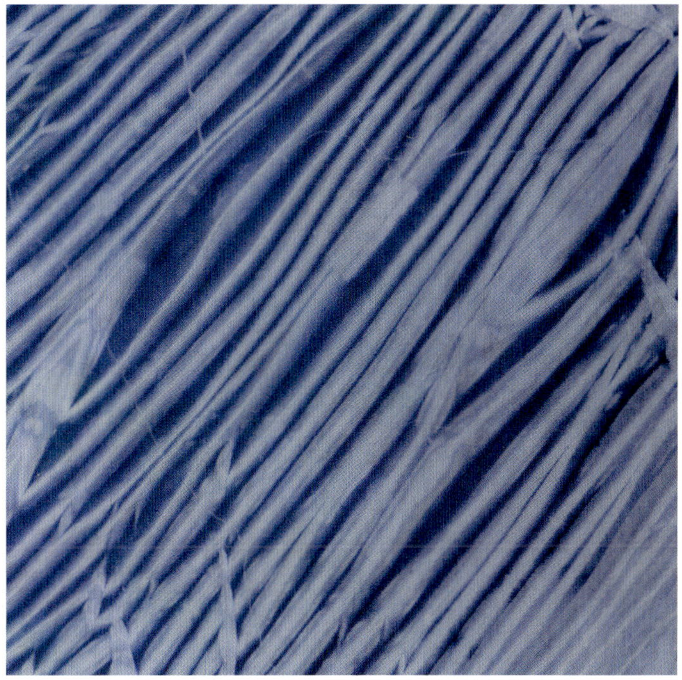

02-62 Pole wrapping (*arashi*) to create diagonal stripes. Diagonal placement of fabric on pole, with a few small pleats cutting across the bindings, creating the illusion of ripples. Single-color, fiber reactive dyebath. Cotton print cloth. Scale: 8" × 7.5.

02-63 Pole wrapping to create diagonal stripes. Single light, subtle-color, fiber reactive dyebath. Cotton print cloth. Scale: 6" × 5.5".

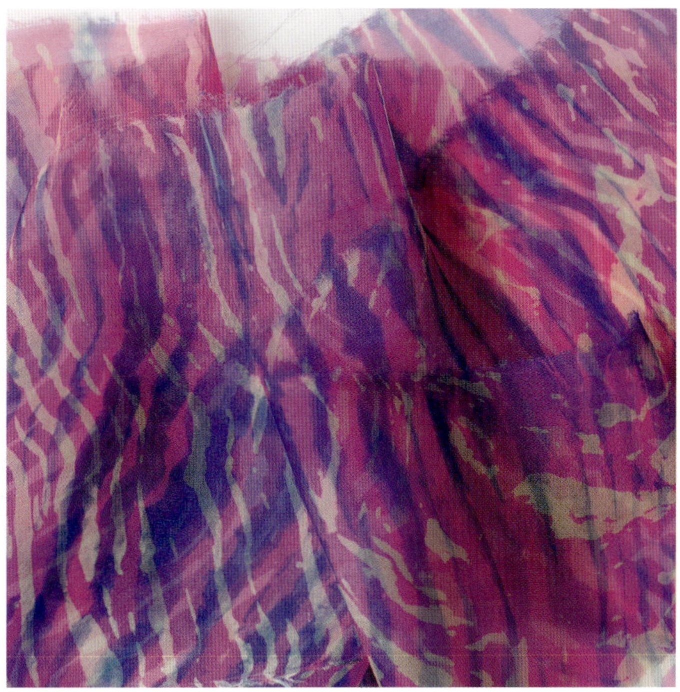

02-64 Sequential pole wrappings (*arashi*), first with magenta dye, second with blue, to create overlapping wood grain (*mokume*) patterns. Fiber reactive dyebaths. Silk organza. Scale: 8" × 12" section of long strip.

02-65 Sequential pole wrappings (*arashi*), to create overlaid subtle wood grain (*mokume*) patterns. Fiber reactive dyebath. Layered silk and cotton. Scale: 15" × 12".

SUPPLY CHECKLIST FOR POLE WRAPPING

- white fabric (cotton or silk)
- Twine, thread, or cord (an entire spool or cone) strong enough to withstand intense pulling and binding tension. Larger-diameter cord binds large areas faster and creates larger-scale resist marks. Smaller threads produce more-delicate resist lines. You can use several layers of thinner cord to provide extra protection in the resist and strengthen the cord.
- scissors: small and sharp pointed, for clipping threads; larger shears for cutting fabric
- washable fabric-marking tools
- masking tape
- tubes (PVC, wood, or other plastic) in several diameters, cut into shorter lengths and thoroughly cleaned
- pole-wrapping device (optional): for making bindings very tight (see image 02-71)
- short metal rod to use as a handle for pulling the cords (for better grip on the binding cord)

Instructions for manipulating and binding for pole wrapping (*arashi*):

1. *Select and prepare the pole (in this case, a tube)*: Choose tubes made of sturdy materials that will not rust (no iron) or disintegrate (no cardboard or paper products) during immersion into water or dye. Wood, aluminum, or plastic are good choices. Thin-walled PVC (plumbing) pipes, a typical choice, come in differing diameters and are easily obtainable at hardware or home improvement stores. Buy large- and medium-diameter pipes, cut them in short lengths (if not already cut shorter by helpful hardware store staff), and clean them thoroughly before and after each use (because dirty tubes will transfer both dirt and unwanted dye to fabrics). If necessary, file off any sharp tube ends to prevent injury to yourself or your fabric.
2. *Choose and cut the fabric*: In the direction it will be wrapped, it should not be longer than one "trip" around the tube, so that the opposite edges of the fabric don't overlap and thereby partially hide one another from receiving dye. Its length in the direction parallel to the length of the tube will depend on whether you intend to just dye the fabric flat (in which case the cut fabric should not extend beyond the length of the tube) or scrunch it up into gathers for extra resist (in which case, you'll need to allow extra fabric—perhaps a lot of it—for those gatherings).

3. *Orient and arrange the fabric on the tube*: To start, lay the tube horizontally on a table or countertop. Arrange the fabric across one end of the tube and use a piece of masking tape to attach the fabric to the tube. The classic method of doing *arashi* uses a *single* continuous length of cord. With that technique, the binding will, of necessity, move down the length of the pole in a gentle spiral as each revolution of cord around tube progresses *uninterrupted* to the next. The orientation of the fabric on the tube will therefore determine the angle of the resist lines produced on the cloth. If you intentionally *align* the fabric *parallel* to the tube, your single-cord binding will then naturally produce parallel *diagonal* resist lines like the spiral winding itself (as in 02-62 and 02-63). (If you wish to offset that diagonal effect, in order to produce resist lines parallel to the *grain of the cloth*, you'll need to do one of the following: rotate the fabric itself off-center [i.e., no longer parallel to the tube, so that the grain *aligns* with the spiraling direction of the binding cords] or, more simply, substitute individual *non*continuous binding, such as rubber bands, which can simply be placed around the cloth and tube at intervals, while leaving the cloth itself parallel to the tube.) See the text box "Binding experimentations with pole wrapping" for other suggestions.

4. *Attach the binding cord*: To begin binding, tie a slipknot in the cord and place it around the fabric and the tube very close to the end where the fabric is taped in place. Tighten the slipknot and also tape it to the tube.

5. *Immobilize the tube*: You will need to immobilize the tube so you can wrap the binding cord with steady pressure. You can set the tube upright on a table and stand beside it, sit in a chair and hold the tube between your knees, or roll the tube across a table or floor as you bind, or you could work with a partner—one person to hold the tube, the other to do the wrapping. (For a helpful alternative, see the text box "Building a homemade pole-wrapping *arashi* device.")

6. *Start wrapping the cord*: Wrap the cord around the fabric and tube in a spiral several revolutions, leaving some space between the wraps. As you wrap, pull very tightly and evenly against the tube. (To help pull tighter without hurting your hands, wrap the end of the cord around a metal rod or a pair of scissors to use as a handle. This will improve your grip and reduce the labor.)

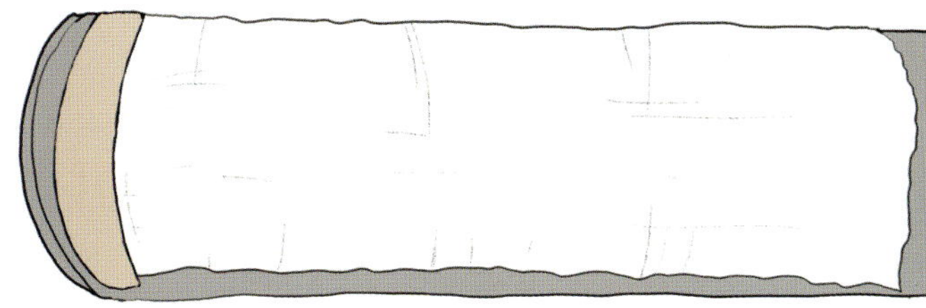

02-66 Step 3: Orient and arrange the fabric, then tape it to the tube.

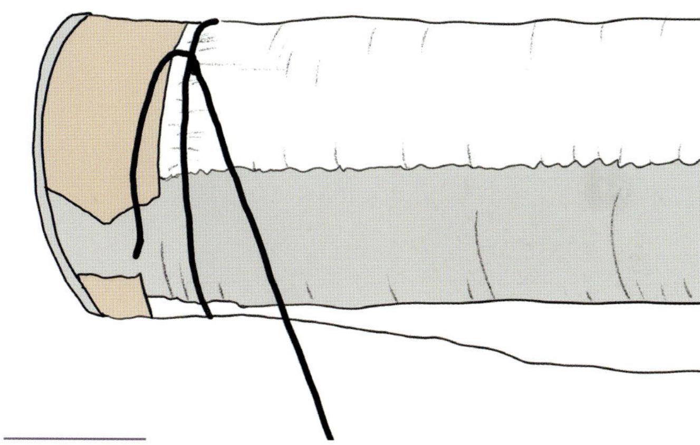

02-67 Step 4: Attach the binding cord with a slipknot.

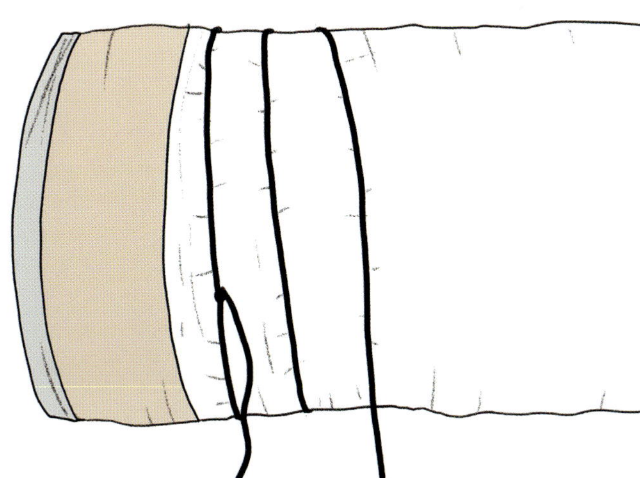

02-68 Step 6: Start to wrap the cord around the fabric and tube.

7. *Start to compress (scrunch) the fabric*: After several revolutions of the cord, and *without releasing the tension* on the cord, push the fabric toward the starting end of the tube. This will scrunch up or compress the fabric into parallel layers. Wrap the cord another few revolutions and then scrunch again. Repeat this alternation of wrapping and scrunching until all parts of the fabric have been bound and scrunched.

8. *Tie off and secure*: When you have finished the binding and scrunching, wrap the cord around the tube several more times to secure it. Then tie off the cord with a secure knot. If necessary, tape the knot to the tube with a piece of masking tape. The pole-wrapped fabric is now ready for dyeing.

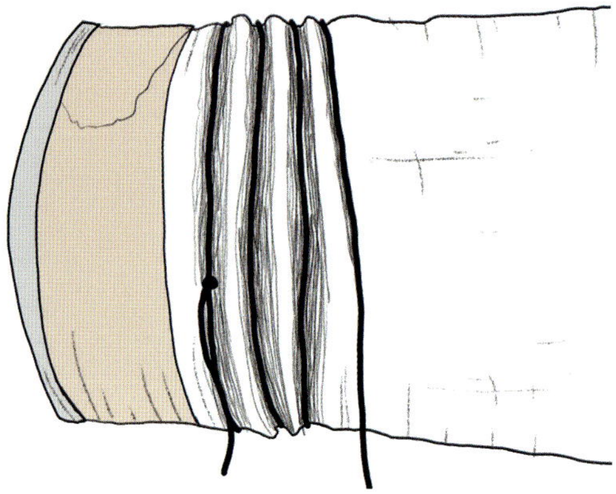

02-69 Step 7: Start to compress the fabric at intervals as you continue to wrap.

02-70 Step 8: Finish wrapping and scrunching; tie off.

BUILDING A HOMEMADE POLE-WRAPPING (*ARASHI*) DEVICE

With this homemade device, you can hold the cord with one hand, spin the tube with the other, and apply the bindings easily and more tightly than you can with your hands alone. And the tighter bindings will easily resist, even when immersed in a fiber reactive immersion dyebath for an hour.

Because you make it yourself, you can construct the *arashi* device in the correct size to accommodate the circumference of your tubes. The version of this device in 02-71 was made with supplies from the hardware store and sized to fit 6" diameter PVC tubes.

The base is ¾" plywood, with two 1" × 6" boards placed upright and screwed firmly into it. Four casters were mounted on upright boards, positioned to support the tube (the distance between the uprights was planned to be several inches *shorter* than the length of the tubes in order to provide good support). A ¾" wooden dowel, inserted into drilled holes in the uprights, provides a guide for "feeding" the cord onto the tube as you wrap.

To use the device: Prepare your fabric through step 4 above, then to immobilize the tube, simply set it on the casters on the *arashi* device. Run the cord under the inserted dowel and start to wrap as instructed in steps 6 through 8.

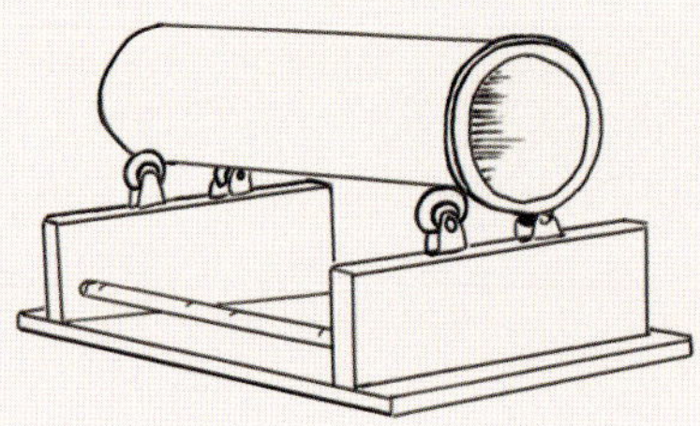

02-71 A homemade *arashi* device.

BINDING EXPERIMENTATIONS WITH POLE WRAPPING

- To create *irregularly spaced* resist lines, vary the spacing between wraps around the tube. Place some revolutions close together and others farther apart.
- To produce more unusual and distinctive marks, including binding lines parallel to the grain of the fabric, *substitute* rubber bands, nylon cord, rope, wire, tape, plastic strips, fabric strips, waxed cords, dental floss, or previously dyed cords (which bleed lines of extra color onto the fabric) for the standard raw cotton twine.
- To introduce *interruptions* in the *arashi* patterning, bind, pleat, fold, or stitch-and-gather selected areas of the fabric *before* binding it to the tube.

Dyeing Pole-Wrapped Fabrics with Fiber Reactive Dyes

Safety guidelines: Always wear rubber gloves to protect your hands and a work shirt or apron (or both) to protect your clothing from accidental spills while painting on the dye paste, removing the bindings, and washing out the fabric. Follow all the dye safety rules discussed in chapter 1.

1. *Dye the bound fabric*: Use stock solutions of fiber reactive dye on *arashi* bound fabrics. You can either use an immersion dyebath (for a single color) or paint on dye paste (for single *or* multiple colors).
   - *Immersion dyebath*: Prepare a fiber reactive immersion dyebath in a bucket that is deep enough to submerge the compressed fabric, *tube and all* (I recommend the kind of 5-gallon bucket typically used by building contractors). Add the water, the dye in stock solution form, and the appropriate dye activator to the bucket. Vertically insert the tube into the dyebath until *all* the bound fabric has been submerged. Allow the fabric to sit in the dyebath for an hour. (If your tube is a lot longer than the fabric, set the bucket in a corner of the room, or against a wall, where any protruding part of the tube can be supported by a solid surface when left unattended.) See chapter 1 for immersion dye recipes.
   - *Paint on thickened dye*: Mix dye paste according to the instructions in chapter 1. Use a *sponge brush* to paint the paste on the bound fabric (you can use one color or several). Cover the painted fabric with a plastic bag or sheet of plastic firmly taped to the tube with masking tape. Allow the fabric to sit undisturbed to batch for 24 hours.
2. *Remove the cords*: Put on your rubber gloves. Starting at the end of the fabric where you *finished* wrapping and tied off your binding, remove the masking tape, clip the knot, and start *unwinding* the cord. When you reach the end where you began, remove the initial piece of masking tape and clip the slipknot. (You can discard the cords or save them for future bound-resist projects. See the text box on "Reusing dyed cords for added colors.") If you used non-traditional individual binding material, such as rubber or metal bands, slip them off the tube one at a time, being as careful as possible not to "drag" any remaining dye across the fabric.
3. Now comes the moment you've been waiting for: open out the fabric to see the patterns your *arashi* bindings created.
4. Rinse out. (See the "Universal Rinse-Out for Resist Dyeing" text box, page 61.)

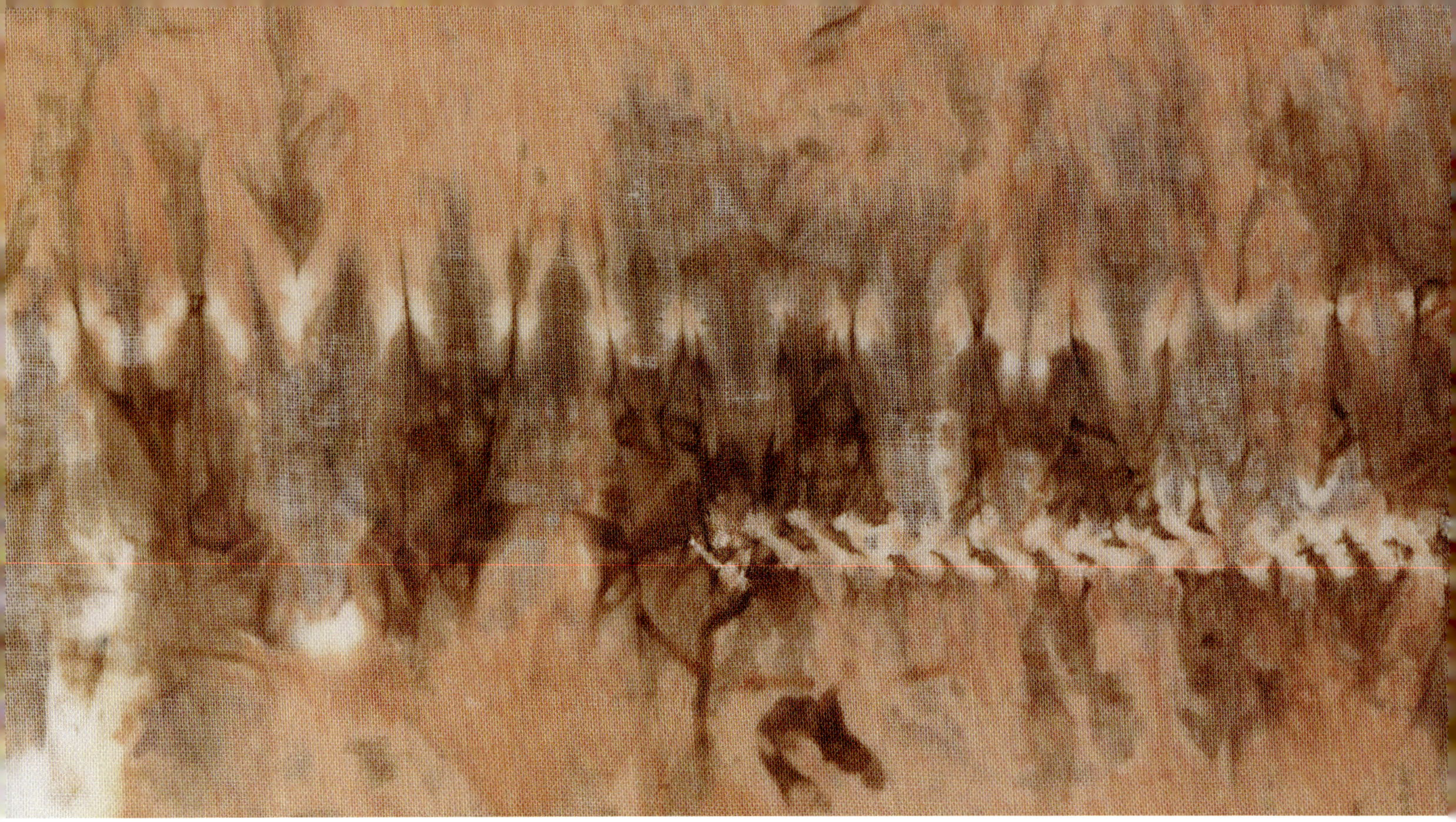

02-72 Stitch resist (*nui shibori* or *tritik*). *Top row*, single line of running stitch (*ori-nui shibori*); *bottom row*, whipstitch on folded fabric (*maki-nui shibori*). Multiple colors of painted, thickened, fiber reactive dye. Cotton print cloth. Scale: 2.5" × 6".

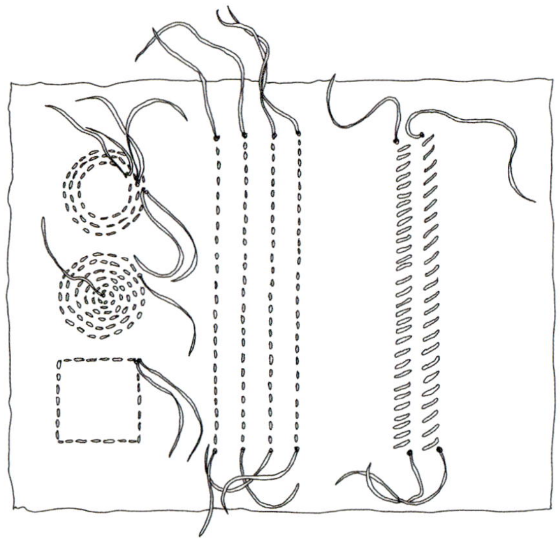

02-73 Sampler of fabric stitched for *nui shibori*, before gathering. Knots with long tails at both ends of each. *Left*: running stitches in concentric circles and spiral, and outlining a square shape. *Center*: rows of parallel running stitches (*mokume* pattern). *Right*: rows of whipstitches (*maki-nui shibori*).

Shibori Method: Stitch-and-Gather (*Nui Shibori* or *Tritik*)

Stitch resist (*nui shibori*, a Japanese term; also called *tritik*, a Malay-Indonesian word) is the drawing up, by hand stitching, of puckers, gathers, and folds along a thread that has been *sewn* into the fabric to resist the dye (02-73). While the process of stitching, gathering, and then subsequently removing the threads is time-consuming, the technique offers unique opportunities for delicate and complex detailing, lines between solidly dyed areas, and fine-scaled drawing.

Stitching Options for Stitch-and-Gather

The running stitches and whipstitches are the most useful for this *shibori* technique. Each stitch is simple to make and easy to gather and creates a distinctive and discernibly different characteristic resist mark.

Running Stitch

This universal linear stitch is useful for straight and curved lines, outlining shapes, drawing, and creating textures (02-74, 02-75). By varying the individual stitches (long or short, even or uneven in size) and changing the spacing (dense or sparse, regular or irregular), the gathers it creates will produce resisted marks with varying characters.

Directions: Bring the needle up from the back of the fabric. Then, with a rocking motion, repeatedly push the

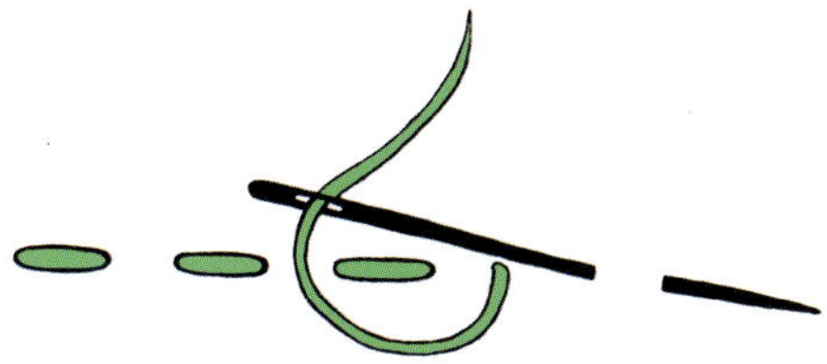

02-74 Running stitch, left-handed.

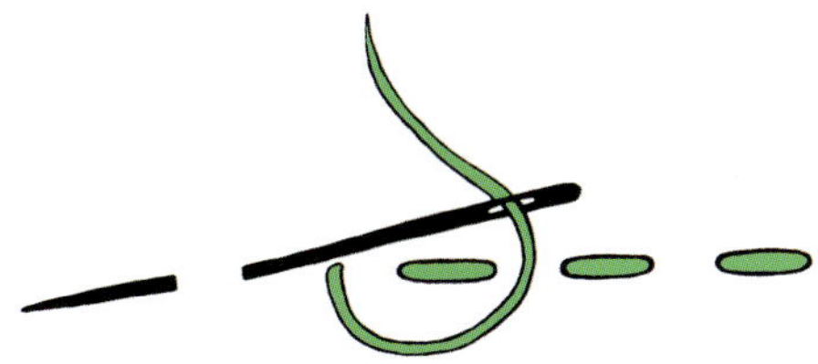

02-75 Running stitch, right-handed.

needle up and down through the fabric along a line. After taking two or three passes through the fabric, pull the thread through these stitches. Continue stitching along the line in this manner. To make very precise and evenly spaced running stitches, use the *stab method* (straight down, then straight up in two motions) to make each individual stitch, one at a time.

Single lines of running stitch can be placed on a single layer of fabric as in 02-82 and 02-91 (*hira-nui*), or along a fold as in 02-78 and 02-80 (*ori-nui*). When stitched in parallel rows, the running stitch creates a wood grain (*mokume*) pattern (02-76) similar to those created with *arashi*.

02-76 Stitch resist (*nui shibori* or *tritik*). *Parallel* running stitch variations, *left*: two sets of three parallel rows to create a wood grain (*mokume*) pattern; *center*: concentric half circles stitched through a fold (Japanese larch or *karamatsu shibori*); *right*: closely spaced, zigzag, and tightly spaced running stitches in parallel vertical rows (modified *mokume*). Single color of painted, thickened, fiber reactive dye. Cotton broadcloth.
Scale: 6" × 6".

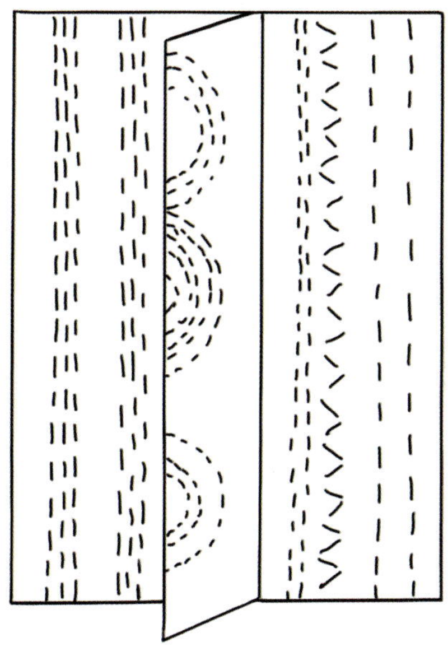

02-77 Stitching diagram. Folding and stitching detail for 02-76. (See also gathering diagram 02-90.)

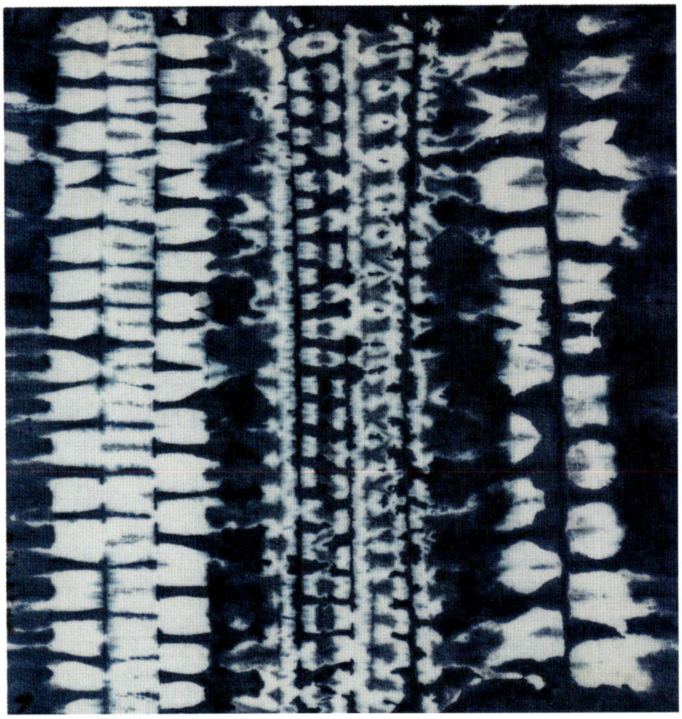

02-78 Stitch resist (*nui shibori* or *tritik*). *Parallel* running stitch on folds, with these variations: *left*: large pleat laid flat, then stitched through all three layers; *center*: three small folds, stitched through two layers; *right*: large fold, large scale stitches at base of fold. Cotton broadcloth. Scale: 6" x 6".

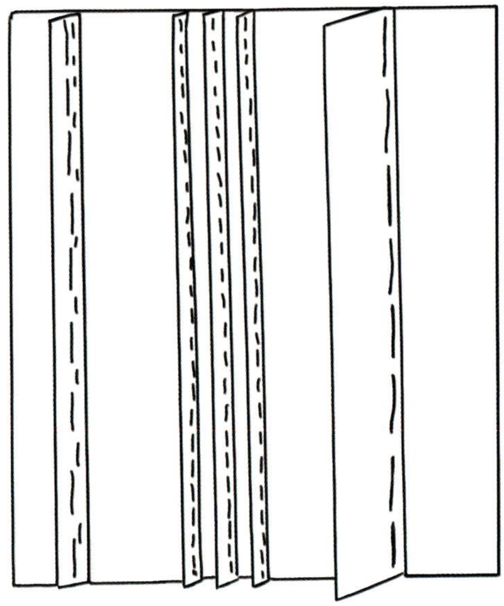

02-79 Stitching diagram. Folding and stitching detail for 02-78.

02-80 Stitch resist (*nui shibori* or *tritik*) in Japanese larch pattern (*karamatsu* pattern). Three rows of parallel concentric half circles stitched through three folds. Creates clear and regularly repeating rings of resist. Cotton broadcloth. Scale: 6" × 6".

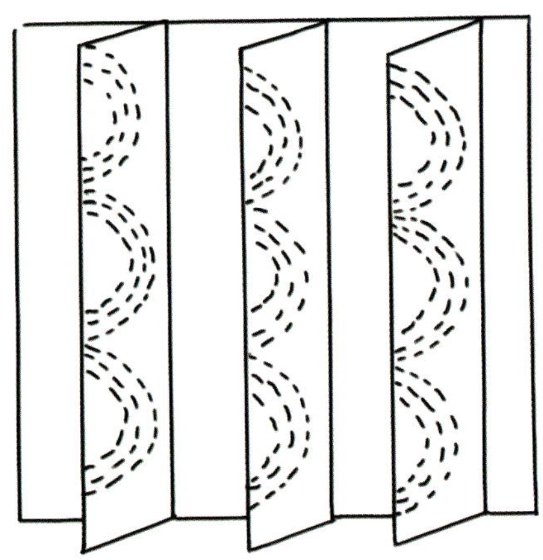

02-81 Stitching diagram. Folding and stitching detail for 02-80.

02-82 Stitch (*nui shibori* or *tritik*) resist. Variation of Japanese larch (*karamatsu*) pattern made with spirals of running stitches on a single layer of fabric. Painted, thickened, fiber reactive dye. Cotton broadcloth. Scale: 6" × 6".

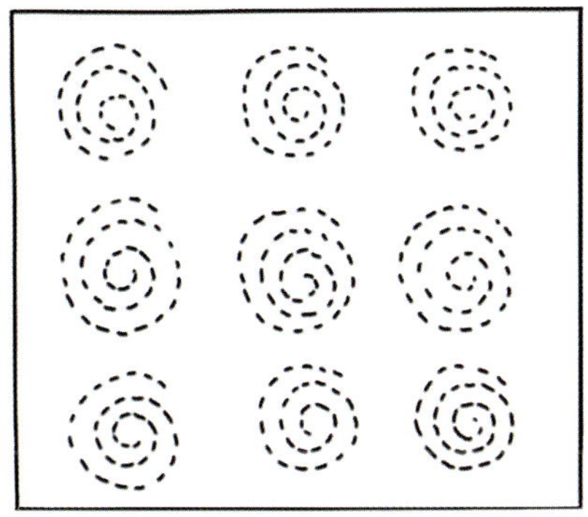

02-83 Stitching diagram. Stitching detail for 02-82.

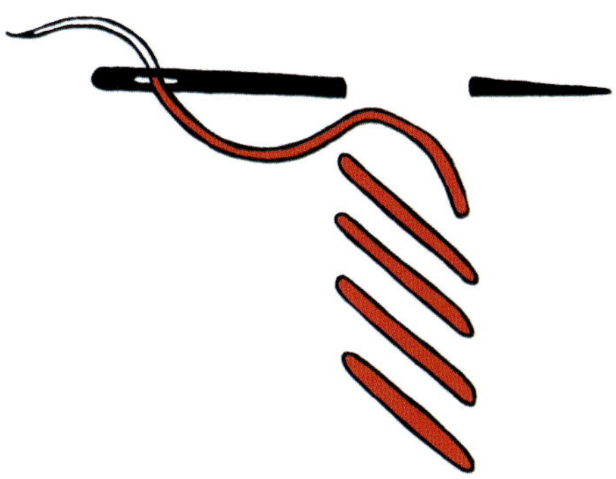

02-84 Whipstitch, left-handed.

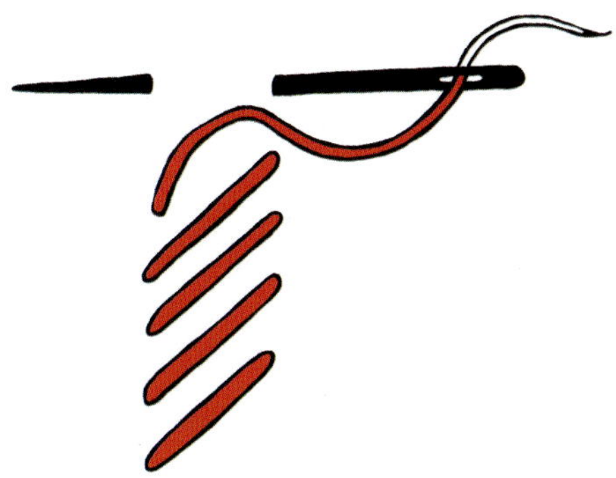

02-85 Whipstitch, right-handed.

Whipstitch

If you have ever hemmed trousers or a shirt, then you have probably used the whipstitch. As easy to learn as the running stitch, it makes a very different kind of mark when stitched, gathered, and dyed (02-84, 02-85). Whipstitching over the peak of a fold creates a series of interlocking chevrons in the resist dye, resembling human vertebrae on an x-ray (02-86, 02-88, 02-91). Whipstitch can be used on flat fabric, on folds, or over yarns or cords, to define organic or geometric shapes.

Directions: Bring the thread up from the back of the cloth at the bottom of the desired line. Insert the needle back down on the opposite side of the line and just a little above (at a diagonal). Thereafter, make a series of stitches straight across and perpendicular to the desired line. This will leave a trail of roughly parallel diagonal stitches on the *face* of the fabric, and a row of parallel vertical or horizontal bars on the *back*.

A single line of whipstitch is called *maki-nui shibori*.

02-86 Stitch resist (*maki-nui shibori*). Whipstitch on folds. *Left*: over single fold; *center*: over three folds together; *right*: alternating long and short stitches. Single color painted with thickened fiber reactive dye. Cotton broadcloth. Scale: 6.25" × 6".

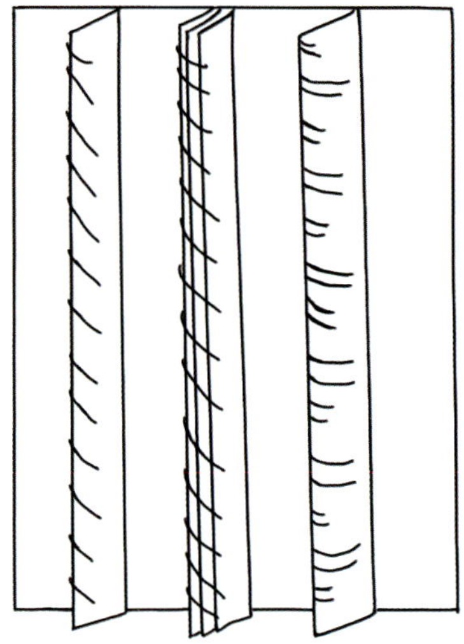

02-87 Folding and stitching diagram for 02-86.

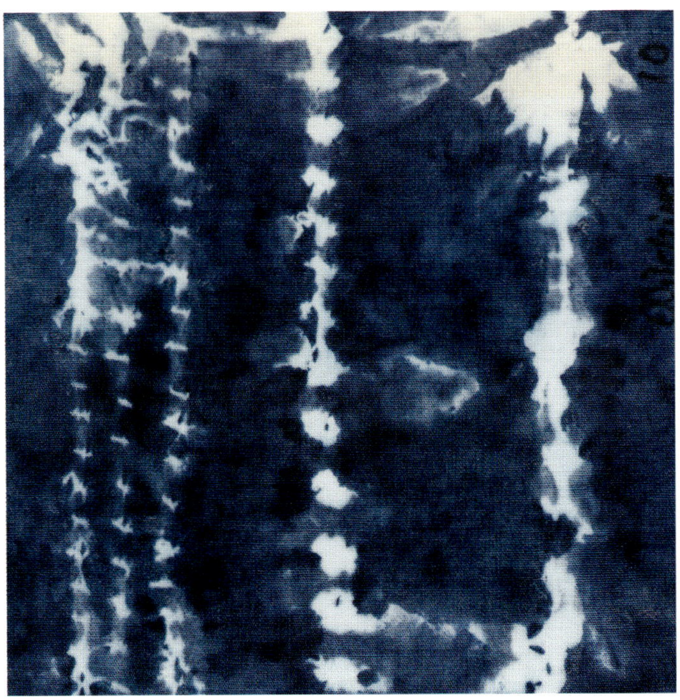

02-88 Stitch resist (*maki-nui shibori*) variations. Different weights of linen cord were laid on flat fabric and bound to it with whipstitches, then gathered up. *Left*: three lightweight cords side by side create small resisted hash marks; *center*: stitching over one larger cord creates a string of resisted dots; *right*: three lightweight cords bound together as one create a long resist mark resembling a cord with knots in it. Cotton broadcloth. Scale: 6" × 4".

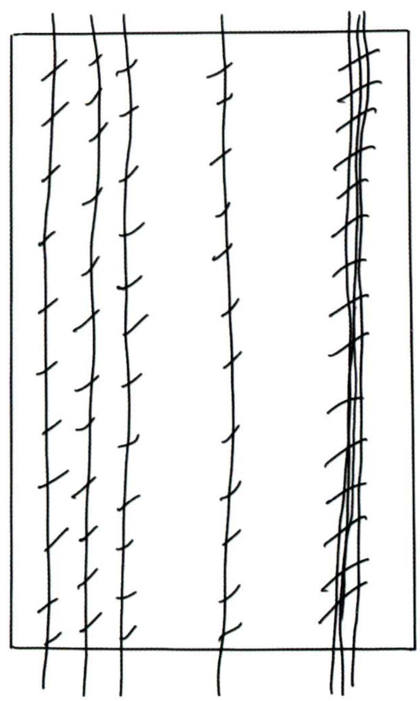

02-89 Folding and stitching diagram for 02-88.

SUPPLY CHECKLIST FOR STITCH-AND-GATHER RESIST

- white or lightly colored fabric, such as lightweight cotton sateen, muslin, lawn, or broadcloth; rayon challis; or silk
- leather gloves to protect your hands and fingers as you pull up the threads to gather
- small, sharp-pointed embroidery scissors
- tweezers with good grip and sharp point
- dyes and chemical assistants
- needles: with eyes large enough to accommodate the thread being used
- Sturdy thread strong enough to withstand firm pulling: button and carpet thread, waxed thread, pearl cotton, dental floss, twine, heavy polyester or nylon. *It should be a different color from the cloth and the color of dye you will be using.* Experiment with threads that work best on the type of fabric being worked.
- thimbles: to protect your fingers as you stitch

Instructions for stitching and gathering:

Because stitch resist is most usually used for creating resisted shapes or for drawing lines and outlines, you should have a plan for the design of the cloth.

1. *Lay out the pattern or marks on the cloth*: Approach the stitching in an organized manner. *Before* you start to stitch, use a temporary marking tool to *draw the entire* pattern, design, or collection of shapes on the fabric. This step is especially useful for large pieces of fabric, or complex designs where you wish to place specific resist lines in specific areas of the fabric surface. Without marking, the gradual bunching of the cloth in the stitching and gathering process will interfere with your ability to control the placement of stitches.
2. *Insert the running stitching or whipstitching across the entire design*:
   - Choose strong thread in a color that *contrasts* with the fabric. To reduce the frequency of unspinning or breaks, cut the thread into pieces about 12"–18" long and tie a large overhand knot about 3" from the end (to leave a "tail"). Thread the needle at the other end.
   - At the *beginning* of each line or section, insert the needle into the fabric *from the front of the fabric*, leave the knot on the surface, and stitch along your design markings. Do *not* gather up along the stitches as you go.
   - At the *end* of each line or section, bring the thread to the surface and unthread the needle. Make a knot in the thread and leave a long tail. (The knots temporarily prevent the thread from pulling out while you proceed to stitch other parts of the design, and the long tails are easy to grab when later gathering the fabric, as in 02-73.)

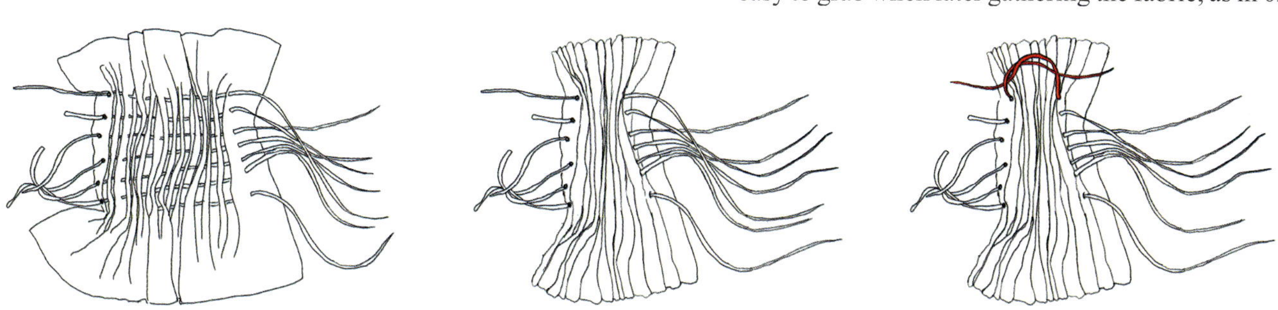

02-90 *Nui shibori*. In this example, running stitches in parallel rows (whipstitches could have been used) have been *partially* gathered (*left*), gathered tight with threads hidden (*center*), and begun to be tied to secure the gathers (*right*). Tails on the right became longer as the fabric was gathered toward the left.

- Insert stitches along all the lines you want to resist, but continue to leave the fabric flat until *all* the stitching on the entire cloth has been securely inserted.

3. *Gather up the stitching*: When the entire design has been fully stitched, you are ready for gathering (02-90).
   - Begin gathering *in the middle* of the cloth and work toward the edges.

   - Grasp the knot at one end of each hand-stitched section. To avoid breaking the thread, gradually and gently slide the fabric along the thread, bunching it up until it is very tightly gathered and compressed in the center. (If you plan to *immerse* the fabric in a fiber reactive dyebath, then the threads must be pulled up *exceptionally tightly* to resist the dyes.) To help prevent blisters on your hands and fingers, wear leather gloves to pull the threads.

   - Continue working toward the edges to gather up all the stitched lines in the design.

   - When gathering is completed, secure the threads to maintain the tight compression by *separately* tying together the ends of *each* thread in the sequence. The fabric is now ready to dye.

Dyeing Stitch-and-Gather Fabric

Safety guidelines: Always wear rubber gloves to protect your hands and a work shirt or apron (or both) to protect your clothing from accidental spills while working with dyes. Follow all the dye safety rules discussed in chapter 1.

1. *Dye the gathered cloth by any of the same methods you use for bound resist.* Choose any one of the following methods for dyeing, depending on the fiber type and project. (Refer to the dyeing information in chapter 1.)

Method 1: Paint dye paste on stitch-and-gather cloth

This painted approach produces an appealingly mottled or uneven color on bound cloth, reflecting the brush or sponge marks and the inevitable inconsistencies in color application. Single dye colors emphasize the marks; multiple combined colors shift attention to the overall color palette. This is the preferred method with fiber reactive dyes because it's easier and produces clearer resist marks.

- Mix your thickener and add the dye in stock solution form (see chapter 1).

- Add dye activator to the thickened dye paste, then apply it with a brush to the stitched and gathered cloth. Experiment to find which thickness of dye paste behaves the best on the specific cloth you are dyeing. Aim for the "sweet spot" between fluidity (the color flows on smoothly) and stability (the dye stays where you put it). The gathered fabric will be dimpled and lumpy, so you will need to carefully work the dye paste into it.

- Insert the painted gathered cloth into a sealed plastic bag.

- After 24 hours, open the bag, remove the cloth, and allow it to thoroughly air-dry. (Dye paste has a slippery consistency, so the drier the cloth, the easier to remove the bindings without smearing dye in places where it wasn't wanted, and the less likely you'll accidentally cut the fabric itself while using scissors to remove the bindings.)

Method 2: Immersion dyeing with acid dyes

For protein fibers (both silk and wool can be stitched and gathered), acid dyes provide the clearest and cleanest resist marks.

- Because of the way that acid dyes bond chemically to the fibers, they don't require the special care concerning fiber reactive dyes, and, if you wish, gathered stitching prepared for acid dyes need only be moderately tight.

- Drop the wetted stitched-and-gathered fabric into the prepared acid dyebath (see chapter 1) and complete the Lanaset dyeing procedure discussed there.

2. *Allow the fabric to dry* thoroughly *after* the dyeing process but *before* removing the stitches.

3. *Remove the stitching*: Even though the fabric is now *dry*, the sequence of wetting, dyeing, and drying the stitched fabric *embeds the stitches* in the cloth, resisting your attempts to pull at them. Be patient; they *will* come out. Remove the bindings *before* rinsing out the fabric: excess dye will rub off on your fingers *regardless* of whether the bound cloth is completely dry or still damp. To minimize this (by maximizing the dexterity of your own finger movements while handling the bundles or clipping the cords), substitute very thin medical gloves for the thicker rubber gloves you wore during dyeing. Work in good light so you can see the stitches clearly.

To more easily catch individual threads when clipping the threads, *but without catching and clipping the fabric itself*, you'll need a tool with a single pointed tip to wiggle under the cords. Use a small pair of very sharp, pointed scissors: nail, embroidery, decoupage, or suture scissors; a carefully wielded seam ripper; or specialty weaver's scissors with a dip cut out from one scissor tip (see 02-57), moving slowly and carefully. In all cases, avoid pointing the tip of the cutting tool directly toward the cloth. Move from section to section, removing the threads in approximately the *reverse order* in which they were originally applied.

To remove the stitches: Begin at the *outside edge* of the fabric and work toward the center (the reverse order of the way you inserted the stitches). Find places where you tied two thread ends together. Carefully slide *one* outside scissors blade against the cloth and under the thread and clip out the knots. Cutting out the knots should release the entire line or section of thread and open out the fabric gathered along it. But you may have to go back and clip threads in other places along the line. To more easily pull out the threads, grasp them with a good pair of sharp-pointed tweezers with a grooved or textured grip. Remove all the threads, carefully cutting away or separating them as needed to get them out. When all the threads are removed, open out the cloth and proceed to rinsing.

4. Rinse out. (See the "Universal Rinse-Out for Resist Dyeing" text box, page 61.)

02-91 Stitch resist (*nui shibori* or *tritik*). *Top*: single line of running stitch (*ori-nui shibori*); *bottom*: single line of whipstitch on a fold (*maki-nui shibori*). Multiple colors of painted, thickened, fiber reactive dye, batched to set color. Cotton print cloth. Scale: 6.5" × 7.5".

Try this!

2.1 Practice resist dye samples

Practice and learn a range of techniques explained above.

- *Fold dye*: Use fiber reactive dip dyebaths and batching to make six samples: simple accordion fold, accordion folds in two directions, rectangular folds in two directions, triangular folds, fold and clamp, and fold and bind.

- *Bound resist*: Use thickened fiber reactive dye paste, painted on and then batched to set the color to make seven samples: random bound resist (two samples), twisted bound resist (one sample), and tie-dye (four samples), to include large rings, spiderweb spirals, and *kanoko* dots.

- *Pole wrapping*, scrunched during binding (one sample)

- *Stitch resist* (two samples), one with running stitch and one with whipstitch

Advanced resist-dyed samples:

Make three samples that combine any of the resist-dye techniques. In each sample, use two to four different colors. Sample 1: analogous colors at the same intensity. Sample 2: complementary colors at any value or intensity. Sample 3: two low-intensity colors with one high-intensity color. Notice which hues dominate in each sample.

2.2 Advanced fold dye experiments

After you've practiced the basic folds to get started, alter and manipulate them to invent new and interesting results on larger pieces of cloth. Make a series of experimental fold dye samples to try any of the following:

- Combine triangular folds with vertical and horizontal rectangular folds, or with accordion folds.

- To achieve a *regularly* repeating pattern, measure, mark, and fold the cloth very accurately.

- For *irregular* results, "eyeball" the folds or encourage odd angles and uneven sizes.

- Fold or pleat on the bias (diagonal to the grain of the fabric).

- Change or reverse the direction of the folds in sequence across the fabric.

- Discontinue folds in the middle of the fabric and leave the rest of the fabric flat. Dye only the folded sections.

- Invent more variations of your own.

2.3 Advanced pole wrapping (*arashi shibori*)

Pole wrapping offers many opportunities to build complex or layered patterns and color blends through binding and dyeing in stages or sequence. If you are working on cotton, try at least two of the experiments below on a series of samples or small cloths, such as handkerchiefs. If you are using acid dyes on silk, use larger pieces of cloth, such as scarves or shawls.

Instructions:

- Layer two different types of binding in sequence, shifting the position of the fabric on the tube to allow resist lines to cross. Use a new color on the second layer of arashi.

- *Add* cords during the dye process: Bind pole-wrapped fabric with sparsely spaced cords and paint on thickened dye. Then, add more cords to increase the density and preserve the first painted color (as in 02-64). Paint on more dye. Batch to set color.

- *Remove* cords during the dye process: Compress and bind the entire cloth in sections of cording (so you can easily remove some of them). Then paint the fabric with thickened dye. Remove some cords, then add more thickened dye in a different color. Batch to set color.

- Bind and apply thickened dye in stripes or sections of the fabric.

- Use saved and *unrinsed* "dirty" cords for binding (see the text box on "Reusing Dyed Cords for Added Colors"). Add your own painted color on top of the residual cord color.

- Combine pole wrapping with other resist-pattern methods (such as bound or stitch resist).

- Experiment with unusual or complex color combinations to match a color source. As you practice, think of other possibilities based on your own experience.

2.4 Advanced stitch resist (*nui shibori*)

Experiment with a variety of stitch sizes and placements.

- Running stitches in parallel rows. Experiment with placing the stitches close together or farther apart, in a single thickness of cloth or on folds, with even or uneven spacing.

- Repeat running-stitch circles, spirals, or concentric circles of increasing or decreasing sizes, close together or farther apart, on a single thickness of the cloth or on a fold.

- Use running stitches in a zigzag, or in an eccentric formation, to make unusual lines.

- Use running stitches to draw geometric shapes (squares, rectangles, triangles, parallelograms, trapezoids, checkerboards), organic shapes (leaves, twigs, flowers, petals, rocks), animals (rabbits, toads, snakes, cats, dogs, etc.), or scenery (landscape or cityscape).

- Experiment with whipstitches in straight lines, in parallel lines, over folds or multiple folds, or to create areas of texture inside running-stitch outlines.

2.5 Stitch resist acid-dyed silk scarves

Create two different resist-dyed silk scarves, each with a different pattern, and each using a combination of bound resist and stitch resist (any variations you like).

Instructions:

- Make sketches to design the patterns for each scarf. You'll be putting both of the scarves into the *same* dyebath, so you'll need to make them look different from each other through their *patterning* rather than their eventual color. Lay out the placement of elements, the composition, and the scale of the marks to intentionally place the pattern elements on the scarves to best advantage when the scarves are worn wrapped around the neck.
- Using a temporary marking tool, transfer the layout of pattern elements to each silk scarf.
- Stitch and bind your design and gather up the fabric ready to dye.
- Prepare a Lanaset acid dyebath in any desired color.
- Dye the scarves according to Lanaset dye instructions in chapter 1.
- After the dyeing, *carefully* remove the bindings to reveal the pattern.
- Wash and rinse according to Lanaset instructions.
- Press the scarves while still damp to remove wrinkles.

2.6 THE CUMULATIVE CLOTH CHALLENGE

The goal: add resist-dyed pattern to one or all of the dyed fabrics from the Cumulative Cloth Challenge in chapter 1. Bind the fabric, using your choice of resist-dye techniques (fold, bound, pole wrap, or stitch) to create an overlay of textures, patterns, or marks. For this resist layer, choose a dye color that will leave clear (even if subtle) marks in contrast to the foundation dye color. If you have selected an overall color palette for this challenge, choose a color from that palette for the resist marks. Make notes about the dye colors and resist methods you used. Take a photograph of the fabric in its new form. Set it aside for the challenge in chapter 3.

3 / DIRECT APPLICATION: DRAWING AND PAINTING WITH PIGMENTS

03-01 Combined direct-application techniques: freezer paper mechanical resists (triangles), sponged texture (in bright pink), applied over screen-printed background pattern. Textile pigments. Cotton print cloth. Scale: 15" × 15".

Direct application is a "catchall" term that includes techniques such as painting, spraying, drawing, sponging, stamping, stenciling, or monoprinting as ways to apply design, color, marks, and details to cloth. The techniques are simple, accessible, and enjoyable. Collectively and individually, these techniques produce spontaneous one-of-a-kind fabrics, whether at large scale or small. When employed with textile pigments, the quickness of color application makes any of these single techniques (or combinations of them) a valuable part of your creative process: to brainstorm and "sketch" ideas or designs, to test specific color overlays or shape combinations, to invent your own marks and shape "vocabulary," or to develop compositions for large-scale digital or screen prints (discussed in chapters 4 and 5).

Direct-application techniques easily create "continuous" effects that are difficult to achieve with screen printing, such as stripes or long continuous lines across the fabric, repeated similar but *not identical* motifs, side-by-side shapes repeated at dramatically different scales, gradations of colors or shapes across the surface, blended or layered marks or shapes with differing amounts of overlap, and placement of single or clustered motifs only in selected areas of the cloth.

With the flexibility to apply pigment and dye spontaneously, work at any scale, and change scales immediately, you have the same latitude of expression as any painter to create gestures, marks, images, and patterns or to tell stories in your own style or in endless variation. With the entire piece of cloth spread out on a padded surface and *fully visible* as you work, you can change lines, colors, shapes, and compositions instantly.

03-02 Combined direct-application techniques. Sponging, stamping, dabbing with shaped brush and dinner fork. Textile pigments. Cotton print cloth. Scale: 8" × 11".

Nevertheless, though the techniques encourage spontaneity, you can also develop your own controlled and precise approach. With tightly woven fabric, careful measurements and fabric stretching, masking tape, and accuracy with pen or brush, you can create detailed representational images or accurate geometric designs or patterns. If you already like to paint on paper or canvas, your skills and ideas will transfer readily to fabric. Whatever your artistic style or subject matter, the texture and three-dimensional characteristics of the fabric can add new dimension to your compositions.

03-03 Sgraffito with painted green pigment, scratched through with both pointed and broad-tipped implements. Textile pigments. Cotton print cloth. Scale: 7.25" × 7.25".

BELOW: 03-04 Combined direct-application techniques. Sgraffito with comb, custom rubber stamps (geometric shapes), found object stamps (yellow), painted with fine brush (red marks). Textile pigments. Cotton print cloth. Scale: 7.5" × 8".

SUPPLY CHECKLIST FOR DIRECT APPLICATION

- pigments (on any fiber type) OR dyes (chosen for specific fiber type)
- transparent extender
- binder
- fabrics (any fiber type with pigments; dyes matched to fiber type)
- small T pins (size 20)
- masking tape
- mixing cups
- containers with tight-fitting lids
- spoons and rubber scrapers
- sponge brushes
- bucket
- soap and water
- application tools:

Look for other likely tools around your house, at garage sales, in the hardware store, or along the roadside. Anything that can be dipped or pressed against pigment will work. Each object will have a distinctive or expressive mark. Some objects can be washed and used again; others must be discarded. *Do not* borrow anything that you will use again in the kitchen or home.

Here are some things my students have used over the years:

1. found objects, implements, tools
2. string
3. shaped stickers, dots
4. tracing paper
5. sponge brushes
6. squeeze bottles
7. masking tape (different widths)
8. salt
9. cheesecloth/meshes
10. empty tin cans
11. mesh-type onion/vegetable bags
12. freezer paper
13. vegetables (carrots, potatoes, onions)
14. natural objects
15. spatulas
16. wire
17. paintbrushes, toothbrushes, sponge brushes
18. scraping implements
19. discarded kitchen tools (potato masher)
20. discarded eating utensils (forks)
21. sponges
22. rollers
23. ruling pen or quill with nibs
24. rubber stamps (commercial or handmade)
25. open silkscreen frame
26. buttons, zippers
27. soles of discarded shoes

Workspace: The Padded Work Surface

We'll start our discussion with an overview of the workspace needed for any direct-application technique, then delve into the individual technical processes later. Most importantly, you will need a padded work surface (a portable board or tabletop) and access to a utility sink with running water for cleanup.

Instructions for making your own padded work surface:

1. *Cut (or buy) a sturdy, inflexible plywood, hardboard, or wooden tabletop to desired size, anything from 12" × 18" to 4' × 4'* (choose a manageable size for you). When it's time to work, clamp the board to your worktable. Or, if you'll be doing this regularly, permanently *pad* the worktable itself (which is also handy for screen printing, discussed in chapter 4). Either way, make sure your work surface is the correct height for your own body (worktable about the same height as your hip joint) and sturdy enough to lean against. Whether portable or stationary, fabric-padded surfaces can also serve "double duty" to press fabrics for piecing, appliqué, reverse appliqué, or fabric manipulation (techniques addressed in the *Dry Techniques* book).

2. *Cut the padding material to the same size as the board or tabletop*: You can use a variety of materials for padding, such as thick (3⁄8") industrial felt, foam rubber (one thick or several thin layers), or several layers of either regular felt, cotton quilt batting, or old blankets. The relative sponginess of the padding material will determine how thick you make it on the board. You will want enough thickness to enable pinning fabric into it. To prevent "ridges" in the eventual pigment application, use single pieces of padding cut to the full size of the work top. Place the padding material directly on top of the board or tabletop and spread it out evenly, with no wrinkles or lumps.

3. *Cut and arrange the covering*: Cut a piece of heavy white cloth or canvas several inches larger than the board on all sides (something to grip as you stretch it tightly). Lay the fabric cover over the padding, squarely aligning the grain of fabric with the edges of the table or board.

   - *On small portable boards* with thin hardboard, arrange the cover straight on the board, then pull and stretch it tightly, beginning in the middle of each side. As you stretch, use packing tape to anchor the edges of the covering to the back of the board.

   - *On larger boards or tables with plywood*: Starting in the center, stretch the covering over the padding and use an electric staple gun to fasten it to the *underside* of the tabletop or wood board. Avoid staples on the edges of the wood (because they'll snag on your clothing) and on the top of the wood (because they'll create unwanted "resist" marks when you paint pigment over them). Insert the first staple in the center of one side, and the second one directly across in the center of the other side. From those points, use pliers to grip and stretch the cloth, and staple every few inches along the sides. To avoid creating ripples or wiggles in the grain, maintain equal tension each time you stretch the cover fabric. Insert staples every few inches, first on one side, then directly across on the other side, as you work toward the ends. Stop within a few inches of the corners. Next stretch and staple each end of the cover, again beginning at the center of one end, then the center of the other end, working outward toward the corners of the board. To finish, miter or neatly fold the corners under and staple them into place (04-07).

   - *Temporary plastic covering*: For extra protection on the canvas cover, wrap a piece of heavy, clear plastic around the board, then tape it securely to the back. The plastic can be wiped off after each work session or replaced as frequently as necessary. It preserves the clean white working surface, ideal for choosing colors without visual color interference from past stains and blots.

   - *Alternative vinyl covering*: Instead of heavy twill or canvas, you can use "scrubbable" marine vinyl to cover the surface. White vinyl will stain over time, so I recommend black or gray as neutral alternatives. This surface is easily washed after each work session and, unlike canvas or cloth, won't collect dye or pigment residues that could be accidentally and unintentionally transferred to future projects.

   - *Caveats*: *Plastic* and *vinyl* covers require masking tape to stretch the fabric (because T pins would leave many holes in the work surface). And you cannot use plastic- or vinyl-covered boards or tables to iron fabrics (because the hot iron would melt the covering).

03-05 Sponging. Dabbed with natural sponge; stamped with cut synthetic sponge triangles. Textile pigments. Cotton print cloth. Scale: 8" × 8".

03-06 Combined direct-application techniques. Sponging (*background*), mesh resist, rubbing. Textile pigments. Cotton print cloth. Scale: 6" × 8".

Introduction to Textile Pigments and Paints

To be prepared for the techniques yet to come, you need to know more about textile pigments and paints, the media of choice for ease of use and safety.

In this chapter we'll focus on textile pigments in water-based extender preparations. However, nearly all the techniques will also work with fiber reactive dyes, in corresponding thin solutions or thick pastes as outlined in chapter 1.

Textile pigments, also called *printing inks* or *textile paints*, provide simple and relatively nonhazardous means to color fabric with direct-application techniques. Unlike dyes, which penetrate and lock into the fibers, pigments *lie on top* of the fabric, adhered with a *binder*. After air curing or heat setting, textile pigments are brilliant and relatively lightfast and washfast. They can be applied to *any* properly prepared fabric surface, of any fiber type (natural or synthetic). Because pigments sit only on the cloth surface, the back of the fabric carries only a ghost image or pattern.

Textile pigments can be purchased in several forms: as pre-mixed colors in small jars or large cans, in powdered form ready to mix into a separately purchased *extender*, or in concentrated liquid form, also to mix into an extender. (The latter gets my vote for cheapest and most flexible for precise color mixing.) The extender is a white gelatinous substance (roughly the consistency of yogurt), already containing the binder, to suspend and distribute thoroughly mixed concentrated pigment (color) for smooth application. When they dry, extenders can be transparent (which allows optical mixing of colors when one pigment is layered over another) or opaque (which block out the fabric color and any shapes or patterns beneath them). Selectively using both transparent and opaque extenders yields a more diverse result than can be achieved with dyes, which are always transparent.

Products marketed as *fabric paints* are thinned-down versions of textile pigments (their watery consistency causes them to resemble dye solutions), but they still contain a binder and possess the same physical properties as other textile pigments. However, their thin consistency causes them to flow like gouache or watercolor paint and thus facilitate smooth lines and even color surfaces. Fabric paints are often marketed in small costly bottles, but you can mix your own "textile paints" less expensively by thinning full-strength textile pigments with a water-and-binder mixture (more on that later).

03-07 Combined direct-application techniques. Canning (blue), stamping with corrugated cardboard (green), dabbing with scrunched netting (black). Textile pigments. Pale-yellow-dyed cotton print cloth . Scale: 8.5" × 11".

Textile pigments and paints are easy to use, require no chemical assistants, and clean up quickly with soap and water. They are relatively nontoxic (no more toxic than acrylic paints) if you avoid handling them in dry powder form (or eating them). Nevertheless, good ventilation and rubber gloves are still advisable. They dry quickly when laid down in a thin, even layer (as in screen printing), but a bit more slowly when applied thickly with brushes or stamps. Air curing for 10 days to two weeks sets the color, though you can speed up the process with a dry hot iron.

Placed in tightly sealed containers and climate-controlled conditions, textile pigments usually store indefinitely without deteriorating. Thus, avoid storing them in attics, garages, and outdoor storage sheds where conditions fluctuate, and avoid storage containers that admit air. In warm, humid climates, stored pigments may grow a bit of mold, especially during a hot, humid summer. It looks bad, but you can use a rubber scraper to skim off the mold and discard the affected areas (again, just as you would with a bit of mold on top of yogurt). The mold will not usually affect the usefulness of the rest of the batch. If you routinely stock and store large quantities of textile pigments for lengthy periods, ask the manufacturer, at the time you order them, to add a mold inhibitor to the pigments and the extender, then make note of that addition on your copy of the Materials Safety Data Sheet for the product. Occasionally, if subjected to unusually poor conditions (extreme heat, freezing, wetness, or rapid fluctuations), the pigments may begin to break down or separate and will then need to be discarded.

Because of their essential composition (particles suspended in an extender containing a plastic-like binder), most textile pigments *do* change the surface qualities of any fabric to which they are applied. The change may be slight or quite noticeable, depending on the type and amount of pigment and the binder in the product, and the kind of cloth you use. Touching the cloth or examining its drape will tell you how much the pigment product has stiffened it. The same combination of factors (pigment, binder, cloth type) may also change the way that light reflects off the printed fabric surface, a characteristic most visible on *shiny* fabrics, such as rayon satin, where the pigment will register as a *matte* color area less glossy than the fabric itself. All these outcomes can be either advantages or disadvantages, depending on how you want the printed cloth to appear in the projects where you'll use it. For example, a rather thick, plastic-like extender can be used to *intentionally* stiffen fabric or give it more "body," while thin and fluid *paints* preserve the texture and drape of soft, flowing silks.

Safety Guidelines for Textile Pigments

- Follow the usual safety methods outlined in chapter 1 to protect your hands and clothing: cover your clothing with a work shirt and apron and wear *close-fitting* latex or rubber gloves (both to protect your hands and maintain manual dexterity). Because pigments are safer to use, as you gain some experience you can relax *somewhat* and devise your own ways to control the work safely.

- Protect any textiles you care about (i.e., wear old clothes and shoes on which you'll be content to see pigment splashes and smears).

- Spilled pigments and extender are *very slippery*. Wipe up all spills *as they happen*. (I speak to you as someone who has almost lost her balance, more than once, by sliding on patches of wet pigment while walking through a classroom.)

03-08 Combined direct-application techniques. Monoprinting, stamping, stenciling, painting, sponging, mechanical resist with torn masking tape, fine lines drawn with a syringe. Thick and thinned textile pigment. Heavy cotton twill. Scale: 10" × 8".

SOME THOUGHTS ABOUT OPAQUE PIGMENT EXTENDERS

A great advantage: Opaque extender and pigments allow you to mix any colors (including very light colors) and layer them on a dark background, without the color of the cloth showing through to change the applied color. This opacity adds considerable flexibility to the visual effects and color relationships possible on the fabric and extends the range of fabric colors with which you can begin your projects.

A headache: Opaque extender is more difficult to work with than the transparent variety. It is sticky, emits odors that *require* good ventilation in the room, and dries *very quickly* on anything it touches, and it is difficult or impossible to remove once dried on anything. Cleanup needs to be immediate and thorough.

A related warning: White pigments and white color concentrates automatically contain an "opaquing agent." *White pigments are therefore the only ones that are almost never transparent*. Used alone or in mixture with other pigment colors, white will still smell of chemicals and will dry quickly on your fabric and tools (and even more quickly if there is any fan in the room) but will still exhibit the usual opacity, which blocks out colors beneath it. Some people love working with white pigments. I personally prefer to avoid them and to achieve "white" by leaving areas of the fabric itself unprinted.

USING ACRYLIC PAINTS ON FABRIC

Straight from the tube, acrylic paint will significantly alter the original hand of the fabric, rendering it stiffer and more paperlike. Applied too thickly, acrylic paint, once dry, will also be inclined to flake, crack, or even fall off the surface. However, if you want to get started experimenting with direct application right away, and you already have acrylic paints on hand, here is a simple alternative:

Add *fabric/textile medium* to the acrylic paint. This acrylic polymer liquid blend essentially transforms the paint into a softer and more flexible textile pigment. The results can be washed by hand or machine. Use this mixture with any of the techniques in this chapter.

Mixing Custom Colors with Pigment Concentrates

Textile pigments in extender are nearly the same consistency as acrylic paints straight out of the tube. If you have used acrylic paints, the feel of the pigment medium will seem familiar, and the *color-mixing strategies are much the same.* Differences lie in the specific composition of the *binders* in each colorant: the binder in acrylic paint is formulated to hold color to *stationary* surfaces such as prepared canvas or paper; the binder in textile pigments is a softer formulation for *flexible* surfaces (such as fabrics and threads) where movement stretches the contact between colorant and underlying threads. See also the text box about "Using acrylic paints on fabric."

Inventory of colors: To get started, buy a small range of *color concentrate pigments* (cyan, magenta, yellow, black, white, brown) and a bucket of transparent extender. This inventory allows you to mix desired amounts of individual custom colors for each project and in the long run costs less to stock than individual jars of pre-mixed colors. The latter seldom supply the nuances and varieties of colors you want; they cede the control of precise color mixing to the manufacturer, and (not least!) they generally take the fun out of the color mixing. Rely on your own eyes, instincts, and color-mixing skills. (But it's fine for beginners to buy pre-mixed colors until they become accustomed to using direct-application techniques and want to "branch out" into mixing their own colors.)

Mixing strategies and predicting finished color: All colorants shift hue, value, or intensity as they dry, air-cure, or undergo heat-setting processes, but with textile pigments these shifts of color are minimal, and their stability and predictability give you greater color control. When the pigments are *still wet* immediately after application, they *do* appear slightly darker and more intense, but (unlike fiber reactive dyes) when they dry, the colors should not surprise you. When used on white cloth, what you see in the mixing container is pretty much what you get on the finished cloth, even after air curing or heat setting, and washing. (Direct application on colored fabrics, however, is a different matter. Because all pigments except white are transparent—see the text box about opaque extenders built into white pigments—if you put a yellow pigment on a pink cloth, you'll get some type of orange.)

For simplicity, mix your custom colors directly in small plastic storage containers with tight-fitting lids. Cleaned-out yogurt, cottage cheese, and deli containers work well. Or purchase small, lidded plastic containers specifically for this purpose. I use the smallest and least expensive food storage containers.

Start the mixing with the extender! Since the volume of the extender determines the volume of the resulting custom color, start the process with a measured (even an estimated) amount of the extender and *then* add the pigment concentrate *in small increments*. (There is a reason these pigments are called "concentrates." If, for example, you wanted to mix only a tablespoon of custom color, a pinhead's worth of concentrate in a tablespoon of extender might be all you need. Or, for larger amounts of custom color, ¼ tsp. of concentrate might be enough for 2 or 3 cups.) If, on the other hand, you were to place the concentrate in the container first, you would then have to keep adding extender until you "diluted" the color to the value and intensity you actually want, which would generate much more custom color than you're likely to need. So start with a *finite* amount of extender and *then* add concentrate, mixing thoroughly until you reach the "right" color. And when you mix two colors of different values, *start with the lighter color* mixed into the extender, then add the darker color in *small* increments until you arrive at the right combination.

Test each custom color on a scrap of the same fabric that will be receiving the direct application. After each addition of color concentrate, and after mixing thoroughly, smear a small amount on the fabric scrap. Continue to add or adjust the color, mixing and testing with a smear each time, until you get the exact color you want. If you have a color chip, photograph, or piece of material, or another object to match, have it close at hand and compare the fabric smears to the color source.

To mix *very small amounts* of custom color (less than a tablespoon), use a palette knife or a small rubber scraper and mix on a *white* surface: a white painter's palette, a white metal butcher's tray (my own preference), heavy white paper, or white plastic plates. (If you've ever mixed paints, this process will be familiar to you.) A white surface minimizes color interference that could change your perception of the colors as you mix them.

Storing the custom colors: After you mix each color, cover the container tightly and label it with the color name or attach the scrap of fabric with the color smear to the lid with a piece of masking tape. This will let you identify colors without opening their container lids. Between working sessions, store your custom colors in their tightly sealed containers in a cool place away from sunlight. Tiny amounts of color can be stored in similarly tiny containers with tight-fitting lids, such as old film canisters (sometimes still available at local camera stores), plastic spice containers, or plastic condiment containers from the salad bar.

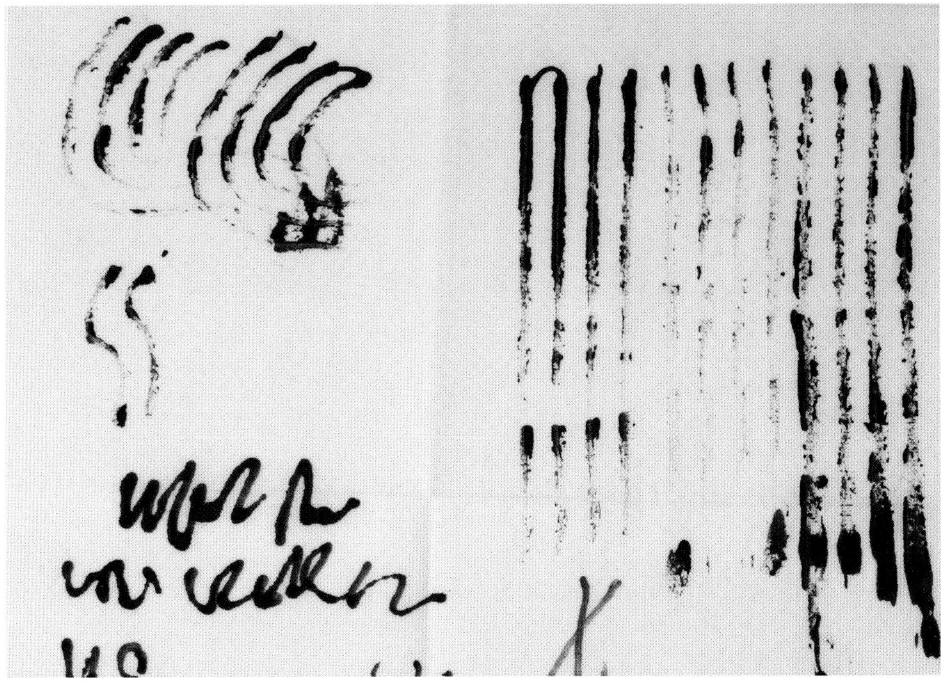

03-09 Drawing. Differing hand pressures alternately create thinner or fatter lines, or solid or broken lines. Thinned textile pigment in squeeze bottle. Cotton print cloth. Scale: 5" × 7".

Thick vs. Thin Custom Color Mixtures

Custom colors can be mixed into various consistencies, from thick to thin. If you are working with a transparent extender and mixing your own colors, you also control the thickness of the "paste." The eventual use for the fabric (clothing, quilt, wall hanging) should largely determine the thickness of your paste application. If the fabric will be worn and washed repeatedly, keep the application relatively thin and even. If the fabric will *not* be washed, build up color on the surface in any way you wish, just as you might build up paint on a canvas.

For each project, test the application thickness on a sample of the exact fabric you plan to use. Allow the sample to dry thoroughly, air-cure or heat-set it, then wash it. Does the color retain the look you wanted? Is the surface texture what you expected? Was the pigment so thick that it cracked off the surface? Can the fabric be moved, rolled, or handled as you intend without damaging the surface? Make adjustments to the paste, according to your test results, before you apply paste to the final project.

Caveat: Extender already includes a measured amount of binder, which is formulated to stick to bare *fabric*, but *not* necessarily to stick to *itself* in areas where a previous layer of paste has already been applied. Therefore, too many layers of custom color built up on the surface may cause the color to rub away or detach and fall off in chips. In general, the thinner you keep overlapping colors, the more physically resilient they'll be. (But sometimes you want to build up a design with overlapping colors and you just can't keep the paste thin enough. If you intend to overlap colors of thick paste, you can ameliorate by adding a bit more liquid binder, purchased separately if it didn't already accompany the extender.)

To Prepare Thick Applications

Textile pigments in extender are usually the consistency of yogurt. They can be made thinner than the way they came from the manufacturer, but not thicker. So think of these as store-bought "thick" pastes. They are ideal, without altering their thickness, for painting, stamping, rolling, sponging, stenciling, monoprinting, canning, mechanical resists, and sgraffito (all of which are discussed below). The thickness of the paste will hold an edge (won't wick or "run"), and color will stay where it's placed.

To Prepare Varying Thick/Thin Applications

You can customize the consistency of the extender to become less yogurt-like and more "creamy." This will facilitate direct-application techniques such as drawing with a squeeze bottle or syringe, or putting pigment in an airpen or airbrush.

Mix up a liquid concoction of water plus binder. (Order a bottle of binder from your supplier when you order your pigments and extender; follow the mixing ratio indicated on the bottle, usually one part binder to nine parts water.) Use the liquid binder mixture (*not* additional plain tap water) to thin down the extender into a measured amount of "slurry" or "thin cream." When you've achieved the desired consistency, *then* add the color concentrate incrementally.

For Thin Applications

For thin applications, omit using extender at all. Instead, mix up a combination of binder and water in the correct ratio, usually one part binder to nine parts water. Add color concentrates, in small increments, directly to the binder/water mixture to make thin custom colors. This combination will have the consistency and mixing characteristics of watercolor paint, but the softness of the made-for-textiles binder. Use it to make very thin applications of any colors (light or dark, bright or dull) that blend and soak into the fabric, producing the *appearance* of dye. It's very effective for painting, sponging, spraying, watercolor washes, overlaying and blending colors, or painting warp or weft fibers (even with the threads already on the loom).

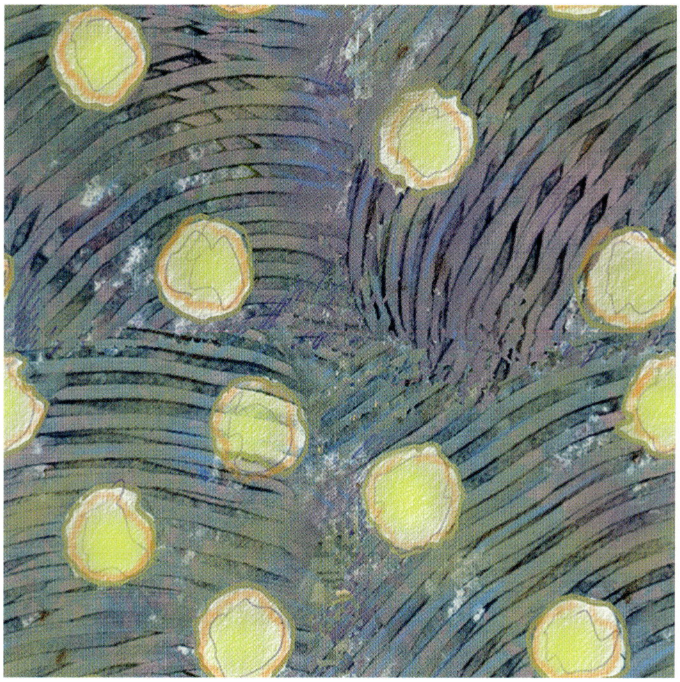

03-10 Combined techniques. Sponging, mechanical resists with press-apply stickers (large adhesive dots), sgraffito with rubber scraper, painting. Textile pigments. Cotton print cloth. Scale: 6" × 5".

Setting the Color of Textile Pigments

Whether the consistency of the applied paste is thick, thin, or in between, textile pigments must be dry in order to set. Allow fabrics printed or painted with textile pigments to air-dry for at least 24 hours before any further handling. Then use one of the following methods to set the color:

- *Air curing:* This is the easiest of the setting methods (because, given enough time, air curing alone can set color), but also the slowest (because setting color by air curing alone requires the fabric to cure undisturbed for two weeks). Just let the cloth hang in a warm room (perhaps 70ºF or more) for two weeks.

To set more quickly, use one of the following *dry-heat* options (*after* the fabric is already dry to the touch) but do *not* use steam heat, which may dissolve colors and make them "run."

- *Dry iron*: Set the iron to the appropriate temperature for your fabric's fiber content. Cover the front of the fabric with a press cloth to prevent scorching. Moving the iron continuously, press the entire surface for five minutes, taking care not to miss any areas or spots.
- *Clothes dryer*: In a very hot, *gas-fired* dryer (electric home dryers don't generate enough heat), tumble on the highest heat setting for 20–30 minutes. If you don't have a gas dryer in your studio location, large commercial ones may be available at public laundromats.
- *Mangle (rolling iron) or heat press*: If you have access to one, you can use an old rolling iron or a commercial mangle (once commonly used for ironing sheets, pillowcases, and other flat household items) to set the color. Sandwich the painted fabric between press cloths to prevent the iron plate from contacting the print directly, and mount it on the roller with pins. Set the time and temperature for the fiber content of your fabric and let it roll around for the requisite time (each mangle will be different in this regard). For small prints, a heat press (also referred to as *dry mount press*) will work similarly. Sandwich the print between press cloths and process at moderate heat.

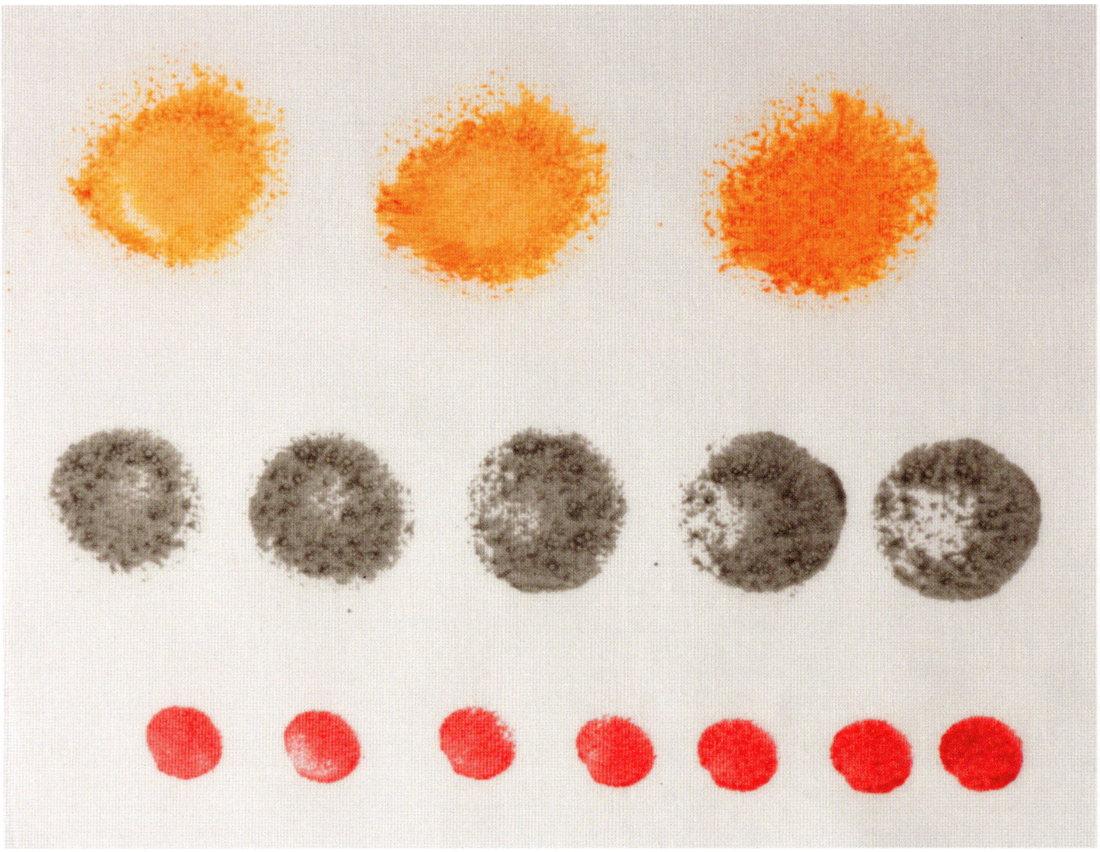

03-11 Sponging. Shaped sponge daubers, large, medium, and small. Textile pigments. Cotton print cloth. Scale: 7" × 8".

USING DIRECTLY APPLIED DYE PASTES AND PIGMENTS ON THE SAME CLOTH

Thickened dyes (see chapter 1) create marks that *sink into* the fabric visually, while textile pigments create marks that *sit on top* of the fabric surface visually. These subtle surface characteristics add to any color contrasts on the cloth.

- Wear rubber gloves to protect your skin from the *dyestuff*. If you feel clumsy painting, drawing, or stamping in ordinary rubber gloves, try inexpensive latex medical gloves for greater dexterity.

- If you are using dyes for direct application, *don't forget to add the activator to the dye paste or solution just before you use it.* And remember that once you activate the paste, use it within an hour. Keep track of the color proportions in the paste, so that if the paste "expires," you'll have the information to remix the color.

The binder in pigments forms a barrier that hinders dye penetration. This means that you can apply pigment on top of dye, but not dye on top of pigment. The color-setting process for dyes (discussed in chapter 1) is also different from, and in conflict with, the color-setting process for pigments. Therefore, when combining dyes and pigments on the same cloth, you must complete the *entire* application and processing of dyes *before* proceeding to pigments.

- Apply the dye *first*, then set, wash out, and dry. (See chapter 1 for instructions.)

- Then stretch the fabric on the padded table again, apply the pigments, and process using one of the "setting" methods above.

03-12 Combined direct-application techniques: torn-paper mechanical resist, stamping, sponging, fan-shaped brush marks, outline drawn with squeeze bottle. Textile pigment, thin and thick concentrations. Heavy cotton twill. Scale: 5" × 6.5".

Individual Direct-Application Techniques

Directly applying textile colorants (thick or thin pigments or thickened dyes) to fabric, using handheld tools, both mimics and relies on the traditional techniques of drawing, painting, calligraphy, and more-direct forms of printmaking on paper. The techniques allow you to create one-of-a-kind effects on cloth with the movements of your own hand and arm, with a minimum of simple equipment. You control the lines, shapes, colors, and layout as you work in your own style, spontaneously or precisely. Patterns, compositions, or images build on the fabric much like watercolor or oil paintings, block prints, or pages of text (i.e., one stroke, mark, or shape at a time).

If you have been traditionally trained in fine arts, you may already have good control of pencils, pens, markers, paintbrushes, and printing processes. If you don't, the direct-application techniques outlined here for fabric will introduce you to the basics.

The techniques below are grouped into five general categories: (1) large color areas, (2) repeating shapes and patterns, (3) mechanical resists, (4) linework, and (5) monoprinting (one-of-a-kind single-impression prints). The section closes with some thoughts about combining various techniques to build custom surfaces, create patterns, or compose images.

Gather your tools, materials, and supplies and practice the techniques with an adventurous, playful, and experimental spirit. Each technique can be used with precision or abandon. Embrace the methods that fit with your way of working and expressing.

Instructions for using the padded work surface:

1. *Before* each work session, place a clean heavy-fabric drop cloth over your padded table or workboard, to protect the work surface from an overspill of pigment or a leakage of dye. (Stains and leftover color on the work surface can both interfere with your color perception *and*, when remoistened as you work, transfer unwanted leftover color smudges to the underside of your fresh cloth or completely through it.) Make sure the drop cloth is spread flat and free of creases. If needed, pin it in place to stabilize.

2. Lay the project fabric on top of the drop cloth, front side up, and smooth out any wrinkles with your hand.

3. Stretch the fabric straight and taut, then use small (size 20) T pins to secure it. Insert the pins through the fabric and into the padding, at an angle *toward* the center of the fabric and *against* the direction of the stretch. (You will have to determine the correct angle to both secure the pin in the padding and not bump the hardboard underneath. Each padded surface will be different.) Place the pins at close intervals around the edges, continually stretching the fabric gently to prevent wrinkles, folds, or skewed grain as you keep pinning. Pin each corner first, keeping the sides straight. If you have a plastic- or vinyl-covered padded surface, use masking tape to attach the stretched fabric to the surface in the same sequence as described for the pins.

4. To cover the pins and preserve a clean border on the fabric, apply masking tape over the fabric edges. Now you are ready to experiment!

Direct-Application Techniques: Large Color Areas

With the entire fabric stretched out and visible, it's the perfect moment to lay out background colors, create color fields, or overlap large areas of color. No color has to cover the whole space, and any color already on the cloth can be altered, enhanced, or shifted in hue, value, or intensity. Using the versatile techniques we'll explore in this category, you can make changes immediately and spontaneously. To produce transparent overlays of color, apply the following techniques to *dry* fabric. To blend the colors or create gradations across *a single piece of cloth* (as opposed to the immersion-dyed *sequence* of separately gradating fabrics we discussed in chapter 1), apply them to fabric dampened with binder and water mixture. Have your custom colors mixed and ready to apply with any of the following tools and techniques.

Sponging

Sponges, both synthetic and natural, used with thin or thick pigments or dye pastes, will add textures (see 03-24) or large color areas to fabric. Thinner applications will distribute uneven swaths of background color (03-06); thick applications will leave mottled textures across the surface interspersed with the ground color of the fabric (03-02). Cut sponges of all types into custom shapes and use them like stamps. Combine differently shaped or textured sponges, in contrasting color, to build spontaneous compositions (03-05, 03-13). Or layer the colors and textures with other direct-application techniques to create complex surfaces (03-41). Gather sponges in a diverse array of types, sizes, and textures; each will have a unique character you can exploit.

Synthetic sponges come in many sizes, shapes, and textures, available in stores for housewares, home improvement, or hardware, and from dye vendors themselves. They are usually cut into rectangular slabs (large ones for washing cars and houses, and smaller ones meant for indoor household cleaning). For expressive purposes, use scissors or a utility knife to cut those dull rectangular slabs into your own custom shapes. Occasionally you'll find synthetic sponges (usually meant for children's bathing) cut into fun or recognizable shapes, such as animals or plants.

Natural sponges, usually left in their living organic forms, vary widely in size from small cosmetic sponges to large bath sponges. You can usually find these in bath and body shops, department stores, and big-box stores, and anyplace that sells makeup or cosmetics. Some natural sponges have a lot of irregular surface texture; others are very smooth. The character of the sponge governs the character of the pigment transfer.

Shop at craft supply stores for *sponge daubers*, round-

HELPFUL HINTS FOR DIRECT APPLICATION WITH PIGMENTS

- *Enjoy the mess!* You may find direct-application techniques a bit messy. It's easy to get yourself into the work (literally), transfer considerable dye or pigment onto yourself, and sometimes even smear the work. Just remember, textile pigments are meant to cling to *any fabric*—that includes the clothing you are wearing, and any carpeting, draperies, or furniture in the vicinity. Think of the mess as part of the fun and spontaneity of direct application. (If you liked finger painting in your childhood, you're going to love this!)

- *Before* you pick up tools to work on a project, make a rough sketch of your ideas with pencil on paper, or a few trial marks on paper or fabric scraps. Feel free to follow, elaborate, or change this "plan of action" as you work on the cloth.

- Each mark made with pigment on fabric is a *commitment*. Since the colorant attaches to or sinks into the fibers, it cannot be removed. Changes to the composition or design become increasingly difficult. Keep your eyes open, respond to the marks you've made, and compose "on the fly." You may discover new ideas that weren't in your original plan of action.

- Generally you'll apply pigments to *dry* fabric, an approach that also produces clean edges of color. But you can also *dampen* fabric (with liquid binder mixture, *not* water) for fuzzy or softly blurred edges.

- To overlap (thin or thick) layers of applied color and maintain their separate characters or distinct pure colors, allow each layer to dry a bit before applying the next.

- To encourage overlapping colors to mix or blend, apply all layers of color while previously applied colors are still wet (but remember that the wet pigment from the previous color can transfer to everything you touch with it).

- Use a fan to hasten the drying process. Or, to dry *small areas* even faster, use a blow-dryer. To avoid causing burns or scorch marks on your fabric, set the dryer on low heat or "air" and keep the focus of the dryer *moving* back and forth across the area being dried.

- While the pigment is still wet on the fabric, it can smear easily or deposit color in unwanted areas. Allow wet pigment to air-dry *to the touch* (about 15 minutes) before you remove tape and pins or move it off the padded work surface. When you move it, keep it from folding back on itself (more of a problem with large pieces of fabric).

- Hang the fabric on a line to dry thoroughly for 24 hours before heat setting. Then cure it, using one of the methods in "Setting the Color of Textile Pigments" (page 121).

- Unused pigments (which are visible) and extender (which is not) that remain on your tools (paintbrushes, syringes, sponges, stencils, meshes, etc.), if left long enough to harden, will damage them. The crusts will not soften with water and can render the tools unsalvageable. You should clean tools as you stop using each of them, but without breaking your work rhythm. Keep a small bucket of warm soapy water close at hand and drop in each dirty tool or implement as you finish with it. Let the tools soak until you clean up at the end of the work session.

- *Dye* pastes left on your tools can, if left to dry, damage your tools in the same way as hardened pigments. Follow the same throw-them-in-soapy-water practice as for pigment-coated tools, but in a *separate* soapy-water container.

- After each work session, *thoroughly* scrub pigments and dyes from the tools and yourself, with soap and water (a "utility" sink or other deep sink is helpful for this). If necessary to scrub out crevices in the tools, use an old toothbrush. Then clean the sink itself. Or, if you don't have the right sink but the weather is warm enough, you can clean tools outdoors, using a garden hose with a spray nozzle.

shaped synthetic sponges glued to the ends of small pieces of wooden dowel. They are easy to hold as you dip into pigment and stamp on fabric (03-11).

Sponging instructions: To begin, dampen the sponge in water, then squeeze out the excess moisture. Dip the damp sponge into the dye or pigment as often as necessary and press the color directly onto the fabric surface. To get a more delicate layer of color on the sponge, spread the pigment out on a metal tray with a large sponge brush or a brayer, then press the sponge into it.

To build a delicate-textured background, dip and press lightly and repeatedly over the surface. For greater drama, use stronger dabs separated by open spaces. To mimic large paintbrush marks or lay down larger swaths of color, draw a "loaded" sponge across the surface with large arm movements. Change directions, vary the pressure, and layer the color to create color fields.

Wash out sponges with soap and water promptly and thoroughly after use. To avoid mold and mildew, allow sponges to dry completely before storing them. *Do not* use these sponges for personal hygiene or household cleaning after having used them with pigments or dyes.

03-13 Sponging. Stamped circular- and triangular-shaped synthetic sponges, overall texture with larger natural sponge, circular sponge daubers. Textile pigment. Cotton print cloth. Scale: 9.5" × 7.5".

Spraying

A simple spray bottle will distribute a light haze of very finely dotted color over large areas, perhaps including some larger dotted textures at the edges. Use sprayed color to "tweak" an underlying dyed color, construct a gradation of colors across the surface, or optically mix overlapping areas. The outcomes will differ according to the fineness of the spray bottle's nozzle, the consistency of the colorant, the distance from the fabric surface, and the number of times the color is sprayed.

Instructions: This is messy, so protect the area around the fabric with plastic and wear your protective apron, rubber gloves, and face mask when doing any kind of spraying. Prepare a thin application (see that section on page 121) or (using a bit of extender) a slightly thicker "slurry" and load it into the spray bottle; fasten the bottle cap tightly. Work slowly and take careful aim to confine the spray where you want it. Some spray bottles have a twisting valve that allows you to change the fineness of the mist or width of the spray. Play with that to find the best setting for your fabric. Spray firmly and smoothly. Experiment to find the optimal distance from the cloth. Usually, the farther from the surface, the wider the spray will cast; the closer, the more concentrated the coverage. In addition, the more repeatedly you spray color in one area, the more solid the color and the more saturated the fabric will become. To preserve their usefulness, carefully clean out the spray bottle nozzles with soap and water before they dry (in other words, immediately).

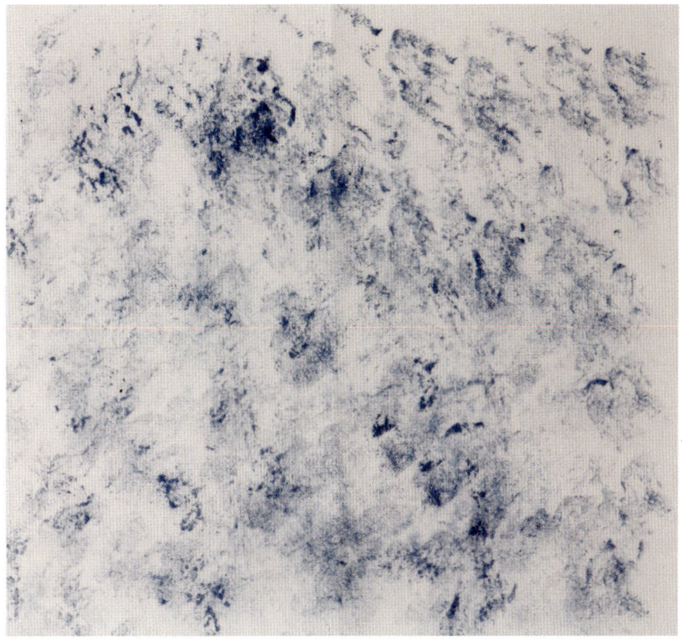

03-14 Sponging. Textile pigment lightly applied with a natural sponge lays down a more subtle background for other marks. Cotton print cloth. Scale: 8" × 8".

03-15 Canning to create background colors (green and purple), squeeze bottle for linework, fan-shaped brush for light-green feathered marks. Textile pigment. Cotton print cloth. Scale: 7.5" × 10".

Canning

This is a technique straight out of your finger-painting days. It is a simple, direct, but more random way to spread or *smear* pigment densely and slightly unevenly across the surface of the fabric (03-15). Where they contact the fabric, the can edges produce visible "drag marks" and capture the direction of movement in the applied color. Canning lays down large swaths of color that can be overlaid with drawn lines, brush marks (03-15), or stamping (03-07).

Instructions: Start with an empty tin can, any size that fits in your hand easily. Use a can opener to remove both ends. Remove the can's paper label, thoroughly clean the inside of the can, and allow it to dry. Place one end of the can in full contact with well-stretched and stabilized fabric. Drop pigment or thickened dye paste through the can. (Yes, the paste will be sitting in a blob directly on the fabric!) You can use a single color or drop in several colors side by side. Without lifting up the can, move it around in any direction on the fabric to spread the paste, until the paste runs out or until you achieve the desired result. To keep going, reload with more of the same colors and apply with similar movements across the surface. To distribute the color with intention, orchestrate your hand movements in arcs, circles, lines, or sweeps in predetermined paths.

To finish smoothly, move the empty can to the edge of the fabric, then off the side onto a large spatula, paper plate, or flat baking sheet. Try to avoid scraping leftover pigment onto the floor or onto the padded work surface. Discard the can or wash it for future use.

Painting with Large Brushes or Sponge Brushes

Just as you might create large background color fields in watercolor or acrylic painting, use wide (3"–6") paintbrushes and thinned pigment or dye to create wide swaths of background color (03-16) or lay down gradations across the cloth. Paint with pigment slurry or thin binder mixtures for smoother watercolor washes; use thick applications to leave crisp edges, texture, or brush marks in the color. To reveal more of the texture of the fabric, dip large sponge brushes in a small amount of color and drag lightly across the fabric surface. Drop used brushes in your handy soapy-water bucket as you work. After the work session, wash them *thoroughly* with soapy water.

03-16 Combined direct-application techniques. Painted ground, sponging, freezer paper stencils (squares and diamonds), fan-shaped brush marks, stamping with circular sponge daubers. Textile pigments. Cotton print cloth. Scale: 8.25" × 8.25".

Direct-Application Techniques: Repeating Shapes and Patterns

Next we turn to *stamping*, the technique best used to repeat identical or similar shapes, either in a pattern or scattered randomly around the cloth. Hand-placing shapes with small blocks or stamps is a precursor to screen printing, but the stamping process is both *more* spontaneous and *less* structured, complicated, and expensive. Slight variations of spacing, outline, and shape create a liveliness in hand-constructed pattern, accentuated or diminished by uneven coloration from natural variations in pressure on the stamp. The patterns you invent with these techniques, along with their irregularities and variations, can be translated onto screens for printing yardage that has a hand-painted aesthetic (discussed in chapter 4).

Rubber Stamps

The variety of commercially available or custom-prepared rubber stamps is vast, but the stamps themselves are expensive. If you are handy with a precision craft knife or carving tools, you can create your own unique custom-carved stamps. Most art and craft supply stores (and some pigment/dye vendors) offer thick adhesive-backed rubber sheets (choose the thickest varieties), which can be carved and applied to wood blocks to make your own stamps in any size (as used in 03-17). Thick and sturdy large plastic erasers (1.5" × 3") can also be carved and, while smaller, are thick enough to use as stamps without mounting (03-18 and 03-19).

03-17 Stamping. Hand-cut rubber stamp material, carved and adhered to wood block; corrugated cardboard used for stripes. Textile pigment. Cotton print cloth. Scale: 7" × 11".

03-18 Stamping. *Clockwise from top left*: cardboard tube, scraped; circular sponge daubers; commercial spiral rubber stamp; pattern-carved rubber, adhered to wood block; carved plastic eraser. Textile pigments. Cotton print cloth. Scale: 7" × 6.5".

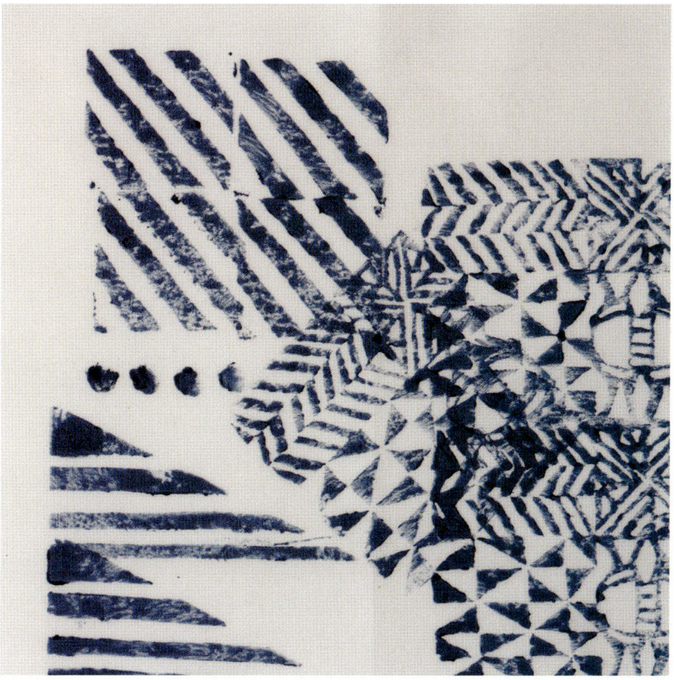

03-19 Stamping. Carved plastic erasers and circular sponge daubers (*left*); pattern-carved rubber, adhered to wood block (*right*). Textile pigments. Cotton print cloth. Scale: 7.5" × 8".

03-20 Combined direct-application techniques. Sponging, stamping with found objects: rubber stamp (spiral), dinner fork tine marks, large- and medium-size circular sponge daubers. Textile pigments. Cotton print cloth. Scale: 6.5" × 11".

The larger stamps approach the size and complexity of printing formats you may find familiar: *wood blocks* and *linoleum cuts*. Instruction in those printing processes is beyond the scope of this book; however, with the right textile pigments, you can use either of them on fabric. The increased size of the printing surface provides more freedom for detail and image development. The materials, tools, and instructions for preparing these blocks are available from most art suppliers.

Nontraditional Implements as "Stamps"

The scrapbooking, paper, or book arts sections of your local craft store stock a wide variety of implements meant for creative stamping, such as shaped foam or sponge blocks, sponge daubers (see 03-11 and 03-13), and textured decorative rollers. But almost any found object, once dabbed with pigment or dye and pressed onto the fabric surface, becomes an improvised "stamp." Use whatever interests you. For variety and quirky marks that reflect your own environment and interests, try using found objects or discarded household tools: cardboard tubes, clothespins, kitchen tools (such as potato mashers), eating utensils (fork, spoons, knives, as in 03-20, 03-42), bottle caps, household or garden tools (screwdrivers, hammers, awls, trowels), *raw firm* fruits and vegetables (potatoes, carrots, apples, artichokes), leaves, and sticks.

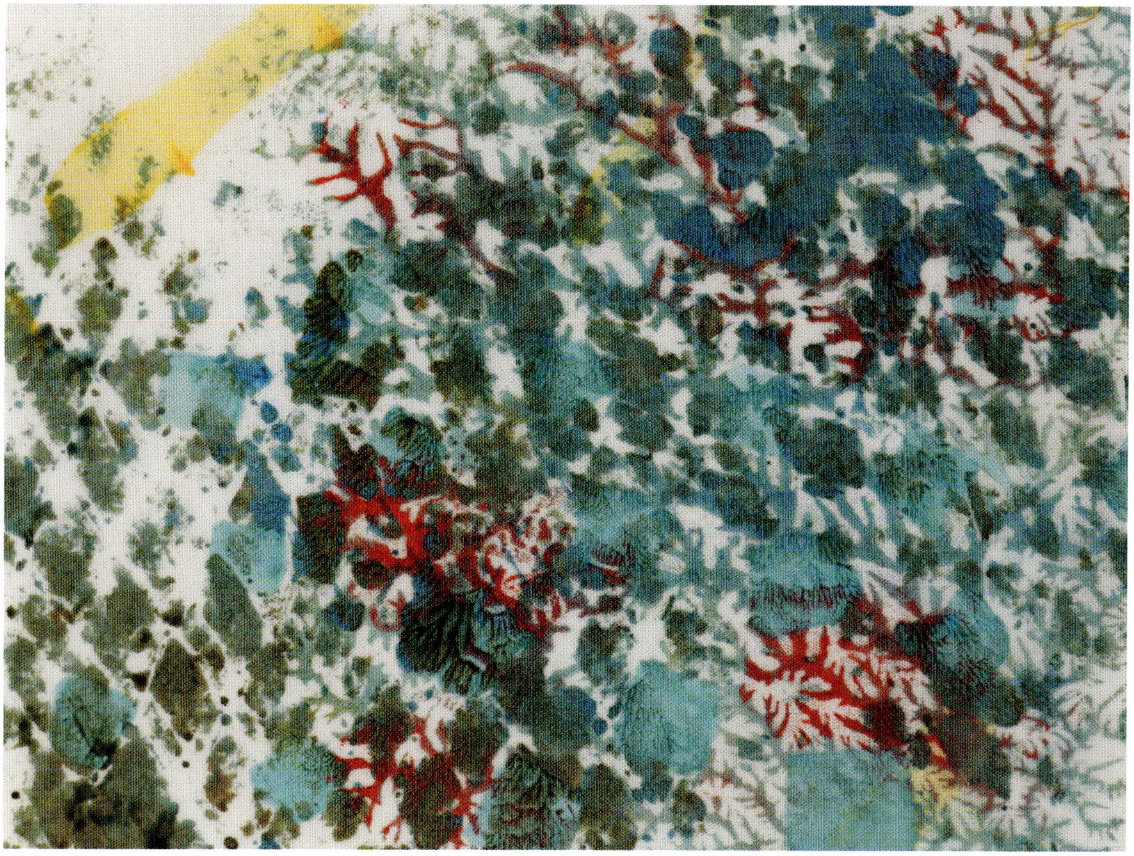

03-21 Stamping. Round and square sponges, plastic mesh, layered on monoprinted ground. Textile pigment. Cotton print cloth. Scale: 5" × 6.5".

Instructions for inking and stamping:

"Inking" any stamp with pigments or dye paste presents some challenges and opportunities. Do you want the color applied thickly or thinly, evenly or unevenly? Your choice of inking method will determine the outcome.

Traditional rubber stamps are meant to be inked with a stamp pad or print roller. Most vendors that sell rubber stamps also sell "fillable" stamp pads, plain pieces of foam intended for ink to be added later. Instead, you can fill those pads with either dye paste or pigment for ease of coating stamps. If you need a larger inking surface, make your own stamp pad by saturating foam rubber or soft cotton cloth with colorant and place it in a plastic deli container.

Some nontraditional implements can be *dipped* directly into moderately thickened paste, and enough color will automatically adhere to them. While this approach is quick and direct, it tends to pick up excess pigment paste that, when pressed to the fabric, will squeeze out from beneath the implement—for better or worse, depending on what you want.

To achieve thinner and flatter layers of color on the fabric, use a sponge, sponge brush, or printing roller to apply the paste exactly where you want it on the object, tool, or stamp. Or, with a printing roller, spread an even layer of pigment on a piece of hard acrylic or plastic cutting board and press your stamp or tool into it. For a "marble" effect, you can also stripe or swirl separate colors onto the hard acrylic, roll over the mix with the print roller, and then dip the stamp.

Experiment with different ways to press the "loaded" implement onto the cloth. To get the most clear and accurate imprint of the stamp, hold it in place, then rock it around *slightly* in all directions, to make full and even contact. For quick impressions, hold the stamp or found object obliquely to the surface and dab quickly. Rotate and ink different sides of the same found object to create unexpected stamped marks or shapes; for example, the end of an old toothbrush instead of its bristles.

As you work, drop used stamps of all kinds into your bucket of soapy water. In the final cleanup, wash the implements carefully to preserve them for future use. Use an old toothbrush to scrub out cracks, edges, joints, and depressions in stamps. If you "borrowed" any household implements or tools, consider them permanent studio tools and never again use them for personal use or food preparation.

Direct-Application Techniques: Mechanical Resists

Many types of flat materials will create *mechanical resists*, physical barriers to the pigment that selectively preserve the underlying fabric color. You simply put the "resist" material on the fabric and then apply pigment around it (stickers), through it (stencils), or over it (tape or paper) with brushes or sponges. After the pigment dries, you remove the resist to reveal the preserved color. The contours of the resist material are faithfully recorded on the fabric.

03-22 Combined direct-application techniques. Dyed fabric ground, sponging, stamping, painting. Textile pigments. Cotton print cloth. Scale: 9" × 12".

03-23 Mechanical resists with masking tape. Cut strips and torn bits, canning and brush-painted background colors. Textile pigments. Cotton print cloth. Scale: 7" × 7.5".

Tape

Use masking or painter's tape for quick and spontaneous mechanical resists (03-23). Tape is flexible, is easily removed once the pigment dries, and can be found in various widths from ⅛" to 3". To make long lines or repeating stripes, use long strips. You can tear or cut the tape into short chunks, uneven or narrow strips, wavy or serrated lengths, or small shapes. Always apply tape to *dry fabric*. To create interesting variations in line or mark character, press the tape against the fabric flat, straight, curved, wrinkled, folded, or twisted. Press tape firmly in place along its length to make complete contact with the cloth. (Note: Remove masking tape promptly once it has served its purpose and the fabric is dry, because masking-tape adhesive will stain, "eat," and degrade cellulose fibers over time.)

Cut or Torn Papers

Almost any kind of paper can be cut in any shapes and arranged on the fabric as a mechanical resist, although it is challenging to *keep* the paper shapes in that arrangement as you work. With plain (nonadhesive) papers, thinned pigment or dye in a spray bottle disperses the color and captures edge details, without disrupting the composition or shifting individual paper pieces.

Freezer Paper

Freezer paper (available at most groceries) makes a great alternative. It is waxed on one side and absorbent on the other side. Cut or tear separate shapes or make a temporary stencil with the freezer paper. Place the paper, *waxed side down*, onto the clean dry fabric. Using a hot iron, briefly press the paper to the cloth (the wax provides a very light temporary adhesive). The paper will stay in place as you apply the pigment with a spray bottle, sponge, brush, or sponge brush (03-01, 03-12). Take care not to push pigment up under the adhered edges of the shapes. To prevent smudging or smearing, wait until the pigment is dry to peel the paper off the fabric.

Clear Contact Paper

The strong adhesive on clear contact paper makes firm resists or stencils. It comes with a paper backing, so you can cut the shapes you want and then peel the paper backing off to apply the shapes to the fabric. Contact paper can be reused until its adhesive begins to fail.

Found Objects as Resists

A wide variety of relatively flat found objects can be *laid* directly on the fabric to create a resist: string, cheesecloth, lace, onion bags, dry pasta, meshes, washers or screws, window screening, leaves, feathers, paper bits, artificial leaves or plants, burlap with threads pulled out. Experiment with spraying, sponging, daubing, or painting around or through the materials. Remove the objects after the pigment has dried.

"Rubbings"

When you were a child, you may have done texture rubbings for school projects: placing paper against tree trunks, sidewalks, gravestones, or other rough surfaces and then rubbing crayon, pencil, or charcoal across the paper to "magically" transfer the underlying textures or images to the paper. In much the same way, you can place found objects or textured materials *under* your fabric to generate an impression of their surface textures, in colors of your own choosing. Materials with minimal thickness such as leaves, lace, meshes, and bark work best. Simply place the items under the fabric, aligned where you want their textures to appear, then use a roller or daub with a sponge to apply a light, thin, even layer of pigment over the top. Quickly clean up the roller and sponge to preserve them for future use.

Manipulated Fabric Resists

Instead of *adding* something to the fabric to resist the colorant, you can use the fabric's own properties to create a resist. Scrunch, pleat, tuck, gather, or fold the fabric and pin it down to the work surface in that form *before* applying the pigment with spray bottles, sponge brushes, or rollers. The areas of fabric inside the three-dimensional manipulations will be protected from the colorant. You can also do a second manipulation and application of pigment, in the same or different color, *after* the first has dried to the touch.

Stickers or Adhesive Sheets

Press-apply stickers or dots (03-10, 03-24, 03-25) can be stuck directly to the fabric and pulled off after the pigment has been applied and dried, making a "negative" shape in the original color of your fabric. Self-adhesive labels come in a wide variety of sizes and shapes: dots, labels, shapes, letters, and numbers. Cut your own shapes from large labels, adhesive sheets, or contact paper. To avoid disturbing or smearing the colorant, wait to remove the stickers or adhesive shapes until the pigment is dry. If desired, the resisted area can then be filled with other colors and markings.

03-24 Sponging (*background*), mechanical resist with large press-apply dots, drawing with thinned pigment in squeeze bottle (red accent lines). Textile pigment. Cotton print cloth. Scale: 7.5" × 9.5".

ABOVE: 03-25 Combined direct-application techniques. Painted ground, mechanical resist with press-apply stickers and tiny dots, sponging (black), sgraffito with fork tines. Textile pigments. Cotton print cloth. Scale: 11" × 8".

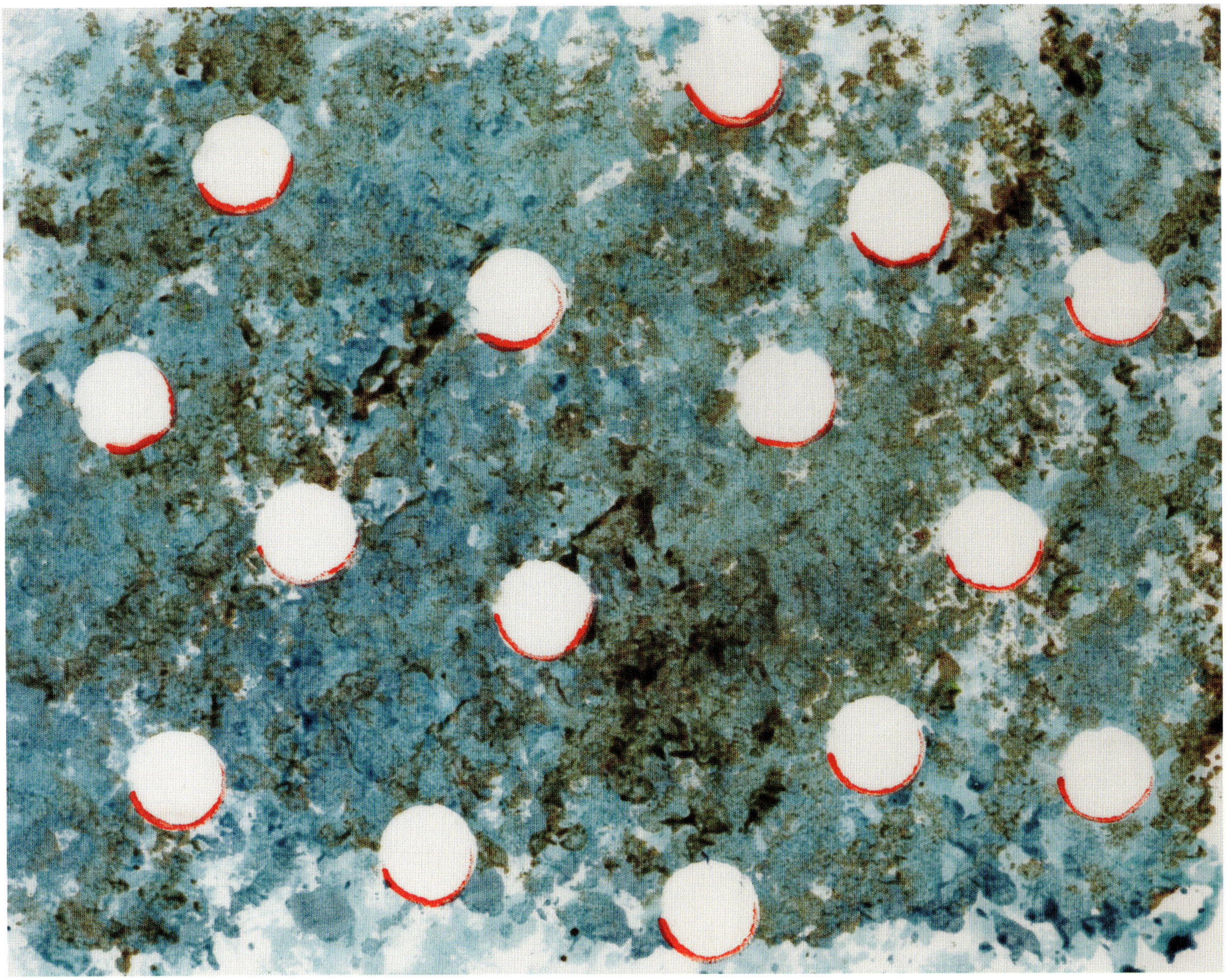

Stencils

Stencils allow you to design your own specific shapes and then admit pigment to the fabric only through those cutout shapes. Although you can purchase many plastic stencils in art supply and craft stores (as used in 03-26 and 03-27), it's easy to make your own custom stencils with materials from home. Nearly any thick paper will work, such as waxed paper, freezer paper, food packages, gift boxes, or index card stock. Check your waste or recycling bin for options.

Freezer paper makes stable and *fixed* temporary stencils when ironed onto the clean and dry fabric before adding the wet color. To make more durable handheld *movable* stencils, use cardboard or card stock and reinforce it with clear contact paper on both sides to maintain the shape to "waterproof" the stencil. For *washable* custom stencils in any size, use mylar or plastic sheets from your local art and craft store and hand-cut your own designs with a precision craft knife.

Stencil edges acquire the character of the cutting or tearing method. For example, cut edges tend to be crisp and clear; torn edges tend to be soft and fuzzy. Stencils can be simple or complex, spaced densely or sparsely across the surface, overlapped slightly or fully, and repeated endlessly in any location or orientation to layer and combine transparent colors and shapes.

03-26 Combined direct-application techniques. Monoprinting, painting, pigment forced through plastic checkerboard stencil with sponge. Textile pigment. Cotton print cloth. Scale: 5.5" × 6.5".

Instructions for using stencils:

Iron freezer paper stencils onto the clean dry fabric to keep them in place. If using cardboard or plastic stencils, use your hand to press them firmly against the cloth. If using the same stencil on multiple areas of the cloth, carefully lift and move it to avoid smearing previously applied pigment. Apply the paste by dabbing straight downward repeatedly with a sponge or sponge brush until you have deposited the desired amount of color. Avoid brushstrokes toward the edges of the holes, which will force color beneath the stencil edges, and avoid excessive amounts of pigment for the same reason.

To save and reuse the stencils, clean them (I actually wash plastic stencils with soap and water but use a wet cloth to wipe the contact paper faces of cardboard stencils). Let them dry *flat* on a tabletop. Once they're dry, store them flat but with some pressure, perhaps in a file folder between two heavy books. (This is true even for plastic stencils, which, if their material is thin, can still curl.)

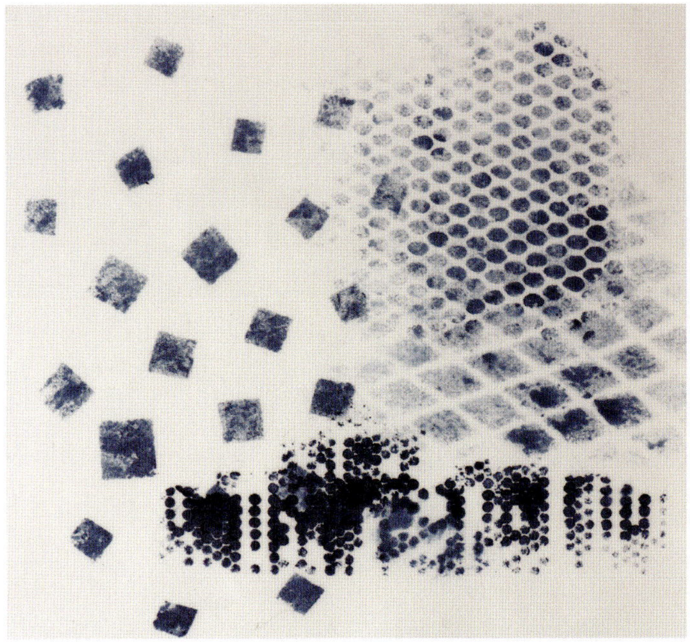

03-27 Stencils. Hand-cut freezer paper (squares), commercial stencil (very tiny dots), two sizes of plastic mesh (ovals and diamonds). Textile pigment. Cotton print cloth. Scale: 8" × 8".

03-28 Linework. Sponged background, large painted strokes using fan-shaped brush, gestural drawing (red) using thinned pigment in squeeze bottle. Textile pigments. Heavy cotton twill. Scale: 4" × 4".

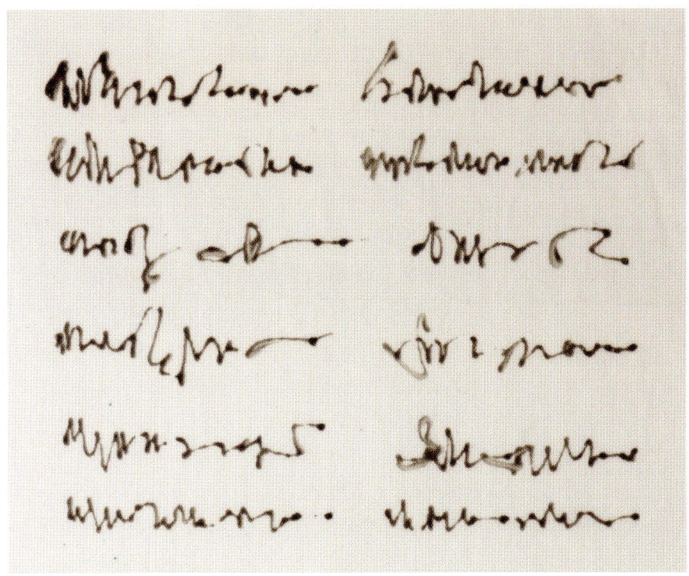

03-29 Linework. Drawing with thinned textile pigment in squeeze bottle to create marks that resemble longhand text or script. Cotton print cloth. Scale: 7" × 8".

Direct-Application Techniques: Linework

This category of direct application includes three major categories: drawing, painting, and sgraffito, all of which produce bold or delicate lines, realistic or abstract images, longhand writing or printed text. The techniques come directly from the traditional fine arts, though translated with tools and colorants appropriate for and permanent on fabric. In linework, you mark directly on the cloth, leaving traces of the inconsistencies, peculiarities, and unique qualities of your hand—a figurative or literal "signature."

Drawing

Drawing on fabric is very much like drawing on paper, with the exception that paper usually stays put as you work, while the more flexible structures of cloth stretch, shift, and expand with the addition of pressure from your hand and moisture from the pigment. Thus, for drawing, choose tightly woven cloth *stretched taut*, then pinned or taped *firmly* in place. (On loosely stretched fabric, the pressure of your drawing tool will raise up wrinkles of fabric and impede forward motion of the line.) Once the fabric is flat and stationary, you can draw lines of any length, dimension, color, or character on it. When dried and unpinned, the fabric will resume its naturally occurring folds and drapes and distort, hide, or enhance parts of the drawing. The intimacy of drawing brings you in close physical contact with the tools and the cloth, thus capturing your own gestural idiosyncrasies along with the particular characteristics of the tool you choose and the fabric's surface qualities.

You can do linework directly on dry fabric with the same tools you might use on paper: pencils, colored pencils, crayons, and markers.

- *Drawing with pencils*: Plain graphite pencils are permanent on fabric, which you will have discovered if you have ever tried to wash pencil marks out of your clothing. Choose those with softer lead to accommodate the weave of the fabric more easily as you draw. Use them as you would on paper: to sketch, to draw in great detail, to add precise outlines, or to add accents. If the resulting fabric will be handled a great deal or washed, brush or screen a layer of transparent extender over the drawing to preserve it from possible smudging.

- *Drawing with colored pencils*: If you like to use colored pencils, you will be delighted to know that they can be used directly on cloth. If the fabric will not be washed, you can use any kind of colored pencil you like. If you want something more permanent, draw with *watercolor pencils* directly on the stretched cloth, then screen or brush over the drawing with transparent extender to seal the marks to the cloth.

03-30 Linework. Drawing with watercolor pencils directly on fabric, overprinted with solid square of transparent extender. Cotton print cloth. Scale: 7.5" × 7.5".

- *Drawing with crayons*: If you like the characteristic marks of crayons (03-30), buy the ones specifically formulated for cloth (lines using regular crayons flake or rub off over time). To seal the marks to the cloth, paint over them with a layer of transparent extender.

- *Drawing with pre-inked markers*: The colored markers now common in the artist's toolbox for illustrating and drawing on paper are equally useful on fabric. Both washable and permanent varieties exist, some formulated specifically for fabric, and others for use on any surface. If the idea appeals to you, try an assortment of markers in a single color and test their characteristics, until you find the tip size, material, and flow you like the best for your purposes. Note that some markers have a strong smell and can leave behind an unpleasant odor that is hard to remove from cloth.

You can do linework with textile pigments by using refillable pens, dip pens, ruling pens, squeeze bottles, and syringes.

- *Drawing with "refillable" pens and refillable markers*: You can load the receptacles of refillable pens and markers with a pigment "slurry" (thinner than heavy cream but not watery) in your own custom colors. You want the color to flow through the pen but not run out all at once. Draw directly on tightly stretched cloth with a steady pressure. The tool may require frequent refilling. Follow the manufacturer's instructions for cleaning the tool immediately after use.

- *Drawing with dip pens*: These are still in wide use by calligraphers, so they're available with assorted sizes of interchangeable tips. Dip them directly into pigment or dye paste thinned to about the consistency of cream. Wash the tips thoroughly after use.

- *Drawing with ruling pens*: Once the technical tool of choice for graphic designers, a *ruling pen* has two curved flexible writing "blades" or jaws that meet at the tip and are connected by a screw that controls the spacing between them. The screw controls the amount of open space between the blades and provides a place where ink or pigment can be "stored" before flowing down the pen and onto the paper or cloth (this requires practice and some skill). Thinned textile pigment works quite nicely in a ruling pen, allowing the same kind of control over the drawn line as you would have with a pencil, pen, or marker.

- *Drawing with squeeze bottles and syringes*: To make large marks or work on larger pieces of fabric, you may want a continuous stream of pigment that makes long lines *without re-inking*. In that case, thin the pigment or dye paste to the consistency of cream and load it into a squeeze bottle (as used in 03-09) or syringe (03-08) with a selection of interchangeable tips in different sizes. While both these tools require some practice to control, they are very effective at making marks (03-32), making fluid lines (03-28, 03-31), and writing text (03-29). Clean out the bottle or syringe and its tips quickly after each use, before the pigment dries to a permanent clog.

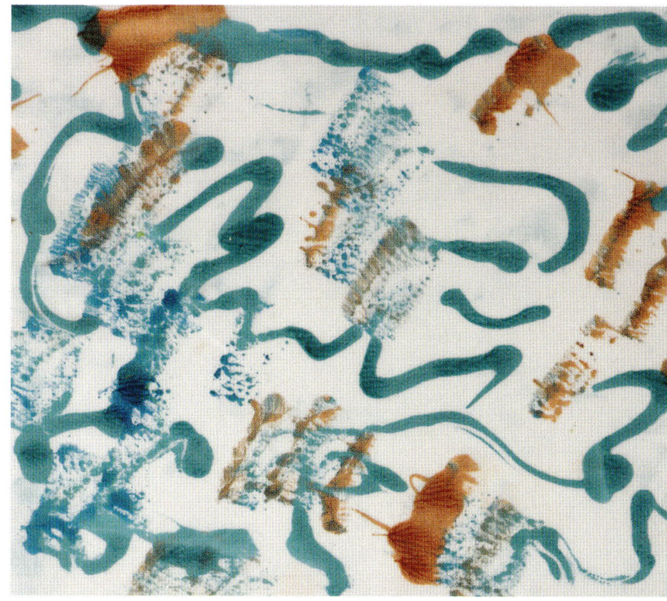

03-31 Linework. Drawing with thinned textile pigment in squeeze bottle to create fatter lines. Cotton print cloth. Scale: 8" × 8".

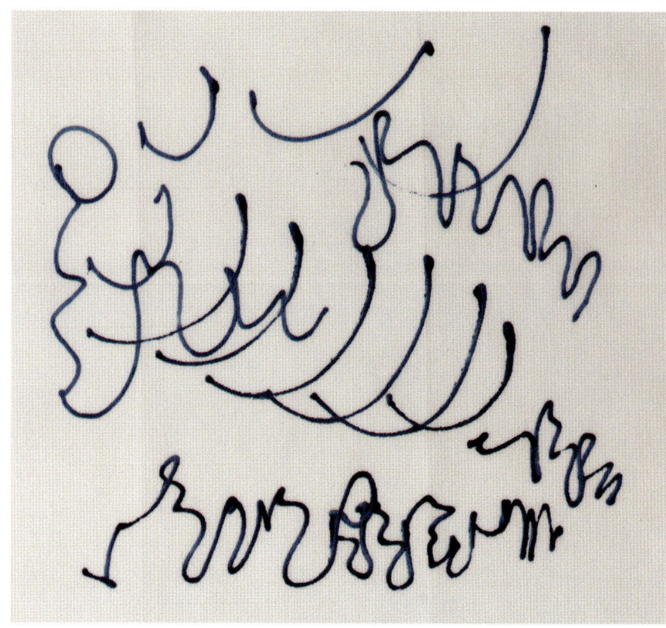

03-32 Linework. Thin looping lines, drawn with thinned textile pigment in squeeze bottle. Cotton print cloth. Scale: 8" × 8".

Painting

Dragging a loaded brush across a fabric surface feels very much like painting on canvas or watercolor paper; the grittiness of the surface radiates up through the tool. In fact, the texture of the fabric surface in large part determines the type of mark left behind. Consider this when selecting both fabric textures and brush types. Styles of painting range as widely as the hands wielding the brushes. Choose your tools and work in ways that express your ideas.

Generally, you can use the same brushes with textile pigments as you would for acrylic or watercolor painting on canvas or paper. A visit to your local art supply store or online supplier will reveal a wide variety, each with an identifiable characteristic shape and *brush mark*. Try round (03-34), flat (03-28), fan-shaped (03-12, 03-16), angular (03-22), pointed, and blunt brushes (03-33) in a variety of sizes or combine them for a complex result (03-02). To add a small dash of life to a composition, use a fine brush to apply highly contrasting colors (03-04).

Try some *unconventional* brushes to work color into fabric: toothbrushes will produce either rough parallel marks or long scratchy lines, scrub brushes can make large gestures or swooshes of color on a large fabric, and if you are working *really large*, try using a whisk broom to make lines and gestures! A tip: protect the work surface and surrounding floor with sheet plastic to catch spatters and drips from vigorous brushing.

Painting invites the creation of a color palette, a collection of colors, perhaps derived from a source or visual influence, that you assemble on a single cloth. Depending on the type and scale of your projects, choose an approach to mixing that makes sense: (1) mix custom colors in small amounts as the need arises, and use each one immediately; or (2) lay out a palette of large globs (2–4 T.) of pure colors (mixed in extender) on a metal tray or plastic dish, then dip into each one in a "painterly" way to mix custom colors in rapid sequence as you need them; or (3) start with equal amounts of extender (¼–½ c. each) in small containers with tight-fitting lids and mix an entire color palette to store for future use.

03-33 Linework. Painting with a variety of brush types (round, flat, fan shaped) and strokes (dabs, swooshes, twists), varied amounts of color in the brush. Textile pigments. Cotton print cloth. Scale: 7" × 7".

03-34 Painting. Monoprinted and sponged background; painted swoosh with fan brush (brown) and small round brush (blue). Textile pigments. Heavy cotton twill. Scale: 3.5" × 3.5".

Sgraffito

Sgraffito is essentially drawing *into* or *through wet paint*. (Think of it as a more sophisticated version of finger painting!) On fabric, it consists of drawing into *thickly* applied *wet* textile *pigment* to create a subtle drawing revealing the color(s) beneath the applied pigment. (Dye pastes usually don't work well with sgraffito, because they wick too quickly into the fibers.) Because bits of the thick layers of pigment will fall off if washed, sgraffito is best used on fabrics that will *not* be washed (for example, don't use sgraffito on clothing or linens).

03-35 Sgraffito. Multiple colors painted onto fabric surface, scraped through with large marking implement. Textile pigments. Cotton print cloth. Scale: 10" × 13".

Instructions for sgraffito:

Use pins to stretch your fabric tightly on the work surface. Apply masking tape over the pins and cover the edges of the fabric. Use a sponge brush to apply a thick layer of pigment in either a single color (03-03) or multiple colors (03-36). Work quickly while the pigment is still wet; draw through the pigment with almost any implement that achieves the kind of mark you want. For example, try the handle end of a paintbrush, the tip of a knitting needle, a comb, a fork, or the scraping tools used to make decorative end papers for books (03-04, 03-10, 03-37). The sgraffito marks will reveal any underlying colors on the fabric. For example, in 03-35 the fabric had first been painted in several colors with a large brush. Then the blue was laid over everything and scraped through with a large implement. Play with tools and combinations to develop your own visual "vocabulary." Wash off the implements as soon as you are done with them. Let the fabric sit undisturbed to dry thoroughly (at least overnight) before you move it to cure.

03-36 Sgraffito. Multiple colors daubed on surface with sponge brush, scratched through with blunt end of a paintbrush. Textile pigment. Cotton print cloth. Scale: 9" × 8".

03-37 Sgraffito. Painted and sponged colors, scraped through with rubber comb. Textile pigment. Cotton print cloth. Scale: 5.5" × 11".

Direct-Application Techniques: Monoprinting

Once again we'll borrow, and modify, a technique from the world of improvisational printmaking. In monoprinting on *paper*, a design painted on glass is transferred with direct contact to the paper surface with pressure. For fabric surfaces, we'll use pigment in extender or thickened dye paste, painted on a piece of Plexiglas or regular glass (with edges taped for safety).

Unlike stamps, which can be reused to produce the same image again and again, monoprints create one-of-a-kind painted gestures, images, and spontaneous marks. In monoprinting you're painting the plate itself, which is the reason a specific image or color arrangement can be printed on fabric only once, but monoprinting also offers a built-in "safety net" to adjust or change details *before* they're pressed onto the fabric. If you don't like what you've painted, you can scrape off the pigment, reapply it to the plate, change its position, or completely wash the plate and start over. Designs can be simple and spontaneous, or very complex and multicolored.

Caveat: Because this is a printing technique in which fabric and plate are in face-to-face contact, the *image will be reversed* in the print (like a reflection seen in a mirror). This is especially important to remember with images that include text or numbers.

03-38 Monoprinting with a pair of pressed plates. Color applied to a Plexiglas plate, then pressed against a second plate, then separated and printed side by side. Textile pigments. Cotton print cloth. Scale: 5.25" × 11".

Instructions for monoprinting:

Buy or cut pieces of Plexiglas (or real glass with taped edges) to the size you want. (For the illustrations in this section, I used 6" square Plexiglas plates, but you can actually use round, triangular, hexagonal, free-form, or any shape of your choosing.) Mix all the pigment colors (thick application) for your design and have them at hand. Place a drop cloth on the worktable. Place the plate on top of the drop cloth so that the side to be painted is facing upward. Use any tools or implements you wish to apply the color to the plate (brushes, sponge brushes, stamps, found objects). If you apply the color in layers, those applied first will lie in the background of the final print; those applied last will be in the foreground. The flatter the application of color to the plate, the less the pigment will squeeze sideways and distort the marks when pressed against the fabric. The thicker the pigment application, the more likely to squeeze (03-38 and 03-39).

If you work slowly, add a *retardant* (available at print supply companies) to the pigment to slow its drying time until you are ready to print. When you complete the design to your satisfaction, you are ready to transfer it to the fabric by either of the following approaches:

- *Monoprinting with small plates (those easily held in one hand)*: Place the fabric, *front side up*, on the padded surface. Hold the painted plate by the edges, *turned facedown*, and press it against the fabric. Slightly rock the plate in various directions to make full contact with the fabric in all parts of the design. When you are convinced that the print is complete, begin from one side of the plate to carefully peel it up and away from the fabric in a single, slow, smooth action. Set the plate aside. Hang the print to dry. Clean the plate thoroughly with soap and water.

- *Monoprinting with large plates*: Unlike small-plate monoprinting, in which the plate is moved onto the fabric, in this procedure the fabric is moved onto the plate. Leave the painted plate lying *faceup* on the worktable. Drop the *front* of the fabric, as *evenly* as possible, onto the painted plate. Then, starting in the *center* (to minimize any movement of the fabric on the plate) and using your hand or a brayer, press the cloth against the glass, working outward to make sure that all parts of the fabric come in complete contact with the plate. When you are convinced that the print is complete, pull the *fabric* up and away from the plate in a single, slow, smooth action. Hang the print to dry. Clean the plate thoroughly with soap and water.

- *Monoprinting with a pair of pressed plates*: This fun patterning alternative with monoprinting starts with two *equally* sized and identically shaped Plexiglas plates. Drop or deposit dollops of various colors onto one of the Plexiglas plates, then, with plate edges aligned, press the other one straight and firmly down onto it. This will make the pigment spread out in unplanned directions. *Without twisting them* against each other, pull the plates straight apart. There will be a bit of suction when you do this, and it will pull up the pigment into tiny points. The plates will now bear interesting organic designs, in mirror image. Each plate can be pressed onto fabric in any alignment, location, or orientation. Like ink blot patterns, no two of these are the same (03-38, 03-39). These squiggly patterns can stand on their own or provide a background texture for added marks and gestures (03-08).

03-39 Monoprinting with a pair of pressed plates. Color applied to a Plexiglas plate, then pressed against a second plate, then separated and printed side by side. Textile pigments. Pale-green dyed cotton print cloth. Scale: 5.5" × 11".

03-40 Shaving-cream resist. Combed. Fiber reactive dye paste. Cotton print cloth. Scale: 9" × 8".

03-41 Combined direct-application techniques. Sponging (ground), stamping (green spirals), stencil (orange squares), and drawing with squeeze bottle (black outlines). Textile pigments. Cotton print cloth. Scale: 8" × 13".

- *Monoprinting with shaving cream and thickened dye paste*: I learned this easy-to-do technique from my good friend and colleague Christine. It mimics paper marbling on fabric (see 03-40). Cover your table or printing surface with a sheet of plastic. Apply *foam-type* shaving cream directly to the plastic surface and smooth it out and down into a thin layer as large as your intended piece of fabric. (If you find that you still don't have enough shaving cream, add more and smooth it out again.) Place thickened, activated dye paste in a couple of areas (pigment paste usually doesn't work well for this technique). Then drag a comb or fork with widely spaced teeth back and forth through the paste and cream. When you have an arrangement you like, place your piece of fabric on top of the cream and *lightly* press it down (only enough to make full contact but not squirt shaving cream and dye across the table!) to make a monoprint of the surface. Pull the fabric up off the table and allow it to dry completely. Set the dye (see chapter 1) before washing and rinsing appropriately.

Postscript: Combined Techniques

I created most of the illustrations in this chapter by combining several interacting direct-application techniques (for examples, see the image captions of 03-41 and 03-42). For me, and I hope for you, the excitement of direct application arises from mixing and layering the different techniques for expressive purposes, interesting compositions, decorative patterns, detailed borders and bands, or layered marks. The more you experiment, the more ideas you'll develop. The way *you* wield the tools, combine colors, and apply pigment will carry forward the gestures of your hand and reveal your way of thinking. Because the techniques are fast, you can experiment very widely in a relatively short period of time.

03-42 Combined direct-application techniques. Dyed, screen-printed, and discharge-printed background; stamped with sponge dauber; dinner fork tines; painting (black brush marks); sgraffito with fork and comb. Textile pigments. Cotton print cloth. Scale: 9" × 12".

Try this!

03-43 Example of color-mixing test strip in progress, showing the marked rectangles and labels for color categories.

3.1 Color-mixing test strip

This exercise introduces the physical properties and mixing characteristics of textile pigments. The goal: reduce color theory to practical and expressive applications. In the process it will broaden your understanding of color interactions, focus your eye on specific rather than generic colors, improve the accuracy of your color-mixing skills, and sharpen your ability to observe, and then match, specific colors.

This is a challenging exercise, but even beginners can "get it," and over the course of many years my surface design students have told me it was one of the most important exercises I ever gave them, and established the foundation for their understanding of color on fabric. When you see that it involves mixing 43 different colors, your first reaction may be *"43!!???"* But there is a reason for that number: to move you beyond obvious and easy "color" (your "favorites," or the very first things that pop into your mind) and into more nuanced mixing of *color*.

To start: Tear a 6" wide × 45" long strip of white cotton fabric. Use size 20 T pins to stretch it tightly to a drop-cloth-protected padded surface (if your padded surface is less than 45", you can move the strip as needed during the exercise). You're going to draw a series of small rectangles, each of which will contain a separate color sample. With a permanent black marker and a metal yardstick, moving quickly to prevent too much wicking (or a graphite pencil, which, being nonliquid, won't require you to move as quickly), mark off a 3" × 44" rectangle centered along the length of the fabric (leaving space at the fabric margins, in which you'll later label the color samples) and divide that 3" rectangle into 43 segments of 1" × 3" each (see 03-43 for a strip in progress).

Mix and paint: Mix *small* amounts of 43 *distinctly different* colors (not simply tints, tones, and shades of one or two hues) in the categories listed below. As you mix, some colors may be transparent and some (generally those containing white) will be opaque. Fill each 1" × 3" strip with a single custom-mixed color in the categories listed below. You can do the categories in any order you wish, but for simplicity and visual clarity, group *together* the colors within any single category (all of your primaries, all of your tints, all of your tones, etc.). Don't be tempted to make a second strip. Using only one forces you to mix carefully and to pay continuing attention to the way surrounding colors influence the look—"in context"—of each new color added. The most important part of the challenge: when the strip is complete, no color should repeat or *seem* to repeat by its context. Keep a color wheel and value scale at hand for reference.

The 43 color categories:

- 3 primary colors: cyan, magenta, yellow
- 12 colors containing black, white, or gray, of which 4 are tints (light/high-value colors *clearly* containing white), 4 are tones (medium-value colors *clearly* containing gray), and 4 are shades (low/dark-value colors *clearly* containing black)
- 12 value samples: 4 high value (near white on the value scale—think pastels; light, airy colors), 4 medium value (corresponding to middle grays on the value scale), 4 low value (near black on the value scale, very dark)
- 8 intensity samples: 4 high intensity (bright colors—think Hawaiian shirts); 4 low intensity (dull colors—think camouflage or colors you can't name)
- 8 temperature samples: 4 warm colors and 4 cool colors (in a variety of values and intensities)

A few technical tips for the exercise:

- In the unmarked border of your color strip, use pen, pencil, or marker to write the names of the categories (three rectangles under a notation "Primary Colors," four rectangles under "Tints," and so on).
- Keep a separate test fabric alongside your strip, to practice your brush technique and colors *before* you paint on the strip.
- You'll need to completely fill each rectangle with color in order to fully see its color in context with the others. (Just placing a little shapeless "blob" of pigment in each rectangle won't be sufficient.) To maintain straight edges on your color rectangles, use masking tape to temporarily separate each rectangle from its neighbor. This means you'll have to "hop" down the strip, leaving alternate rectangles dry while you fill others, then return to fill the rectangles still left empty. (Yes, after the first round of painted rectangles has dried, you can put masking tape on *them* while you paint *their* neighbors.)
- Apply the color with a sponge brush.
- Excess water in the sponge brush will make the color leak under the masking tape. You'll need to wash out the brush each time you move to a new color, but make sure to squeeze excess water from the brush into a paper towel, rag, or old cloth towel. Better yet, have several already-washed brushes in different stages of air drying as you move from color to color.
- Colors already painted in the strips *can* be changed by painting over them with other color, but *only* to darken, intensify, or de-intensify them. They can't be easily or invisibly lightened, even with white (opaque) pigment.

Make some notes about what you learned in this exercise. Could you remix the colors in the strip if challenged to do so? Did you move out of your "comfort zone" with the colors you mixed?

3.2 Practice direct-application techniques with textile pigments

To test and familiarize yourself with the basic direct-application techniques, gather your supplies, tools, pigments, and fabrics and set up your padded print surface in an area where you can spread out and work without having to stop and clean up until the session is over. Prepare your print surface, cover it with a drop cloth (unless you added the plastic cover), and have T pins and masking tape ready. Wash, cut to size (about 8" × 8" is a good size), and press a stack of 10 to 12 simple white cotton fabric pieces, ready to pin to your print surface. Use a fresh piece of fabric for each new technique or idea. String a clothesline (not necessarily a full-fledged laundry line; it could just be heavy cord tied to two chairs or two doorknobs) and have a bag of clothespins nearby to hang each completed print to dry.

The goal: using textile pigments, mix a palette of colors drawn directly from and matching those in your color mixing strip from exercise 3.1. Include a range of light and dark, bright and dull, warm and cool colors in your palette. Choose and practice at least two techniques in each of the five categories discussed in this chapter: large color areas, repeating shapes and patterns, mechanical resists, linework, and monoprinting. Be inventive and spontaneous and work quickly. Don't think too much right now! Combine and overlay colors to see what happens. Make the samples as complex or simple as you wish. Get your hands dirty and play!

3.3 Practice direct-application techniques with dyes: Predicting color shifts

This is a quick exercise to practice using thickened dye for direct application. Prepare five 8" × 8" pieces of white cotton fabric. Using thickened dye (see chapter 1), make one sample from each category of direct-application techniques: large color areas, repeating shapes or patterns, mechanical resists, linework, and monoprinting. Use two warm colors and two cool colors to create any kind of gestures or shapes you wish. While each sample is still wet, *cut it in half.*

Set aside one-half of each sample to air-dry. With the other half, complete the processing (instructions in chapter 1): batch or heat set, wash, dry, and press. Compare the color in the two halves (one fully processed, one not) of each sample. What percentage change or color shift do you observe? Did the hue change? The value? The intensity? Does the *amount* of change alter with different dye colors? Make some notes in your sample book (see Appendix C).

3.4 Expressive compositions: A collection of direct-application "prints"

Direct-application techniques provide many ways to experiment with ideas, techniques, and color interactions, but they can also be used to create spontaneously composed *finished* compositions on cloth. Now that you have tested a variety of techniques (in 3.2), you are ready to precisely match colors and develop your own fresh imagery in a set of unique "prints."

The goal: create a set of six prints, one for each of the different compositional goals (with their supporting color requirements) listed in the chart below. Use an 8.5" × 11" piece of white fabric for each of the prints. On each one, combine *at least three* direct-application methods and *at least six* different hues based on a specific photograph or color source (see chart below).

Steps:

- Sketch compositions: With a pencil on paper (*not* the fabric itself), develop several (three or four) alternative rough (black and white) thumbnail (2" × 2") sketches for each print's composition. The composition should convey the goal or effect in the right column of the chart above. This is a chance to combine marks, shapes, and color for personal expression.

Compositional Structure	Color Palette	Goal/Effect
1. Change in density or concentration of elements across the surface	Complementary color relationship	Eye popping, energetic
2. Organic shapes, packed into the space, with little background showing	Neutrals	Subtle, quiet, calm
3. Overlapping shapes	Analogous color relationship	Gradations, blending, transparency
4. Geometric, hard-edged shapes in combination	High contrast of either value or intensity	Dramatic, crisp, and clear
5. Texture contrast	Low-value contrast + consistent intensity	Texture changes across the surface (such as rough to smooth, scratchy to silky: your choice)
6. Composite stripes (stripes composed of linear formations or repeated elements)	Triad color relationship, with value and intensity range	Lively and directional, vibrating

- Choose photographic color sources: Find one *separate* complex photograph as a color source for each print according to the *color palette* column on the chart. Choose six photographs (one for each print), using the chart. Then choose six colors from each photo that you'll *match precisely* to create your print. Some tips for choosing the photos: Work from actual "hard copy" photographs that you've taken yourself or cut out of high-quality magazines. Avoid using images on a computer screen or phone, online stock photos, preorganized color palettes, other people's printed textiles, and advertising photos (which often use very simplistic colors). Look for photos with complex and well-distributed color stories.

- Mix pigments: Mix the colors to match each of your sources as exactly as possible, allowing for the differences caused by surface slickness or dullness on the photo. To help convey the total color feeling of the source, try to apply the colors to your prints in nearly the same proportion as you find them in the source. Have the colors mixed and ready to go before you start to work. Then start printing and have fun. Process when done.

- Evaluate: When all six prints are completed, put them up on the wall and make notes about their relative success. Check each one against the goals or effects listed in the chart. Which print meets the challenge best? Why? Which print needs more work? What is needed to improve its quality?

3.5 THE CUMULATIVE CLOTH CHALLENGE

Start with at least one of the resist-dyed fabrics you completed in chapter 2. This fabric should already have an overall dyed background color, and resist-dyed markings. In this part of the challenge, with selected direct-application techniques, add marks and shapes that enhance, contrast, define, detail, expand, or embellish the resist-dyed marks already present on the cloth. Think about what areas you might most like to emphasize, and others you might want to hide or de-emphasize. Develop these areas of the design or composition. Air-cure or heat-set and wash. Make a note about the pigment colors and methods you used, and take a photograph of the fabric. Set it aside for the challenge in chapter 4.

4 / SCREEN PRINTING: REPETITION AND COMPOSITION

04-01 Custom screen-printed fabrics, pieced and machine appliquéd. Textile pigments. Cotton broadcloth and heavy twill. Scale: about 8" × 12".

From the relative spontaneity of direct-application techniques such as stamping, stenciling, block printing, or monoprinting, we now move to *screen printing*, a more formal, orderly, and faster technique for repeating images, motifs, and continuous patterns, especially on larger images and longer lengths of fabric. *Screen printing* replaces *handheld* stencils with stencils affixed to fabric mesh, supported by a rigid frame. Using either textile pigments or dye paste, the screen allows you to repeat the stencil image as many times, and in as many orientations or placements on the fabric, as you wish. While screen printing is strongly connected to repeat pattern yardage, and placing all motifs lined on a grid, there are far more fun and spontaneous ways to use the technique. In this chapter, we'll explore the more free-form approaches first but, for those interested, will cover the repeat pattern approach later in the chapter. For your purposes in building a cumulative cloth, screen printing produces quick repetitions of shapes and motifs.

This chapter focuses on screen-printing techniques suitable for the individual maker in a home or group studio, which do not involve toxic chemicals (lacquers, drawing fluid, mineral spirits) or specialized equipment (for example, access to a photo darkroom). It will also focus on temporary block-outs (stencils) for their flexibility, ease of use, and safety. If you have a genuine need for permanent stencils to be used for extensive repeat printing, or in production work, the supplies are available from screen-printing companies and art supply stores. Consult the manufacturer for appropriate techniques, MSDS, and safety precautions. Use them only in an appropriately safe and well-ventilated studio environment such as a university, community college, or professional print studio that can provide the appropriate studio support and safe disposal of used chemicals. If you wish to produce *photographic* images on fabric, consider having custom photo-emulsion screens prepared for you, or use a commercial service that can transfer your own digital photographic file to printed cloth. (See also chapter 5 for a brief discussion of digital printing at home.)

From the time people first made images on cave walls, they used handheld stencils (or their own hands) to repeat shapes (as we did in chapter 3). What we would recognize today as true *screen printing* had its roots in China and Japan (about 960–1279 CE), where stencils attached to meshes made of human hair and stretched on wooden frames added stability and a firm grip for the artist. By the 18th century, screen printing made its way to Europe and finally became widely used when *silk mesh* was reliably available in trade from the East and could be stretched over a wooden frame (that's why early references described this process as *silk screen* printing, and many people still do). Stiff brushes were originally used to force colorants through the screen stencil but were replaced by rubber *squeegees* in the 19th century. Held in the hand, these rubber blades disperse a thin, even layer of colored paste on the fabric in clean and even sweeps.

In practice, screen printing provides the means to efficiently and reliably print things in multiples, editions, sequences, or series. This characteristic of the technique offers a natural vehicle for storytelling, pattern construction, decoration, fabric books (04-02), editions of prints, and personal expression. In addition to a wide choice of image types, you control the expressive character, quality, and relationship of the custom-mixed colors you use to print.

Screen-printed goods are ubiquitous in modern life, whether produced in industry or in an artist's studio, in the form of repeated identical images or patterns on a variety of surfaces and products: fabric yardage for clothing or quilts;

04-02 Fabric book. Hand-dyed, screen-printed, discharge-printed, fused, appliquéd, stitched. Textile pigments, Procion MX fiber reactive dyes, discharge paste. Silk noil, torpedo silk, silk organza, cotton broadcloth, Lutradur, cotton velveteen, fusible web. Scale: 8" × 12" × ½".

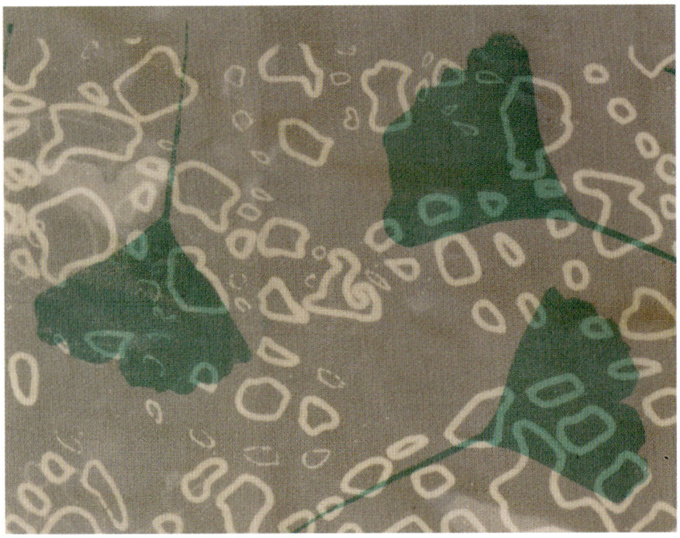

fabrics for pillows, accessories, and wall hangings; T-shirt logos, hats, scarves, dinner napkins, or tablecloths; prints on various types of paper for playing cards, napkins, tablecloths, greeting cards, and wallpaper; and even adapted for use on ceramics, metals, and wood surfaces. You can find inspiration in any of these, but above all I encourage you to think of screen printing as an *artistic tool.*

04-03 Single-element ginkgo leaf stencil image allows flexible repetition and free placement. Overprinted on dyed and discharge-printed fabric. Procion MX fiber reactive dyes, discharge paste, textile pigments. Cotton print cloth. Scale: 3" × 4".

Studio Setup for Screen Printing

Screen printing requires a few additions or alterations to your dye workspace. If you restrict your printing to very small screens (under 8.5" × 11"), the setup is relatively simple. However, bigger screens and more ambitious large-scale projects require more substantial equipment, supplies, and space to print. Support for production printing (for example, yardage, limited-edition fabric prints, production lines of scarves or table linens) is a major investment.

In addition to the screens and stencils, at a minimum you'll need access to a large, deep utility sink with a sprayer (to wash out screens); a squeegee whose handle feels comfortable in your hand and whose blade is slightly wider than the open (printing) area of your stencils; and a padded printing table or portable printing surface large enough to stretch out your fabric at full size. We'll explore each of these in detail.

04-04 Three layers of overlaid contrasting (not interlocking) patterns. Textile pigments. Cotton print cloth. Scale: 8" × 8".

BUYING SCREEN-PRINTED FABRICS: AN ALTERNATIVE TO SCREEN PRINTING

If you like the idea of using printed fabrics in your work but don't want to print them yourself, there is a reasonable alternative, one that will still allow you to use the various "dry" techniques in the companion *Dry Techniques* book: buy commercially printed or artisan-printed fabrics. While you'll sacrifice control of color and precise image, you can still find much on the market to satisfy your needs. You'll find the greatest selection of printed fabrics in quilt shops (mostly printed on the 100% cottons that quilters prefer), in fabric stores (in the quilting section), and at textile or quilting conferences and trade shows. Prints are available in a dizzying array of colors, scales, and layouts; pattern types in multiple colorways range from stripes, checks, and small novelty patterns to batiks, figures, and seasonal holiday patterns.

If you choose this alternative, think about the way you want to use the fabric, then select appropriate patterns, scales, and colors for your projects. Wash the fabric before using it. Use the fabric as it is printed, or use textile pigments to directly apply your own marks and colors (as discussed in chapter 3) to enhance or transform the cloth into your own creation.

SUPPLY CHECKLIST FOR SCREEN PRINTING

- padded print surface
- large sink with sprayer
- screens
- stencils
- squeegees
- drop cloths
- sample fabric or newsprint
- fabric to print
- rags, sponges, towels
- paper towels
- freezer paper
- plastic containers with lids
- spoons and rubber spatulas
- scissors
- utility or precision craft knife and blades

Textile pigments:

- print base extender (transparent, opaque, or both)
- color concentrates or mixed colors

Dyes:

- fiber reactive dyes
- chemical water
- thickener
- activators: soda ash or (for silk) citric acid crystals

Let's start by talking about the various components of fine screen printing: a worktable, screens, block-outs (stencils), and finally the printing process itself.

The Print Table

Screen printing on fabric is best accomplished on a sturdy padded wooden table (04-05), either custom built or reinforced for this use. Typically you must stand at a worktable and lean forward to screen-print. The worktable should be firmly level and sturdy enough that you can lean against it without the table moving, rocking, wobbling, swaying, wiggling, or (most disastrously) collapsing. To recycle an existing table, reinforce or brace the top and legs with extra wood or metal pieces. Your "table" can even be a padded board firmly clamped to sawhorses. Very small print projects can be accomplished on a portable padded board, of the type discussed in chapter 3.

Since you are standing to work, adjusting the *table height* for your size will minimize body stress from the work. Ideally, the table edge should be opposite your hip joint. (To check the height, stand at the edge of the table, with your back flat and heels on the floor, and bend forward at the hip. You should be able to lay the top half of your body flat onto the tabletop.) This height allows you to bend and reach over the work surface without rolling or hunching your back (all too common if the table is too high or too low for you). If you build a custom print table, it's a simple matter to measure from the floor to your hip joint and use that as your table height. (For example, I am 5 feet tall and my custom-built print table is 29" high.) If you want to adapt an existing table, you may need to shorten or extend the legs to achieve the right height for you.

Screen printing on fabric often requires working from both sides of the table, especially on large pieces of fabric or yardage. The *table width* should allow you to reach a bit past the middle of the surface. For a custom-built table, measure your reach to find the width limit. (For example, I am 5 feet tall and my own print table is 48" wide.)

Whether your tabletop is made from plywood, hardwood, or an adapted existing wooden table, its surface should be flat and free of large joints, holes, or seams. Fill minor irregularities and small holes with spackling compound, allow them to dry, and sand them smooth.

04-05 Print table (yours doesn't have to be this large or have legs) made with ¾" plywood sheet (4' × 8'), padded with ⅜" industrial felt cut to plywood size, and covered with stretched painter's canvas stapled to underside of tabletop (see detail in 04-07).

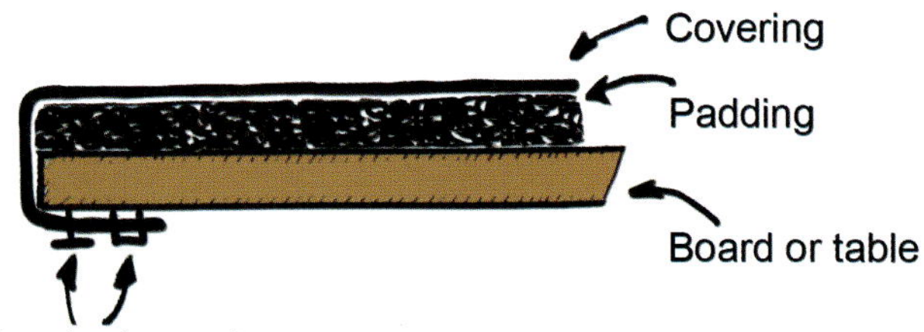

04-06 Section view of a printing surface made with a wood or plywood board, ⅜"–½" of padding, and a tightly stretched cover.

Padding the Printing Surface

Screen printing on fabric, unlike its counterpoint on paper, requires a slightly padded and *resilient* printing surface, of adequate size to tightly stretch your fabric to its full size. The padding provides a cushion for the squeegee as it presses against the screen mesh and flexible fabric surface to ensure complete contact and coverage with the paste. For the top of your prepared wooden table, you will need thick padding material (⅜"–½") that is free of bumps, gouges, and seams. Choose from a variety of alternative padding materials: multiple stacked layers of quilt batting, ½" thickness of foam rubber (but too much foam rubber can be *too spongy*), multiple layers of old blankets, or a single layer of wool or synthetic industrial felt. The latter comes in ⅜"–½" thicknesses and is the most durable, even, and substantial choice (my own table uses ⅜" wool industrial felt).

Cut the padding to fit the tabletop. Trim it as necessary to make it precisely meet the *very edge* of the table.

Covering the Padding and Table

Once you've fitted the padding to the tabletop, you need a covering to keep the padding firmly in place.

Fabric covers allow you to use small (size 20) T pins to stretch the cloth you want to print; they are easy to insert and hold the stretch in the cloth securely. I favor a white or natural-color cotton fabric, such as *heavy* painter's canvas found in art supply stores. But any sturdy, heavyweight white fabric with a smooth texture will work. When you are not printing, fabric table covers can also be used for pressing fabrics during piecing, appliqué, or reverse appliqué (discussed in the *Dry Techniques* book).

Plastic or vinyl covers provide a surface that repels water, meaning that dye or pigment overspill can be easily wiped away, and the table can serve "double duty" for arranging dye pots for immersion dyeing. Thick clear *plastic sheeting* over a white fabric cleans up easily and can be replaced with little expense. Cloth-backed *marine vinyl* scrubs clean but collects pigment or dye stains that do not wash away (more a visual than a practical problem). A disadvantage: plastic or vinyl coverings require that you stretch the fabric with (less trustworthy) masking tape, because using T pins on plastic will leave a profusion of small holes in the surface that may show up as dots in your prints.

Whether you use fabric, plastic, or vinyl, cut your covering material at least *6" larger* than the tabletop on each side, enough extra to get a good grip with your hands when you stretch it across the table.

Spread out the covering on top of the padding. If you use a fabric covering, align and square the grain with the edges of the table. Starting in the *center*, stretch the covering over the padding and staple, nail, or tape it to the *underside* of the tabletop or wood board (see 04-07). To ensure straightness of grain, alternate stretching and stapling from side to side, moving from the center toward the ends of the table and stretching with equal tension at each step along the way. Continue attaching the covering along the sides until you get close to the corners. Miter or neatly fold the corners under and staple them in place (04-07). The cover should be straight, taut, and flat.

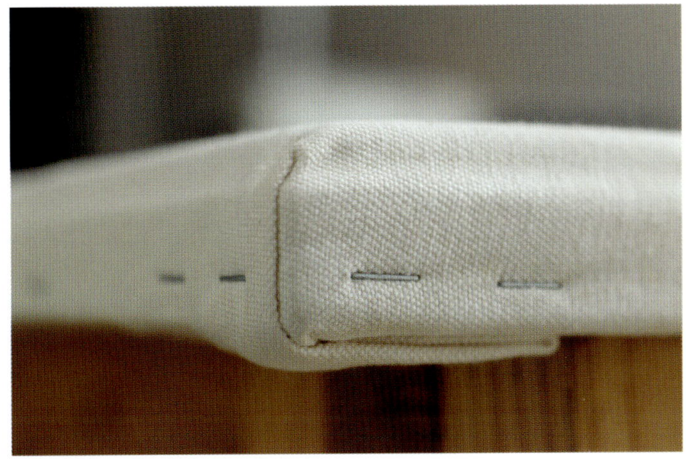

04-07 Detail (corner view) showing canvas covering pulled, stretched, and stapled over the layer of padding on top of the table.

A smaller padded board is handy for small projects (such as the direct-application techniques discussed in chapter 3) and for limited workspaces. It has the added advantage of being portable and easily stored. When you need it, set on your worktable, clamp it to cross braces (sawhorses, chair arms), set it in your lap, or carry it to workshops and group work sessions. Pad and cover your board with the same range of materials suggested for large tabletops; however, at this scale, instead of staples, use packing or duct tape to adhere the covering to the back of the board.

TIPS FOR USING AND MAINTAINING A PADDED PRINTING SURFACE

- Clean the surface. With each use, and before stretching down your cloth for printing, make sure the print surface is clean and free of dye, wet pigment, threads, scraps, wrinkles, pins, and grit. Anything *dimensional* beneath the cloth will make an impression or resist in your print; leftover dye can restain your fabric when the moisture from your print medium reaches it.

- Use a drop cloth. On *cloth-covered* tables (but skip this step for *plastic-* or *vinyl*-covered tables), spread a *clean* thick fabric drop cloth (larger than the piece of fabric you'll be printing) that is free of wrinkles, seams, and tears. The drop cloth adds more padding and will also protect your table cover from gathering stray overprints and bleed-throughs. In group workspaces, individual drop cloths protect the work of each person sharing a table.

- Wash drop cloths frequently. This keeps the buildup of pigment and dye paste to a minimum and also protects your prints from unwanted contamination when remoistened during printing.

- Protect fabric covers from damage and cuts. Do *not* use the padded print surface for other activities that may damage it, such as cutting with knives or scissors. Cuts or tears in the covering or padding, which will appear in your prints as mars or blemishes, completely ruin the surface for screen printing. There is no way to repair the damage, short of recovering the table. If you need to use the *same* tabletop for a cutting work surface, protect it with some pieces of hardboard, plywood, hard plastic, or large self-healing cutting mats.

- Maintaining a plastic or vinyl surface. If you cover the print surface with plastic, cloth-backed vinyl, or marine vinyl, scrub the surface clean with a brush and soapy water after every use. To remove dye stains from a vinyl surface, an occasional scrub-down with a cleanser or scouring powder *containing bleach* may be necessary.

- Whatever the material used for your table cover, protect it from dust and dirt. Between work sessions, drape the cover with plastic or heavy fabric drop cloths.

- Ironing on the print surface. If your table has a canvas or cotton fabric cover (but *not* plastic or vinyl subject to melting), it will serve "double duty" for ironing, a great advantage for constructing quilts, wall hangings, and clothing. Press on a clean white drop cloth placed over the table cover, and keep iron settings sufficiently low to protect the cover from burns and scorches (as you would an ironing-board cover).

- If this table will serve "double duty" as a work surface for your dye pots, use plastic sheeting to cover it temporarily for those purposes.

The Screen

Today, *screen frames* are usually made of wood or aluminum, with a durable, porous, polyester or nylon mesh. The mesh holds the *stencil* firmly and flatly in place, while the frame gives the printer a way to hold and move the stencil to different areas of the fabric (as we'll explore in this chapter). As you probably discovered in chapter 3, *handheld* stencils also have a "design fault" that limits the kind of images they will produce. Specifically, they cannot capture a "trapped shape." For example, the unconnected "hole" in a donut shape, once cut, simply falls away from the stencil, leaving a circle behind. However, on a screen, the mesh stabilizes the stencil and holds even trapped shapes precisely in place.

Your first consideration in screen-printing equipment should be the quality of the screen, which will in large part determine the quality of the prints you can make and the seamlessness of your printing experience. The frame should be sturdy, waterproof, and accurately squared; its fabric should be tightly stretched with its straight of the grain aligned precisely with the frame's edges (see 04-08). Frames that wobble and fabric that is insufficiently stretched (leaving small sags or ripples) inevitably cause printing problems and image errors. The side of the frame with the stretched mesh is the *front side or face*. The side with the well, where you will put the printing paste, is the *backside*.

The simplest and best screen option is to buy commercially stretched, waterproof screens from reputable sources. These come in different sizes, depths, and grades of quality, from those at general art supply warehouses (cheapest, in all senses of the word) to those made for the professional hand screen printer (more expensive, but very durable). Because they are all machine built and stretched, even the cheaper screens are usually far sturdier, more accurately squared, and more tightly stretched than screens you can make for yourself. Homemade screens take a good deal of time to construct but may end up actually costing more than those made commercially (but if you want to make your own screens, see the text box for instructions). Wooden frames should be sealed to repel water; otherwise they will eventually warp and pull out of square, thwarting your attempts to accurately register, orient, and print images. Buy screens with waterproofed frames to save time and aggravation. If you make your own screens, waterproof the frames with polyurethane.

04-08 Commercially built screens with waterproofed wooden frame.

Frame Size

Commercial frames are sized by their *outside* dimensions—*not* by the smaller available printing area *within* the frame. Choose a frame size at least 4"–6" larger, in both directions, than the size of your stencil. (This leaves room for maneuvering the squeegee and temporarily holding print paste aside—but within the frame—during the printing process.) For example, if you buy an 18" × 20" screen, the open area of the screen mesh will be about 14.75" × 16.75" and allow a maximum of 12" × 14" of *actual printing space*. Develop your images and stencils and take measurements before you buy your screens.

Frame Weight, and Why It Matters

You may already be familiar with printmaking methods on paper where the screen is held by a clamped hinge that both bears its own weight and registers the image properly. By contrast, with screen printing on fabric, you hold the screen with both hands, with yours arms extended outward from your body; bend over to locate the screen precisely on the cloth; force the print paste through the stencil with a handheld squeegee; lift and relocate the screen; and repeat those actions many times *on a single piece of cloth*. It's physical work, a cumulative challenge for your hands, arms, back, and legs. To make the process more manageable and less exhausting, *minimize the weight of your screens*. When you choose frames *sizes*, also think about their *weights*. Consider how much screen weight you can personally manage (depending on your physical size and strength) in the kind of printing you want to do (for example, occasional small prints vs. long lengths of yardage in production mode).

Wood is heavy; aluminum is lighter. The thicker or larger the frame, the heavier the screen will be, no matter what the material. I find that repeating a smaller screen and image more frequently is less tiring than trying to shift and accurately place a large, heavy screen (even if it covers more fabric area). If (like me) you are a short or small person, I recommend that you keep your stencil sizes small so you can limit yourself to relatively small and lighter weight screens (18" × 20" or smaller). These not only will make the process easier but will improve your control over image placement and registration. However, if you are a tall or large person, you can probably handle much larger screen sizes (20" × 24" or larger). If possible, try several different sizes of screens to test your own limits. Whatever your own size, you may just want to keep an assortment of screen sizes on hand, for times when you want to print smaller or larger images. But screens beyond a certain size become too unwieldy and awkward to be practical for anyone to handle unassisted.

BUILDING YOUR OWN SCREENS

There are several reasons you might want to build your own screens: you need only one or two screens, you want screen sizes not available commercially, or you just like to build your own equipment. Screens require some woodworking skills and a bit of time to construct, waterproof, and stretch. Unless you already stock the component materials, the screens cost just as much to make as to buy commercially. However, if you take this option you can patronize your local lumberyard but will most likely have to order the screen mesh from a screen-printing-supply or art supply company. The fabric is sold by the yard in a range of *mesh sizes* (see section on mesh sizes).

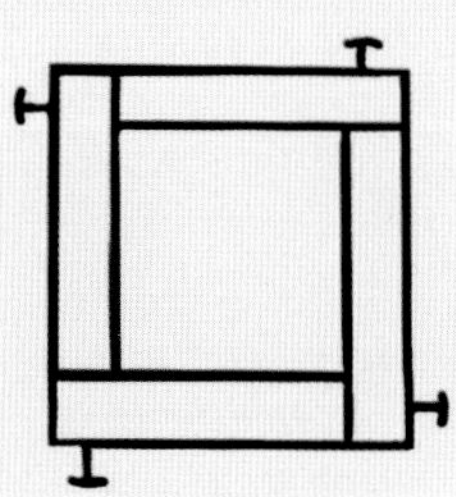

04-09 Butt joint frame.

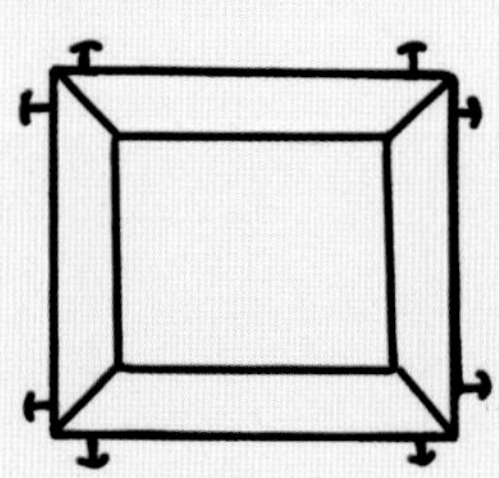

04-10 Mitered joint frame.

Construct the frame: Use four 1" × 2" clear white pine or birch boards (free of knots, chips, and warps), cut to the desired lengths. (Alternatively, use precut painting stretchers for quickly assembled, though shallower and less sturdy, screen frames.) To create the deepest well possible with the wood, assemble the 1" × 2" frame with the 2" dimension of the boards oriented *vertically*. Miter the corners or use butt joints (04-09 and 04-10). Apply glue to the joints, then nail them firmly together, using a carpenter's square to make sure that the corners are true 90° angles. Sand any rough spots. Pieces of wood are rarely completely straight, but make sure that at least one side of the constructed frame lies very flat and will make full contact with the print table.

Waterproof the frame: To waterproof the frame, apply three coats of polyurethane, allowing each coat to dry before applying the next. Let the frame dry overnight, then *lightly* sand its surface (to remove any air bubble "pimples" in the coating) before proceeding to stretch the screen fabric over it.

Stretch the mesh and staple it to the frame: Place the wooden frame on a table with the *flattest side facing up* (this will become the *front side* or *face* of the screen, which contacts the fabric). The goal is to get the mesh stretched taut and even, without ripples or buckles, and with its straight of grain aligned with the frame. Start with a piece of fabric larger than the frame by several inches. Measure and tear the fabric mesh along the grain (as opposed to cutting it) to retain the grain line. To square the grain, lay the mesh on the frame, aligning two adjacent torn (or selvedge) edges with two adjacent frame sides.

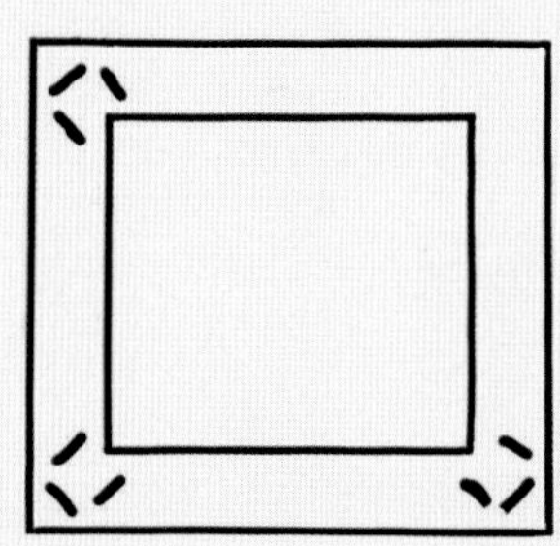

04-11 Staple positions for first three corners. First set of staples at lower left, second set at lower right, third set at upper left.

Using an electric staple gun and ¼" or ⅜" staples, place three staples, at angles to one another, in the corner adjoining the two adjacent sides. Aim the staples straight down into the 1" edge of the frame.

(Unlike stretching a painting canvas, where the fabric is wrapped around and stapled to the edge, the screen fabric need be attached only to the face of the frame with no wraparound.)

Next, pull the fabric taut along one edge and place three staples at the second corner. Then, pull the fabric taut along the adjacent edge and place three staples in the third corner (04-11). Leave the fourth corner temporarily unstapled.

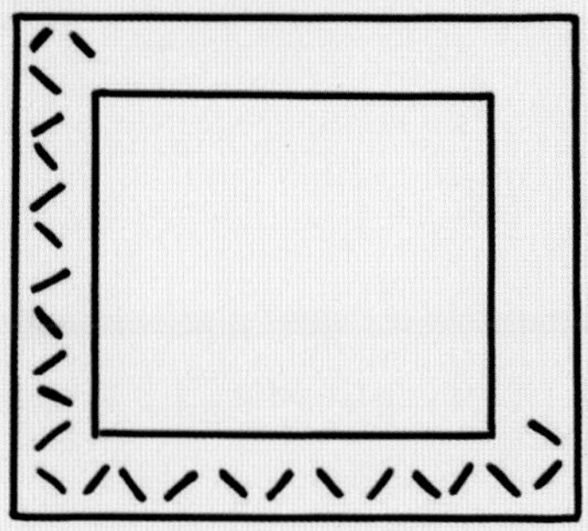

04-12 Staple positions when inserted in a zigzag on first two sides.

Insert a *zigzag row* of staples (at about a 45° angle to the edge of the frame, and no more than ½" apart) to fill in the space between the corners on both adjacent sides (04-12). If any of the staples go in crooked or stick up, either pull them out and insert new ones or tap them flat with a hammer so they will not later protrude into the printing fabric. Center the staples along the frame edge, keeping them *away* from the *inner edge* of the frame, where an off-target staple could rip the screen fabric. Use needle-nose pliers to pull out any staples that hang off the edge of the frame, and insert new ones.

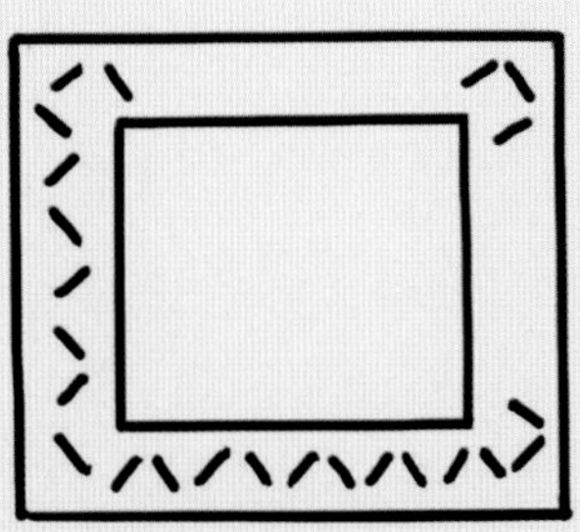

04-13 Mesh stretched to fourth corner and anchored with three staples.

To complete the stretching, tightly pull the screen fabric *diagonally* across the frame to the fourth corner. Keep the grain of the fabric straight. Then insert three staples in the fourth corner (04-13).

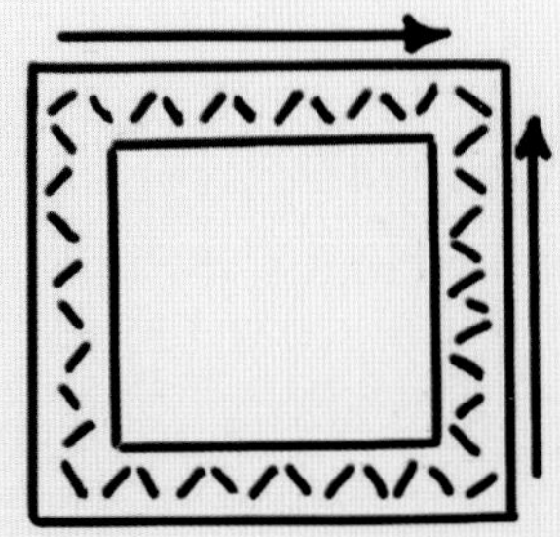

04-14 Staples inserted in zigzag on remaining two sides according to direction of arrows.

Then, starting *from* the corners stapled in 04-13 (*not* from the fourth corner itself), work toward the fourth corner, inserting staples in the same zigzag arrangement (see arrows in 04-14). As you insert each staple, pull the mesh tightly and straight away from the edge of the frame. Finish stapling the mesh tightly to the remaining edges of the frame (04-14). Hammer down any staples that stick up, then use scissors to trim away excess mesh protruding beyond the frame edges.

To prevent rusting or protrusion of the staples, you can paint over them with two coats of polyurethane or gel medium. For extra protection, cover the stapled edges of the mesh with strips of duct or packing tape that wrap around the edges toward the *outside* of the frame.

As described below, clean, caulk, and prepare the homemade screens as you would commercially prepared screens.

Screen Mesh Size

When you buy a commercially made screen (or buy mesh to make your own screens), you must choose its *mesh size* (the size of the openings between the component threads in the fabric's weave structure). Whether the screen fabric is polyester or nylon, you will find a gradation of mesh sizes, intended to capture the differing levels of detail demanded by your images. The mesh-numbering system will vary with the type of fabric and the company.

The mesh number and the openness of the mesh are *inversely* related. Generally, the *smaller* the number, the more *open* the mesh, the less detail it will hold, and the easier it will be to force print paste through it. Fairly open mesh, such as 8xx to 10xx (or 110 mesh) will suffice for most images with moderate-to-large-scale marks, lines, and shapes.

On the other hand, the *larger* the number, the tighter or *finer* the mesh size, the greater the detail it will hold, and the harder it will be to force the print paste through the mesh. Thus, for very detailed images, fine lines, halftones, or four-color printing you will need at least the fineness of 12xx to 16xx (or 155 to 200 mesh).

Rule of thumb: choose the most open mesh (smallest number) that will successfully reproduce the image you want to print. To avoid accidentally affixing a stencil that requires tighter mesh than is attached to that screen, use a permanent marker to label the outside of each screen frame with its correct mesh size.

Cleaning Screens before First Use

Whether you buy commercial screens or make your own, they need to be cleaned before use. To remove dirt, fingerprints, and grease from production and handling, thoroughly scrub both sides with a brush and hot soapy water. Alternatively, use *screen degreaser*, a commercial screen-cleaning product sold by screen-printing suppliers. Place the degreaser in a spray bottle, spray it on both sides of the screen (it will foam slightly, like soap), and scrub thoroughly with a brush. Thoroughly rinse off soap or degreaser. Let the screen dry *completely* before affixing a stencil. After this thorough cleaning, do not handle the screen mesh again, since this will leave behind new fingerprints (yours, because even the "cleanest" hands still bear traces of oil) that may resist the adherence of block-outs.

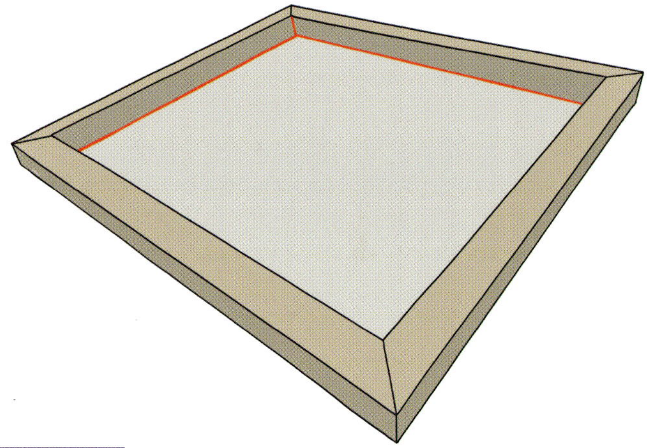

04-15 Apply *clear* silicone caulking to the inside joints, corners, and edges (red lines) to prevent colorant seepage into any remaining interior gaps between frame and mesh.

Blocking Out Corner Gaps on the Frame

If you have purchased a screen with a commercially waterproofed frame, the areas where the mesh and frame overlap should already be firmly adhered to each other with glue, leaving no gaps. Nevertheless, examine the screen carefully. If you locate any remaining gaps between the mesh and the frame (or you have made and stretched the screen yourself), apply *clear* silicone caulking, working in the well on the *back* of the screen, to the inner corners of the frame and then to the linear edges where the mesh and frame meet (04-15). Allow the caulk to dry thoroughly before using the screen. This should prevent trapped water from warping a wooden screen, or print paste from hiding in gaps, where it waits with malice in its heart for the moment when it can seep out to ruin the next fabric you print.

04-16 Temporary block-out with freezer paper and masking tape, leaving space between tape and frame to apply gel medium as a permanent edge block-out.

Sealing Edges of the Mesh

There is one more step to seal off gaps that could allow print paste to seep between the edges of your stencil and the screen frame, thereby leaving unwanted straight lines of color on the fabric. To provide an additional barrier on the *front or face* of the screen mesh, paint a 1" border of polyurethane or gel medium directly onto the mesh and completely around the frame perimeter. To paint this line without dripping on the open area of the screen mesh, cut a piece of paper 2" smaller than the interior frame and then attach the paper, using masking tape, to the center of the mesh on the face of the screen as a *temporary* block-out (04-16). Once taped in place, this taped paper should leave a gap of about 1" all the way around. Using a small brush, paint with polyurethane or gel medium to fill in the untaped border of the mesh. Make sure you coat it *thoroughly*. Allow the sealant to dry completely before removing the masking tape and paper block-out. Now you can size the outer edges of your stencils to overlap the blocked border (instead of trying to meet the frame edge), minimizing the chance for print paste to seep into any gaps at the stencil edges.

With solid, squared, tightly stretched, cleaned, and prepared screens in hand, you are now ready to attach your stencils.

Block-Outs (Also Called *Stencils*)

In this section, we'll explore *temporary*, hand-cut block-outs for simple shapes and images, small print runs, fewer repeats, quick sequences of image changes using the same screen, and a generally more spontaneous approach to screen printing. You can make these stencils from freezer paper (waxed on one side), tape, thin plastic, or contact paper. All these materials are safe, easy to prepare, and inexpensive and require very little setup, equipment, or supplies.

Most temporary stencils are essentially *disposable*. Except for plastic sheets, they usually deteriorate quickly with use, can stretch or wrinkle when damp (especially paper stencils), or become too distorted to use over a long period of time. Much will depend on the image and the way you handle the stencils.

The image or subject matter in your stencil design sets the tone for the expression you make; the layout, spacing, rendering style, and coloration combine to complete your meaning. Use any type of image, shape, or motif that you can draw or cut out: geometric or organic, abstract, or representational shapes; motifs drawn from your environment, family history, reading, or hobbies; and images infused with personal meaning, social symbolism, political beliefs, or historical references.

Generally speaking, the fewer the number of elements on the screen stencil (such as single shapes, marks, or gestures), the more flexible its combinations and orientations. A simple stencil can be used to compose, to lead the eye along the fabric, to create patterns or textures, to selectively place elements on clothing pattern pieces or parts of constructed textiles, or to tell a story.

Think of a screen with a single, simple image as a paintbrush and use it to build the fabric surface incrementally, print by print, image by image. For example, a stencil of a single leaf can be easily turned or used asymmetrically in various orientations or floated on top of another printed pattern (04-03). The less rectangular and more amorphous the contours of the stencil image, the more naturally and seamlessly they combine and overlap. If your stencil of a leaf also contains a scattering of smaller, sparsely dispersed leaves, printing the stencil overlapped and in various orientations will simultaneously overlap the small leaves to create an interesting textured background.

For *all* the stencil-making methods discussed below:

- Remember that screen stencils should block out all areas *except* those you wish to print, because the "holes" in the stencil are the "positive image" that will actually appear on the printed fabric, while areas blocked out by the stencil will not.

- Directional stencil modules narrow the possible uses of the screen, almost always necessitating an *upright orientation* in which the "top" of the image will also be uppermost in the viewed fabric after printing. For example, a stencil featuring groups of plants or leaves, especially if the image includes the entire plant from the ground up (roots, stalks, leaves, flowers, all reaching skyward), more naturally suggests one-directional placement and regular repetition instead of rotations and random printing (see 04-31).

- Select block-out methods according to the kinds of images or marks you want to print (simple to complex), how many times you plan to repeat them (one, two, dozens), and the studio facilities to support your choice (size of sink, availability of sprayer, and support for the dyes or print pastes you'll use).

- Screen stencils can be made from a range of materials that vary widely in their permanence, methods of preparation and screen adherence, ease of use, and safety procedures. Look for thin, nonporous materials that are easily cut with a precision craft knife or scissors but will block the paste sufficiently to provide a clean print. Each material largely dictates the type of image or marks that can be cut through it, the tools needed for the cutting, and the method necessary to adhere the stencil to the screen.

- Regardless of material, all stencils must be adhered to the *front side* or *face* of the screen, because if the stencil were placed in the screen well, the squeegee would snag on the stencil or degrade it from friction.

- Cut all temporary stencils large enough to meet and cover the screen mesh to the edge of the frame or to overlap the painted strip of gel medium, as described on page 161. But if you have a stencil that's smaller than your frame, cover the unused portion of the mesh with masking tape, on the *face* of the mesh, to seal it out from printing. (You can also do this if you discover small leaks through the mesh during the actual process of printing.)

- Because you'll want extra space within the well to temporarily "park" pigment before drawing it across the stencil with a squeegee, the stencil *material* should extend the full width of the screen frame (from each inner edge of the frame to its counterpart on the opposite side), but the stencil *image* should be 2" smaller on all sides.

- With any new stencil, run a few test prints on paper, newsprint, or scrap fabric to make sure the ink saturates the screen properly and passes through the mesh evenly across the image.

- Because dye pastes and textile pigments (other than those containing opaque white) are transparent, overlapped printed elements will mix colors optically or build textures (04-04).

TOP: 04-17 Screen print block-out made from torn strips of masking tape. Single screen, printed in alternating color blocks and overprinted in rotating orientations to create a plaid. Textile pigments. Cotton print cloth. Scale: 30" × 30".

04-18 Masking-tape block-out being smoothed into place on the screen front.

Masking-Tape Block-Outs

Masking tape provides an immediate and extremely easy way of making a temporary block-out on a screen (04-17, 04-18). In a pinch, other types of packing and shipping tape may also work, but avoid drafting tape and ordinary office tape, which wrinkle when wet and easily peel off. Masking tape is most appropriate for spontaneous or experimental images, lending itself particularly well to geometric shapes, bars, and stripes. You can experiment with a variety of configurations and combinations.

Masking tape is sold in widths from ⅛ inch up to 3", which can be applied in long strips straight off the roll or cut or torn into irregular strips or specific shapes. Always apply masking tape to a thoroughly dry screen mesh to help ensure it will continue to stick reasonably well during the printing process, despite the moisture that accumulates. Remember to apply the tape to the *front side* or *face* of the screen, safe from the friction of the squeegee.

Wherever you place it, the tape becomes the *negative image*, and everything around it will print. In 04-17, I tore the masking tape lengthwise and used the strips as boundaries and divisions in a single 6" square on the screen, with the stripes running in only one direction. During printing, I rotated the square module to cross and overlay the stripes as I simultaneously changed colors. (Of course, this required thoroughly *washing out* the screen *before* each change of color.)

Freezer Paper Block-Outs

Cut-paper stencils are inexpensive, fast, and easy. They are great for quick, spontaneously cut shapes, simple images, and impromptu experimentation (04-19). However, most papers have a short life when damp and are therefore best considered for one-time use. Therefore, the best kind of inexpensive paper to use for screen stencils is *freezer paper* of the type found in grocery stores. It is waxed on one side, simple to adhere to the screen, and strong enough to hold together under pressure and moisture. Remember that paper stencils, like those we used in chapter 3, do not accommodate "trapped shapes" (remember the "donut hole" example) or extremely fine detail (because hand-cutting precise, delicate lines and marks with a knife is a challenge).

Instructions for cutting and adhering freezer paper stencils:

1. Cut a piece of freezer paper large enough to cover the face of your screen. Draw the stencil design on the *waxed* side of the freezer paper, oriented as you wish it to appear on the fabric (*no reversing* for letters or numbers to print correctly), and leave a 2" border without cuts around the perimeter of the stencil. The waxed side will eventually adhere to the *front side* of the screen for printing (i.e., you are looking at the stencil as it will print).

2. Using a small, sharp utility or precision craft knife, and working with the waxed side of the paper *facing up*, and the paper taped to a self-healing mat or mat board surface, carefully cut out the positive shapes you wish to print. Intricate images and patterns will take more time to cut than simpler ones. Leave the remainder of the paper intact. (To cut an identical "backup" stencil, stack two pieces of freezer paper on the self-healing mat and cut the shapes through both pieces of paper at the same time. This will save time in case your first stencil "wears out" during the printing.)

04-19 Paper block-outs (leaf shapes) laid over masking-tape block-out stripes. Textile pigments in split fountain (04-29). Scale: leaves are life-size.

04-20 Freezer paper stencil being cut and adhered to a screen.

3. Place the cut stencil on a padded ironing surface, *waxed side up*. Make sure no edges are folded, curled, or wrinkled. Set the *dry* screen on top of the stencil, waxed side of paper against front side of screen, correctly squared with the image. Heat your iron to the nylon or polyester temperature setting (relatively "cool" to match the fiber content of your screen mesh, enough to adhere the waxed paper without melting the screen mesh). (If you have a small tacking iron or travel iron with sensitive temperature control, it may prove more maneuverable inside the well of your screen than a full-sized iron.) Working on the inside of the well, use your iron to press the back of the mesh and melt the wax of the freezer paper onto it. To avoid melting a hole in your screen, *keep the iron moving* around the well, without lingering longer than necessary in any one spot.

04-21 Layered prints made with plastic stencils. Textile pigments. Cotton print cloth. Scale: 2.75" × 7".

Plastic Stencils

Plastic stencils are a bit thicker than paper ones and may feel a little lumpy to use with the screen, but they have the advantage of being waterproof and stable and, unlike paper, won't expand or wrinkle when wet.

Anything that can be cut from paper can also be cut from thin plastic (04-21). To design and cut your own custom stencils, buy sheets of thin plastic (at your local art supply or craft store) at least large enough to fit the front of your screen. Tape the plastic sheet to a self-healing cutting mat and draw your design on it with a pencil. Cut the images one by one with a small, sharp utility or precision craft knife. Remember that the areas you cut *out* will be the ones that print. (While you're at the craft supply store, also check out selections in precut plastic stencils that might work for your project.)
Tape the cut stencil to the front of your screen mesh, securing all edges with masking tape (04-22). If your plastic stencil is smaller than the printing surface of the screen, continue adding masking tape to the edges of the screen frame, to eliminate any nonstencil areas that would otherwise allow pigment to come through to the fabric.

04-22 Applying a plastic stencil to a screen with masking tape.

Contact Paper Stencils

Clear contact paper comes on rolls, temporarily adhered to a paper backing. Because it is adhesive on one side, any stencil cut from it will stick to the entire surface of the screen mesh and hold the image in place for printing. It's more durable than paper, flatter than plastic. Contact paper stencils can be meticulously designed and carefully cut or spontaneously created with a craft knife. As long as the screen mesh is completely dry when the stencil is first applied, contact paper stencils hold their shape when wet; thus, you can capture relatively detailed marks that will hold up reasonably well during repeated printings. You can store and reuse the screen over time, although you cannot successfully remove and reapply the stencil, because the removal process would stretch it.

Instructions for cutting and adhering contact paper stencils:

1. Place a piece of contact paper, large enough to cover the entire front of your screen, on a self-healing mat, with the *paper backing side facing upward*. Draw your image on the backing. (This will be the orientation of the printed image, including any letters and numbers.)

2. Cut out the positive shapes (the holes in the stencil) with a small, sharp utility or precision craft knife, piercing through both the paper backing and the contact paper itself. (If you intend to use the stencil image again in the future, cut an identical backup stencil. Stack two pieces of contact paper on the self-healing mat, tape them firmly in place, and cut the shapes through both pieces of contact paper at the same time.)

3. When the entire stencil is cut, it's time to remove the paper backing and adhere the stencil to the *front side* of a thoroughly clean and dry screen—in a careful and combined action.
   - Place the screen on a worktable, with the *front side facing upward.*

   - Working from one end of the contact paper, slowly peel back about an inch of the backing from the top of the stencil. Then flip the contact paper so that the exposed sticky edge is facing the top front rim of the screen frame (the rim farthest away from you). Use your fingers to *very lightly and temporarily* press the exposed sticky edge of the contact paper onto the screen mesh covering the rim.

   - Gently *roll* the still-backed part of the contact paper away from you, then grasp the edge of the paper backing. Pull off the backing in a slow, smooth motion (toward yourself), allowing the remainder of the now-sticky and backless contact paper to *settle* lightly onto the screen mesh as you unroll the backing paper inch by inch.

   - Next, working from the center of the paper outward, carefully smooth out any wrinkles and folds as you press the paper a bit more firmly on the screen mesh.

   - When the contact paper has been placed as you wish on the *front* of the screen, turn the screen over and, working from the *inside* of the well, use your fingers or a small brayer to press the mesh itself firmly against the back of the stencil. Make sure to contact the entire surface evenly and to eliminate any air bubbles.

LEFT AND ABOVE: 04-23 Attaching a contact paper stencil to the screen front.

Adhesive Labels

Small self-adhesive labels, stickers, dots (all in their original geometric shapes), or custom shapes cut from very large self-adhesive labels can function as mechanical resists to create negative shapes. Adhere them directly to the *front side* of the screen, or directly onto the dry surface of the cloth you are printing. The rest of the screen will print, while those small shapes preserve the original color of the fabric beneath them.

Texture Rubbings

A messy process, although fun. Place the front of the screen against a textured surface (concrete, brick, wood, tree bark) and then, working inside the well, lightly rub a piece of paraffin or beeswax across the mesh to capture the texture. Repeat the rubbing to increase the amount of detail in the texture. Tape around the edge of the rubbing to create a temporary storage area for your print paste. You can reuse this waxed stencil for repeated printings, but as long as the waxed image remains in place, you can't use the screen for any other image. For that, you will need to remove the wax from the mesh. To do this, set your iron to a very low heat to avoid melting holes in the screen mesh. Place several sheets of unprinted newsprint or craft paper on a padded ironing service, then place the screen on the paper with the front side down. Place several more sheets of paper, cut to fit, inside the well. Working in the well of the screen, move the iron around carefully and slowly to melt the wax. Because the wax will melt out in both directions (front and well), discard the papers as they become waxy, and replace them with fresh paper. It will take many pieces of paper and patient, slow, prolonged ironing to remove all the wax. When all wax residue has been removed (the papers are no longer picking up melted wax), scrub the screen thoroughly with a brush in *hot* soapy water, followed by scrubbing with screen degreaser (see directions earlier in this chapter).

04-24 Layered screen prints. Hand-dyed, discharge-printed, screen-printed, reverse appliqué and bead embroidery. Textile pigments (the white is opaque). Cotton broadcloth. Collection: Gregg Museum of Art and Design, North Carolina State University.

THERMO-FAX SCREENS

Thermo-Fax screens provide an option for detailed *photographic images* on small, flexible screens for home use, without the investment of studio equipment to support using photo emulsions and films.

Thermo-Fax screens are very flat, small (usually 8.5" × 11"), flexible, and easy to manage; require very little print paste; and are easily washed out in a small sink. The stencils are cut by means of face-to-face contact between *riso paper* and a high-contrast (no grays) black-and-white photocopy of your image, as the two are fed together through a Thermo-Fax machine. Very small tools will suffice for the printing, such as old credit cards or small rubber scrapers.

Thermo-Fax machines were commonly used decades ago to prepare mimeograph copies for distribution in offices and schools but are still available today. (Readers of a certain age will remember those purple-printed Thermo-Fax sheets.) The expensive option is to buy your own machine (new or used). A variety of sellers advertise on the internet, where you will also find considerable information and instructional videos to lead you through the easy steps. If you find the cost prohibitive to own the equipment yourself, there is another more affordable and easier option: have the custom Thermo-Fax screens made for you, to your own design specifications, by any number of small-scale manufacturers who do business either on the internet or in your own area.

04-25 Four layers of printed patterns. Textile pigments. Cotton print cloth.

Instructions for Screen Printing

This section discusses the basic techniques of applying a printed image to cloth, for a single print of the image or for multiple prints that are randomly placed on the fabric (i.e., not contiguous with one another even though they use the same screen). If you will want to repeat the same image across the entire piece of fabric, or an entire part of it, with multiple printings contiguous (a practice called "registration"), read first in the several sections below whose titles begin with "Repeat Pattern."

If you are accustomed to printing on paper, the shift to printing on fabric presents some surprises and challenges. Paper, made of compressed interlocking fibers, is flat and *stable*. You can tape it down and it won't move.

By contrast, fabric is composed of a loose and movable grid of interlacing threads (woven) or loops (knitted). They are not "frozen" in place but shift and seem "alive" under the screen. Fabric fibers also absorb moisture from the printing paste and swell in size, filling or further loosening the joints of the structure. When you lift the screen to pull away from the table, the fabric can grab on to the screen face and lift up from the table too. Thus, when you first print on cloth, you may feel that it won't stay put—and you'd be right! In fact, it simply *does* move. Looser fabric structures move more, and tighter structures move less; fibers that absorb water more readily swell more, and those that repel water swell less. To minimize the migration or movement of the fabric during printing, choose more tightly woven cloth, stretch it evenly and tightly on the table, and don't make your print paste too thin. Printing on cloth may still require some adjustment in your printing techniques but can be mastered with practice.

Comparing Colorants: Textile Pigment vs. Dye Paste

You can screen-print with *textile pigment paste* or with *dye paste*. Each requires different procedures and will render different results. With either type of colorant, the amount of paste needed and the amount of pressure on the squeegee will change with the type of fabric chosen. For example, it will take more pigment to print on cotton velveteen than on sheer silk scarves. (See chapter 1 for thickeners to make dye paste, and chapter 3 for information on pigment paste.)

Textile Pigment Pastes	Dye Pastes
Adhere to any fabric type and fiber content with a binder.	The correct dye must be chosen to chemically bond with the type of fiber.
Prepared pastes are the correct consistency to hold a sharp printed edge (no bleeding).	You must mix your own dye thickener to the correct consistency, using a compatible thickener.
Easy to use directly from the jar with no chemical additions.	Must be activated with the appropriate chemical assistants just before use. Printing must progress quickly before the dye paste is rendered inactive.
Custom colors can be easily and quickly mixed. Much like acrylic paints, what you see is the color you get on the fabric.	Custom colors can be mixed, but the colors will shift a certain amount during color-setting and post-printing processing, making exact color matching more challenging.
Safe to use; no rubber gloves needed during printing.	Safety precautions necessary in mixing and handling; rubber gloves essential during printing.
Clean up with soap and water.	Clean up tools and screens with soap and water. Must use a safe and effective specially formulated dye remover for your skin (but never bleach).
Allow the deposit of a thin, even coat of color on the fabric.	Allow the deposit of a thin, even coat of color on the fabric.
Color concentrates can be mixed into either a transparent or opaque base.	Always produce transparent colors.
Permanent set with air curing or dry heat.	Permanent setting requires steam iron, electric blanket, or batching processing.
The print will appear to sit slightly on top of most fabrics and will not physically penetrate the cloth.	The print will appear to sink into the fabric, rather than sit on top, and may well penetrate the cloth.

PERSONAL POSTURE TIPS FOR THE SCREEN PRINTER

The problems caused by incorrect posture during screen printing are *cumulative* and difficult to correct later, when your way of working has become ingrained and automatic. If you intend to print frequently or repeatedly, I recommend that you establish good habits of body mechanics from the beginning (the one-time printer can probably afford to ignore them).

- Wear flat, well-padded shoes; athletic shoes are a good choice.
- Stand flat on your feet, not rocked forward on the balls of your feet and your toes.
- Use a good-quality rubber mat on the floor around your table to ease stress on your feet and back.
- Bend forward from your hip joint, not from the middle of your back.
- When you lean over the table, try to keep your back straight and don't roll your shoulders forward.
- Instead of relying solely on pressure applied by the *muscles* and *joints* of your wrists, hands, forearms, and the tops of your shoulders, take advantage of the combined *weight* of your arms and upper body, and the strength of your shoulder blades, to do the work of pressing with the squeegee.
- Take time out to periodically rest and stretch. Even one minute out of every 30 can make a huge difference to your body.

1. Have your squeegees(s) ready.

   - In screen printing, you force the print paste through the screen with a rubber or plastic blade called a *squeegee*. Most squeegees have wooden handles into which a rubber blade has been inserted. Squeegees specifically made for fabric work have rubber blades with squared-off edges (04-26).
   - Alternatively, you can choose simple solid plastic or rubber squeegees, in which the handle and blade are formed in one piece, which work well for small designs. Even a window-washing squeegee with a short handle can work and may be easier for you to grip. For very, very small printing, even an old credit card can function as a squeegee. In any case, the key components are a straight edge, a flexible blade material, and a firm grip.

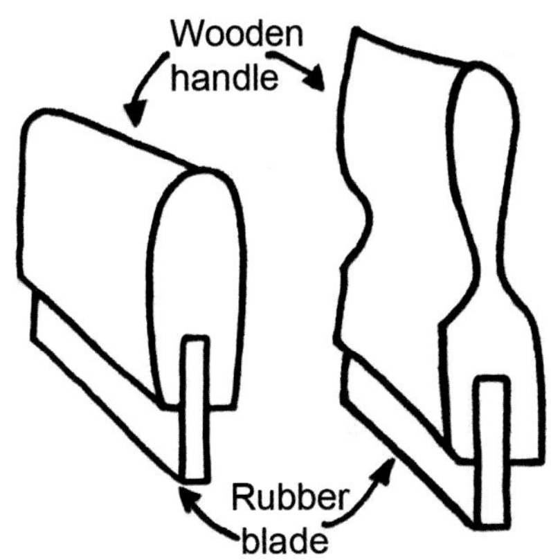

04-26 Wooden-handled squeegees. *Left*: a smaller rounded wooden handle, best for people with smaller hands; *right*: a larger and more commonly found squeegee.

   - Choose a squeegee that is the right size for *your hand*, one you can grip and hold easily without strain or undue tension. (I raise this point because commercial squeegees often have very large handles, which are inappropriate for small hands.) If the handle is too large or too small, your hand will tire easily or cramp from the grip needed to control the squeegee. To avoid the possibility of unwanted irregularities or uneven lines of color across your images, use a squeegee slightly wider than the image being printed.

2. Mix your color palette.

- Screen printing proceeds most efficiently when you have all print paste colors for the project mixed and ready to go *before* the print session. Custom color mixing takes longer than you might think. It depends on the number of colors in the palette and your skill with color mixing or matching colors to a color source. Set aside at least an hour to prepare the colors.

- To make your printing pastes easier to use and safe from cross-contamination, mix each color in a separate plastic container with a tight-fitting lid. Label the container with a color name or number. To provide a quick glimpse of the color in the container *without* taking off the lid, smear a swatch of white fabric with the custom color and tape the swatch to the container lid. Once mixed, textile pigments are then ready for immediate use but should be capped or covered until you're ready to start work, and after you're done. Provided they don't dry out in the container, pigments will last indefinitely.

- Dye pastes can also be mixed ahead of time (make them slightly more intense or darker than you intend the final color), but wait to add the activating chemicals to each color until immediately before you start using each one. Once it's activated, use dye paste within an hour.

- As you print color, remember that *wet* print paste always appears darker or more intense than when it dries.

- *To ensure color consistency across an entire cloth, complete the application of each different color in one printing session.*

3. Clean off and protect the printing surface.

- Brush or vacuum off the printing surface to prevent dirt, debris, bits of tape, or stray T pins under the fabric from making unwanted resists or irregularities in your print. Use a lint roller or a piece of masking tape wrapped around your hand (sticky side out!) to remove stubborn threads. On cloth-covered print surfaces, lay down a thick fabric drop cloth that covers the entire surface or at least extends 12" in each direction beyond the edges of the fabric you intend to print. Spread the drop cloth out smoothly and tightly to remove wrinkles and folds. Use small T pins (size 20) to pin it in place around the edges. Check to make sure its surface is clean, and use the lint roller or masking tape on it, as you did on the table cover.

4. Pin or tape the fabric to the printing surface.

- On *cloth* table covers, you'll be pinning the fabric to the clean and protected print surface, stretching it evenly and tightly, and keeping the grain of the fabric straight and square with the table edges. Use small T pins (size 20), inserted at an angle *away* from the direction of tension, through the drop cloth and fabric cover, angled into the table's padding (use a metal thimble to protect your fingers as you push against the pins).

- For *plastic* or *vinyl* table covers, you'll be using masking tape to fasten down the stretched fabric. Choose a good-quality brand of tape that is 1½" or 2" wide. Overlap ¼"–½" of the tape over each fabric edge.

- To square up the fabric for pinning or taping: First, align one selvedge edge (or a torn edge if you don't have any selvedges) equidistant from the straight edge of the printing surface or table. To be completely accurate, measure the fabric's distance from the edge every few inches along the selvedge and pull the fabric tightly to stretch it taut along the selvedge as you pin or tape the edge in place. Insert pins or apply small pieces of tape at least every 4"–6" along the edge.

- Next, stretch and pin or tape the *opposite* selvedge or torn edge, squaring the grain evenly as you go. Then, finally, stretch and secure the ends with pins or tape. When the fabric is stretched correctly, there should be no evident wrinkles, bumps, or pulls in the grain; it should look completely flat, tight, and straight.

- If you used pins to stretch the fabric, adding a continuous strip of masking tape to cover the pins and the selvedges of the fabric produces a cleaner and more professional-looking finished print.

- If you used small pieces of masking tape to stretch the fabric, leave them in place but now add a *continuous single long strip* of wide masking tape along each of the four edges of the fabric to make sure it is firmly and securely attached to the table. Press the tape down firmly with your fingers or use a large bone folder to press harder.

5. Check the screen for pinholes or leaks.

• Hold the screen stencil up against a bright light (lamp, window, or flashlight) to make a last-minute check for any pinholes, tears, or blemishes in your block-out. If you find any that might allow unwanted print paste to leak through, carefully block them out. Masking tape on the screen *face* is a quick solution.

• You may wish to print only a section of the image that is on your screen. If so, this is the moment to block out any parts not to be printed. Use masking tape or cut freezer paper on the *face* of the screen fabric as temporarily block-outs.

6. Squeegee technique

• Use your *dominant* hand to hold the squeegee, grasping it in the middle of its handle to evenly distribute the pressure you will place on it. (Use your *nondominant* hand to hold the screen itself in place on the fabric.)

• Start by placing the squeegee blade at the *top* of the screen (the end farthest from you) directly in the line of paste you will have loaded there, and then pull *toward* yourself. Pull *only* in this direction. Do *not* push print paste *away* from yourself with the squeegee, since this will cause thicker, uneven globs of paste to deposit across the well of the screen.

• Pull with the squeegee itself tilted *toward* you at approximately a 45° angle to the screen. This position uses the sharp *edge* of the squeegee blade (as in 04-28), not its flat bottom, and makes the best contact with the screen. *Avoid* pulling the squeegee with its blade perpendicular to the screen, which will cause misprints, "skips," and shudders that leave ridges of color alternating with unprinted areas. (The squeegee will literally vibrate in your hand from the perpendicular friction of its flat bottom against the screen mesh.)

• As you pull the squeegee across the screen (and toward yourself), press downward against the screen mesh, with a firm, even stroke, making sure that the print paste is distributed along the entire width of the squeegee blade. (Squeegee pressure is a skill you develop with practice. Generally speaking, if you've placed *too much* pressure on the squeegee or made too many pulls, the paste will squeeze from under the edges of the block-out to fuzz and darken the contour lines of your shapes, usually leaving a telltale thick, often-smeary deposit in the image areas. On the other hand, *too little* pressure on the squeegee results in some areas not printing, printing too lightly, or printing unevenly.)

04-27 Loading the screen with print paste.

• After you pull the squeegee across the screen for the first time, with the squeegee tilted at a 45° angle *toward* you, and have reached the bottom of the screen, intentionally tilt the squeegee handle *away* from yourself, use its blade to scoop up surplus print paste, and then *redeposit* that paste at the top of the well in preparation for the *next* squeegee pull, in which the squeegee will again be tilted *toward* you.

• When you have pulled the squeegee across the image a sufficient number of times to achieve a good even print, you will end with the squeegee at the bottom of the screen (closest to you) with excess pigment again sitting in the masked-and-blocked area of the screen well. (If you will be using the same screen to print on another area of the cloth, temporarily leave this surplus paste in the nonprinting area of the well—but you'll be moving the paste to the top of the well again when you begin printing in the new location.)

• Even if you are using a nontraditional "squeegee," such as a credit card or spatula, or a store-bought single-blade plastic squeegee, the technique is the same: pull in only one direction (toward yourself), with the squeegee angled toward yourself, then reverse the angle of the squeegee upon reaching the blocked-out end of the screen well closest to you and use the squeegee to scoop up paste and redeposit it to the blocked out screen border at the top of the well.

- If you are new to screen printing, you'll find that with practice, these squeegee motions will eventually blend into a seamless and natural action. Feel free to practice your technique with a dry screen that hasn't yet been loaded with paste.

7. Make test prints.

- Until the mesh has been saturated with print paste, the first few pulls you make with the squeegee will not print clearly and completely. *Before* you ever place the screen on the fabric, you must first saturate the mesh in the well with print paste, and you must do this every time you start printing with a fresh, dry screen. (Professional screen printers call this "flooding" the screen, but it doesn't actually involve pouring large amounts of pigment into the well. You just need to make sure that paste has been pushed through all printing areas of the screen, so that the paste will "flow" through the mesh when the actual printing begins.)

- Gather several pieces of newsprint or other scrap paper. Place the screen on the first sheet of paper, screen *front side down*.

- Load the screen with print paste. (If you are using *dye paste*, remember to *activate* it, just before printing, with the appropriate chemical; i.e., soda ash or citric acid crystals.) Place a moderate amount of paste (2 to 4 T.), arranged in a long line across the width of the screen, at the top of the well (04-27). Make sure the paste is sitting on the *blocked border* of the screen and *not* in an open area that will print. With each printing project, you will learn how much paste each particular image requires, and you can adjust the amount for that screen accordingly, adding more paste if needed (the larger the open area in your image, the more paste you'll need).

- Holding the screen stationary against the paper, and using the squeegee techniques described in Step 6, make several passes of the squeegee to saturate the entire screen while also making a *test print* on the paper.

- Lift the screen and inspect whether the image is clear and even and has printed completely in all areas. If not, repeat on another piece of paper and keep repeating until you are satisfied with the quality of the printing. (These test prints may also reveal some gaps or blemishes in the stencil, which require further blocking to *prevent* them from printing. If so, wipe off the *front* of the screen with a dry rag and repair the gaps with masking tape.)

04-28 Screen printing with wooden-handled squeegee, held tipped at an angle and pulled toward the body. Note overspill of print paste to the sides of the squeegee, which is prevented from seeping through by block-out and painted gel medium stripe previously applied to the front of the mesh.

- To finish up your tests, try printing the now-saturated screen on a *scrap* of the actual fabric you're about to print for your project. This last test will tell you how many pulls of the squeegee should deposit the required amount of paste (not too little, not too much) on this *particular* fabric.

8. Set the screen on the fabric to be printed.

- Your saturated screen will now leave traces of your test-printing color wherever you happen to place the screen down on the fabric you intend to print. Therefore, *carefully* place the screen, *well side up and mesh side down against the fabric, exactly* where you want the first print to be located. The *registration* of subsequent screen placements will be discussed in more detail below.

9. Print the fabric.

- Continuing to hold the screen to keep it from moving, use the squeegee with firm downward pressure to force print paste through the stencil as you pull across it. The goal is to apply even layers of print paste and well-defined images on the fabric. This will require that you pull paste across the stencil more than once, but the *exact number* of pulls will depend on several variables: the fabric texture and structure, the density of the screen mesh, the type of block-out, the extent of open areas in the stencil, the type of squeegee, the degree of padding on the printing surface, and the characteristics of your own body movements and hand or arm strength. Run some more tests each time you change the fabric or stencil image. Usually no more than two to four pulls should be required to deposit enough colorant on the fabric. If more pulls are required, your paste may be too thick (which you won't actually know until you do it), or you may not be applying enough pressure on the squeegee. You can adjust either the paste consistency or your squeegee pressure to compensate.

- Paste consistency: At the correct consistency, a dollop of textile pigment or dye paste should not move: no leaking, bleeding, or disappearing into the fabric. If the paste is too thin, it will run under the stencil and bleed outward, leaving a ragged or faded edge around shapes or marks. If the paste is too thick, you will have trouble forcing it through the stencil, and it will not print evenly. Thin or thicken your paste as appropriate, using the instructions in chapter 1 (for dyes) or chapter 3 (for pigments).

- Take note (literally, in writing) of the number of pulls required to produce even color on this specific fabric. This is important if you want to achieve the same color results (which will also involve the same number of squeegee pulls) in *multiple* printings from the *same* screen on different areas of the *same* fabric.

10. If you wish to make more prints of the same image, move the screen to the next location.

    Note: This section assumes, for now, that you want to make multiple prints that are randomly placed on the fabric (i.e., not contiguous with one another even though they use the same screen). If you will want to repeat the same image across the entire piece of fabric, or an entire part of it, with multiple printings contiguous (a practice called "registration"), read first in the several sections below whose titles begin with "Repeat Pattern."

    - When you have completed the *first print* on the fabric, you are ready to move the screen to the next location (if desired) and repeat the process.

    - Before you move the screen to the next location, set the squeegee out of the way, preferably somewhere it will not drip on your project. (For example, you could lay the squeegee down on a drop cloth, set it aside in a plastic trough, or even firmly clamp it against the inside of the screen with your hand and move it, along with the screen, to the next printing location. Just keep a watch on it; squeegees can easily topple over, fall onto the fabric, or flip print paste everywhere. It's not the end of the world, but it's a real mess, and potentially expensive.)

    - Use a dry or slightly damp rag to wipe clean the screen face and frame before each new placement of the screen. You want to remove any stray bits of paste still clinging to the *front* of the screen, so that only the image itself will print in the new location and there will be no unwanted transfer of stray lines or globs of paste left over from the previous printing.

    - Set the screen down in the next location. Reload with additional paste, if needed, and print with the same number of squeegee pulls you noted after the first printing. Repeat as desired across the fabric.

11. Clean and dry the screen.

    - Remember that excessive amounts of print paste will clog drains. Use a rubber scraper to remove all remaining paste from the screen well. *Dye* paste cannot be reused and should go directly in a waste container. *Pigment* paste can be saved in a container (perhaps including the one in which it was mixed) with a tight-fitting lid.

    Before you can reuse the screen, you must clean it thoroughly and do so before print paste begins to dry on it. The method of cleaning depends on the stencil material, but the method of drying described on page 176 is the same for all:

    - *Freezer paper (disposable)*: Because of freezer paper's tendency to swell and wrinkle when wetted, and because you melted its wax when you ironed it onto the screen, it is best treated as a stencil for one-time use. Peel the stencil from the screen and discard. Then, to remove any vestiges of melted wax, scrub the screen with *hot* soapy water.

    - *Masking tape and contact paper (gently washable)*: If you'll want to reuse the screen, leave the stencil on the screen. Gently and carefully wash *both* sides of the screen and its frame with *cool water* and careful *hand rubbing*. Avoid spraying these adhesive block-outs with water, especially from the *backside* of the screen, which would irretrievably loosen the adhesive. Blot the screen carefully and allow it to dry, then store it for future use. (On the other hand, if you'll want to use your screen for another kind of image, immediately remove and discard adhesive stencils but still wash the screen thoroughly to prevent the tape leaving a sticky residue. The screen is now ready for a new stencil.)

- *Plastic (washable and reusable)*: Even if you're going to reuse the stencil for a future printing, I recommend removing it from the screen until then. (This is one of the advantages of plastic stencils: unlike masking tape, contact paper, and freezer paper, the stencil material doesn't degrade with repeated use.) Pull off the tape. Remove the stencil and wash it by rubbing with warm soapy water. Then wash and scrub the screen with *hot* soapy water.

- Drying the screen: wipe the screen carefully with a dry towel and place it in front of a fan to complete the drying.

12. Wash and dry your tools.

    Using warm running water, wash the squeegee, rubber scrapers, spoons, or anything else that came in contact with the printing paste. Attend carefully to the edges and grooves where the blade meets the handle, so that no residual print paste will remain before your next printing project. Wipe the tools carefully with a dry towel and allow them to air-dry, or place them in front of a fan.

13. Remove the fabric from the print table.

    - After printing, the fabric is still wet, and handling will cause it to fold back on itself, smearing colors or images or transferring color onto unprinted areas. Whether you used dye paste or pigment, allow the fabric to dry to the touch *before* unpinning it from the table or moving it (however, if for some reason you *must* move freshly printed wet fabric, have someone help you lift it vertically off the table and then hang it on a line to dry).

    - To remove the fabric from the table, first carefully remove the masking tape from the edges of the fabric. Pull the tape gently and steadily. Remove the pieces in approximately the *reverse order* they were applied.

    - To protect your fingers, use a pair of needle-nose pliers to pull out the T pins, one by one, around the perimeter.

    - Because the pressure of the squeegee may have pressed print paste *through* the fabric and caused it to stick to the drop cloth beneath, gently pull up the *edges* of the fabric first and work toward its center. Once loosened, the fabric can then be moved with ease.

14. Cure the fabric.

    - Allow fabrics printed with *textile pigments* to air-dry for at least 24 hours before heat setting (see chapter 3), or for two weeks to completely air-cure (with no heat setting required).

    - Fabrics printed with *dye paste* can immediately be wrapped in plastic for electric-blanket heat setting, batching, steam ironing, or commercial steaming (see chapter 1).

15. Clean up the workspace.

    Thoroughly clean up all spilled pigment, dye, tape, and papers. Remove and wash the drop cloth.

SCREEN PRINTING WITH "SPLIT FOUNTAINS" OF COLOR

When you print with two or more colors of print paste, placed *simultaneously* side by side in your screen well, you create what is called a *split fountain* of color. As you pull the squeegee toward you, it deposits the colors in long swathes that mix where they meet on the fabric (04-29). This allows you to play with printing multiple colors, using a single screen and stencil. Analogous colors of similar value or intensity will blend almost seamlessly into a printed gradation, while contrasting colors usually form stripes or wide bands across the print.

04-29 Split fountain (green and blue) using a single pass on the shell pattern. Note at center, where the two colors mix on the shapes. Low-immersion-dyed with Procion MX fiber reactive dyes; textile pigments. Cotton print cloth.

Instructions for printing with a split fountain:

1. Place two or more colors of print paste (dye or pigment), side by side, in a line at the top of your screen (where you would normally place only one color to begin printing). For example, in 04-29 I placed medium green on one side of the screen and dark blue on the other side.

2. *Before* you print on *fabric*, make a test print *on paper* to encourage the colors to slightly blend where they meet. Then move to print on the fabric.

3. Place the squeegee squarely down into the line of print paste and pull it steadily *straight* toward yourself from the top to the bottom of the screen. For the next pull with the screen in the same location, replace the squeegee at the top of the screen, in the *exact same position*. Repeat until you are ready to move the screen to the next location.

4. For each successive pull, continue to exactly realign the squeegee with the different colors and pull straight toward yourself evenly. (While the colors will blend where they meet and overlap, care with placement of the squeegee will help keep the colors purer during the process.) (For example, in 04-29, the green and blue met and mixed in the middle of the squeegee. The more times this split fountain was printed, the more they would mix.

5. With repeated pulls of the squeegee and color mixing, the overall printed color can become increasingly "muddy." To keep the colors fresher through repeated pulls, frequently scrape out spent paste from the screen well with a rubber scraper and then replace it with fresh paste.

Screen Printing in Repeat

Both in the natural world and the man-made environment, repetition of motifs draws attention to itself and often creates a sense of unity, harmony, and visual potency. So too in printed fabric, and the ability to *repeat* images or stencil designs is one of the main advantages of screen printing. The repeated image itself can be almost anything and can be placed anywhere on the fabric.

This process of *repeating* a printed image across a piece of fabric, whether informally or in a grid-like way, is called *registration*.

04-30 The pleasures of pattern.

04-31 Print created with an image of a single tree on the screen, repeated to suggest a natural winter landscape. Fiber reactive dye paste printed on cotton broadcloth previously sprayed with a diluted gray dye solution to suggest "winter sky."

Registration: *Informal* Screen Placement for "Painterly" Composition

Screen printing can, if you wish, be wonderfully spontaneous. Think of your print fabric as a "canvas," stretched out in front of you, and your screen stencil as a "shaped" paintbrush. Use your stencils to "paint" images (04-31), blend or contrast shapes, overlap colors, and build textures incrementally, moving and turning the screen in each new location to build images with "brushstrokes" of the screen. Locate, orient, and repeat images *irregularly* and wherever you wish on the fabric: scattered far apart, densely clustered, lined up, overlapped, layered, unevenly repeated, partially blocked out, rotated, or printed with multiple colors in a split fountain (04-29). You have the flexibility to make design decisions in the moment, place colors and images intuitively, layer prints on the cloth, and play with space and composition based on your own artistic ideas and personal design sense. In this way, you can use your screen stencil to create painterly compositions, soft books, custom-printed lengths of cloth, or intentionally composed pattern pieces for clothing or three-dimensional textiles.

You can choose any type of fabric as the ground for your printed images, deliberately selecting for its texture and surface qualities, which will enhance the printed image in the final project. Printing on cloth offers the same artistic potential as paper and stretched canvas. The images and ideas come directly from your own vision and imagination.

Nearly any *type* of image on your screen stencil can be used in this manner, but the size of the piece of fabric should allow the stencil to function as a small incremental mark (like a brush mark), rather than so large by comparison that it dominates the composition. Then, as you mix and layer, turn and overlap, play with color and placement, even simple images combine in unexpected ways.

If you regularly create one-of-a-kind clothing, sculpture, or other three-dimensional textiles, rather than quilt fabric or work for the wall, you're *unlikely* to want rectangular pieces of cloth printed border to border. Instead, stretch your fabric for printing, then lay out and align the pattern pieces with the grain of the cloth (see chapter 7 in the *Dry Techniques* book). Then use a pencil to draw around each pattern piece *directly on the cloth*. Now compose your images and print *only inside the boundaries* of these drawn pattern pieces. Turn and rotate the stencils, printing and overprinting where you wish, direct-

04-32 *Left*: single-image fern leaf placed and oriented spontaneously; *right*: module of plant stalks and flowers printed in repeat pattern. Screen-printed, pieced, and reverse-appliquéd. Procion MX fiber reactive dyes, textile pigments. Cotton broadcloth (*left*), silk noil (*right*), and wool felt (*brown vertical in center*). Scale: about 8" × 14". Collection: Cindy Speicher, Des Moines, Iowa.

ly apply color accents, and compose to suit the overall design of the final printed textile. (You could, for example, print only in selected areas, cluster small single motifs in one place and larger images in others, overlay open areas with contrastingly light textures, or add words on sleeves or edges. This "engineered" approach to printing the fabric saves time and labor because you print only selected areas of the cloth instead of an entire piece of yardage.

04-33 Two layers of printing, overlapping separate patterns on low-immersion-dyed fabric. Procion MX fiber reactive dyes, textile pigments. Cotton print cloth.

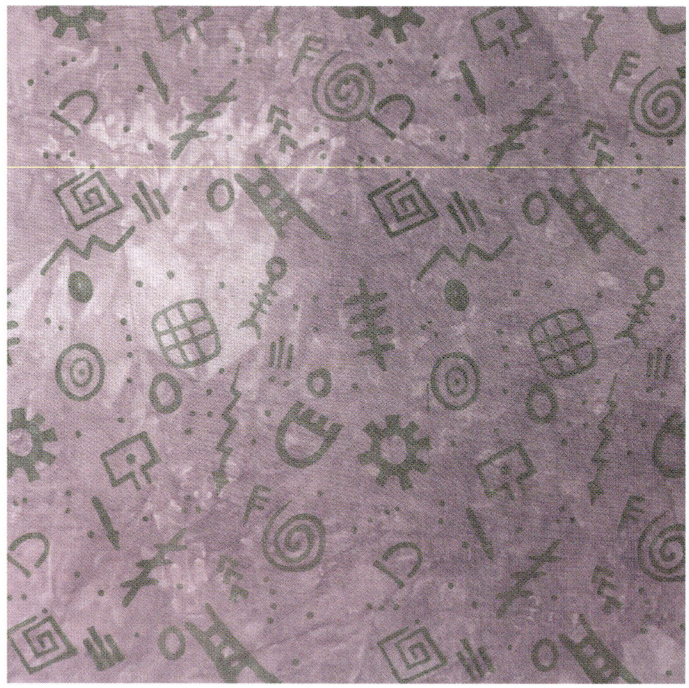

04-34 Motifs on a single screen stencil, registered loosely (not aligned) in repeat printings on previously dyed yardage. Procion MX fiber reactive dyes for low-immersion dyeing, textile pigments for screen printing. Cotton.

Registration: Custom Yardage Using an *"Eyeball"* Approach to pattern

This very direct and intuitive approach uses your own ability to look through and around the screen and then place the image or module in a loose repeat pattern. In this approach, each print is placed contiguous with the last to create a repeating pattern but is done so entirely by your in-the-moment visual judgment as you print repeatedly across the fabric (i.e., you don't seek to align the multiple prints of the screen in a formal or perfect grid-like way). Even if the modules don't touch, the act of repeating them will create a perceived pattern (04-34). This method is especially appropriate for use on fabric that will be cut up for piecing in quilts, wall hangings, or clothing.

04-35 Loose (nongrid) repeats using overlapping screen prints, with slight changes in color of pigment. The fabric was not dyed first. Its perceived color was achieved solely through the printing. Procion MX fiber reactive dyes. Cotton.

Similarly, you can use your screen stencils to print long lengths of fabric that change in color, image, or density of repeats along their length in large, long, single compositions (04-35).

Collections of custom-printed fabrics, with complementary images and color palettes, can be combined into a single pieced composition. For example, to produce the work in 04-32, all the printed images were inspired by a single natural site but varied in scale and type: a single fern leaf, textures from plant stalks, and clusters of small flowers. The loose and overlapping textures were printed as a delicate ground pattern, then overlaid with the larger fern shapes.

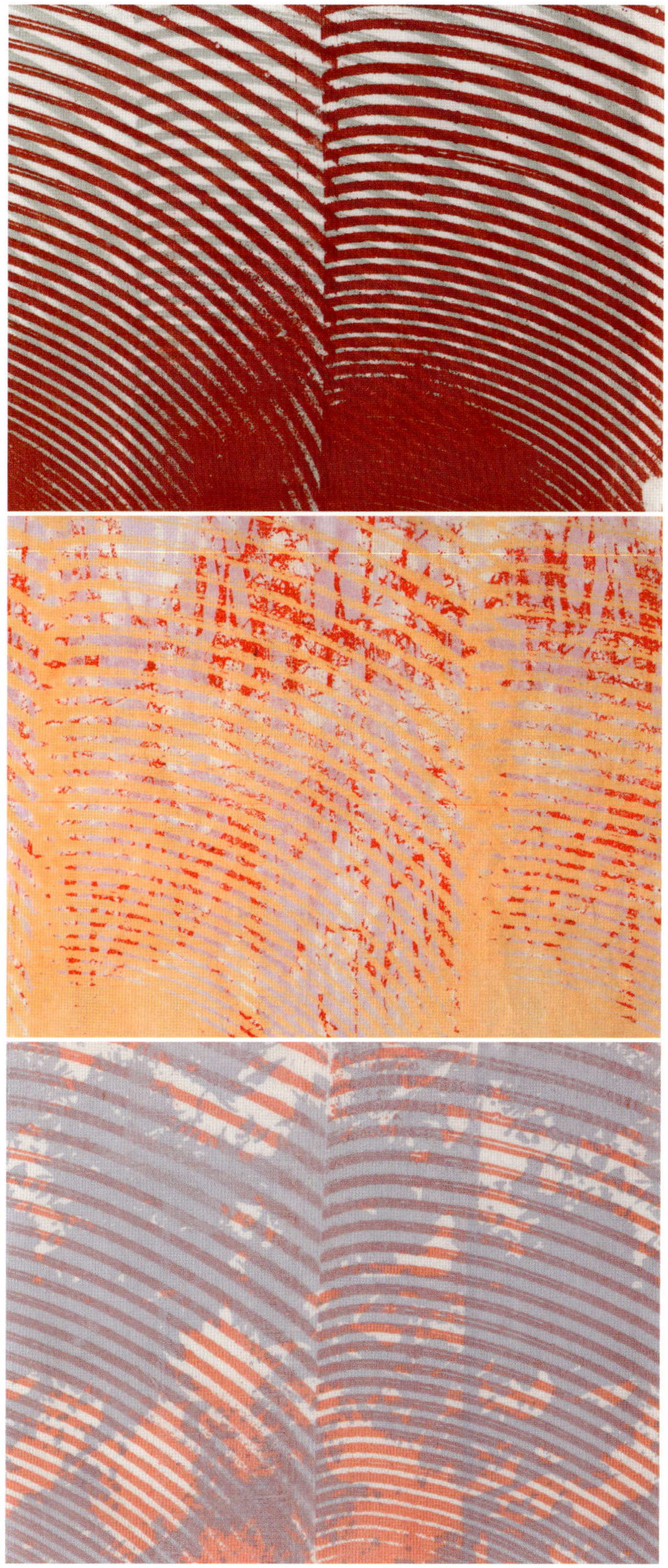

04-36 Loose (nongrid) repeats from the same screen, printed twice over a previously printed background pattern. High contrast (*top*), medium contrast (*center*), and low contrast (*bottom*). Textile pigments. Cotton broadcloth.

04-37 Screen-printed fabrics from 04-36 cut and pieced to form a background for appliqué. Textile pigments (patterned pieces) and Procion MX fiber reactive dyes (solid colors). Scale: about 12" × 18".

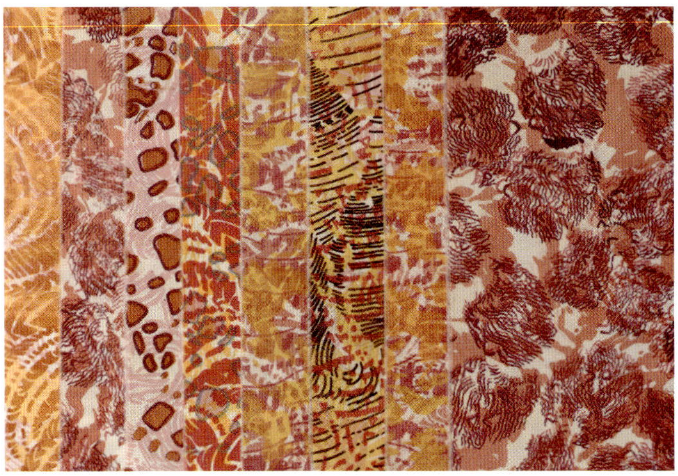

04-38 Collection of related prints combining a set of seven screens and warm, gradating colors (used to create the background for 04-39). Screen printing on white ground. Textile pigments. Cotton print cloth.

04-39 Screen-printed fabrics from 04-38 cut and pieced to form a background for appliqué.

The motifs in the stencils themselves can also be *thematically* related. For example, all the stencils used on the *collection* of fabrics in 04-38 were derived from the patterns on seashells. On each cloth, several stencil images were mixed and overprinted in subtly blending colors. When the fabrics were cut, interspersed, and pieced, their colors and images combined to create the pieced background in 04-39. When applied and assembled at a much larger scale, this approach can create large atmospheric and evocative color fields (04-01).

Registration: Repeat Pattern

Perhaps the most common use for screen printing on fabric is the *exact* and *orderly* repetition of marks, elements, images, or modules to create yardage. We'll define *pattern* as the *systematic repetition* of an element, a motif, or a group of elements called a *module*. Patterns rely on geometry, underlying lattices or networks that organize and place elements or modules in *regularly* repeating spatial relationships and orientations. This results in an even distribution of elements without variations (that is, each repetition is identical in both size and spacing).

At a deeper level, you can incorporate visual effects into the structure of the pattern modules and repeat systems themselves. For example, you can manipulate the density of the element placement: Sparser placement (leaving larger unpopulated spaces between repeated elements) will suggest airiness or lightness, and the pattern will just barely dimple the surface. Denser placement (proximity of elements) will attract more attention, "speak" more aggressively on the cloth, or even suggest congestion or crowding (which are not "bad" things if they're what you actually seek).

All printing of repeat pattern involves the use of an organizing grid (network) on the fabric, so that the printed images (modules) will be in linear alignment with each other across the yardage, regardless of whether the grid itself is intended to be visible in the printing.

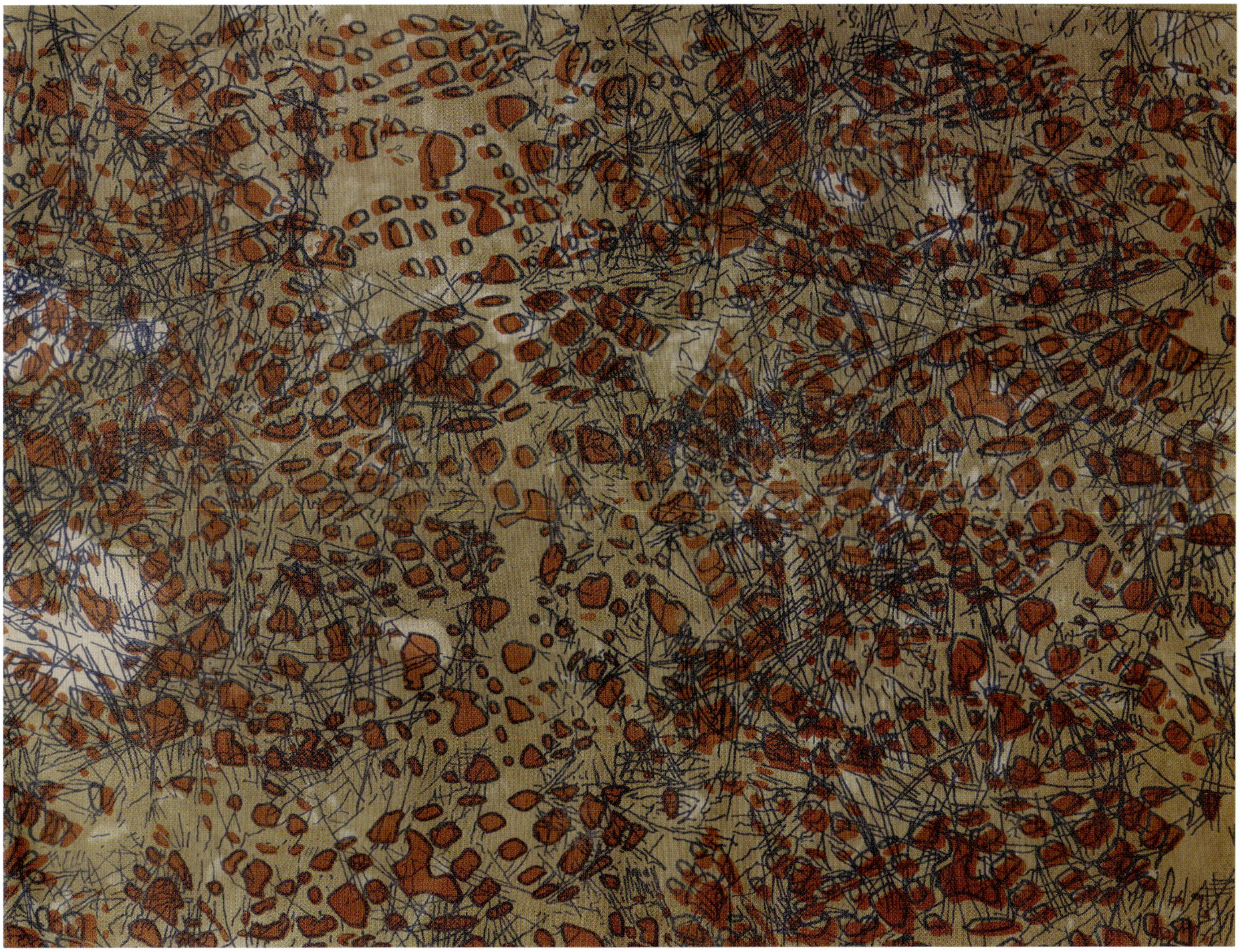

04-40 Previously low-immersion-dyed background fabric, overprinted with dark outlines of seashell fragment shapes, then again with a companion screen to fill the shapes, then a third time with blue pine needle shapes. Textile pigments. Cotton print cloth.

Repeat Pattern: Grid (Network) Visible on the Printed Fabric

Repeat networks serve as basic frameworks for the repetition of a motif or module to create a pattern. They are the means by which you *organize* the repetitions (i.e., exactly where you will place the screen on the cloth, *before* repeat screen printing ever begins). Each type of network imposes a specific geometric relationship among the repeated elements and suggests a certain kind of underlying orderliness, regularity, or flow in the pattern itself, contributing significantly to the expressive potential of the pattern arranged on it. The network may be well defined and quite *visible* in the finished fabric design, *or* it may be used only for registration purposes (to guide placement of the screen) and thus essentially invisible in the finished fabric. Geometric pattern networks, in particular, are meant to eliminate gaps or unorganized "leftover spaces" between the repeated placements of the screen. While you may most typically use square and half-drop networks (see the definitions below), the most common types, here is a broader list of possibilities you might consider.

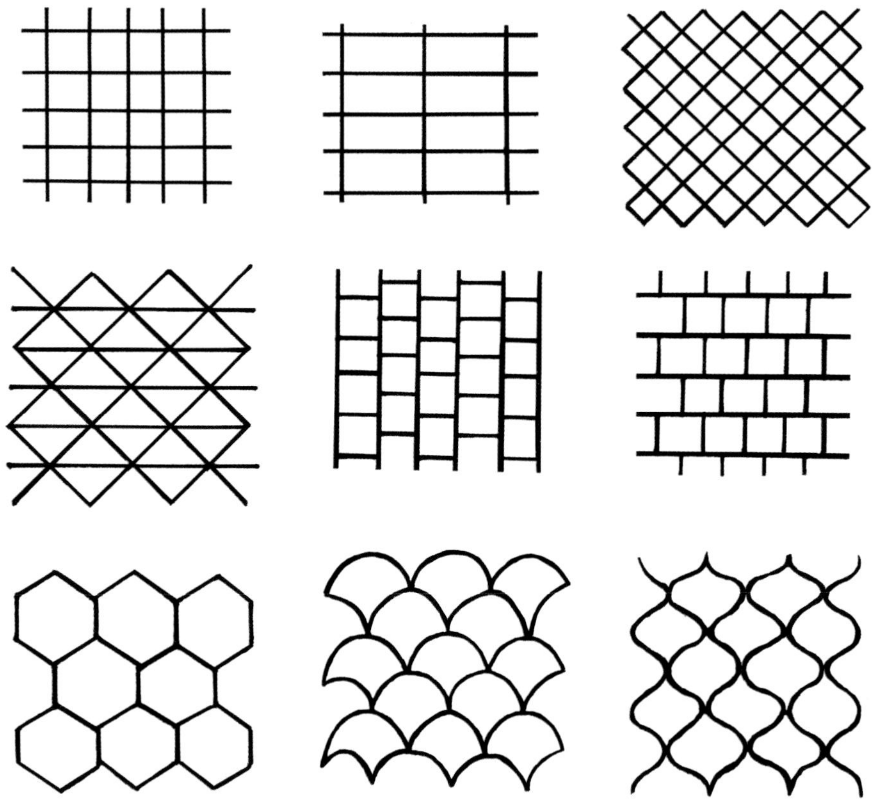

04-41 Repeat networks to be drawn on fabric before printing, as guides to screen registration. *Top row*: square, rectangle, diamond; *center row*: triangle, half drop, brick; *bottom row*: hexagon, scale, and ogee.

- *Square* (04-41, *top row, left*): A square grid is simple, direct, straightforward, and easy to use. It provides the greatest solidity, rigidity, and symmetrical order for organizing and containing a pattern. Real-life examples: graph paper, tile floors, checkerboards.

- *Rectangle* (04-41, *top row, center*): A rectangular grid, oriented either vertically or horizontally, rivals the square grid in orderly organization and additionally introduces directional movement into the layout. Real-life examples: accounting spreadsheets, information tables.

- *Diamond* (04-41, *top row, right*): A diamond grid made from squares turned 45º to rest on their points, in half-drop and dovetailed alignment, to fill space without any gaps. Real-life examples: plastic mesh vegetable bags, Italian mosaic tiling.

- *Triangle* (04-41, *center row, left*): Triangles alternate positions and dovetail to create repetition without gaps. Some types of triangles will combine to form other geometric networks, such as squares, rectangles, diamonds, parallelograms, hexagons, and octagons. Real-life examples: decorative ceramic tabletop, bathroom floor tiles.

- *Half drop and brick* (04-41, *center row, center and right*): A square or rectangular grid in which alternate rows *shift* the repeat one-half unit vertically (half drop) or horizontally (brick). Real-life examples: brick sidewalks and walls, polka dots, "subway" tiles.

- *Hexagon* (04-41, *bottom row, left*): A network created by interlocked and dovetailed hexagons (six-sided geometric figures composed by joining six equilateral triangles). Real-life examples: tiny ceramic bathroom tiles, tortoiseshells, honeycombs.

- *Scale* (04-41, *bottom row, center*): A network created by overlapping tangential circles (also referred to as a *scallop*). The direction of the scale's *point* will change the overall visual effect: pointing downward suggests energy, tensioned balance, and accentuation; pointing upward suggests calmness, rest, and suspension. Real-life examples: fish scales, bird feathers, drapery or bathroom tile patterns.

- *Ogee* (04-41, *bottom row, right*): A network in which double S curves (both convex and concave) create a serpentine contour. The orientation of the two points will emphasize either vertical or horizontal movement in the pattern. Real-life examples: damask table linen patterns, crocheted doilies, wallpapers.

Let's make this a bit less theoretical. And, for the sake of simplicity, let's remove it from the realms of screen printing on fabric, and let's also remove the variable of color. *Each* of the following patterns was made with a *single* motif cut into a *single* rubber stamp inked from an ordinary office-type ink pad, and the motif was then repeat-printed on *paper* across an ordinary *square* network. 04-42 shows a straight repeat, with the stamp and its motif placed continuously in the same orientation across the entire network. In 04-43, the motif was *rotated* 90º clockwise when printing each *alternate* cell across the network rows. In 04-44, the printed motifs were *rotated* in four separate 90º rotations around points where cells of the network intersected. Voids were intentionally left between these clustered motifs, but the voids are the same size as the printed clusters (i.e., the voids incorporate the same number of cells in the overall network as the printed motifs themselves), and therefore the voids still "read" as part of the square grid. In 04-45, the motif was printed a first time in each cell of the network, in the same format as 04-43, and each cell was then *overprinted* with the motif rotated 180º relative to the first printing of that cell.

In other words, although you may think at first that ordinary square networks and their regular systematic repetition would be quite limiting, with a little invention and experimentation you can create lively variations. **And all the patterns shown here could be done with screen printing instead of rubber stamp, and all of them could be done in one or more colors. Here's how:**

04-42 Ink on paper.

04-43 Ink on paper.

04-44 Ink on paper.

04-45 Ink on paper.

Instructions for screen-printing a simple motif in repeat in one color on a grid:

1. Make several sketches to develop a single motif. To make it easy to register on the square network and to print on a square grid on the fabric, make sure your design has at least one edge that completely touches the boundary of the square, as with the motif in 04-42 (which actually touches parts of *three* edges of the square). Choose the best of your sketches to enlarge to full scale, and then draw it on graph paper. Draw vertical and horizontal lines on the graph paper, parallel to and equidistant from its sides, top, and bottom. The intersection of those two lines should be the exact center point of the graph paper. Tape the graph paper motif sketch to a light table or bright window, so that you can see through it.
2. Choose freezer paper, contact paper, or sheet plastic for your stencil material but choose only *one* of these. Each of these materials is sufficiently thin that light can pass through it (see the earlier section of this chapter on "Block-Outs"). Cut a piece of stencil material at least 2" larger on *each* of its four sides than the size of your motif. (For this purpose, your stencil can, if needed, be larger than the graph paper itself.) Draw vertical and horizontal lines on the stencil, as you did on the graph paper, parallel to and equidistant from the stencil's sides, top, and bottom. The intersection of those two lines should be at the exact center point of the stencil.

3. Arrange the stencil material on top of the graph paper drawing so that the lines and center point completely match. For freezer paper or contact paper, the *back* of the paper should be facing you. Then tape the stencil material firmly in place over the graph paper drawing.

4. Using the light passing through these materials, trace the contours of your motif on back of the stencil material.

5. Using a precision craft knife, follow your contour drawing to cut the stencil as precisely as possible.

6. Choose a screen size that is at least 2" larger on *each* of its four sides than the size of the stencil.

7. As you did on the graph paper and the stencil before it was cut, use a pencil to lightly draw vertical and horizontal lines on the screen mesh (preferably on the face rather than the well), parallel to and equidistant from the sides, top, and bottom of the screen (it's easier to measure from the outer edges of the screen frame). The intersection of those two lines should thus be at the exact center point of the screen.

8. Attach the stencil to the face of the screen, aligning the axis lines on the cut stencil with the axis lines you drew on the screen mesh. The stencil itself should also now be perfectly centered on the face of the screen. Use the appropriate attachment method for the stencil material you have chosen. As discussed in this chapter's main screen-printing instructions, use masking tape on the face of the screen, and overlapping the frame itself, to block out any gaps of exposed open mesh outside the edges of the stencil.

9. Mix your colored print paste and have it ready to use. Tightly stretch the fabric you want to print, with its grain straightly aligned and parallel to the edge of the print table (see instructions on page 172). Place masking tape along the sides and ends to cover T pins and preserve clean selvedges and ends.

10. Using the dimensions of the motif you're actually going to print (*not* the outer edges of the stencil into which it was cut), calculate the size of grid you will need on the amount of fabric you intend to print. Measure the maximum dimension of your motif in each direction but then *subtract* 1⁄16" from the vertical measurement of the motif, and 1⁄16" from the horizontal measurement of the motif, and use the resulting numbers as the size of cells in the grid you're about to draw. (Yes, that's right, you will make the grid cells just *slightly smaller* in each direction than the module itself. Subtracting this tiny amount from the grid measurements eases the precision of the hand-printing process by allowing the modules to touch or overlap "by a hair" even if your hands are vibrating a bit as you place the screen on the fabric—which they will, assuming that you're breathing and have a heartbeat. That little 1⁄16" of forgiveness also offsets the tendency of fabric to swell slightly from the moisture in the print paste.) For example, if your motif, at its outermost dimensions, measured 6" × 6", then each cell of the grid you draw on the fabric will be a 5 15⁄16" square. Because all measuring tools vary slightly, use the *same* tape measure, ruler, or yardstick to measure the cells of the fabric grid as you used to measure the dimensions of the motif.

11. Use a *temporary* marking tool (such as washable graphite, washable marker, or disappearing marker) and a yardstick to draw the square grid, horizontally and vertically, *directly* on the fabric. This grid will guide the repeated placement of the screen on the fabric to create a repeat.

12. Practice registering your motif on the grid. Place your screen, with stencil attached and while both are *still clean and dry*, at either of the lower (nearest to you) *corners* of the fabric grid, and align the motif with the contours of the first cell in the drawn grid. (Remember that your motif design has at least one straight edge, and, looking *through* the screen, *use* that straight edge to align the straight edge of the motif with the straight edge of the grid cell.) Repeat this action when you move the screen to the next cell. (When you print, you'll be doing this each time you move the screen, but the stakes will be higher because the screen will be loaded with paste. Hence the importance of a literally "dry" run as practice.)

13. Following the main screen-printing instructions earlier in this chapter, load the screen with colored print paste and do some test prints on paper to make sure the screen mesh is saturated with paste and the entire motif image is printing completely. Now you're ready to print on the fabric.

14. As you did when practicing with a dry screen, place the screen on the fabric in that same first lower corner cell. Print the first cell. Then, lift the screen and set it down again, aligned with the next *vertical* cell of the grid (i.e., one grid cell farther away from yourself), and print the module again.

15. When you lift the screen after printing the second cell, the screen will have picked up (in nonprinting areas of the screen mesh) some of the paste from printing the first cell, which, if not removed, will produce "ghost images" of unwanted paste on subsequent cells. Therefore, beginning from the time you lift the screen from printing the second cell, and continuing for the entire rest of the print run on this grid, *wipe off* the *face* of the screen with a dry rag *before* setting the screen in the next cell.

16. Keep moving from one vertical cell to the next in this manner, until you have completed printing the motif in the first vertical column of the grid.

17. Move the screen to the bottom cell (closest to you) of the next *adjacent* vertical column. As in the first column, register and align the motif with each cell of the grid as you proceed to print upward on the vertical column, remembering to wipe the screen face between prints.

18. When you have finished printing on the fabric, clean the screen and set it aside to dry. Allow the entire fabric to dry to the touch before removing it from the table. Cure or set as appropriate for dye pastes (chapter 1) or textile pigments (chapter 3).

Notes for screen-printing a simple motif in repeat and then printing a second time with the motif rotated (as in 04-43) or in multiple rotations (as in 04-44):

- In the instructions above (a single printing, in straight repeat across a grid of rows and columns), it didn't matter whether the dimensions of your motif formed a rectangle instead of a square. The motif was simply being repeated in the same orientation each time, and if your motif was a rectangle with unequal sides, then your fabric grid was also drawn accordingly. But if you wish to print the fabric a second time with the motif *rotated* (as in 04-43 and 04-44), your fabric grid and the motif itself must be *a square*, so that even after rotation, the motif will still align with each cell of the original grid.
- Follow all the instructions in the section immediately above, *except this*: To achieve the effect in 04-43, you will do the first printing in *alternate* cells of the grid (as in a checkerboard), and the *second* (rotated) printing will then fill the cells remaining unprinted by the first. Or, to achieve the effect in 04-44, each grouping of the motif represents *four* cells of the grid (clustered around a single point), as do the cell clusters left unprinted, and the printed motif was rotated multiple times around that shared point.
- Note that any of these rotations of the image could also use a different color from the first (in 04-43) or multiple colors in rotation (04-44), but you will need to thoroughly clean and dry the screen before proceeding to the next color and do the next printing only after all the previous printings have dried.

Repeat Pattern: Multicolor Printing with Grid (Network) Invisible on Fabric

To print pattern that flows continuously across the fabric *without* an obviously visible grid (network), you must create a "dovetailed" repeat in which the organizing grid (network) exists only temporarily to guide the screen placement itself, while this dovetail printing method renders the grid invisible on the resulting yardage.

Designing a Pattern Module for Dovetail Repeat

To accomplish this seamless, continuous flow of pattern with interlocking dovetailed modules, you must adjust the external edges of the module (rendering them *irregular* rather than straight), carefully measure the repeat, precisely align the elements on the network, and check for accuracy along the dovetailed edges where the repeats come together.

While thinking about this in the abstract may cause you to feel that your head may explode, the following instructions describe what I consider to be the simplest (and most enjoyable) approach. The designing requires only paper, pen, ruler, scissors (or, if it's in your skill set, a drawing tablet attached to a computer), and ordinary office tape. You can, of course, find many other approaches to creating repeats in the literature, but they may not be aimed at printing that pattern *by hand*. (See the Bibliography.)

Instructions for designing a pattern module to be put in dovetailed repeat with hand screen printing in multiple colors:

04-46 Step 1: Initial drawing for a module to be put into dovetailed repeat. This example was drawn by hand on a piece of 6" square white paper.

1. Begin with a *square* of paper the *exact final size* as you'll you want for the module itself. (If you're using a tablet and computer, set the image dimensions to the exact final size.) Make note of the dimensions of the square, so that you can use them to construct the repeat network for printing the fabric with the module you're about to design. After you have decided on the individual motifs you wish to put in repeat, draw them in your square, laying them out in relation as you wish (tossing, flipping, rotating, and orienting them in any way you like). However, in laying out the drawn image, make sure that your design elements *touch the center of all four sides of your square* (leaving empty the corners of the square), but also make sure that no element of the image extends *beyond* the edges of the square.

04-47 Step 2: Precisely cutting the image from step 1 into four pieces, with design elements in all four parts, but without bisecting any of the individual shapes.

2. If the image from step 1 were simply placed on a screen and printed "as is" (even if the drawn image had completely filled the white space), the result would still be a recognizable grid across the fabric. But in dovetailing, even though the screen will be printed repeatedly across a grid, our goal is to render the grid itself *invisible* in the finished printed fabric. So the initial image must be broken up, supplemented with more imagery, and then reassembled. Therefore, when you are satisfied with the *partially finished* module design from step 1, cut it into four parts (manually with scissors, or digitally with your software's "cutting" tool). Start in the center of each edge *but do not cut through any of the shapes*. That is, as you come to shapes, twist and turn your scissors to cut precisely around the shape edges. This should produce quadrants that are slightly unequal in size.

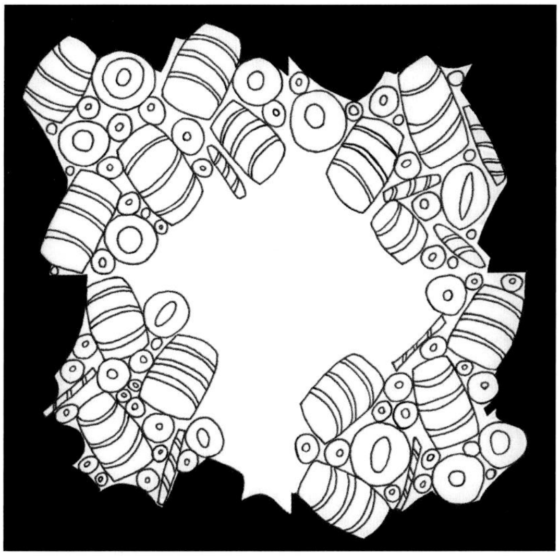

04-48 Step 3: Putting a pattern module in repeat. The four pieces from step 2 have been rotated 180º and taped together. Traces of the joining lines are visible in the four places (north, east, south, west) where the vertical and horizontal joining axes extend just slightly beyond the edge of the image.

3. Once the four pieces are cut apart, rotate each of them 180º so that the original corners of the paper meet in the middle. Align them so that their edges are butted together and the vertical and horizontal joins are perpendicular and straight. Use ordinary office tape to join the pieces together on the back. This now leaves irregular edges on all sides and also creates an empty space in the middle.

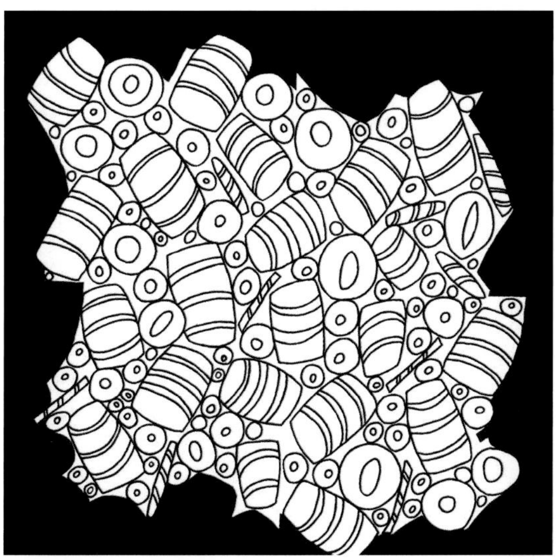

04-49 Step 4: Filling the white space from step 3 with more of the same design motifs to create the black-and-white master module.

4. But you also don't want to print the image from step 3 "as is," because you'll still have large areas of unprinted cloth corresponding to that white space in the middle. So now you need to do additional drawing to fill in that open space, placing the same motifs in approximately the same relationship as in step 1, making adjustments of shapes and placement as necessary to achieve balance and harmony.

   You now have a "master module," in outline format, to be placed in dovetailed repeat *for hand printing*. If you look at the left edge of module 04-49, you will see that it will neatly dovetail into the right edge when the module is repeated *horizontally*, as will the top and bottom edges of the module when repeated *vertically*, leaving no visible seams, grid marks, or interruptions in the pattern. The *convex* extensions of each motif will inevitably "fit" the *concave* indentations of its printed neighbor.

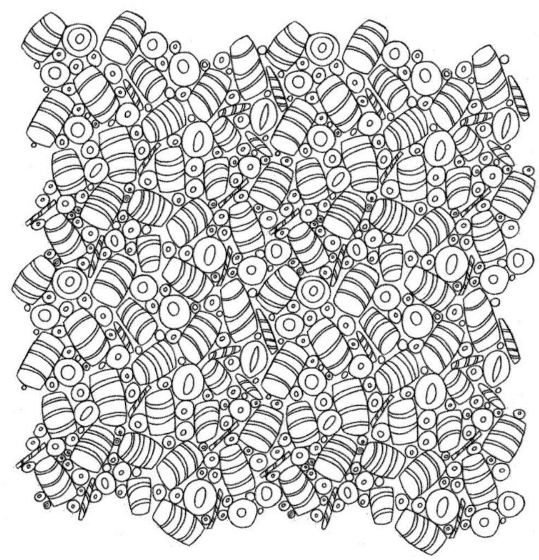

04-50 Step 5: Testing the accuracy of the repeat, using four cut black-and-white photocopies of the master module of 04-49.

5. Run a test for accurate repeat. Make four black-and-white photocopies of the entire master module. Cut *precisely* around the image edges of each copy of the module and lay out the four cut copies in a block (two vertical, two horizontal), each interlocked with the edges of its companions. This is how the pattern will look when actually placed in repeat on fabric. If you see any gaps in the aligned edges, the four modules have not completely interlocked, and any gaps between their edges will be left unprinted on the fabric. So check now for gaps, misalignments, or any unattractive or unwanted results in the layout of the motifs and correct them by returning to the master module itself (not these multiple photocopies) to do additional drawing as needed. Then, make four new black-and-white photocopies of the corrected module and test again (or, if working on a computer, scan the module into a digital-image management program to test the fit for needed corrections).

Although the dovetail method creates repeats in which no grid is visible on the resulting fabric, it does in fact use an accurately measured geometric network to *organize* the printing (i.e., the precise placement of the screen each time the stencil is printed on the fabric), in order to create a seamless and visually exact pattern in which the repeats of the module interlock and align with each other, as intended, when repeat-printed across the fabric. The grid organization remains *especially* important in repeat patterns because the printed image itself is not a square, and, therefore, exact printing in interlocking rows depends *entirely* on the accuracy of screen placement on the fabric. (Any irregularities will be multiplied exponentially down the length of the cloth. That is, with each new row of printed modules, any gaps, overlaps, or misalignments will increase in size.)

Printing the Module in Repeat, Using Multiple Colors

With your master module completed, you're now ready to choose the colors you'll actually print with it to create multicolored patterned yardage—such as you would find in the fabric store, but with your *own* design ideas, custom motifs, and colors.

To print multicolor repeat patterns, *each individual color* in the design will require its *own* screen and stencil (a technique called, naturally, *color separations*), which, when printed in sequence in *precise* registration with one another across a grid, will interlock with all the other stencils printed in other colors.

The example in 04-51 shows the color separations I chose for the master module in 04-49. To use the minimum number of color-separated screens for the maximum number of resulting colors in the pattern, I designed two of the stencils to partially *overlap and overprint* (04-52, 04-53, 04-54, 04-55) so that selected shapes on the red screen stencil, when printed over blue and gold, created, respectively, red violet and orange. (When printed, the red stencil would therefore perform "double duty" to create a total of *five* colors in the printed module, from *four* colors of pigment.)

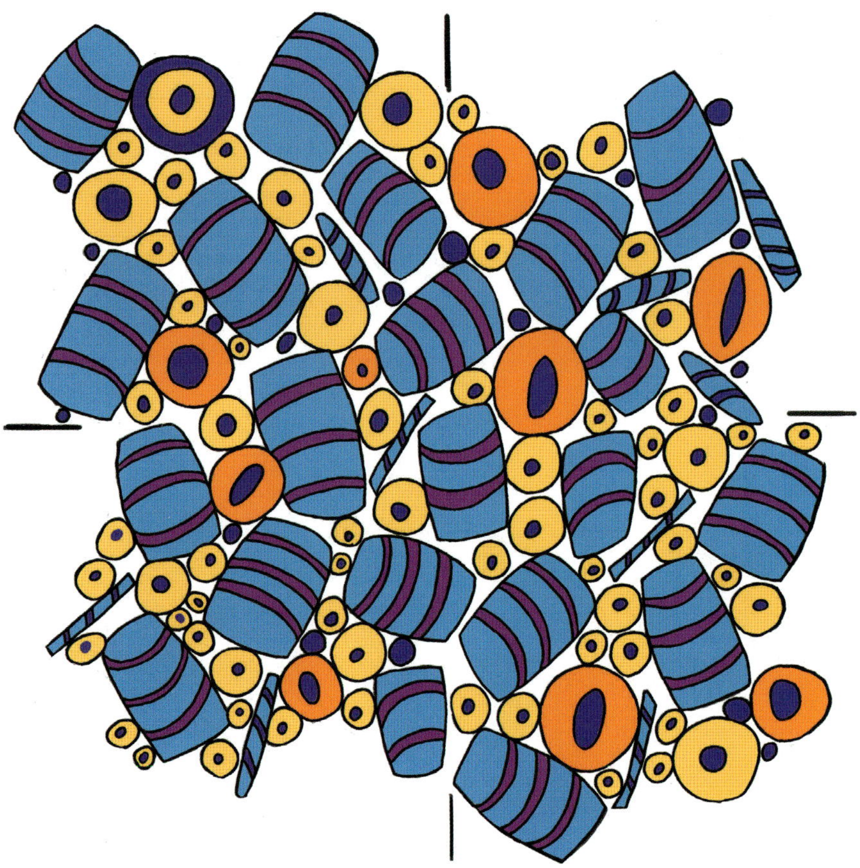

04-51 Master *color* module, with registration marks: illustration of chosen color distribution on the "master module" from 04-49. Color #1 is blue, color #2 is gold, and color #3 is purple. Color #4 is red and will be overprinted on the blue to produce the red-violet "stripes" on the "barrel" shapes, and overprinted on *selected* gold circular areas to produce orange.

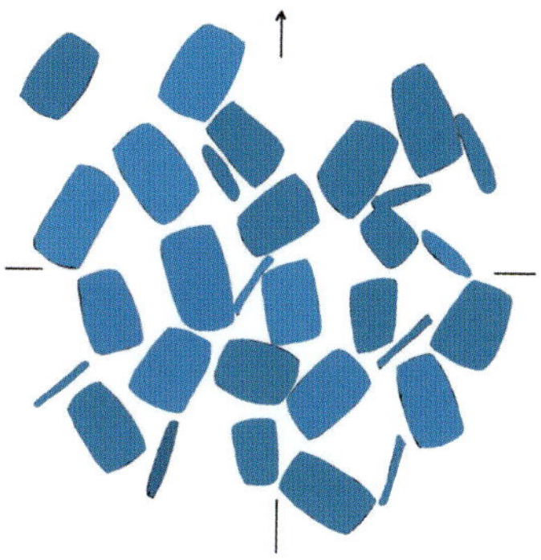

04-52 Separation for color #1 (blue).

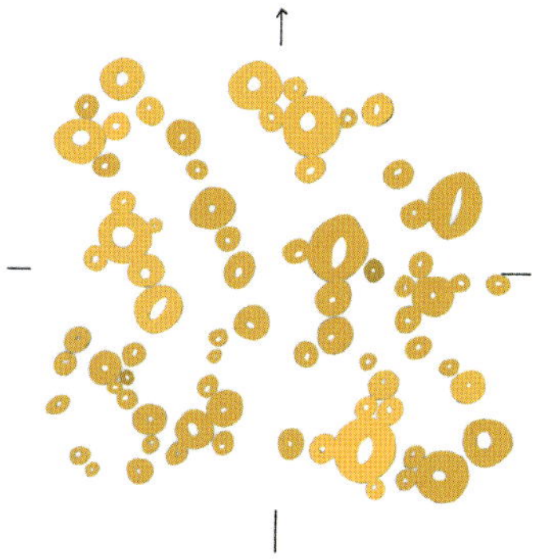

04-53 Separation for color #2 (gold).

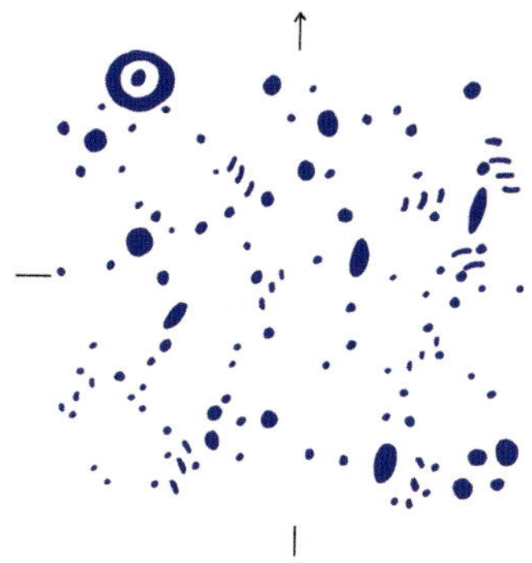

04-54 Separation for color #3 (purple).

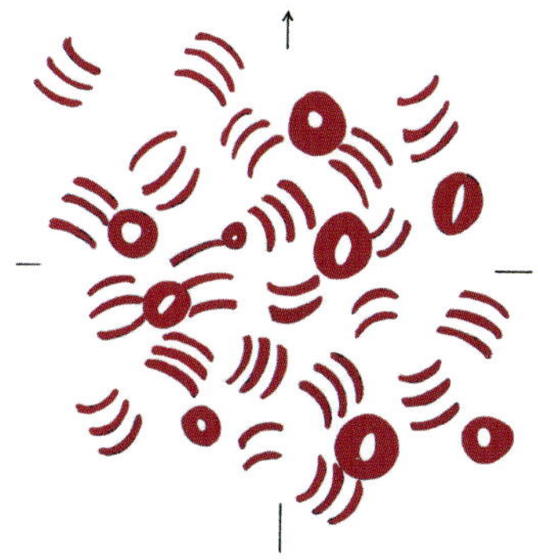

04-55 Separation for color #4 (red), an overprint.

Instructions for making color-separated hand-cut stencils:

1. Decide how many colors you want to use in your module. There is no "right" or "wrong" number. Your choice will depend on the imagery and motifs you've chosen, but remember that you'll need a separate screen and its stencil for each color to be printed, so perhaps limit the number of colors to what you find necessary to make an interesting and attractive pattern.

2. On a copy of the master module (04-49), distribute (fill in) your chosen color for each element. (In this example, I chose a color for the "barrels," a color for the circles, a color for the centers of the circles, and so on.) To visually balance the pattern, space the individual colors *evenly* across the surface in both directions. You'll be using this color distribution as the new *master color module* to create a separate stencil (literally, a *color separation*) for each color in the design.

3. From your black-and-white photocopy test (above) when originally constructing the module, you've already ascertained that the module components properly interlock with others adjacent to them. Now you also need to run a test to ascertain that the *color repeat* is harmonious. Make four *color* photocopies of the entire master module with the colors you propose. Cut *precisely* around the image edges of each copy and lay out the four cut copies in a block (two vertical, two horizontal), each interlocked with the edges of its companions. This is how the colors on the module will look when actually placed in repeat on fabric. If you see any color imbalances, or any unattractive or unwanted results in the layout of the colors, correct them now by returning to the master module itself (not these photocopies) and redistribute the colors as needed. Then make four new color photocopies of the corrected module and test again for the desired color distribution. (Or, if working on a computer, scan the master module into a digital-image management program, add the colors, copy and repeat the module in a block, and make any changes needed.)

4. Prepare the master module to use as a template for stencil preparation:
   - Work directly from the *master color module* (04-51), which was "colorized" on the dovetailed *master module* (04-49).

   - On the master color module, place registration markings (straight lines) just outside the centers of the top, the bottom, and each side of the master module (as shown in 04-51). You'll be using these marks to ensure that the stencil for each color is centered on its screen and perfectly aligned in its vertical and horizontal dimensions, so that the printing of each of the successive color-separated stencils is aligned with its predecessors during printing. And you'll be transferring those registration marks to the *same* location on *each* color-separated stencil you prepare.

   - You will need light from behind the module drawing to accurately transfer the correct shapes onto your stencil material, and you'll also need to keep the module from shifting as you work. I recommend physically taping the module to a light table or a brightly lit window, *after* making sure that the vertical and horizontal registration lines you made on the module are also aligned with the vertical and horizontal axes of the window frame or light table. Then leave the module taped there for now.

5. Choose freezer paper, contact paper, or sheet plastic for your stencil material (but choose only *one* of these). Each of these is sufficiently thin that light can pass through it. (See the earlier section of this chapter on "Block-Outs" for instructions on attaching a stencil to a screen.)

6. The stencil that will generate the largest single color area among the sequence of stencils should become your color #1. This will also help with the registration of subsequent color-separated stencils during their own printing.
   - Cut a piece of stencil material at least 2" larger on *each* of its four sides than the size of your master module.
   - Place your stencil material *over* the module drawing taped to the light table or window, then tape the stencil itself firmly in place. (If you are using freezer paper, tape with the waxy side facing you. If contact paper, with the backing paper facing you. If plastic, the side facing you doesn't matter.) Your light source should now be transmitting through both the module and the overlying piece of stencil material.
   - With a pencil or pen, trace the registration marks from the master module onto the stencil material. Add an arrow to the top registration mark as a reminder of which side of the module should always be *oriented upward* during printing. Label the stencil with its color number (in my example above, the stencil to be printed in blue was color #1).
   - With the stencil material still taped in place over the master module, trace the contours of all the shapes that will be printed in color #1. These will become the guides for cutting stencil #1 itself. Leave the master module in its taped place, but you can now remove the stencil you taped over it for tracing areas of color #1.

7. Repeat the actions in step 6 for *each* of the other colors to be printed. Tape a fresh piece of stencil over the taped master module, trace the registration marks, add the directional arrow, label the stencil with its color number, and then trace all the shapes or lines to be printed with that particular stencil and color. When you are done with the entire series of stencils, you can remove the master module from the window or light table.

8. Recheck all of your drawings to make sure that each stencil is correct (it's important to do this now, before actual stencil *cutting* begins). Stack up the separate stencils on the light table or the window and *align* all of their respective registration marks and orientation arrows. Make sure the stencils fit together as they should, so that when one stencil is printed over another, all the shapes and colors will match the composite multicolor image you created in the master module. You can still adjust the drawn lines (if necessary).

9. Using a precision craft knife, accurately cut each stencil, one at a time.

10. Choose your screen size. Provided that each screen is sufficiently large to encompass the entire area of the master module (plus the taped borders of the screen), it's not imperative to use screens of the same size for all of your colors. However, it's simpler to do so. Remember that you will need extra space in the screen well for "parking" pigment during printing, and that you'll be taping around the perimeter of the screen face to prevent paste leakage outside the stencil image. Therefore, your screen size actually needs to be 2" larger on each of its four sides than the outside edges of the stencil.

11. With a light hand, use a pencil to draw a vertical line on the mesh of the first screen (the face side of the screen is best), parallel to and equidistant from the sides of the screen frame. Then do the same for a horizontal line, parallel to and equidistant from the top and bottom of the screen frame. The intersection of those two lines should therefore be the exact center point of the screen. Attach the stencil for color #1 to the face of the screen, aligning the registration marks on each of the four sides of the cut stencil with the lines you've just drawn on the screen mesh. The stencil itself should also now be perfectly centered on the face of the screen. Use the appropriate attachment method (discussed earlier in this chapter) for the stencil material you have chosen.

12. Repeat the actions in step 11 for each of the other colors and their respective stencils and screens. Once you have attached all of your stencils to screens, you are ready to proceed to the printing instructions below.

Instructions for printing color-separated pattern:

1. Decide on the amount of fabric you want to print. Tightly stretch the fabric with its grain straightly aligned and parallel to the edge of the print table. Place masking tape along the sides and ends of the fabric to cover T pins and preserve clean selvedges and ends. (When you print a dovetailed repeat on a fabric grid, some of the printed areas will extend beyond the edges of the fabric, and that's what your drop cloth is for.)

2. Measure the maximum dimension of your module in each direction but then *subtract* $\frac{1}{16}$" from the vertical measurement of the motif and $\frac{1}{16}$" from the horizontal measurement of the motif and use the resulting numbers as the size of cells in the grid you're about to draw on the fabric. (Yes, that's right; you will make the grid cells just *slightly smaller* in each direction than the module itself. Subtracting this tiny amount from the grid measurements eases the precision of the hand-printing process by allowing the modules to touch or overlap "by a hair" even if your hands are vibrating a bit as you placed the screen on the fabric—which they will, assuming that you're breathing and have a heartbeat. That little $\frac{1}{16}$" of forgiveness also offsets the tendency of fabric to swell slightly from the moisture in the print paste.) For example, if your module, at its outermost dimensions, measured 6" × 6", then each cell of the grid you draw on the fabric will be a $5\frac{15}{16}$" square. Because all measuring tools vary slightly, use the *same* tape measure, ruler, or yardstick to measure the cells of the fabric grid as you used to measure the dimensions of the motif.

3. Use a *temporary* marking tool (such as washable graphite, washable marker, or disappearing marker) and a yardstick to draw the square grid, horizontally and vertically, *directly* on the fabric. This grid will guide the repeated placement of the screen on the fabric to create a repeat.

4. Once printing begins, you'll no longer be able to see the vertical and horizontal lines you drew on the screen mesh when you centered the stencil on it. And the frame of the screen, being substantially larger in its dimensions than the module actually being printed, will overlap more than one cell in the grid as you move the screen around to print. Therefore, you'll need to place *new* registration marks *on the frame* of the screen in order to guide your screen placement. Here's how:

04-56 Adding registration marks to screen frame in multiple locations. The marks align with the grid drawn on the stretched fabric to ease accurate repetition on the cloth.

- Place the still-clean and dry screen for color #1 at either of the lowest (nearest to you) *corners* of the grid on the fabric. Look through the screen to center the module in that first cell of the drawn grid (the ragged edges of the module will *not* fit neatly inside the cell).

- With the screen still in place, find the points where the grid lines on the fabric *intersect* each side of the screen frame.

- Place a small piece of masking tape on the side and back of the screen frame at *each* of those points.

- Using a fine-point permanent marker, place a registration line on the masking tape at each of these "match points," up the tape on the side of the frame and across the tape on the back of the frame, as if each drawn line was a *continuation* of the fabric grid lines *onto the screen frame itself*, as in 04-56. (When you print, you'll be matching up these screen frame registration lines with the grid lines on the fabric in each new printing location, thus allowing precise repeated alignment of screen and grid even though you can't *see* the grid immediately *beneath* the screen.)

5. You're finally ready to print! Mix your color #1.

6. Make test prints:
   - Until the mesh has been saturated with print paste, the first few pulls you make with the squeegee will not print clearly and completely. *Before* you ever place the screen on the fabric, you must first saturate the mesh in the well with print paste, and you must do this every time you start printing with a different screen for a different color separation.

   - Gather several pieces of uninked newsprint or other clean scrap paper. Place the screen for color #1 on the first sheet of paper, screen front side down.

   - Load the screen with print paste. If you are using *dye paste*, remember to *activate* it, just before printing, with the appropriate chemical (i.e., soda ash or citric acid crystals). Place a moderate amount of paste (2 to 4 T.), arranged in a long line across the width of the screen, at the top of the well. Make sure the paste is sitting on the *blocked border* of the screen and *not* in an open area that will print. (The larger the open area in your module, the more paste you'll need.)

   - Holding the screen stationary against the paper, and using the squeegee techniques described earlier in this chapter, make several passes of the squeegee to saturate the entire screen while also making a *test print* on the paper.

   - Lift the screen and inspect whether the image is clear and even and has printed completely in all areas. If not, repeat on another piece of paper and keep repeating until you are satisfied with the quality of the printing.

   - To finish up your tests, try printing the now-saturated screen on a *scrap* of the actual fabric you're about to print for your project. This last test will tell you how many pulls of the squeegee should deposit the required amount of paste (not too little, not too much) on this *particular* fabric.

7. Print color #1 in repeat on the fabric:
   - Once again matching the registration marks on the masking tape to the lines of the grid on all sides of the frame, align the screen with that first lower corner cell (*carefully*, because as soon as screen touches fabric, some pigment will be deposited, so your goal is to place the screen in exactly the right place on the first try).

   - Print the first module.

   - Lift the screen and set it down again, matching registration marks on frame to lines on grid, in the next *vertical* location on the grid (one grid cell farther away from yourself), and print that cell.

   - When you lift the screen after printing the second cell, the screen will have picked up (in nonprinting areas of the screen mesh) some of the paste from printing the first cell, which, if not removed, will produce "ghost images" of unwanted paste on subsequent cells. Therefore, beginning from the time you lift the screen from printing the second cell and continuing for the entire rest of the print run of color #1 on this grid, *wipe off* the *face* of the screen with a dry rag *before* setting the screen in the next cell.

   - Continue registering and printing from one vertical cell to the next until you have completed the first vertical column of printed modules.

   - Move the screen to the bottom of the *next* adjacent vertical column. Register the screen with the grid in the bottom cell of that column and print modules up the column, wiping the screen face between prints and also checking by eye that the modules are correctly dovetailing together both in the vertical and horizontal directions. If you move to the other side of your print table to better reach the printing locations, remember to rotate the screen in your hands accordingly, so it continues to align correctly with the printing you already did from your original standing position.

   - When you have finished printing color #1 on the fabric, clean that screen and set it aside to dry. Allow color #1 to dry to the touch before proceeding to color #2.

8. Preparing to print color #2:
   - When you prepared registration lines on the screen for color #1, you needed only to match those lines to the drawn fabric grid. But, beginning with color #2 and continuing through each of the subsequent colors, you need not only to match the screen with the grid but also to ensure that, when printed, color #2 will align with the actual printed motif of color #1. (And then do the same with color #3 after completing colors #1 and #2, and then with color #4 relative to colors #1, #2, and #3.)

   - While the screen for color #2 is still clean and dry, place it on the same lower corner of the fabric where you started the printing of color #1. Align the screen by looking through it to make sure that the color separation for color #2 is perfectly placed in relation to color #1.

   - Add registration marks on masking tape on the sides and back of the screen frame for color #2, as you did for color #1, above.

   - Load the screen with paste and make test prints on paper, as above, until the screen is printing as you intend.

9. Print color #2 in vertical columns across the fabric, as you did color #1, continuing to wipe off the front of the screen mesh before printing another cell. Each time you move the screen to a new location on the grid, even if you have already matched up the registration marks, also look *through* the stencil to check its alignment before you squeegee the print paste. (Even with the screen sitting on the fabric, you can sometimes still make *subtle* shifts in the screen position without smearing the paste.) Allow color #2 to dry to the touch.

10. Repeat this procedure for all of your subsequent color separations, allowing the print paste from one color to dry to the touch before proceeding to the next color.

11. After printing the final color, allow the entire fabric to dry to the touch before removing it from the table. Cure or set as appropriate for dye pastes (see chapter 1) or textile pigments (see chapter 3).

And here (04-57) is how the original module in 04-49 appeared when put into repeat using color-separated screens.

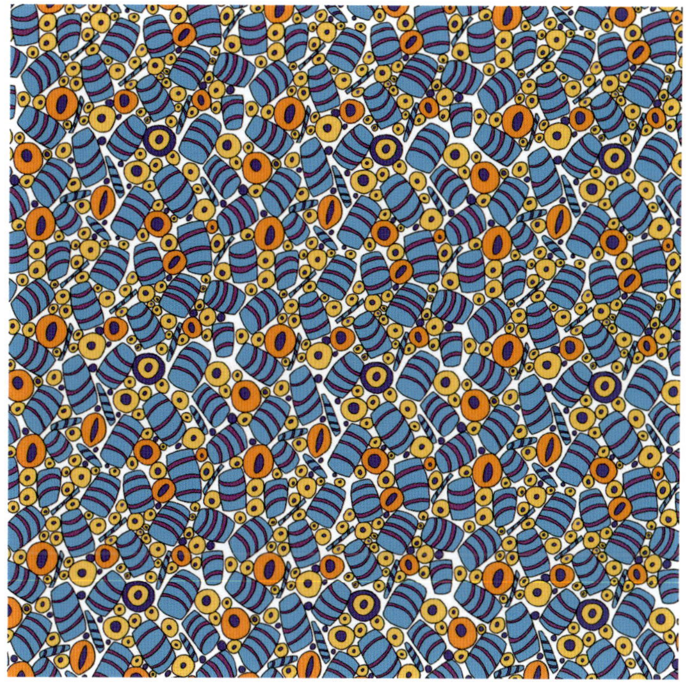

04-57 Repeat pattern created with the module illustrated in 04-49 through 04-52. A dense, visually active, and playful pattern in high-intensity colors.

Try this!

4.1 Repeat pattern experiments on paper

The goal: create a variety of 12 black-and-white patterns using *only* a single module (repeated, rotated, or overprinted inventively). See 04-42 through 04-45 for examples.

- With pencil and paper, sketch several ideas for a small *asymmetrical* motif and choose the one you like best to be made into a printing stamp. You'll be carving this image into rubber stamp material (available in sheets at craft stores) or a white plastic eraser. (If you make a rubber stamp, you'll have to adhere it to some kind of wooden block in order to hold it when you eventually print. Many white plastic erasers are made with 1.5" as one of their dimensions, and 1.5" × 1.5" is also a good size for this small-scale experiment.)

- Draw your sketched image onto the stamping material.

- Using a precision craft knife, cut away the "negative space" around the motif (i.e., all the stamping material you *don't* want to print).

- Using ruler and fine-point marker, lay out a grid on a piece of white paper. (You want a *dark* marker because, to avoid drawing the grid again and again, you'll want to see this *single* grid *through* other pieces of paper you'll be laying on top of it—and I'll get to that in a moment.) Each cell in the grid should be the same size as your stamp, and the grid should have enough cells to accommodate printing the motif *at least* four times horizontally and four times vertically. Therefore, the number of cells in the grid also needs to be a multiple of the size of the stamp. If, for example, your stamp is 1.5", your grid will have 1.5" squares, and in order to print at least four times in each direction, your grid will also need to be at least 6" × 6", or it could be 6" × 9" or 9" × 12". The same rule would apply if your stamp was 2" × 2": each cell in the grid would be 2" square, and in order to print at least four times in each direction, each dimension of the grid would need to be at least 8".

- Using drafting tape or "painter's" tape (avoid masking tape or office tape, because you need a tape that can later be peeled off *without* damaging your grid sheet or your stamping), tape down the grid sheet to a firm (i.e., hard, not spongy) worktable.

- Tape a piece of white paper, at least as large as the grid sheet, over it. You should now be able see through the overlying paper to the grid beneath.

- Using your stamp and an ordinary black ink pad, print the motif in *straight repeat* (i.e., across the entire grid without varying its orientation or spacing aligning the stamp with the grid cells as you go). When you are finished, carefully untape this printed sheet of paper (carefully, without touching any wet ink) and set it aside to dry. Leave the grid sheet still taped in place.

Print the stamp again in the following ways. Use a fresh piece of white paper for each, taped down over the same original grid sheet, as you did in the straight repeat above.

- *Rotation*: Experiment with several different ways of rotating the module while repeating it. For example, rotate 90º in alternating square cells (as in 04-43). Then start again and rotate 180º in alternating cells. Or rotate 360º around a point where four grid cells meet, as in 04-44. Or invent your own systems of rotation and repetition.

- *Voids*: Print the stamp while skipping certain locations where the module could have been printed but wasn't.

- *Overprint*: Repeat the module in such a way that a second printing on the same sheet of paper is rotated to overlap the first printing. (This is most effective when the overlaps create darker areas of black in contrast to the lighter areas of the single layer of stamped ink.)

- Combine any of the above approaches or invent more.

4.2 Masking tape block-outs

Use a pencil to draw a 4" square (or 6" or other, but start small) on the face of a screen.

- Design a square stencil, in the same dimensions as the drawn square, using torn or cleanly cut masking tape to be placed within the drawn square on the face of the screen. The shapes you form with the tape can be anything you wish (jagged strips, circles, triangles, etc.), and it is not necessary that each piece of masking tape meet the drawn square. But remember that you are using the masking tape to define "negative space" (i.e., the areas of the drawn screen square where you *don't* apply masking-tape block-outs are the areas that will actually *print*). Aim for an asymmetrical contrast of open and blocked spaces.

- When you are done applying tape for your design *within* the square, use more masking tape to completely block out everything *around* the square, out to the frame itself, so that no screen areas outside your design will be allowed to print.

- Print the module in repeat on fabric large enough (taking into account the size of your drawn square) to allow at least six to eight repeats in each direction, but also rotate the screen to overprint with other colors to achieve "optical blending" (see 04-17 for one example).

4.3 "Painterly" composition with screen printing

Goal: choose a direct-application experiment from chapter 3 to serve as inspiration for a compositional screen print. Use *informal* (nongrid) screen placement to create a large fabric print (for example, 36" × 44"). Your print may be purely compositional (as for a wall hanging, art book pages, or quilt component) or may have the potential for functional use (inclusion in clothing, accessories, or household items). Use any type of stencil, and as many different stencils as you wish.

- Use a specific *multicolored* source (photo or object) for inspiration and color matching.
- Brainstorm several different ways to lay out and repeat your stencil(s) on the fabric by sketching a few basic arrangements (some random, some intentional) in your sketchbook. Play with multiple ideas before committing yourself to the fabric. Choose one of your ideas to guide your printing, even if you won't precisely follow what you drew.
- Choose a fabric of any fiber type (cotton, linen, silk, wool, synthetic), fabric structure, or color you wish.
- Choose at least five colors from your source image and mix a color palette of at least five colors of textile pigments to match them.
- Work with all five pigment colors in your palette and your screen stencils to compose spontaneously by repeating the motif on the fabric in many various orientations and locations. Focus on keeping the composition balanced and aesthetically pleasing.
- After printing, you can also add marks or details with direct-application techniques to define, enhance, or spark the composition (see chapter 3).
- When the print is complete, thoroughly dry and air-cure it for two weeks, then wash and press it.

4.4 Experiments with overprinting

Printing one repeated stencil over another, or *overprinting*, will produce many interesting color combinations and patterns. Try some of these possibilities:

- Overprint your own printed patterns (with pigments or dye pastes) to blend colors, contrast images of different sizes, interrupt color blocks with linear patterns, or create complex textured surfaces.

- Overprint your own immersion, rainbow, or resist-dyed cloth (with either pigment or dye pastes). Respond to the dye colors and patterns (the dominant color background) to add accents and textures. Remember that adding new colors to a dyed ground requires adjustments in your color mixing as you put the printed color in a context other than white.

- Overprint commercially printed cloths (with textile pigments). If you have a lot of unsatisfactory or dull commercially printed fabrics, liven them up by printing your own patterns, marks, or images *on top of* them. Enhance, contrast, or alter the commercial print's overall color story or pattern as you play with scale, color, texture, and layering. (Remember to first wash commercial fabrics to remove finishes that might resist the textile pigments.)

4.5 Repeat pattern screen print

The goal: Print 1 yard of fabric in repeat pattern (for example, 36" × 44"). Design and execute a 1-yard hand screen print in repeat pattern in one color. Develop one of your more successful direct-application prints further or choose a theme of personal interest to develop the motifs and shapes for the stencil. Keep the module design simple and leave space around the central shapes so they don't have to touch or match when printed. Use any kind of block-out you prefer. Print with textile pigments on white fabric, using a square grid and any registration method to place the repeats. Thoroughly dry and air-cure the fabric.

Advanced try: Prepare a dovetail module that will use three color-separated stencils. Use three colors of textile pigment (one for each color-separated screen) to print a three-color pattern (for example, 36" × 44"). When done printing the module in repeat, you can add details and other colors in small amounts with direct-application techniques, as you wish.

4.6 THE CUMULATIVE CLOTH CHALLENGE

Start with the piece of fabric completed from one or more previous Cumulative Cloth Challenges. (Depending on how you responded to the challenge, this fabric may already have a general dyed color, a resist-dyed layer, and some direct-application markings combined as a *ground* for printing.) In this part of the challenge, screen-print with textile pigments on top of the colors and marks already present on the cloth. Repeatedly print a motif to create a pattern, or to emphasize certain areas with clusters of motifs and colors. Dry, air-cure, and wash. Make a note about the colorants, pattern, and methods you used, and take a photograph of the fabric. Set it aside for the challenge in chapter 5.

5 / DIGITAL PRINTING: SCANNED OR PHOTOGRAPHIC IMAGES ON CLOTH

Among all the topics discussed in this book, the specific types of hardware and software for digital printing are among the most certain to change, quickly and repeatedly, both after this book is in print or even while it was being written. Therefore, this chapter will not cover specific hardware and software products or attempt to provide technical instruction for them. Instead, it is intended to provide useful information—whatever the hardware and software available on the market when you first encounter this book—on how to think about, prepare for, and creatively use digital file making for fabric printing.

In *digital printing*, an image is assembled and manipulated with a computer and then printed, all at once and in its entirety, onto paper-backed fabric fed through an inkjet printer. This technique surpasses hand screen printing for the creation of complex compositions and diverse color palettes and is the best approach for transferring photographic images to cloth. The process of digitally printing on fabric can be conveniently broken down into two separate parts: imagining and developing the image (at home on the computer) and the actual printing on the fabric (at home or at a commercial printing establishment).

Digital printing on *cloth* is a relatively new creative tool, requiring admittedly expensive equipment (computer, digital camera, scanner, image management software, inkjet printer) and some computer software *knowledge*. The techniques can safely be done at home, perhaps even with the equipment you already have on your desk.

However, bear in mind that printer inks suitable *for fabric* haven't been around long enough to establish a truly long-term record concerning permanence or stability over time. If you want to make a digitally printed textile that you would

05-01 Layers of digitally printed cotton sheeting and silk organza, embellished with hand and machine embroidery and glass beads. Digitally printed with Procion MX fiber reactive dyes. Scale: 18" × 24". Collection: Duke University Medical Center, Durham, North Carolina.

characterize as a keepsake, be prepared for the possibility that the color in these inks *may* begin to fade over the course of many years—a characteristic that may yet improve with future generations of ink products.

The image management *software* provides a "virtual workspace" to reproduce, alter, or manipulate images, whether introduced to the software from physical *or* digital sources. (We'll talk about a variety of possibilities later in this chapter.) Once the image is in your computer program, you can alter, manipulate, and change it in any way you wish.

If you are already adept at using computers and a variety of software programs, the transition to printing on fabric will be easy. However, if you are new to this kind of use for a computer, you'll need some time to acquire the equipment, learn to use image management software, and feel comfortable with the tools available.

Fortunately, there are many books, local courses, workshops, and online tutorials available that provide excellent and *up-to-date* information and instruction in this fast-changing technological realm.

05-02 A simple desktop digital printing setup: scanner, computer, keyboard, mouse, desktop inkjet printer, graphics tablet and stylus (laser printer in background). An adjacent worktable to the right (just out of picture frame) provides a place to apply the paper backing, trim the edges, and process the fabrics.

The first section of this chapter discusses the basic equipment and supplies you'll need for digital printing.

The second section of the chapter offers approaches, expressive possibilities, and inspirations for *developing images* for printing, all of which are things you can do in a home studio or group workspace. Once you have completed that part of the process, you could decide to have your files printed on fabric professionally and delivered to your doorstep.

The third section of this chapter is for readers who also want to print their digital images at home. It provides a discussion of matching image types to fabric types, and the basic instructions for preparing the fabric, adding a paper backing, and choosing printer and color settings.

"The icing on the cake" is that any digitally printed fabric can also be combined with other wet or dry surface design techniques in this book to construct a cumulative cloth.

Studio Setup for Digital Printing

The equipment needed for digital design and printing is expensive compared to the simple tools needed for the handwork techniques discussed elsewhere in this book. But the basic setup requires relatively little space and poses no known safety issues beyond screen fatigue for your eyes and posture challenges from sitting for long hours.

When you buy any of the following equipment, take the time to carefully research each component to make sure it will suit *your* purposes, then make sure it will be compatible with all the other components in your overall *system*. (You may need a "computer geek" to help you with these decisions.) The following are usually essential:

- computer with significant storage space (image files are large)
- image management software, such as Photoshop, Photoshop Essentials, Painter, or any of the less expensive or free open-source alternatives
- flatbed scanner with a glass bed and professional-level scan control options, to transform physical image sources (e.g., photographs) into digital files
- graphics tablet if you intend to make digital image files from your own digital drawing or painting
- internet service to your computer system
- cords, connectors, and backup drives, and surge protectors to support your system

- Desktop (or wide-format) inkjet printer, if you're going to print the digital images yourself, instead of sending your files to a commercial fabric-printing service. Note that a home studio inkjet printer should be capable of using *pigment-based* inks, because they will print on cloth of any fiber content. *Caveat*: Inkjet printers of *all types* work properly only if they are run *frequently*. If allowed to sit idle for a week or two, their print heads may clog with dried ink, which then requires clean-out. Left for a month or more, the print heads can clog permanently. If you don't have any fabric-printing jobs "in the pipeline" for the near term, regularly print something anyway (on paper) just to keep the inks flowing through the jets.

- Desk or worktable. You will need a place to arrange and connect your equipment, as well as a place to prepare fabrics for printing.

- Comfortable adjustable desk chair. As you prepare images, you'll be spending a lot of time in that chair. Make sure it fits your body and supports good posture.

TOP: 05-03 Scanned screen-printed fabric sample using masking tape and paper block-outs. The sample was quick and messy but captured some good colors. Cotton print cloth. Scale: 6" × 9".

05-04 Color chip sampler drawn from the printed sample in 05-03, with identifying RGB color numbers for each separate color to allow reconstruction of the palette. Cotton print cloth. Scale: 8.5" x 11," chips each 1.5" × 1.5".

Imagery for Digital Printing

The development of original and unique images constitutes the heart of creative possibility in digital printing. Virtually any kind of image can be transferred to fabric by digital means. Whether you do the printing yourself or send the files for commercial production, you are in charge of the content, style, and preparation of the images. To create the most original and personally expressive images for your work, generate your own images *from scratch*, whether this means starting from existing *physical sources* that you've photographed or scanned into the computer or from *digital sources* such as your own digital drawings or digital photographs. The potential range of images is limited only by the capabilities of the hardware and software, and the scope of the creator's imagination.

Caveat: The technological ability to scan, photograph, or download images for your work is entirely separate from your *legal* right to do so. Avoid "borrowing" or copying the work of others without explicit written permission from the original author. Typical copyrighted materials include magazines, books, postcards, artworks, musical scores, and websites on the internet. If you want to borrow images, select them from *copyright-free* internet sites where you can use anything you find, without cost, legal obligation, or ethical transgression (or, better yet, create your own digital images and "own" them from the beginning).

Some Thoughts on Color Reproduction

Reproducing accurate color in the transfer from computer screen to fabric is an enormously complex topic. Not only are the color ranges and capabilities of each printer different, but you will have the additional variables of fabric structure, pretreatment chemicals, color settings, and post-printing washing. Each step along the way, colors can slightly shift. You can rely on the printer settings to get *close* to the color relationships you see on the screen, but the results will always be slightly different. If great precision is *not* an issue for you, but you want a reasonably saturated color to correspond to the monitor image, then I recommend that, just before printing, you set the *color intensity* about 15% to 25% higher to help compensate, then simply accept the results. However, if you want greater accuracy or color matching, especially as you advance in sophistication with the digital tools, you can invest in color calibration software for your computer to control the color more methodically and precisely. This is a solution *only* for the serious digital printer. (Note: The density and fidelity of blacks is often a problem when printing digitally on cloth. If you have a choice of black inks, *matte black* will produce the best-quality black on fabric.)

You can use your computer to capture colors from a source and insert them into a separate new image. First, scan the color source. In my example, it was an improvisational screen print made with masking tape and paper stencils (05-03). The sample was a mess (haphazard composition, printing smears), but the *color palette* was appealing, and I wanted to use it again. Most image management software will let you identify each specific color and capture it (usually with a tool that looks like an eyedropper) along with specific identifying RGB (red, green, blue—the additive primary colors) or CMYK (cyan, magenta, yellow, black—the printer's primary colors) numbers. You can choose any colors from an existing image by clicking on the image with the eyedropper, then drop them into a *chip sampler* (05-04) (squares on a page). After taking a broad sampling of the colors, you can choose among the entire chip sampler for the most appealing ones. Once again, you just need to click on the chip with the eyedropper and then drop that color into your new image wherever you want (05-05).

05-05 Selected colors from the chip sampler in 05-04 inserted into a new design in roughly the proportion of their use in the original fabric sample (05-03). Cotton print cloth. Scale: 7" × 7".

Scanned Images from Physical Sources

If you are accustomed to working with traditional or tactile materials, you can transition more smoothly into digital work by converting those *familiar* materials into digital files. With physical sources, your *flatbed scanner* becomes a "translation tool" at your service. Scanners are relatively inexpensive machines that come in handy for a variety of tasks in your home office and creative workspace. Choosing physical materials to place on the scanner bed is simple and is limited only by your imagination and the size of the glass bed on your scanner. If you don't have access to a scanner, then digital-device cameras (handheld, pad, phone) can also be used to transfer many kinds of images and also allow you the leeway to capture originals larger than your scanner's glass bed.

Most scanners have lids that will accommodate rather thick items on the bed (the manufacturers were thinking of books, of course), but you should avoid placing excessively lumpy items on a scanner bed (because they won't scan well), or jagged items that puncture the cover or scratch the glass bed (a blemish that will then show up in any future scans but is impossible to remove from the glass).

Materials must be placed *facedown* on the glass scanning bed, and the scanner lid should be closed. However, if the shape or thickness of the object requires the lid to be left in a relatively upright position, place the object on the bed and then, before scanning, cover it with a thick white cloth to prevent extraneous room items (such as furniture, ceiling, walls, and lamps) from making background appearances in the scan.

Before scanning, use any available tools in your scanner's software to customize your scans as you'll want them to appear. For example, most scanner software allows you to take the "raw" scan and then frame, crop, and set resolution (dpi), and also to adjust the hue, saturation, contrast, or color balance. (Using image management software separate from the scanner's own, you may have later opportunities to further modify the image, but the "raw material" is still provided by the original scan.)

As you scan, keep in mind that the better the detail and quality of the scan, the greater the amount of *visual information* available when preparing the digital file for printing, and the better the final print. Use the scanner software to scan the original materials into your computer at a relatively high resolution and save them as .jpg or .tiff format files. During the actual process of printing, the structure of the fabric weave itself will reduce the original level of image resolution. Therefore, it may be advisable to err on the side of a higher resolution in the scan. I recommend 300 dpi or greater, although resolutions above 600 dpi are rarely useful, because the increase won't be captured on the fabric.

Once your materials have been converted from physical objects to digital files, you can open them in your image management software, manipulate them at will, and print them at any scale your printer accommodates or your ideas suggest.

05-06 Digital image file scanned from pencil drawing of topographical map on tracing paper over Bristol board. Scale: 12" × 9".

05-07 Digital image file scanned from colored pencil drawing on smooth paper. Scale: 1.5" × 2.75".

05-08 Digital image file scanned from composition in pastels on Bristol board. Scale: 9" × 12".

Consider tapping the following types of original sources.

Hand Drawing

If you keep a sketchbook, you can directly scan pages from it. If you regularly draw or doodle, whether you use pencil, pen, marker, charcoal, colored pencils, or pastels, the scanner will pick up and transfer not only your unique style, marks, and gestures, but the textures of the original papers and drawing media. For example, delicate pencil drawings can be preserved in a scan (05-06) and transferred to the fabric with digital printing, to convey the soft fuzziness of graphite. Colored pencil drawings will transfer their waxiness and interaction with rough-surfaced papers (05-07), and pastels will transfer their essentially chalky character (05-08). With messier materials, such as pastels or Conté crayons, cover the scanner bed with clear plastic before placing the item on the bed for scanning.

Painting

If you already make paintings on paper or canvas, you can scan them complete or as selected details. Any kind of paint you normally use will transfer beautifully—watercolor, acrylic, gouache, oil, watercolor pencils—along with the surface textures of the paper and the paint. (Make sure the paint itself is *dry* before putting it facedown on the scanner glass.) If you wish to scan completely, but the original is too large for the scanner bed, you can still scan it in sections and then "reassemble" it in the computer, but you must also adjust the size of the final image to fit the capabilities and limitations of your *printer*. Simple painted gestures (05-09) or quick watercolor sketches (05-10) can be scanned and printed "as is" or further modified (including additional "painting") with your image management software.

05-09 Digital image file scanned from hand-painted gesture in textile pigment on paper, which was then scratched through with comb and fork.

TOP: 05-10 Digital image file scanned from travel journal drawing in watercolor and colored pencil.

05-11 Digital image file scanned from assorted textured materials on hand in the home: waxed paper, crumpled paper (newsprint), aluminum foil, bubble wrap.

Textures

Create and capture textures by placing textured materials directly on the scanner glass. The possibilities are nearly endless; try crumpled papers, handwoven fabrics, bubble wrap, grass clippings, aluminum foil, or waxed paper (05-11). Large fields of digitally printed textures can make wonderful backgrounds for other software-generated marks and images.

Found Objects

When you choose found materials to scan into the computer, confine yourself to those that are relatively flat and clean (i.e., things that can go on the scanner glass without damaging it). Search your house, garden, local walkways, and wastebaskets for likely materials. Expand beyond the obvious or closest at hand and let your imagination run wild with possibilities: slivers of tree bark, buttons, cut papers, candy wrappers, cork, corrugated cardboard, jewelry, beads, gift wrap papers, lace, wood splinters, twigs, leaves, eggshells, feathers, floor coverings, boxes, chewing-gum wrappers, waxed paper, aluminum foil, paper napkins, hair, maps, dog tags, matches, toothpicks, textured fabrics, memorabilia (ticket stubs, programs, invitations, cards, postcards, party favors), metal pieces or bits, sheet music, metal washers, newspaper and magazine text, handwritten letters and notes, playing cards, business cards, netting, mesh bags, nutshells, pebbles, charms, photos, plants, recycled fabric fragments, plastic, sand, sawdust, seashells, seeds, dried beans or peas, shavings (wood, metal, plastic), straw, string, veneers, wallpaper, wire mesh, *very* flattened aluminum cans. Reminders: avoid copyrighted items and cover the scanner bed with clear plastic before placing any sharp object that could scratch the glass.

05-12 Digital image file scanned from tree leaves placed directly on the scanner bed.

05-13 Digital image file scanned from shells and a sea plant, string, hair, buttons, crocheted doily, lace.

TOP: 05-14 Digital image file scanned from close-up photograph of lichen on rock.

05-15 Digital image file scanned from photograph of petroglyphs on rock face.

Physical Photographs

Many of us already have a collection of photographs on hand, and many other artists use photography to document subject matter or inspire work. You can scan any of your own physical photographs into the computer, make them digital files, and manipulate them to print on cloth. This is especially useful for subjects that no longer exist or cannot easily be rephotographed (05-14, 05-15), including, for example, archived "historical" photos of family, friends, pets, vacation destinations, and such. Choose any photographs from your existing collection that catch your eye for content, colors, textures, patterns, composition, or personal meaning. Instead of scanning an entire photograph, you can also scan details to magnify or combine with other images.

If you still use a film camera, you can shoot a new series of physical photographs specifically intended for digital development. Have the photos printed and then select the best among them to scan. Explore your daily surroundings for interesting textures, patterns, or images. Photograph subjects that particularly attract you. Shoot each subject from a variety of viewpoints: close-up or far away, from different angles, or from above or below. If you don't know where to start, try focusing on photographs of patterns and textures in your environment: tree bark, pine needles, pebbles, grasses, shells, manhole covers, leaves, stone walls, old building walls, geometric shapes. A photo tip: shoot your photographs close enough to the intended subject to cut out extraneous information and (because whatever is blurred in a photograph will correspondingly blur in a scan) keep the entire image in focus.

Fabric Samples

Fabric samples made from any of the wet techniques discussed in this book (or in its "Dry Techniques" companion volume), and fabrics you may already have on hand (for example, quilt blocks or stitched samplers), can be scanned and reproduced. The technology allows the multiple *reproduction* of *single* images created by hand, and the printing will reproduce both the overall impression and the individual details (both the glories and the imperfections) of the original object scanned, so that the resulting cloth will still *appear* to have been hand-produced. (See also "Fabric Collages," page 210.)

ABOVE LEFT: 05-16 Digital image file scanned from a fabric sample of potato dextrin resist.

ABOVE RIGHT: 05-17 Digital image file scanned from screen-printed fabric sample.

RIGHT: 05-18 Digital image file scanned from direct application fabric sample (the areas in color). Shapes in white were then created by using a software "sponge" or "stamping" tool to selectively subtract color before digital printing.

Fabric Collages

Collage is a term that usually refers to a hands-on technique of combining and adhering papers and other mixed or random materials onto a two-dimensional surface. Collages made with fabrics are usually sewn to a sturdy fabric ground but are built in similar ways with contrasting materials (05-19, 05-20). Entire fabric collages can be scanned to capture contrasting textures, details of threads, and weave structures on freshly *printed* fabric. (See chapter 8 in the *Dry Techniques* book for instructions and suggestions about fabric collage.)

ABOVE LEFT: 05-19 Digital image file scanned from collage of fabrics variously using screen printing, discharge printing, dyeing, appliqué, and hand and machine stitching. Cotton print cloth and thread, silk organza, rayon satin, commercially produced plastic-studded velveteen. Scale: 11" × 14.5"

ABOVE RIGHT: 05-20 Digital image file scanned from collage of fabrics variously using dyeing and hand screen print. Cotton print cloth, heavy twill, and silk organza. Scale: 9" × 12".

ABOVE LEFT: 05-21 Digital image file scan of cut paper collage of recycled magazine photographs. (For the fabric printed from this scan, see 05-44.) Scale: 4" × 6".

ABOVE RIGHT: 05-22 Digital image file scan of paper collage of recycled magazine photographs, assembling unlike images in contrast. Scale: 4" × 6".

Paper and Mixed-Media Collages

If kept relatively flat, paper and mixed-materials collages scan very well. You can make collages from any materials you find interesting, then scan to convert them into digital files that capture and freeze the collage construction. Once in the computer, the collage image can be further manipulated and changed: distorted, rotated, re-colored, textured, or drawn on.

05-23 Digital image file scan of spontaneous collages of cut paper and postcard strips arranged directly on the scanner bed. Scale: 9" × 12" each.

Spontaneous Scanner Collages

This approach to collage making is more playful and captures a sequence of related, but not identical, spur-of-the-moment collages made with *unjoined* materials (05-23). To start, cut, tear, or fold a variety of interesting papers, foils, plastics, or other flat materials into shapes that can be laid down in combination directly on the scanner bed. For a wide range of papers and textured materials, visit the scrapbooking section of your local craft store to discover translucent, textured, and beautifully colored rice papers; lacy cut papers; paper doilies; marbled book papers; patterned papers; and a variety of more unusual materials. From your own home, you can gather paper towels, aluminum foil, paper bags, labels, sandpaper, sheet foils, construction paper, plastics, vinyls, and acrylics. All of these materials can be cut into geometric or organic shapes.

Remember to place all materials *facedown* on the scanner glass. Unlike a paper collage, where you would build the background materials first and then add the materials to be seen on top of them, you must do the opposite if composing a collage directly on the scanner bed: Arrange *first* the materials you'll want in the *foreground* of the scan, and arrange *afterward* those you want in the *background*. Close the lid and scan. Those separate materials will appear to be visually *connected* in the scanned image. Before removing them from the scanner, look at the generated image. If you're satisfied with the placement of shapes and colors, you're done. If not, since none of the materials are actually fastened down, move them around on the scanner bed and make another image. And, of course, you can continue to "play" with the scanner bed collage to do as many new compositions as occur to you, or reuse some elements of the original collage but introduce others for follow-up scans.

When you have completed all versions of your spontaneous collages on the scanner bed, you can also make a *separate* scan of *each* of the original collage *elements*, building a *collage element library* if you want to generate future collages directly in the computer's imagery software (see section on "Digital Collage," page 212).

Drawn or Photographic Images from Digital Sources

You can also begin your digital-printing experimentation by creating digital files "from scratch" with a graphics tablet, digital camera, phone, or pad. If you have strong computer skills, high tolerance for time spent at a screen, and interest in imagery with a characteristic "digital look," this may be a good approach for you.

Digital Collage from Bits and Pieces

Now we'll expand our definition of *collage* beyond assemblages of paper and other physical objects, to include any combination of separate images or segments brought together in composition with a computer. Working on collage solely with image management software requires having a small library of images capable of being interestingly combined. If you have already set up a *collage element library* (described above), you can tap it now. Or, generate new *bits* and *pieces* from your digital drawings and photographs as ideas occur to you. Use the software (which may even have a function explicitly called *layers*) to place collage elements, or groupings of elements, as if they were actually in different physical planes, so that you can separately move and manipulate while combining multiple elements and layers into *digital* collages. Draw with colored marks or add new elements or images on each layer or on the assembled collage. Print from a flattened version of the digital collage but save the layered version for future manipulations and play.

TOP: 05-24 Digital collage from details of photographs of rocks on the Oregon coast. Scale: 4" × 4".

05-25 Digital collage layering a pine needle pattern over a paper stencil screen print (see 04-19 for the original improvisational screen print).

Digital Drawing and Painting

You can use a *graphics tablet* with your image management software to draw, paint, or create textures, images, marks, shapes, and color palettes. If you're new to graphics tablets, begin by playing with all the different tools, to learn how to vary the character and weight of the lines and marks (05-26). Then apply those tools to your ideas. Many graphics tablets allow you to see the drawing in progress directly beneath the stylus on the tablet itself (which feels like drawing on paper). Others, less conveniently, require you to look at a separate monitor to see the drawing. Either way, you capture the motions and gestures of your hand but can then still alter their character with the software as you create drawings (05-27, 05-28). With enough practice, you should be able to use a graphics tablet as comfortably as you would a pencil or pen.

05-26 Mark-making experiments with image management software. The marks mimic traditional tools: chalk, charcoal, pen and ink, pencil, and many different stylus shapes.

05-27 Digital image generated with a graphics tablet and stylus, using drawing and painting tools in Photoshop software. Different colors and software paintbrushes used in succession and worked spontaneously in response to a garden scene.

05-28 Digital image generated with a graphics tablet and stylus, using Painter software, intended to create the impression of a colored pencil drawing.

Digital Photographs

Photographic transfer is by far the most widely used approach to digital printing on fabric, and it was the initial spark that lured me into learning to use the technology. In its essentials, you can shoot your own custom digital photographs of any subject of interest (nature, close-up textures, words, numbers, portraits, travel images, details from the man-made environment) and then load the images directly onto your computer with a cable or a card reader. Once loaded, the photos can then be imaginatively layered, re-colored, distorted, rotated, dissected, or otherwise manipulated (05-29). This approach to photography allows you not only to use your own photographs as the inspiration for your textile work, but also to print the images themselves (or your custom manipulations of them) directly onto fabric at any image scale.

05-29 Two digital photographs, layered. *Bottom layer*: rocks and sand; *top layer*: fibrous cactus plant. Original images intentionally distorted, re-colored, and adjusted for opacity (top layer more "see-through") in image management software.

TOP RIGHT: 05-30 Digital image. *Left*: selected petroglyph symbols, originally photographed in color, flattened to intentionally eliminate sense of texture, and changed to black and white; *right*: then re-colored with image management software.

05-31 Digital image. *Left*: selected images of fern fronds, originally photographed in color, flattened to intentionally eliminate sense of texture, and changed to black and white; *right*: then re-colored with image management software.

LAYERING AND MANIPULATING IMAGES IN THE COMPUTER

Any types of digital images, whether the original sources were physical or already digital, can be combined, layered, or manipulated in the computer before printing. Be inventive and playful in testing the possibilities. Here are some starting points:

- Re-color or change hues, values, or intensities to differentiate balance or atmosphere in an image (05-30, 05-31).
- Rotate, distort, skew, warp, or otherwise manipulate the image (05-29, 05-32).
- Layer images, patterns, gradations, photographs, hand drawings, marks, or textures (05-25).
- Change and manipulate the levels of transparency and opacity in each layer (05-29, 05-32).
- Insert color gradations (difficult to achieve in hand printing) (05-42).
- Create patterns with your images.
- Crop and magnify parts of images to use (05-38).
- Use the special tools in your image management software to re-style or draw on the image (05-32).

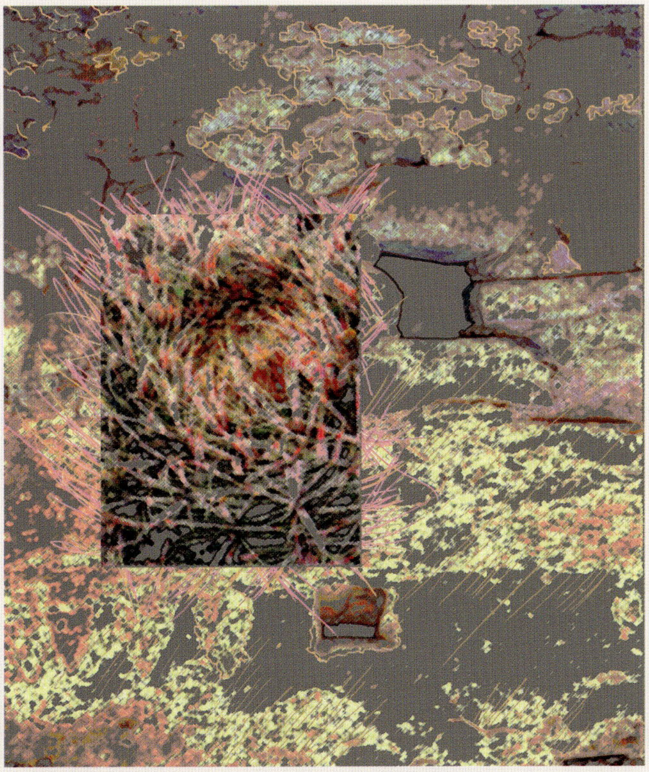

05-32 Digital image. Two scanned photographs, re-sized, layered, re-colored, and distorted, with added layer of digital drawing. (See the original scanned photographs in 05-33 and 05-34.)

05-33 Photograph of rock wall with two small windows, scanned, re-colored, and enlarged to serve as the background of the composite image in 05-32.

05-34 Detail photo of cactus, scanned and reduced in size, overlaid on rock wall image shown in 05-33 to serve as the foreground of the composite image in 05-32.

Printing Digitally

If you want to print your fabrics at home on your own inkjet printer, the following sections will provide basic guidance. Nevertheless, you will need to experiment with the specific printer to see what actually works for your ideas.

See also the sections on "Advanced Printing Technique for Small Sections to Construct a Larger Work" and "Mixing Digital Printing with Other 'Wet' Techniques," which follow these general instructions.

Choosing Fabrics for Digital Printing

A wide range of fabrics can be fed through an inkjet printer. The size of the *platen gap* (the space between the printing bed and the ink nozzles) defines the limit of the fabric thickness it will accommodate. In some printers, a choice of settings allows the gap to be manually widened or narrowed to match the gap with the thickness of the fabric to be fed through it.

The marriage of fabric and image is crucial to the success of the printed image—that is, finding the right kind of texture, the right fiber content, and the right surface characteristics (dullness/shininess, open weave / tight weave, light/dark color, and hand). I have worked with a range of fabric weights, from thick (heavy cotton twill) to thin (silk organza). All worked well in my small desktop inkjet printer, which does *not* have an adjustable platen gap, but that same characteristic also would have prevented me from using any fabric *heavier* than cotton twill. *Test* a range of fabrics with your own printer to understand its limits.

Because fabric itself is made from a grid of warp and weft threads, there are necessarily parts of the printed detail that will "fall through" the woven intersections of the fabric structure. This physical reality will almost inevitably reduce (or even slightly distort) the resolution of the image, as printed on fabric, compared to its original digital form. (Only an *exceptionally* tight weave structure will *approximate* the image resolution achievable on smooth paper.) Accepting this slight loss of ultimate resolution is just part of being satisfied with the outcome of digitally printing on cloth. A rule of thumb: the larger the image in relation to the scale of the fabric structure, the more of its detail you will capture. If, for example, you make a digital image at 300 dpi resolution and print it on linen (a fairly loose weave), much more of its detail will be captured if printed on a 3' square than if printed on a 6" square of the same fabric.

SUPPLY CHECKLIST FOR DIGITAL PRINTING AT HOME

- fabrics to print
- self-healing cutting mat
- precision craft knife and blades
- rotary cutter and blades
- freezer paper
- card stock (8.5" × 11" sheets)
- artist's tape
- iron

05-35 Lightweight, open-weave cheesecloth. Printed image of tiny marks broken up by the open structure, and the instability of the weave clearly (and, in this case, desirably) visible in the wavy distortion of the rows from the original scan. Cotton. Scale: 9" × 7".

05-36 Thin tightly woven cotton conveys flat images especially well, behaving much like paper. Edges of shapes and details are crisp and clear; ink lies flat on the surface. Scale: 6.25" × 6.5".

05-37 Digital printing on a semitransparent silk organza lends an aura of impressionistic mystery to the image of a tide pool. Organza also makes an excellent see-through overlay on other images and fabrics. Scale: 9.5 × 8".

Lightweight Fabrics

These vary in openness and tightness of weave, fiber content, and structures but include such *cotton* fabrics as lawn, sateen, muslin, gauze, and cheesecloth, and varieties of *silk* such as organza, shantung, and dupioni. Silk organza in particular captures a ghostlike impression of the original image, as in 05-37, and is thus well suited as an overlay allowing other fabrics to be seen through it.

Most of these fabrics are relatively flat, conform snugly to the paper backing needed for printing, and easily feed through an inkjet printer without platen adjustments. They accept a wide variety of image types without interference. (Lightweight cotton muslins are especially good for generating inexpensive test prints.)

The more open the weave structure, the likelier the color will seem to disperse slightly, and the softer or more blurred the resulting printed image (05-35, 05-37). Conversely, the more tightly woven the fabric, the better it will capture fine detail and color intensity (05-36). Tightly woven fabric will even capture subtle textures from the image, and the resulting print can *appear* to have a physical texture greater than the texture of the fabric itself. For example, the image in 05-38 was originally hand-screen-printed on *linen*. After scanning, it was printed on a thin *cotton*, but the resulting *printed* image still retained the visible weave structure of the linen original.

Sheers or semitransparent fabrics need to be arranged carefully on the backing paper to retain straightness of grain. (On the other hand, depending on your source imagery and intended printing outcome, you may actually want the pleasant wavering of a thin weave structure, as in 05-35.) Many sheers and semitransparent fabrics (such as silk organza) require heavier paper, a hot iron, lots of pressure, and being pressed flat under weights for several hours after adhering. And if you previously adhered paper to thin fabrics but then stored them, bubbles or edges may have appeared, and you may need to re-adhere them with an iron just before printing.

Sheers are best used for delicate or indistinct images, since they take the color *very lightly* (i.e., they'll have a slightly gauzy and washed-out appearance even if printed with vibrant colors). Because their open structure allows excessive printing ink to pass through to the backing paper, you can also economize on your inks by reducing image resolution to 150 dpi, or even 75 when printing on sheers. Allow sheers to dry thoroughly before you attempt to pull them from the backing paper (they dry quickly, *provided* you haven't used excessive

05-38 A tightly woven, thin cotton cloth captures all aspects of a scanned fabric sample: the colors, the image, *and* the texture of the original linen cloth. The flat cotton now looks heavier and more textured than it really is, a trick of the eye created with the print. Scale: 10" × 7.5".

ink). A certain amount of ink will have bled through the sheer fabric to the paper in any case, and the paper can't be reused.

Note that because light colors also reflect more light when viewed, the darker areas printed on sheers will actually be more transparent than the light, and medium values will provide the most transparency of all.

As would be expected, *synthetic* sheers lend a plastic "sheen" to the printed surface. They can be especially difficult to adhere to the paper backing. (To avoid melting the fabric, use a low heat setting on your iron, such as "nylon.") Like natural-fiber sheers, bleed-through ink deposits on the backing paper will prohibit its reuse.

LAYERING SILK ORGANZA

Prints on silk organza (and some other sheers) can be overlaid on other digital prints to add a mysterious sense of depth and interest.

- To avoid visual confusion, the two layers should be designed to interact for mutual enhancement.
- To reduce the possibility of creating an unwanted *moiré effect* (a perceived rippling caused by the misalignment of two grids), which may interfere with the reading of the combined images, carefully line up the grains of the two layered fabrics.
- Adjust the silk organza layer on top to make sure that the grain is straight, and the edges of the print are rectangular before basting or attaching the two layers.
- Remember that when printed on sheers, lighter colors will tend to reflect light, and darker colors (although more transparent than light ones) will tend to absorb it, so that the areas of *highest transparency* in the organza will be those in *medium-value* colors. Think about where you most want the cloth layer beneath to show through the sheer, and plan your design accordingly, making any needed adjustments in the digital image before printing it on the sheer.

Medium-Weight Fabrics

Medium-weight fabrics are undoubtedly the easiest to find, the most flexible to integrate into subsequent works, and the least difficult to feed through the printer. These include such common fabrics as quilting cottons, print cloth, muslin, broadcloth, sateen, satins, damasks, heirloom household linens (napkins, tablecloths, dresser scarves), silk noil, and softened linen. They are more stable than the lightweight fabrics, adhere easily to the paper backing, and accept intense colors very well. They feed through the printer more easily than lighter or heavier fabrics and get *head strikes* (marks where the print heads make unwanted contact with the cloth instead of just spraying ink while passing over it) only when the fabric is not firmly adhered across the entire piece of backing paper. The various fabric structures and fiber contents available in this weight category can add appealing delicate textures to the printed images.

05-39 Smooth medium-weight linen shows its delicate texture beneath this digital print in large blocks of color (re-colored version of 05-25, minus pine needle imagery). Scale: 9.5" × 7".

05-40 Silk noil enhances and exaggerates textures from a photograph of stacked roof tiles. Scale: 9" × 7".

Silk noil (05-40) has a lively hand, a matte surface, and a lovely nubby or gritty surface texture that makes it appropriate for images with equally rough or gritty textures.

Softened linen, similar in weight to silk noil, has a beautiful matte luster and smoother surface and goes through the printer easily, supporting a great range of image types.

05-41 Silk dupioni. Compare the intensity of printed color here with the "airier" impression made when the same image was printed on silk organza in 05-35. Scale: 10" × 8".

05-42 The surface shine of rayon satin enhances pastel colors and helps them shimmer. Digitally printed. Scale: 9.5" × 7.5".

Silk dupioni (05-41) is versatile and has a fluidity of hand and sheen of surface that enhances either straight-edged or textured images. Its lovely floppy drape may be great for clothing and accessories but may not join well with other fabrics in a pieced construction.

Satins are particularly appropriate for high-value (pastel), high-intensity (pure) colors (05-42). However, they tend to be quite slippery and mobile. Their grain must be straightened and pressed flat before the fabric is adhered to the backing paper. All satins have a distinct front and back side—make sure you print only the *front*—and they work best for images that will be enhanced by the fabric's natural shine. Due to the "floppy" drape of most satins, they resist straight seams when joined to other fabric types.

Fabric textures add actual *physical* dimension to any visual textures in the image, either supporting or interrupting them (05-43, 05-44). Like satins, *textured silks* (also called *figured*) are quite slippery and mobile and must be pressed flat and straight before adhering them to paper. To prevent head strikes or jams with textured fabrics, press the surface as flat as possible just before printing (and, if your printer has an adjustable platen gap, use the widest setting possible). Textured silks often have distinct front and back sides. Examine them carefully to make sure you print on the *front*. With

05-43 Ridged textured silk adds linear elements and surface dimension to a spontaneous scanner collage. Vertical ridges in the cloth cut clearly across the printed image. Scale: 9" × 7".

05-44 Tucked silk digitally printed with the image from the scanned paper collage in 05-21. The tucks run horizontally and the color changes in the print run vertically across them. Scale: 6.5" × 9".

05-45 Digital printing on voided velvet. Scale: 8" × 10".

05-46 Heavy cotton twill, with its sturdy hand and distinct, tight ridges in the weave structure, makes an excellent textured ground for an image of rock walls. Scale: 8" × 10".

pin-tucked silk, the tucks will lie to one side as they pass through the printer and create linear mechanical resists with the printing on top of the flattened tucks.

Voided velvets (05-45) provide a lush surface and soften the images printed on them. However, they're especially tricky to feed through a printer. To prevent head strikes, jams, or fabric rips, these dimensional velvets must be ironed very flat, pressed under sustained weight for a while before printing (for example, left overnight under a stack of heavy books), and fed through using the widest platen gap. After the printing has dried, their surface then needs to be rubbed *lightly* by hand to restore their original velvety texture.

Heavyweight Fabrics

Heavyweight fabrics (such as heavy cotton twill, lightweight cotton canvas, heavy kettle cloth, and most handwoven fabrics) are very stable and sturdy and capture lovely intense colors. They require more pressure with the iron to adhere the paper backing, but once adhered they grip the paper well. However, many of them are too thick to feed through the platen gap on desktop printers (test them on your specific printer). In all cases, these fabrics soak up a lot of ink, require a higher dpi resolution in the image being printed, and take longer to dry.

Generally avoid thick or fuzzy synthetics or thick fabrics with deep textures, which are likely to cause frequent head strikes on the surface or gather excess ink from the print heads and smear it across the fabric. Additionally, some heavy synthetics will melt onto the freezer paper during adhering, which will cause individual fibers to pull out of the cloth (in essence, ripping it in the melted places) when you try to pull away the paper after printing.

In my experience, *heavy cotton twill* is an inexpensive and sturdy choice and takes printing inks very brightly. Once paper-backed, it feeds through the printer easily without needing an additional header (instructions for using a header below). On its front, it adds a clearly perceptible diagonal texture that must be taken into account when choosing a suitable image (05-46).

Cotton velveteen works best with images that convey the same kind of lushness that its texture suggests (05-47). While more expensive to use, velveteen's surface tends to increase the sense of depth in the print. However, it can wrinkle up or "crawl" when being adhered to the backing paper. To solve this problem, first press the fabric from the back carefully with an iron, then press it flat under weights (e.g., a stack of heavy books) and leave overnight *before* adding the paper backing. To prevent velveteen pile from catching on the print heads, it must be firmly and flatly adhered to the paper and

05-47 The lush surface of short-pile cotton velveteen adds sheen, depth, and a suggestion of water to this image of seaweed and rocks. Scale: 8" × 10".

05-48 Handwoven jacquard fabric digitally printed with a shadow image of enlarged fern fronds. The flatness, scale, and distinct contours of the leaf shapes are compatible with the scale of the threads and woven structure. Cotton and synthetic fibers. Scale: 8.5" × 11".

again pressed with weight overnight. *Caveat*: Not all velveteens are the same. In some, a shorter pile takes the ink on all sides. On others, a longer pile *may* lie down, which prevents the ink from soaking all the way through to the other side of the fibers, so that if its pile is rubbed in another direction after printing, it will reveal small dots of the original fabric color in areas where the ink didn't penetrate. This is not necessarily a "bad" outcome, if it's appropriate to the image and your intent.

Handwoven fabrics offer some very interesting digital printing options (05-48). Most handwovens are fairly thick and *may* have a front side and backside to their structures. Those that use thinner threads and make a cloth similar in weight to heavy cotton twill will probably work in most printers. Adhere the fabric firmly and press flat onto stiff, heavyweight freezer paper, with the grain straight and parallel with the paper edges. (Printing an image off-grain on a handwoven will immediately look lopsided and uneven.) Most important, before feeding the backed handwoven through the printer, *clip off all loose threads*, whether on the surface, selvedges, or ends (to prevent them catching on the printer's internal rollers) and use a lint roller to thoroughly clean the surface of the fabric. On the printer, use the widest platen gap possible, guide the fabric carefully as it feeds through the printer, and intervene to prevent jams. Perhaps the most important challenge with printing on handwoven fabrics is visual or aesthetic: Because handwovens typically have far fewer threads (what weavers call "ends per inch") than industrially produced fabrics, it is difficult to get the image to sit "in" the fabric of a handwoven, instead of superficially "on" it. In fact, some digitally printed images will look quite disconnected from handwoven fabric—an outcome that or may not be exactly what you sought. As always, it is important to ask yourself what you aim to achieve, then match the nature of the image to the nature of the fabric's scale and structure.

PRINTING ON PRE-PRINTED OR PRE-DYED FABRICS

An inkjet printer doesn't "care" what is already on the surface of the material. Thus, consider overprinting fabrics previously printed or dyed. You can choose commercial prints, recycle heirloom fabrics, or cut chunks from used clothing to concoct imaginative combinations of old and new. And, of course, you can also take advantage of this opportunity to digitally print on top of your own previously hand-dyed or printed fabrics, experiment with feeding the same piece of fabric through the printer in multiple separate passes, or add layers of text or gestures to build a complex layered composition. Be inventive and experiment with a range of combinations.

05-49 Scanned textile pattern, digitally printed on top of a three-color hand screen print. Contrast of shape sizes and optical color mixing. Scale: 10" × 8".

05-50 Scanned paper collage, digitally printed on top of a hand screen print. Complex interference and color contrasts. Scale: 9.5" × 7.5".

Preparing Fabrics for Printing

In this section, we'll review the steps necessary to prepare fabric for digital printing on your home printer: pretreatment for color permanence, adhering a paper backing and optional card stock header, key computer settings, making the print, and what to do afterward. You can expand on these basic tips as you get to know the demands and quirks of your own individual printer.

Pretreating the Fabric for Color Permanence

Generally speaking, printer inks are formulated for paper and not meant to withstand the rigors encountered by fabrics (such as being bent, folded, washed, dried, rubbed, and handled). This characteristic of printer ink leads to necessary procedures to make them more permanent.

As with the hand-coloring and hand-printing techniques discussed in previous chapters of this book, a machine printer can use dye-based or pigment-based inks. I recommend pigment based because they incorporate a binder and can therefore be used on fabric of any fiber content, whether natural or synthetic, they don't require the fabric to be pretreated (although you can, of course, still choose to buy fabric already pretreated, or pretreat your own), and the printed colors will usually become permanent on fabric if air-cured for two weeks (just as you would for textile pigments).

Printers using *nonpigment* inks require that the fabric be pretreated for the inks to become permanent.

Fabrics intended for digital printing, already pretreated, and print-ready with paper backing already applied, are sold by reputable dealers. Such fabrics not only are convenient but will ensure ink permanence and brilliance on fabric. However, they are available in a relatively limited range of sizes, fabric types, and fiber contents.

If you prefer to choose your own fabric type, you can pretreat your fabric at home. The process is slightly messy, but it works well. (Note: Complete all pretreatment and *dry* the fabric *before* adding paper backing.)

Instructions for pretreating fabric for digital printing:

- Soak the fabric in the commercial product Bubble Jet Set 2000, diluted to 50/50 (chemical/water). Similar products may be available from other vendors.

- Press out some of the moisture (do not wring) and lay the still-damp fabric flat on a piece of plastic sheeting.

- Leave the fabric undisturbed until it is *completely* dry.

Adhering a Paper Backing to the Fabric

Printers, nearly all of which were designed to print on paper, must essentially be "tricked" into printing on fabric by temporarily adhering it to a paper backing (in other words, the printer and its settings still need to "believe" they are printing paper). As noted above, you can buy print-ready fabric paper-backed, but you can expand your options by doing your own backing on a wider range of fabric types.

The simplest way to prepare fabric at home is to temporarily iron it onto the *waxed* side of *freezer paper* (available in the grocery store). The following are the general instructions for applying paper backing for digital printing, but see also the section above for comments about specific fabric types.

Instructions for applying backing paper to fabric:

1. Unroll the freezer paper, *matte side up*, on a table. Mark off a number of rectangles of the size that will fit through your printer (for example, 8.5" × 11"), even if this is wider than the image you're going to print. Cut out the rectangles with scissors.

2. Place your fabric *facedown* (especially important on fabrics with a distinct front and back) on a padded surface or an ironing board and press out the wrinkles.

3. Place the rectangles of the freezer paper, *waxed side down*, onto the *back* of the fabric. Square the rectangles with the straight of the fabric grain. Press each rectangle into place with a warm/hot iron (set the temperature consistent with the type of fabric being ironed). Keep the iron moving and *press down firmly* until the paper is adhered across the *entire* fabric surface, including its edges and corners.

4. Transfer the fabric, facedown, onto a large self-healing cutting mat. Using a ruler placed along the edge of the papers, and a rotary cutter (or scissors or a sharp precision craft knife), trim the backed fabric pieces to the paper size.

5. Prepare however many of these backed fabrics you intend to print, perhaps with some extras in case a specific printing doesn't succeed.

6. Stack the paper-backed fabric rectangles in a folder or between pieces of smooth cardboard and place them under a weight (such as a heavy book) to keep them flat ready to use. This is especially important in humid climates.

Note: You can substitute *fusible web* (see the Glossary), which comes on its own paper backing, for freezer paper. In this case, the fused web will *remain* on the back of the fabric even after the paper is removed, so that your digital prints will themselves assume the character of fusible fabrics for potential combination (although not simultaneous printing) back to back with other fabrics.

Adding a card stock header (optional, depending on fabric):
To avoid jamming the printer, you should use the widest platen gap possible, usually the "envelope" setting. However, adding a *card stock header* to your backed fabric will mimic the action of a bevel and thus further help feed the fabric smoothly into the printer.

1. Buy a package of 8.5" × 11" (or larger) card stock (the same thick paper used to make index cards, but also sold in larger sheets) from an art or office supply store.

2. Cut a 1" strip the width of your paper-backed fabric sheet (for example, 1" × 8.5").

3. Lay the paper-backed fabric rectangle on a flat surface, with *fabric side up*.

4. Slide the 1" header piece *under* the top of the backed fabric, leaving half of the header piece still protruding from beneath the fabric.

5. Using artist's tape, *attach* the paper-backed fabric to the card stock header with a continuous strip of tape across the leading edge of the backed fabric. Do *not* take the tape completely to the top of the header itself and do *not* fold the tape over the *edge* of the header on either side, since doing so may lead to exactly the kind of printer jams you're trying to prevent. (Note that you really can't print edge to edge on the entire fabric, and so the small strip of space occupied by this tape is not "sacrificing" any area of the fabric that would otherwise have been printed.)

6. Turn the fabric over with the *paper side up* and put another strip of tape across the *same* header on the back to join the header to the fabric's paper backing. Tape completely across the header but do *not* fold the tape over the edge on either side.

7. With scissors (or a precision craft knife and a ruler), trim off any excess tape protruding from either side, so that the ends of the tape align with the header and paper-backed fabric.

8. Use a lint roller on the front of the fabric to remove any last thread bits or lint that could gum up or clog the print heads. *Now* the fabric is ready for printing.

Making the Print

Using your image management software, open the image you want to print and make the final adjustments:

- Crop the images and adjust the size correctly for the printer and fabric sizes.

- Set the printer's paper-handling setting to the correct orientation (vertical "portrait" or horizontal "landscape").

- If you attached a card stock header to the paper-backed fabric, remember to include the length of the header in the total printer setting for length of print.

- If you are printing on a sheer fabric, reduce the dpi resolution to 75 or 150.

- Leave the number of copies set at "1." All digital printing on a simple home printer requires that the backed fabric be fed into the printer *by hand, one piece of fabric at a time*. You cannot set the computer to print "3," and you can't use its automatic feed or its paper drawer. Instead, print one piece, get ready to feed the next, and again instruct the hardware to print "1."

- The "paper choice" option controls how much ink is laid down. (Remember that we're trying to fool the printer into "thinking" that it's handling *paper*.) The "plain paper" setting uses less ink (and is most economical) but often produces skips in the color of the image on cloth. The "enhanced matte finish" setting (or your printer may have the same type of setting but give it a different name) uses more ink and achieves better color distinctions *on fabric*.

- Change the printing mode to "quality" (or the appropriate setting to make your particular printer move more slowly and lay down more ink, as if it was printing densely on paper). The "speed" setting, although faster than "quality," often leaves stripes across the image. In this case, slower is better.

- Make sure the fabric is still completely adhered to the paper. If not, press it again to adhere any loose places and to flatten any bubbles that could strike the print heads and leave smudges.

• If you attached a card stock header, check to make sure it is *securely* attached on both front and back, also without any loose places, creases, or bubbles.

• Guide the paper-backed fabric, *header end first*, into the printer just as you would load paper. (In most inkjet printers, this will be *face side up*, but if you're in doubt about your own printer, make a test by marking an × on one side of a piece of paper, feed it through the printer, and see which side got printed.) Use only *manual feed* to roll the leading edge of the fabric to the point where the printer rollers will grab it.

• Press PRINT! Keep an eye on the fabric as it moves through the printer, to make sure it doesn't jam. If it does, you'll need to use the stop function of your printer control or just completely turn off the printer, in order to extract the jammed fabric, which is then typically not reusable.

After Printing

When the fabric comes directly out of the printer, the ink is still wet and can smear.

• To carefully remove the print from the printer, handle *only the header* or the *unprinted edges* of the cloth. Do *not* touch any ink-bearing areas and do *not* allow any part of the wet fabric to touch any part of the printer itself.

• Lay the print out flat and allow it to *completely* dry before touching it again.

• Remove and discard the tape and the header. This prevents long-term contact between the fabric and the adhesive in the tape, which will leave a sticky residue.

• Once the header and tape are removed, you can store or *air-cure* your prints (just as with textile pigments) on the paper backing.

• When you are ready to use the fabric, *gently* peel off the freezer paper backing.

• To reuse the freezer paper (which may be possible for two to three print sessions, but not more), place it in a file folder and store it *pressed flat*.

• If you've used *pigment-based* inks for your digital print, let them air-cure (still flat on a table or pinned to a wall) for at least a couple of weeks.

• If you've used *non-pigment-based* inks, you will have had to buy pretreated fabric or pretreat it yourself. Follow the instructions from the fabric vendor, or your own pretreatment solution.

• I've generally found it unnecessary to wash digitally printed cloth bearing the appropriate amount of ink. However, if needed, digitally printed fabric, *once cured*, can be washed to remove *excess* printing ink (which will also prevent excess ink from rubbing off on your hands, or on other pieces of fabric you may wish to combine with the print). Gently hand-wash digital prints with Synthrapol and cool water.

SIMPLE APPROACH TO TESTING LIGHTFASTNESS AND WASHFASTNESS OF DIGITALLY PRINTED FABRICS

After printing, you can conduct some simple tests on your fabrics and printer inks. To be accurate and fully effective, these tests take about a month but require little actual effort or attention on your part. This procedure will work with all kinds of dyed and printed fabrics, whether your own or commercially produced.

To start, cut *three identical swatches* of the printed fabric you want to test. Make sure that you include a representative sampling of all the colors in the cloth. Make notes about the fabric processing completed (such as pretreating or heat setting) and any other important details.

- **Control:** Put the first *unwashed* fabric swatch in a dark place (a thick brown envelope, a large book, or a sealed box) *for a month*. The point is to prevent this "control" fabric being exposed to light. Don't remove it until the time has passed.

- **Washfastness:** Place the second fabric swatch between pieces of white cotton cloth, baste the three layers together, and wash this fabric "sandwich." Make note of the type of detergent used and the temperature of the water. After washing, immediately disassemble the package and check for signs of washout or fading on the fabric sample itself, or bleeding on the attached white fabrics. Make note of any changes or problems. Set it aside in a dark place and, after a month, compare it with the control cloth and note changes, especially if some colors are more stable than others.

- **Lightfastness:** Tape the third fabric swatch to a window, preferably in *direct* sunlight, and leave it undisturbed for a month. Then take it down, compare it to the other two swatches, and note changes, especially whether some colors are more stable than others.

Use the results of these tests in judging how you'll be able to use this digitally printed cloth. Do you need to avoid using it in a garment that will regularly be worn outdoors in strong light? Will you be using it in a wall hanging that will neither be washed nor hang in direct light, so that neither of those permanence factors really matter much? And so on.

Advanced Printing Technique for Small Sections to Construct a Larger Work

Small printers necessarily present size limitations on printing. However, you can use image management software to break up larger images into sections, print the sections separately on fabric, and then join them to assemble a larger *pieced* image. Because the image continues across all the pieces smoothly, the seams will go largely unnoticed in the pieced construction. Ultimate success with this approach depends on your artistic goals, the type and scale of the image, your software and printer capabilities, and your own patience and math skills. Here is a very simple approach, using Photoshop, which you can also adapt for other software programs. If your software has the capability to print sections of an image, the process is very simple.

Instructions for printing an image in sections using the "print selected area" option:

1. Open the image with the software.

2. Size the image to the overall *finished* size you intend when all pieces will have been assembled into one joined fabric.

3. Fit the image on your computer screen.

4. Use the software to lay a temporary grid over the image.

5. Now for some math: Your goal is to break the image into equal parts that will print on the page size your printer allows. To each section you will need to add about ¼" *on each side where there will be a seam.* For example: Suppose you have an image that you want to be 15" wide × 20" high. You can break that image into four equal parts, each 7.5" wide × 10" high, and each one will easily fit on an 8.5" × 11" piece of paper-backed fabric. Since there are only four parts to construct this image, you need to add ¼" seam allowances only on the sides that meet in the middle of the image, as indicated by the red lines in 05-51. Therefore, in this example the size of each selected area will be 7.75" × 10.25".

   - Choose the marquee or selection tool from the software toolbox. If you can choose a fixed size for the marquee tool, set it to the dimensions of the selected areas (in my example, 7.75" for width, and 10.25" for height). This should automatically construct a rectangular marquee of the specified size.

   - Click on the image, and a fixed-size marquee should appear. Align the upper left corner of the fixed-size marquee with the upper left corner of the image. It should snap into place on the screen and align with the correct measurements on the ruler's grid.

   - Print with a preview, which should allow you to choose "print selected area" from among the printing options.

   - Load your fabric (properly prepared, as discussed in the general printing instructions above), using the manual feed option, and press "Print."

   - For the second part of the image, click on the image and align the fixed-size marquee with the upper right corner of the image. For the third part, align it with the lower left corner. And for the fourth (and, in this example, final) part, align it with the lower right corner. To keep the parts organized, mark the parts or their locations on the back of the paper as they come out of the printer.

   - When you are finished with the printing, you should have four pieces of fabric, with seam allowances built in, to sew together with ¼" seams (05-51) to construct the image in cloth. For maximum construction accuracy, pin, baste, and check the image before sewing the final seams.

   - My example had only four parts, but if you have an image with more than four parts, the number of seam allowances needed on each segment of the image will differ (the parts along the edges of the image will need only one extra ¼" seam allowance, but parts in the middle of the image will need two extra ¼" seam allowances). For these larger images, make careful calculations before you start printing.

05-51 Single photograph of ferns (target size = 20" × 15") split into four equal parts. After adding ¼" in each direction, the quarters are each 7.75" × 10.25". Red lines indicate the ¼" seam lines. When these four parts are sewn together, they reassemble the image in a larger format than the printer could accommodate.

Mixing Digital Printing with Other "Wet" Techniques

You can successfully combine digital printing with all the processes discussed in previous chapters of this book: dyeing,

05-52 Digital printing and overdyeing. Bold black curves digitally printed on cotton print cloth, then overdyed (see chapter 1) with low-immersion Procion MX fiber reactive dyes. High-intensity colors behind the black are easily perceptible. Scale: 10.5" × 7.75".

resist dyeing, direct application, and hand screen printing. Digital-printing inks behave much like textile pigments: the color is transparent, is adhered to the surface with a binder, and will combine visually with other marks on the fabric.

Digital Printing + Dyeing and Overdyeing

Fabrics can be dyed *before* digital printing or *overdyed* afterward (05-52). The overdyeing exposes the print to lengthy soaking in the dye pot. To prevent loss of color and detail, fully air-cure digital prints *before* overdyeing.

Whether dyed before or after printing, the dyed color will sit *physically* behind the printing (recall from chapter 1 that dyes *penetrate* the fibers, but pigments, even if they were printed *first*, sit on top of the fabric) but with sufficiently dramatic color contrasts may seem to advance *visually* toward the front of the print. In 05-52, many of the colors appear to be closest to the viewer, but the colors are actually the dyes that lie *behind* the black overprinting.

Carefully chosen dye colors can therefore intentionally connect, blend, or modify the printed colors. However, to avoid completely obscuring the printed image, keep dye colors *higher* in value and *lower* in intensity than the *printed* parts of the image.

INKJET TRANSFER PAPERS

To transfer photographic images onto fabrics or garments that will *not* feed through your printer (for any reason), I suggest *inkjet transfer papers* as the preliminary step. Print your image on the paper, then transfer it to cloth with heat.

General instructions: Prepare the image in the computer, reversing any letters, numbers, or critical right-left image orientations. Use an inkjet printer without a heating element to print your image on the transfer paper. Lay the printed transfer paper facedown in direct contact with the fabric surface. Press with an iron (or place in a heat press) to transfer the image. See package instructions for details.

05-53 Digital printing and resist dyeing. Digitally printed photo of sky and clouds, overdyed using arashi shibori (see chapter 2). Procion MX fiber reactive dyes, silk noil. Scale: 9.5" x 7".

Digital Printing + Resist Dyeing

Digital prints can also be *resist*-dyed, before or after the printing. Depending on the colors in the digital print, the resist marks can appear to sit behind the print or in front of it (as in 05-53, where the *arashi shibori* overtakes the more subtle digital print of sky and clouds). To help find a complementary combination of resist marks and printed images, adjust the scale and layout of each to complement each other.

05-54 Digital printing and direct application. Digitally printed, then stamped with rubber stamps (spirals, striped triangles) and textile pigments. Heavy cotton twill. Scale: 10" × 7".

05-55 Digital printing and hand screen printing. Delicate bubbly marks digitally printed on heavy cotton twill, then screen printed with large blocks of color. Cotton print cloth. Scale: 10.5" × 7".

Digital Printing + Direct Application

With harmonious color choices, directly applied (i.e., stamped, painted, sponged) textile pigments can blend well with digitally printed images (05-54), making the entire composition appear to be hand-printed. Direct handwork with *pigments* should be done *after* the digital printing (when it also helps to restore the tactile qualities of the printed cloth), but direct handwork with *dye pastes* should be done (and heat-set) *before* the digital printing.

Digital Printing + Screen Printing

Screen printing and digital printing are equally flat in appearance. Hand-printed images that contain visual breaks to expose parts of the digital print are often the most successful. Freeform screen printing is useful to isolate and build up selected areas in a digital print (05-55). Hand screen printing with *pigments* should be done *after* the digital printing (when it also helps restore the tactile qualities of the printed cloth), but hand screen printing with *dye pastes* should be heat-set, washed, and pressed, *before* digital overprinting.

Digital Printing + Discharge

As with textile pigments, printer inks do not respond to most bleaching agents. Usually the colors remain the same, although a few individual colors may lighten a bit with a directly applied *bleach pen*. However, if you have access to a digital printer loaded with fiber reactive or acid dyes (*not* regular paper-printing inks), then you can use any of the discharge chemicals you would use to reduce the color of those dyes, as discussed in chapter 6.

05-56 Digital printing integrated into an artwork also using hand dyeing, screen printing, discharge printing, felting, reverse appliqué, appliqué, and machine embroidery. Cotton twill and broadcloth, silk noil and organza, merino wool fibers, cotton thread. Scale: 38" × 76".

Try this!

5.1 Computer play

A good way to start experimenting with digital printing on fabric is to choose a single image and manipulate it on the computer. For this exercise, start with one of your own photographs and scan it into the computer. Then play with the various tools or filters in your image management software to change size, rotate, distort, rebalance or replace colors, or change its focus or viewpoint. Save a few of the best results as digital files and then choose fabrics whose characteristics seem to best enhance those images. Print three to four versions of the same image on several different fabric types. Use these in a project of your own or set them aside to embellish with some of the techniques in chapter 11 of the *Dry Techniques* book.

5.2 Scanned paper collages

Start this exercise by gathering a variety of interesting materials from which you can make six to eight small-scale collages. (See the list of suggestions in the section above on "Imagery for Digital Printing.") Choose a convenient size for the overall compositions and cut six to eight pieces of heavy paper or card stock to that size. Set out some adhesives (glue, glue stick, rubber cement, or double-stick tape) and a pair of scissors or a precision craft knife. Cut and arrange shapes and materials and adhere them to the piece of paper or card stock. Work quickly and spontaneously, without overthinking the compositions. Generally, place larger, more important shapes on the composition first, then add the smaller supporting shapes next.

Use an appropriate adhesive to attach all the collage parts in the first composition to their respective places on the backing. Let the adhesive dry thoroughly while you move on to the next composition. Try a variety of ideas to create contrasts from one collage to another.

Still looking for a focus and guide for your actions? Try choosing from among the following *organizing ideas* for your collage compositions:

- *Point of view*: looking through, looking down, looking up, looking around a corner, or looking from multiple directions

- *Contrasts*: close/far, hard/soft, hot/cold, warm/cool, opaque/transparent, lush/spare, bright/dull, light/dark, density contrast, texture contrast

- *Context*: camouflage or assimilation, anomaly (emphasis on a lone element), sequence

- Scan all of your collages into the computer. Print them on fabric types that either enhance or interrupt their rhythms and compositions. Either approach should yield some interesting results.

5.3 Improvisational collage on the scanner bed

Since you can move, rearrange, and repeatedly scan the results, this more spontaneous collage exercise makes flexible use of *limited* or special original materials (things you might not want to cut up or would like to save for future use). Gather a range of relatively flat materials: papers, found materials, fabrics, anything flat that appeals to you. Working directly on the scanner bed, arrange and rearrange the *unattached* pieces of original materials, facedown, *starting* with those you want to appear in the *front* of the image and *ending* with those you want in the *background*. Use the preview function of your scanner to check the arrangements. Each time you come to a particularly pleasing arrangement, lower the lid and scan. Or, try moving the software's marquee tool to select interesting sections from the arrangements, then scan those. Repeat this process, changing the arrangement of the elements each time to get a selection of 10 to 24 scanned collages. Choose from among these; make any additions, subtractions, or manipulations you wish; and print the best six on fabric. *To finish*: make an individual scan of *each* collage element to build a "collage element library" for use in future digital collages.

5.4 Digital collage from library elements

This exercise draws on the images in your digital "collage element library." Looking for contrasts or connections among the elements, choose at least a dozen and use them to compose a series of collages in the image management software on your computer. For maximum flexibility, work in layers, placing each element on a separate layer so you can move, rotate, distort, or repeat them. Assemble at least six digital collages and print them on fabric.

5.5 THE CUMULATIVE CLOTH CHALLENGE

Start with a fabric from the challenge in chapter 4, or any fabric that you have dyed or printed in the exercises in previous chapters. Make sure the fabric has been heat-set or washed and dried (or both). Design and refine a digital image to print on top of your dyed/printed fabric. Perhaps overlay an image that would not be possible to construct with hand techniques, but look for harmonious combination of the hand and digital techniques, so that, although created separately, they now seem "meant" to go together. Then print. Make a note about the printer settings and take a photograph of the combination fabric. Set it aside for the challenge in chapter 6 or use in other exercises in the *Dry Techniques* book.

6 / DISCHARGE: REMOVING COLOR

06-01 Layers of discharge printing (fern leaves and tiny marks) on low-immersion, hand-dyed fabric. Rongalit ST discharge paste, Procion MX fiber reactive dyes. Cotton broadcloth. Scale: 6.25" × 9.5".

After the previous chapters discussing the many ways to *add* color and pattern to fabric, we'll now look at an opposite process: chemically based *discharge* (bleaching) techniques to reduce, fade out, lighten, or completely remove previously applied color, whether across the entire cloth or only in selected areas. Discharge *removes* color from commercially dyed or hand-dyed fabric, either as an end in itself or to leave the fibers able to receive new layers of dye or pigment.

In the process of building a cumulative surface, think of discharge as a way to rethink the color without completely starting over, or a means of returning to that "Oops!" moment to correct a mistake or just to proceed in a different color direction. In 06-01, for example, the entire cloth was dyed in green, and because low immersion leaves portions of the fabric protruding from the main dyebath, the dyeing process itself produced a mottled effect among lighter and darker shades of green. But individual shapes of fern leaves still required emphasis to make them stand out from the background, and discharge was used to lighten them.

Until recent decades, discharge chemicals were confined to the textile industry, and out of reach for the studio practitioner. But you can now buy the chemicals from a variety of reputable dye and chemical vendors who cater to the small studio market. You can apply discharge chemicals in liquid form (for immersing the cloth), thin solutions (for dipping, painting), or thick pastes (for resist bleaching, stamping, screen printing) to create complex and unexpected reversals and visual textures. (Note: Rongalit ST, the specific discharge paste I used for many years and have cited in some of this chapter's image captions, is now difficult to find on the retail—as opposed to industrial—market, but the newer commercial discharge pastes are comparable.)

However, discharge chemicals of all types are toxic to breathe (requiring especially good ventilation and face masks that may need to filter vapors, not just particles) and irritating to the skin (requiring elbow-length rubber gloves). I do not recommend them for use in the home or small-group studio, unless you have a truly robust overhead ventilation system or can work exclusively outdoors (and still aided by fans). Because this book focuses on materials and processes suitable and (with proper precautions) generally safe for the home or small-group studio, this chapter does not discuss highly hazardous methods of discharge.

Discharge *paste*, selectively applied with screen-printing or direct-application techniques, allows you to insert light-colored shapes, patterns, or marks on a darker fabric ground, difficult to achieve with other forms of printing. Paste is the most common way to perform discharge, and the most precise in design terms.

While there are several types of discharge chemicals on the market, in this chapter I'll restrict discussion to *chlorine bleach* and commercially prepared *color removal paste*. These chemicals will reduce the color of fabric toward its pre-dyed color, although rarely to the original "industrial white." The chemicals work *only* to discharge on *dyes*. They will *not* work on pigments. (You can still discharge on a fabric you dyed and then printed with pigments, but the discharge will affect only the dyed areas around, or under, the pigment-printed areas, not the pigments themselves.) Viewed as a possibility instead of a limitation, this fact—the imperviousness of pigments to discharge—can be quite useful in building an evocative or "mysterious" cumulative fabric surface. For example, marks or images can be discharged from the dyed surface with a discharge paste that will leave intact areas previously printed or painted with pigment, creating dramatic or subtle (06-09) contrasts.

Immersing an *entire* piece of dyed cloth in a discharge *bath* will raise the *value* of the main color (on a fabric that is too dark) or lower the *intensity* (on a fabric that is too bright). In this sense, discharge is the opposite of overdyeing, which can only make a fabric darker, not lighter. I'll discuss discharge baths later in this chapter.

06-02 Discharge-printed fern shapes applied to multiple overlapped fabric layers. Handwoven, dyed, then discharge-printed, pieced, bead-woven, embellished. Cotton and silk fabrics, Procion MX fiber reactive dyes and Rongalit ST discharge paste, glass beads. Collection: Helen Moran, Bellingham, Washington.

Beyond this general lightening of color, *predictable* or *repeatable* results with *discharge pastes* are infrequent. The specific *colors* produced by discharge will vary from fabric to fabric, and from dye color to dye color, depending on several variables: fiber type, cloth structure or thickness, dye type used, the specific discharge chemical used, and the specific color already on the cloth. For example, in 06-04, 06-05, and 06-06, three *different* results resulted from printing the *same* discharge paste on three pieces of the *same* dyed fabric, in three separate working sessions. In 06-04 the discharged color is gray; in 06-05, tan; and in 06-06, yellow. How, you may ask, can three different discharge colors be generated on the same underlying cloth? These interesting variations could be the result of impurities in the water, traces of detergent left on the fabric, the particular dye colors mixed to achieve the original color, or differences in the type, age, or strength of the discharge paste applied. But in all cases, regardless of the actual color results, paste-discharged areas usually contrast clearly and distinctly with the dyed background. Occasionally, on some fabrics, the area discharged will be the *complement* (i.e., the color *across* the color wheel) of the original cloth color, but even this is usually not predictable. Bottom line: when you discharge, you'll always get something lighter, but you never know exactly what—and even a surprise can be viewed as a creative opportunity.

06-03 Screen-printed discharge on fold-dyed fabric. Cotton broadcloth, Procion MX fiber reactive dyes, Rongalit ST. Discharge chemicals reduce different dye colors differently. Here, the degree of reduction varies from nearly white in the areas originally dyed with magenta to light yellow in the areas dyed with green. Scale: 8" × 10.5".

06-04 Hand-dyed maroon fabric (same ground as in 06-05 and 06-06), discharge-screen-printed with Rongalit ST in thickener. Note the gray discharge result. Cotton broadcloth. Scale: 9" × 11".

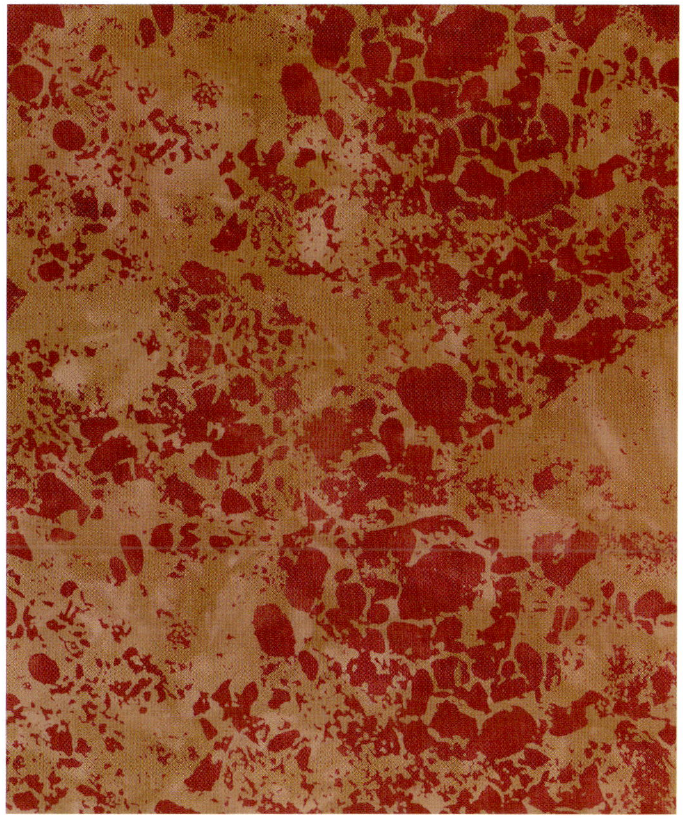

06-05 Hand-dyed maroon fabric (same ground as in 06-04 and 06-06), discharge-screen-printed with Rongalit ST in thickener. Note the tan discharge result. Cotton broadcloth. Scale: 8.5" × 12".

06-06 Hand-dyed maroon fabric (same ground as in 06-04 and 06-05), discharge-screen-printed with Rongalit ST in thickener. Note the yellow discharge result. Cotton broadcloth.

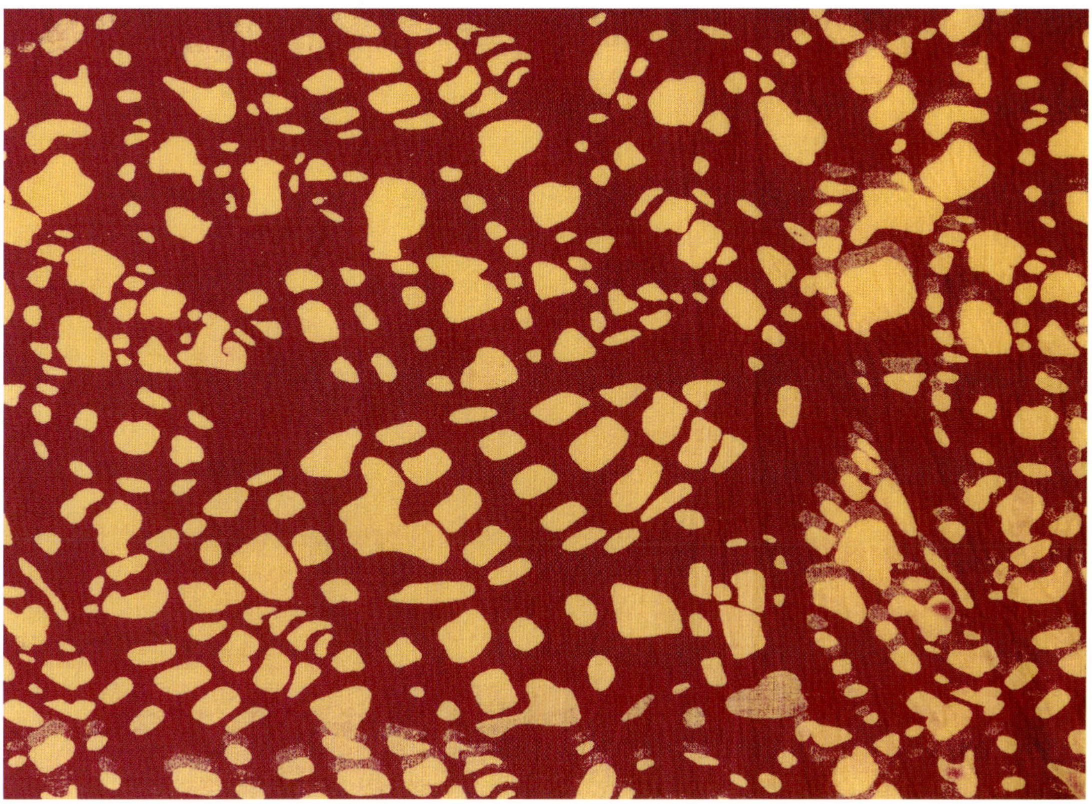

06-07 Screen-printed discharge on commercially dyed black rayon challis. Areas discharged with a dilute paste in one screen pattern turned the black to dark brown; others at full strength in a different screen pattern turned the black to light gray. Rongalit ST discharge paste.

Depending on the dyes originally used to produce them—technical manufacturing information usually unknown to the retail buyers of the cloth—some *commercially* dyed fabrics can't be discharged at all. Others will produce color surprises (pleasant or unpleasant). For example, commercially dyed black fabrics may discharge variously and unpredictably to brown, tan, gold, gray, red, or pink (although in 06-07 the black rayon challis simply reduced to gray). Commercially dyed greens may turn to orange, and blue may turn green. *Test* your discharge paste on a small sample of your commercially dyed cloth *before* applying the paste to larger pieces of yardage. If you'll be using commercial fabrics, I recommend that you accept the apparent serendipity of the color that discharge produces on the cloth, and respond by adding new layers of dye or pigment to further transform the fabric surface.

06-08 Screen-printed discharge on low-immersion, hand-dyed green fabric. Cotton broad cloth, Procion MX fiber reactive dyes, Rongalit ST. Discharge color shifted to a flat light turquoise across the cloth, in spite of the uneven original dyeing. Note: Turquoise was a composite dye color in the original dyebath.

A few specific colors of *fiber reactive dyes* will resist discharge, while others will discharge nearly to white. Turquoise and green often lighten just a bit or shift hue slightly (06-08, 06-09, 06-14). This is a great advantage in trying to achieve *subtle* color shifts and low contrast of delicate or elegant colors and patterns. In 06-09, the fabric for the large leaves on the left side of the image began with a medium-value green cotton velveteen. The discharge printing reduced some areas to a light blue/green, providing just the right kind of texture and low color contrast to convey a leaflike surface. Similarly, in 06-12 the discharge printing on a low-immersion-dyed brown fabric created slightly lighter marks on the left, which suggest a closer view of the rock textures captured in the digitally printed photograph on the right.

However, some reds and oranges may discharge more nearly white (06-10, 06-13), as will some greens (06-02), and some blues will do the same on semitransparent fabrics such as silk organza (06-11). This greater degree of discharge opens up additional possibilities for adding new color to the composition or pattern.

06-09 *Left*: Screen-printed discharge on "leaf" shapes in hand-dyed, medium-value green cotton velveteen creates subtle textures and color shifts. *Right*: Screen-printed discharge on background cloth of hand-dyed green cotton with textile pigment overprinting yields complex patterns and textures. Fiber reactive dye, Rongalit ST discharge paste.

06-10 Screen-printed discharge on low-immersion, hand-dyed orange fabric. Cotton, Procion MX fiber reactive dyes. Discharge color varies from light yellow over darker dyed areas to white in more lightly dyed areas, reflecting the unevenness of the original low immersion dyeing itself. Scale: 9" × 11".

06-11 Screen-printed discharge on low-immersion, hand-dyed blue silk organza. Procion MX fiber reactive dyes. The unevenness of the original dyeing, and the sheerness of the fabric, produced discharge colors ranging from white to very light blue. Scale: 5" × 8".

06-12 Screen-printed discharge on the left creates lighter marks on a low-immersion, hand-dyed fabric intended to mimic the rock texture photograph digitally printed on the right. Procion MX fiber reactive dyes, digital printing. Cotton broadcloth. Handmade wool felt (in the center and as the underlying base for reverse appliqué on the left).

ALTERNATIVES TO DISCHARGE

Commercial alternatives: If you are unable to set up a safe working environment to use bleaches or other discharge chemicals, you can find an array of discharge-printed fabrics on the market (shop online fabric vendors and quilt stores). By selecting the fabrics carefully, with an eye for the kind of imagery and marks that serve your ideas, buying prints provides similar visual results without personal health risk.

Mechanical alternatives: There are a number of ways to *simulate* the effects of discharge on fabric.

- Appliqué shapes cut from silk organza, tulle, silk meshes, or other semitransparent sheer fabrics and laid on darker fabrics. (See chapter 8 of the *Dry Techniques* book.)
- Reverse-appliqué on assembled multilayer fabrics, to cut away darker top layers and shapes and reveal lighter colors beneath. (See chapter 9 of the *Dry Techniques* book.)
- Cut away selected threads or shapes on multilayered fabrics, using small, sharp-pointed scissors to make small holes or "windows." (See chapter 10 of the *Dry Techniques* book.)
- Cluster light-colored embroidery stitches on a dark ground. (See chapter 11 of the *Dry Techniques* book.)

SUPPLY CHECKLIST FOR DISCHARGE

- dark-colored or dyed fabric (avoid synthetics if you'll be using chlorine bleach)
- chlorine bleach or discharge paste (such as deColourant)
- cord, string, thread (if doing bound-resist discharge)
- thread and needle (if doing stitch-resist discharge)
- screen-printing supplies
- paintbrushes with *synthetic* bristles, because they won't be "eaten" by bleach
- scissors
- rubber gloves
- fan (for ventilation)
- two-cannister respirator that filters organic compounds (essential)
- hydrogen peroxide (3% solution from drugstore) or commercial equivalent (Anti-Clor)
- steam iron (buy a high-quality professional model with an automatic on/off switch) or handheld clothing steamer
- Synthrapol for washing out discharged fabrics

Safety Guidelines for Using Discharge Chemicals

Discharging color from fabric can be enormously rewarding and enjoyable in aesthetic terms (making rich cloth surfaces), but of all the chemicals covered in this book, the chemicals used for discharge are the most *immediately* damaging if handled improperly. You *must* take precautions against both acute exposure at the time of the work and repeated exposure over time, and you *must* establish a very safe work environment *every* time you do discharge. And note: if you have chronic breathing problems or lung disease, or if you are pregnant, you shouldn't be doing discharge at all.

- Work outdoors (or in a carport or open garage) to avoid breathing the fumes. Wherever you work, use a fan (stationary is better than oscillating) to move air away from your face as you work. If you are unable to avoid working indoors, do so directly under a strong rapid-air-exchange ventilation system, with open windows and a steady source of fresh air across the workspace.
- Cover your skin and clothing: Wear long, thick rubber gloves and a large work shirt and an apron or smock to protect your clothing and skin from splashes. (If you're suitably attired, the discharge chemical should not splash on your skin. If it does, *immediately* flush the area with running water, then wash with soap.)
- Wear an organic-compounds-filtering face mask (the type with two cannisters containing internal filters). Have someone knowledgeable help you fit it to your face. Wear the mask throughout the work session and until the fumes have been thoroughly vented away from the workspace.
- Wear face goggles to protect your eyes, especially if you wear contact lenses, but even if you wear glasses.
- *Never* mix ammonia or vinegar with chlorine bleach. These combinations are toxic.
- Follow all the general guidelines for safe use of dyes outlined in chapter 1.
- If using a commercial discharge product (instead of making your own from ordinary bleach), *scrupulously* follow the manufacturer's instructions and precautions.

Discharge Chemicals and Procedures

Chlorine Bleach

Common chlorine bleach is the cheapest and most accessible discharge chemical. Because it will "eat" silks and other protein fibers, it is suitable for use *only on cellulose* fabrics. Although a common cleaning agent in most households, chlorine bleach at full strength is also aggressive and capable (if you wish) of reducing the color of entire larger pieces of cloth in an immersion bath, but it can also be suspended in a thickener for more dilute and precisely wielded paste applications.

Instructions for chlorine bleach immersion bath to discharge entire pieces of dyed fabric:

1. Begin with dry fabric. If you are using the discharge bath along with resist bindings (fold, bind, pole wrap, stitch), apply them to the fabric before preparing the bleach bath. (See resist-binding instructions in chapter 2.)

2. Wet the fabric thoroughly by soaking it in plain tap water for 15–20 minutes.

3. Put on your rubber gloves, organic-filter face mask, and goggles to protect you from inhaling bleach fumes. As mentioned above, it's best to work outdoors or in an open garage. In any case, turn on a fan to blow fresh air across the working area and fumes *away* from your face.

4. Prepare the bleach bath: Fill a plastic or enamel pan with water of sufficient room temperature to allow submerged fabric to move freely (perhaps 3 gallons of water per 1 pound of fabric). Add the appropriate amount of bleach, based on the fiber type and the speed of discharge desired, as follows:

   - For cotton: 1 part bleach to 2 parts water

   - For linen: 1 part bleach to 3 parts water

   - For rayon (more easily degraded by bleach): 1 part bleach to 7 parts water

   The amount of bleach used is a delicate balance. The stronger the solution, the faster the color will discharge; the weaker the solution, the slower the color change. *At the same time*, the stronger the solution, the more likely it will damage or weaken the fibers. And although a warm-to-hot bleach solution works faster than a cold one, *never boil* a bleach solution, since this would release copious amounts of chlorine gas. If you want to hasten the discharge process, it's safer to use just hot tap water.

5. When you've exposed the fabric to bleach to achieve the desired color reduction, you'll then need to *stop* further action by the bleach. That means "quenching" the fabric, so you'll need to prepare a ready-to-use stop bath *before* you begin using the bleach:

   - *Commercial preparation*: Prepare a bath of sodium bisulfate (Anti-Clor, for example) by mixing 1 tsp. Anti-Clor with 2 gallons of warm water in a plastic bucket. Stir until dissolved. Make a volume of this mixture sufficient to completely submerge the fabric.

   - *Homemade version*: Combine 1 part hydrogen peroxide to 2 parts water and mix well in a container, also in sufficient volume to completely submerge the fabric.

   (You may see other books that recommend vinegar for a stop bath. *Never* add vinegar to a stop bath, because combining vinegar with bleach-soaked fabric will accelerate chlorine gas release.)

6. Place the fabric in the bleach bath.

   - To achieve an *even* discharge across the entire fabric, agitate and squeeze the fabric constantly so the bleach penetrates throughout.

   - To achieve an *uneven* discharge, just let the fabric, folds and all, sit in the bleach bath undisturbed (as you would do if performing low-immersion dyeing).

7. *Watch* the cloth as you agitate it (even discharge) or as it sits in the bath (uneven discharge), to observe when its color has changed as you wish, though not more. (Remember, however, that wet fabric looks darker than dry, so that its final appearance will be lighter than what you're seeing in the discharge bath.)

8. When the desired level of discharge has been achieved, remove the fabric from the bleach bath and plunge it immediately into the stop bath. This neutralizes the action of the bleach and helps preserve the fabric.

9. Remove the fabric from the stop bath and rinse it well (and repeatedly) in a tub of clear running water. Submerge the fabric, move it around, and make sure it doesn't fold over on itself to create spots. Change the tub water several times, then discard.

10. For bound resists only: Carefully cut and remove the binding threads.

11. Refill the tub with hot soapy (Synthrapol) water and wash the fabric to remove all traces of bleach. Rinse repeatedly and thoroughly.

12. Hang the fabric to dry, then press the dry fabric to remove wrinkles.

Instructions for chlorine bleach pastes for selective discharge by painting, printing, stamping, and other direct means:

Unlike immersion bath discharge, a bleaching paste allows you to discharge specific areas of the fabric without changing others. But bleach will dissolve the sodium alginate types of thickeners we previously used to make dye pastes. Instead, use a product called *monagum* (a modified starch gum) to thicken bleach. Monagum is available from most dye and chemical suppliers and comes in granular form, ready to be mixed with water to the desired thickness.

1. When you eventually apply the bleach paste to your fabric, you'll need to complete the actions quickly, and you'll need to terminate the action of the bleach before it proceeds too far. Therefore, whether you intend to discharge by direct hand application on the fabric or by screen printing with the bleach paste, *plan* the specific areas or shapes you'll want to discharge *before* you ever expose the fabric to the bleach paste.

2. Mix monagum paste: Start with 1 cup of warm (105°F) water in a bowl or container for mixing. Sprinkle 1–3 T. monagum in the water and stir with an electric mixer. Let the mixture sit for a couple of hours or even overnight until it smooths out, releases the air bubbles, and cools to room temperature.

3. Put on your rubber gloves, organic-filter face mask, and goggles. As already discussed above, take the necessary precautions to prevent bleach fume inhalation.

4. Prepare a stop bath, as explained in step 5 of the previous section on immersion discharge.

5. Add the desired amount of chlorine bleach to the monagum paste (about 2–4 T. bleach per 1 cup paste) and use the paste immediately.

6. Apply the paste:

   • To paint by direct application, the most common way of doing discharge (see chapter 3), use only a brush with *synthetic* bristles (bleach will eventually eat away natural bristles) and apply as desired. When finished, wash out the brush immediately in hot soapy water.

   • To screen-print (see chapter 4), squeegee the bleach paste through the screen stencil, just as you would if printing with any dye or pigment paste. The bleach paste will not harm the synthetic screen mesh, but you may have to discard the screen stencil after its exposure to bleach. When finished, use hot soapy water to wash out the screen for future use.

7. After applying the bleach paste, whether by direct application or screen print, allow the fabric to sit *undisturbed* while the discharge paste takes action. The paste itself is nearly transparent, so *monitor* the color change happening beneath it.

8. When the desired level of discharge has been achieved, plunge the fabric immediately into the stop bath. This neutralizes the action of the bleach and helps preserve the fabric.

9. Remove the fabric from the stop bath and rinse it well in clear running water. Fill a tub and submerge the fabric; move it around and make sure it doesn't fold over on itself to create spots. Change the water several times.

10. Wash in hot soapy (Synthrapol) water to remove all traces of bleach. Rinse repeatedly and thoroughly.

11. Hang the fabric to dry, then press the dry fabric to remove wrinkles.

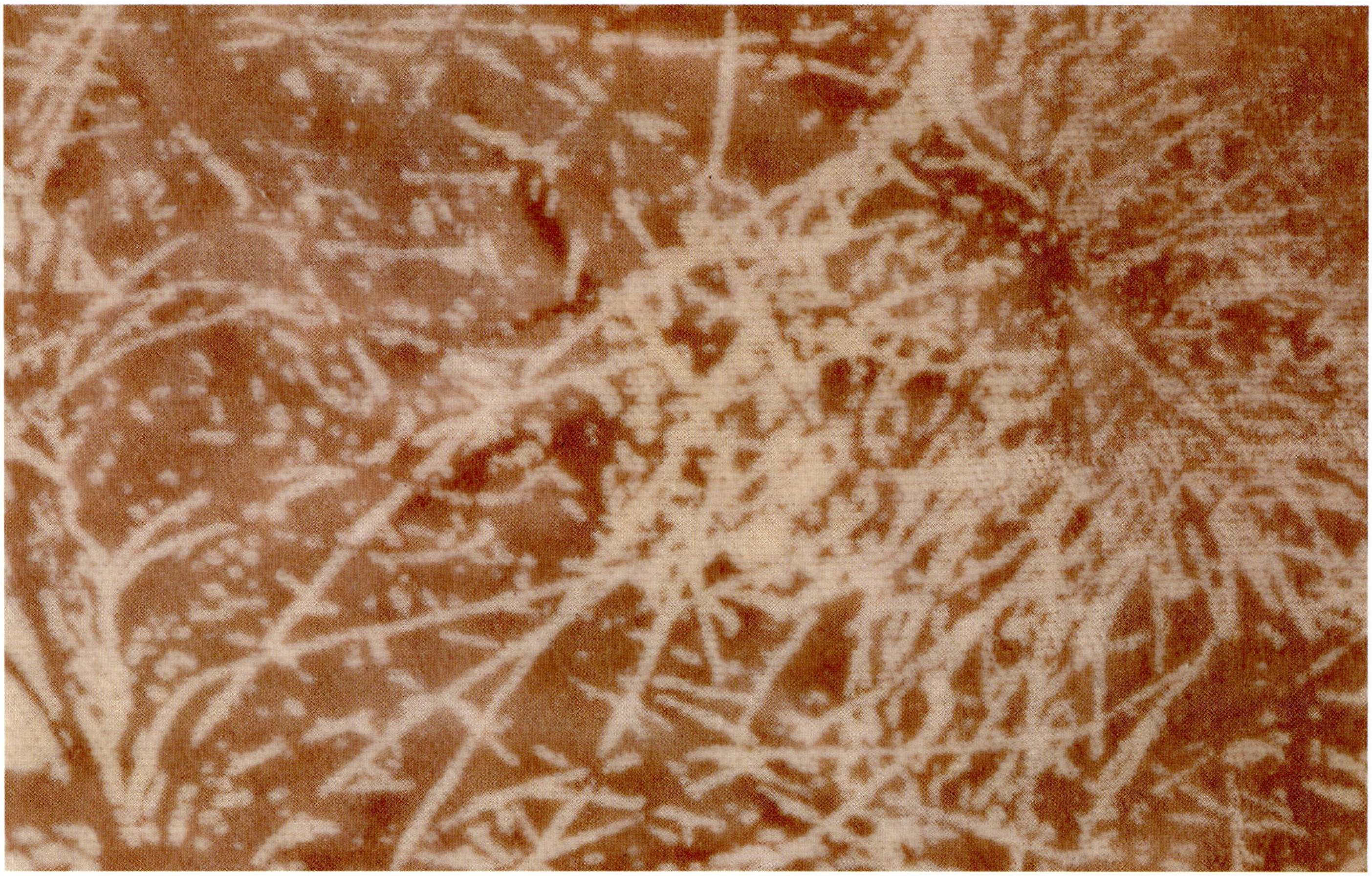

06-13 Cotton velveteen unevenly dyed in reddish browns in a low-immersion bath, then printed with discharge paste through a screen, using a delicate image as its stencil. Procion MX fiber reactive dyes, discharge paste.

06-14 Cotton broadcloth unevenly dyed in medium-value green, then printed with discharge paste through a bolder and more open stencil, which left the original green areas smaller in area than the discharged areas. Procion MX fiber reactive dyes, discharge paste.

Commercial Discharge Pastes

Most dye and chemical vendors also sell a newer discharge paste product called *deColourant* or their own proprietary formulations of discharge paste. Buying one of these is a convenient choice for paste applications (such as screen printing, painting, or stamping). Unlike chlorine bleach, these pastes do not degrade the fibers themselves but work *only* on the dye, so they may be used safely on any natural fabrics—cotton, linen, wool, rayon, and, yes, even silk. In these paste products, the chemicals are activated by exposure to heat *after* application. These products still require stringent safety precautions (outlined above and listed on the accompanying product literature) but are generally less toxic than using bleach. If you want to play with discharge but don't want to mix your own at home, I recommend using a commercial paste but carefully following the vendor/manufacturer instructions.

Try this!

6.1 Whole-cloth immersion discharge

The goal: lighten the color of an entire piece of fabric with a bleach bath. Choose a dark piece of cotton cloth. Match its color against a value scale and note its relative value. Cut a sample of the cloth to set aside for later comparison. Using the instructions above for bleach immersion baths, reduce the value of the color about 20% to 25%. While the fabric is in the bleach bath, monitor the color change closely. Temporarily remove it from the bath and hand-press the water from it repeatedly to check the change (it will look darker while still wet). Remove it from the discharge bath at the moment you think it has changed enough. Plunge it in the stop bath, rinse, wash, dry, and press it.

Match the color of the discharged fabric to the value scale and to the predischarge sample. Make note of the degree of color reduction. Did it change as you expected from the amount of time the fabric was in the discharge bath? More? Less? Did anything else (hue, unevenness of color, speed of color change, or the cloth's texture or "feel") change in expected or unexpected ways?

6.2 Commercial discharge paste to create light shapes on a dark ground

Start with several pieces each of commercial or hand-dyed black, navy, dark-brown, or dark-green cloth. Cut an 8" × 8" square from each fabric.

Design a *simple* pattern, a group of marks or gestures, or a *simple* composition that you can duplicate (with screen printing, stamping, or painting) on *each* of the 8" fabric swatches. Apply your design to each fabric, using a *commercially purchased* discharge paste, following the manufacturer's or vendor's instructions to allow the discharge agent to achieve the desired color change and to end the discharge.

When the fabrics are dried and pressed, compare the results. What color did your pattern or marks assume as the discharge lightened the underlying fabric? Were they different for each color of fabric? Did fabrics of different *types* (cotton, linen, etc.) but the same *color* yield different results? Were there any surprises? Did differing weave structures among the swatches make a difference in the color changes? Compare the degree of color lightening to a value scale to understand the percentage of color change you achieved. Make note of your discoveries.

6.3 Make-your-own bleach paste to create light shapes on a dark ground

Follow the same general approach as Try this! exercise 6.2, but use only *cellulose* fabrics to screen-print, paint, or stamp your motifs or composition, and follow the "Instructions for Chlorine Bleach Pastes," page 243.

6.4 Combining discharge with subsequent color additions

Choose a cotton cloth that has been hand-*dyed* or hand-printed *with dyes* (not pigments). Using large synthetic-bristle brushes, paint it with discharge or bleach paste in large swaths to interrupt, obscure, or create blank areas in the cloth color. Make the discharge marks rhythmic and regular, erratic and irregular, large or small. Use a stop bath to halt the discharge action, then rinse, wash, dry, and press the cloth.

Next, *add more color* to the areas you just lightened! Use any direct-application technique, with either dye paste or textile pigments, to add color back into the open spaces you have created on the cloth and to build a complex patterned surface. Set the color (batch, heat, air cure, etc.) as appropriate for the added colorant.

6.5 Resist dye on dark cloth

Choose a very dark piece of commercial or hand-dyed cotton cloth. Choose a resist dye technique, such as tie-dye, fold dye, stitch resist, or *arashi* (see chapter 2) and prepare the fabric folds or bindings. Discharge the bound fabric in an immersion bleach bath or paint discharge paste onto the bound forms. When the color has changed enough, plunge the bound fabric into a stop bath. Rinse out. Carefully remove the bindings. Then plunge the unbound cloth into a stop bath *again*. Wash, dry, and press.

6.6 Discharge and dyeing

Start with a hand-dyed medium-to-dark-value (cotton) fabric you consider "not very successful." The goal: give that fabric "new life." Use screen printing, stamping, or painting to apply marks or patterns to the cloth with discharge paste. Aim to remove 50% of the color with the paste. Wash the fabric thoroughly. Next, *overdye* the whole cloth in a *contrasting* color.

6.7 THE CUMULATIVE CLOTH CHALLENGE

Goal: using one of the fabrics you dyed for the challenge in chapter 1 or 2 (already heat-set or washed and dried, or both), apply discharge paste to create a mysterious lacelike pattern on the cloth.

To begin, find some *photographs* for inspiration (such as sea fans, ice crystals, snowflakes, disintegrating leaves, bobbin lace). Design a custom stencil based on the photograph, or practice making brush marks that mimic the patterns in it. When you are ready to work on your dyed fabric, apply discharge paste with your stencil or brush. Process according to the discharge instructions above (if you made bleach paste) or the manufacturer's instructions (if you used commercial discharge paste). Take a photograph of the fabric. Set it aside for optional use in chapter 7 of the *Dry Techniques* book.

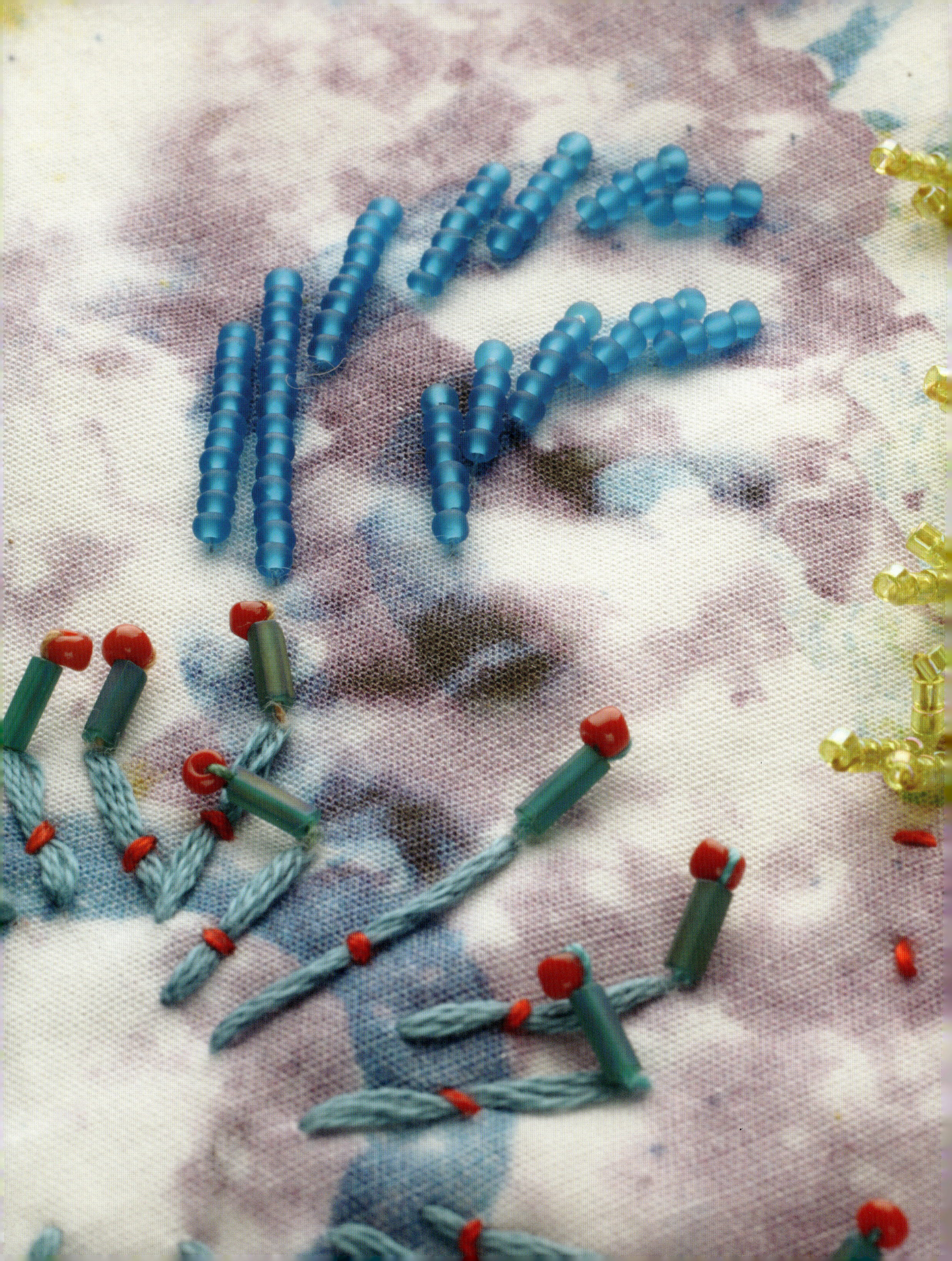

APPENDIX A: FINISHING TECHNIQUES

A-01 Wall hanging with clean, smooth finished edges, achieved with a true-to-grain binding around the perimeter. Hand-dyed, screen-printed, reverse-appliquéd, stitched. Cotton and silk. Scale: 38" × 49.5".

With a few exceptions (reversible fabrics, stitching meant to be seen from either side of the cloth), the chapters of this book have focused on making the "public" part of a cumulative cloth, the surfaces actually *meant* to be seen. But even when the work has been dyed, printed, pieced, appliquéd, embellished—whatever was involved in its making—there are still some necessary additional steps before calling it "done." And those involve actions "behind the scenes," to give a well-crafted completion to the parts that *won't* be seen (or, at least, will typically remain hidden).

Of course, if you've made a work already attached to a finished and hemmed foundation cloth, and if you also *intend* for the edges of the piece to be left slightly ragged (i.e., with some bits of cloth or embellishment extending beyond the rectangular foundation in a tactile and informal way), then your work is already done. Otherwise . . .

Finishing employs a range of sewing techniques to stabilize, protect, or tidy up raw fabric edges: backings, hems, mitered corners, facings, and bindings.

Although finishing is *executed* at the very *end* of a project, you can nevertheless *plan* for the work's finished appearance. With your very first thumbnail sketches or samples, whether the project is a baby quilt for your cousin or a wall hanging for a business office or your own home, try to imagine how it will be seen and used. Will the work be worn, handled frequently, or washed? Will it hang on a wall or sit on a pedestal for long periods? Who will see it, touch it, or care for it? What protection will the materials need to survive over time?

For example, a pieced image with a clean, precise aesthetic might suggest similarly straight, clean, and precise edges or hems, which could be diminished by careless or uneven finishing. On the other hand, a tight, smoothly finished edge treatment could sap energy from a lively and highly textured construction that naturally "wants" to have ragged edges in keeping with its overall informality. As the work literally materializes in your hands, you'll gain additional understanding of what it will "need" to be seen at its best.

Many of the basic finishing techniques listed below are traditional clothing construction or quilt-making methods that can be adapted for any type of work. *Because the chapters in this book encompass so many possibilities for making unique cumulative cloths, I can't specify the absolute best finishing technique for your own specific project.* But I've assembled this chart of general recommendations, followed by discussion of each finishing method.

Finishing Suggestions: Single Layer of Fabric	
Garment edges, straight (bottoms of skirts, shirts, trousers, sleeves)	Hem
Garment edges, curved (circle skirt)	Circular facing
Table linens, rectangular (tablecloth, napkins, place mats, runners)	Hem
Table linens, circular (tablecloth)	Narrow facing
Pillow tops, sachets, small bags	Pillowcase backing
Pieced constructions, rectangular (joined blocks, strip piecing, improvisational piecing)	Add batting, backing, quilting lines, then finish edges with bias or true-to-grain binding
Pieced constructions, unusual shapes	Custom-shaped facing to fit the edge
Finishing Suggestions: Two or More Layers of Fabric	
Rectangular pieced constructions (blocks, strips) with backing already in place	Binding or facing
Quilted image (3 or more layers)	Binding
Foundation piecing (crazy patchwork, strip piecing)	Decorative backing (optional) and binding
Reverse-appliquéd compositions	Binding
Holes cut through fabric layers	Binding or facing
Fabric collage with layers of materials	Binding or facing
Manipulated fabric surfaces	Binding or facing

Backing: Adding a Layer to Cover Construction Stitching

After you've constructed your cumulative cloth, you may want to cover its *entire* back and to hide stitching, construction lines, or padding. Backings are a special category of "finishing" that are best added *before* any of the *edge* finishes that follow. A backing can be attached to a work along the edges, or at spaced intervals across the surface (for example, with quilting lines). A backing can be simple and utilitarian (undyed cotton muslin) or can introduce new colors or patterns. Backings are especially helpful to lend support to works with curved or unusual shapes, such as circles, ovals, or triangles.

Full Backing with Finished Edges

As its name suggests, full backing extends the entire height and width of the work and is tucked under the front edges of the fabric or under edge bindings that have been folded to the back of the work (A-02).

Instructions for full backing with finished edges:

1. Use a temporary marking tool to mark the finished boundaries of the work on its front. (Some of the fabric will extend beyond these marked boundaries.) Fold the front fabric to the back along those marked lines and press them in place.

2. Use those marked boundaries as the measurements for cutting a backing fabric the same size as the *finished boundaries* of the composition itself.

3. Lay the front of the work *facedown* on a table and lay the backing fabric *faceup* on top of it so that the two *backs* face each other. Align the edges of the backing with the finished boundaries of the front fabric (the pressed fold).

4. Re-fold the front fabric *to the back* to cover the edges of the backing fabric. Press the fold in place again, mitering or lapping corners as desired, and pin the folds in place.

5. As needed, measure and trim away any excess fabric from the front of the work to provide the desired width of hem, usually 1"–3".

6. Fold under ¼" hem allowance on the raw edge of the front of the work and tuck it under the hem. Press and pin the edge of the hem in place.

A-02 Construction diagram, full backing (aqua) with edges of the work folded to the back along three of its edges and stitched in place, awaiting the folding and stitching of the fourth edge.

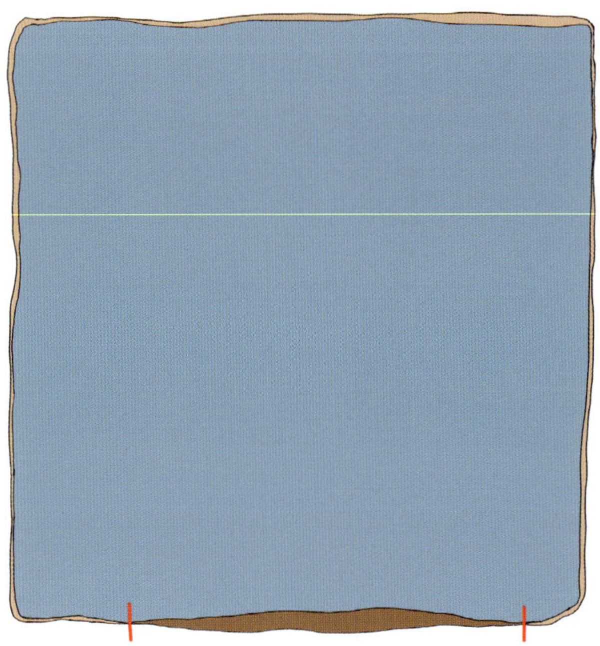

A-03 Construction diagram, pillowcase backing or lining technique. Opening at bottom (*between red lines*) ready for blind-stitched closure.

7. Hand- or machine-stitch the hem in place, following the instructions below for mitering corners, and removing the pins as you stitch.

8. Press the hem to eliminate wrinkles and ease any fullness.

Pillowcase Backing with Finished Edges

In a *pillowcase* backing (or lining), the interior between the front and back remains available for stuffing, and this finishing method is particularly useful for small sachet packets, zippered cosmetic bags, vests, small bags, pillows, or other works too small to hem or face (A-03).

Instructions for pillowcase backing:

1. Cut the backing the same size as your work. Place the work and backing fabric, *front* sides together. Insert pins perpendicular to the edges along *three* sides and *part* of a fourth. (The opening remaining in the fourth side will be used to turn the construction inside out.)

2. Stitch a seam (¼"–½") around all sides, remembering to leave unstitched the opening for turning.

3. Trim and press the seams flat, then clip across the corners to remove bulk.

4. To turn the piece front side out: Reach through the opening and pinch or grab the opposite side of the work and pull it through the opening. With the piece now reversed, insert a pointed tool to poke the corners into square and get the work to lie flat again.

5. Press the seams straight and aligned with the folds at the edges.

6. Finish the opening: Fold back continuous hem allowances on the edges of the opening. Stitch the opening closed with a running stitch that alternates back and forth through the inside of the folds on each side of the opening.

Fused Backing with Finished Edges

To add stability and support to wall hangings, sculptures, or other three-dimensional works, you can use iron-on fusible web to adhere the work to a sturdy backing cloth. Fusing stiffens fabrics and therefore diminishes their natural drape but creates a smooth, paperlike hand in the finished work.

Instructions for fused backing:

1. Use a temporary marking tool to mark the finished boundaries of the work on its back, but leave enough fabric extending *beyond* the marked boundaries to allow for fused hems on all sides.

2. Use those marked boundaries as the measurements for cutting a backing fabric the same size as the *finished boundaries* of the composition itself.

3. Cut enough pieces of fusible web to cover the *entire back* of your work, including the hem allowances. Measure and plan to perfectly abut or slightly overlap individual webbing pieces. (Don't leave gaps, which will appear as depressions on the face of the work.)

4. Place the work *facedown* on a padded surface and lay out the fusible web pieces, one at a time, with their paper backing side *up*.

5. Set your iron to the appropriate temperature for the fabric in your work (follow the webbing manufacturer's specific suggestions). Fuse the web to the back of your work by ironing the paper backing until the web melts onto the cloth.

6. When the first section of the web has cooled, arrange the next section of web abutted on the first piece and iron it in place.

7. Continue to fuse additional sections of web until the entire back of the work is covered with web. After the last web piece has cooled, carefully remove all of the paper backings, one at a time, to expose the side of the web to be adhered to the backing fabric.

8. Press out all wrinkles in the backing fabric, then lay it *faceup* on top of the web-covered work. (The backs of the work and the backing fabric are now against each other.) Adjust the two layers to ensure that the grain lines are straight and that the edge of the backing correctly aligns with the *finished boundaries* of the work as marked in step 1.

9. Working from the *center* outward, and pressing down on the iron with some force to make good contact, iron the backing fabric to fuse it to the web. Press *only* to the edge of the backing fabric but *avoid* moving the iron off the edge of the backing fabric onto any exposed web on the hem allowances, because it will readily melt onto your iron at nearly any temperature.

A-04 Hand blind-stitched hem, showing front and back. Fold-dyed cotton.

10. Allow the fabrics to cool from the pressing.

11. The work's hem allowances are already coated with web, adhered to them but not yet to the backing fabric. Fold the hems around to the back, over the backing fabric, and, mitering each corner as you reach it, iron the hems to fuse them to the backing.

Hems: Folded Edges on Single Layers of Fabric

A *hem* is the folded edge of a fabric (typically ½"–2" wide) meant to hide and protect its raw edges. Hems are simple and quick to execute. They are commonly used to finish garments and household linens (which are usually *single layers* of fabric), providing the most protection with the least thickness at the edge. Sewing books offer many alternative ways to hem, depending on the project, the type of fabric, the contour of the edge, and the scope of the job. I'll focus on the basic hand- and machine-sewn hems, which should meet most of your needs on straight edges. (For curved edges, use either bias bindings or bias facings, discussed below.)

On most fabrics, especially heavy ones, hems wider than 3" will be too bulky and or will distort the edge. On the other hand, except on very sheer fabrics (such as scarf edges), flat hems smaller than ½" are difficult to measure, fold, and stitch in place. If you have less than ½" of fabric available for hemming at the edge of your work, use a *facing* on that edge.

Hand Blind-Stitched Hems

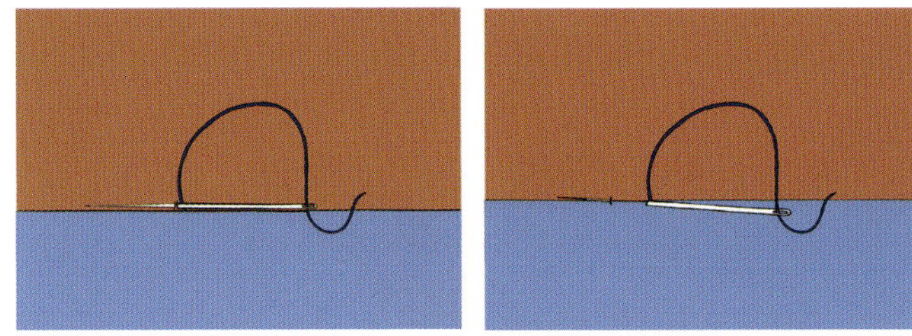

A-05 Construction diagram, steps to make a blind hem stitch (face of the fabric shown in blue, back of the fabric shown in brown).

Traditional blind-stitched hems are neat, regular, and, although often visible on the back of the finished work, not seen on the front, especially when stitched with a matching thread color (A-04).

Instructions for making a hand blind-stitched hem:

1. With the work *facedown*, fold its edge to the *back*. Use a sewing gauge to measure an equal *width* of the hem as you turn the fold along the entire edge, pressing it in place as you proceed. The edge of this fold will form the finished boundary of the work.

2. Fold the top ¼" of the hem under, tuck it *inside* the hem allowance, and press it in place, inserting pins perpendicular to the edge to temporarily hold in place this second fold, parallel to the first.

3. Press the entire hem again.

4. Knot the end of the thread and bring the threaded needle up through the second folded edge of the hem from behind. Then use the needle to catch a *single thread* in the weave structure on the back of the work just opposite the place where the needle emerged from the folded hem. Then take a separate short stitch *inside* the hem fold, emerging about ¼"–½" farther along the hem. Catch another single thread on the back of the fabric and repeat along the entire hem. Knot off the thread invisibly on the back and clip the thread end (A-05).

5. Press the hem to eliminate wrinkles and ease any fullness (A-04).

Machine-Stitched Hems

A-06 Machine-stitched hem, showing front and back. Random bound resist on cotton.

Machine-stitched hems are neat, regular, and *visible* line on both sides of a hem (A-06).

Instructions for making a machine-stitched hem:

1. Place the work facedown and then fold the edges of the fabric to the back. Use a sewing gauge to measure an equal *width* of the hem as you turn the fold along the entire edge, pressing it in place as you proceed. The edge of this fold will form the finished boundary of the work.

2. Fold the top ¼" of the hem under, tuck it *inside* the hem allowance, and press it in place, inserting pins perpendicular to the edge to temporarily hold the second fold in place. (You'll be working with these pins in place, removing them one by one as the fabric advances toward the needle, in order to prevent the machine stitching over them.)

3. Press the entire hem again.

4. With the *back* of the fabric facing *up*, machine-stitch about 1⁄16"–⅛" from the folded edge. (For the most accurate stitched line, use the topstitch foot on your sewing machine, which has a guide you can run along the folded edge.)

5. Press the hem to eliminate wrinkles and ease any fullness.

Seam Tape Hems

A-07 Seam tape hem in progress. Handwoven fabric, cotton twill tape, cotton thread.

Commercially produced *seam tape* is a flat, woven strip (usually cotton or rayon) used to make *very flat* hems. The tape covers the raw fabric edges and minimizes the possibility that fold ridges will be seen on the front of the work. Seam tape is especially useful on fabrics (including handwovens) too thick to fold for a narrow hem with a flat and crisp edge (A-07).

Instructions for making a seam tape hem:

1. Place the work facedown and then fold the edges of the fabric to the back. Use a sewing gauge to measure an equal *width* of the hem as you turn the fold along the entire edge, pressing it in place as you proceed. The edge of this fold will form the finished boundary of the work.

2. Unfold the fabric but *do not* press it flat.

3. Working on the *front* side of the fabric, overlap seam tape about ¼" over the raw edge of the fabric and machine-stitch it in place with straight stitch. If you are sewing around the perimeter of a garment or rectangle, hand-pinch to miter the points where the seam tape changes directions at the corners. When the end of the seam tape eventually meets the beginning, lap them over each other and stitch them in place.

4. Re-fold and press the fabric along the originally pressed line and insert pins perpendicular through the seam tape and the hem.

5. Stitch the seam tape to the back of the fabric by hand or machine:

    - Hand-stitch the hem with a *whipstitch* (*visible* on the back, as in A-07). To keep the stitching *invisible* on the front of the work, catch only a single thread on the fabric back in each stitch.

- Machine-stitch the tape in place with a single line of straight stitching inserted about 1⁄16" from the edge of the seam tape. Note: Machine stitching will be visible on both sides of the work.

6. Press the hem to eliminate wrinkles and ease any fullness.

A-08 Overlapped, hand-stitched corner on faced, padded, and quilted wall hanging. Back view. Digitally printed cotton.

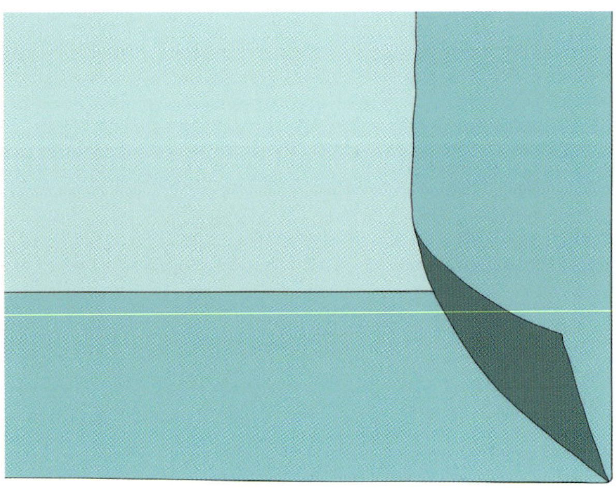

A-09 Construction diagram, overlapped hem corners.

Hem Corners

Hemming rectangular, square, or triangular works (quilts, bags, wall hangings) inevitably brings you to *corners*, where you have two choices: *overlapping* or *mitering*.

Instructions for making overlapped hem corners on rectangles and squares:

Overlapped corners are easy to achieve (A-08) and work well, even on thickly padded quilts and jackets. First, hem across one edge. Then measure and fold the hem on the adjacent edge, overlapping it with the first hem at the corner (A-09). Trim away any excess fabric *inside* the folds to smooth them where they overlap. Stitch the corner hem in place, then continue to hem the adjacent side. Continue in this manner with each corner of the work. (Machine-stitch if you don't mind visible stitching on the front of the work. But to keep stitches from being seen, use blind hand stitching, which catches only a single thread of the fabric back in each stitch.)

Instructions for simple mitering on rectangles and squares:

Mitering the corners on hems and facings creates smoother, flatter, and more precise corners and produces *diagonal folds* that *bisect* each corner on the *backside* of the work. *Simple* mitering is easier, more forgiving, and useful on thick fabrics.

1. Fold and press all four hemlines of the rectangle to the back.

2. The raw edges of the cloth are now folded to the back but still exposed. Fold under the top 1⁄4" of each edge, tucking it *inside* (under) the hem allowance, and press it in place.

3. Then, temporarily *unfold* the pressed hem, in order to clearly reveal again the pressed lines (as represented by dashed lines in A-10).

4. Working on the *back* of the fabric, miter each of the four corners in succession:

   - Fold back the corner at a 45° angle to the seam lines (shown in light pink in A-10) and press the fold in place.

   - Then re-fold the two adjacent hems along the pressed fold lines (the dotted lines) so that the two angled folds neatly touch at the corner.

   - Press and then insert pins to hold the diagonal corner folds in place.

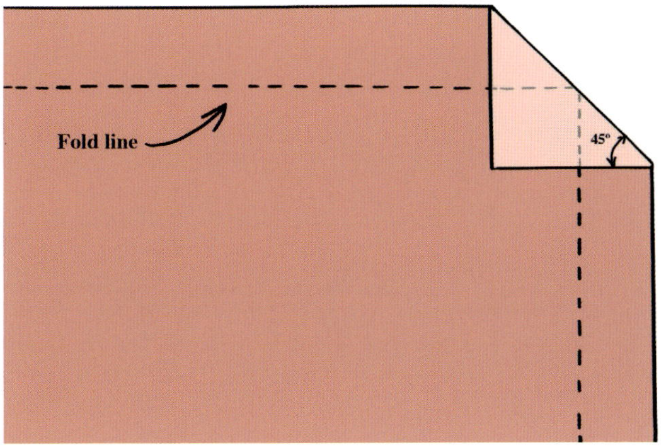

A-10 Construction diagram, simple approach to mitered hem corner. First fold 45° at corner, then second fold along dotted lines.

- Use a carpenter's square to check that the corner is 90°, and adjust the mitering and repin the corner if necessary to make it square.

- Miter, press, and pin each of the other three corners in the same manner, again using a carpenter's square to check angles of all corners.

5. Fold and pin the hems along their original fold lines along all four edges.

6. Stitch the hems in place by hand or machine, including the angled folds on each side of each mitered corner (A-11).

Note: If your work is a different geometric shape with straight edges (for example, triangle, parallelogram, trapezoid, octagon, pentagon), the mitering will still *bisect* the corners, although the degree of the angle will differ.

A-11 Construction diagram, simple mitered hem corners, machine-stitched.

Instructions for complex mitering on squares and rectangles:
Complex mitering takes more time and works best on *single thicknesses* of *lightweight* fabrics to make very precise corners. The method requires accurate measurement and marking.

1. For *each* corner, fold and press the hems of the two adjacent sides *to the back* of the fabric. Press one side first, then press the second side, allowing the two pressed hem folds to cross at the corners. Once both sides hems are pressed, temporarily open the fabric out flat so the creases show easily. (Do not press them open.)

2. With the *front side* of the fabric facing, fold the fabric so the two adjacent edges align (the left edge and the top edge in step 1), matching the edges and fold lines. This will create a triangle with a 45° fold into the corner.

3. With a pencil or other marking tool, and a carpenter's square, draw a line on the fabric perpendicular to the newly *folded* edge (the bottom edge in A-13, step 3).

4. Stitch along that drawn line through both layers of the folded fabric. Then trim the seam and clip the threads.

5. Press the seam open. One corner is now mitered.

6. Repeat steps 1 through 5 for the other three corners.

A-12 Complex mitered corner, ready for turning and hemming. Hand-dyed cotton.

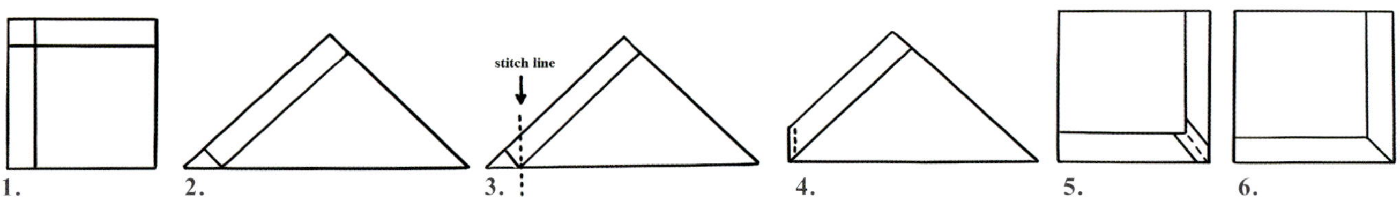

A-13 Construction diagram, complex mitered hem corners

7. Turn the mitered corners *inside out* to lie on the *back* of the work. This will now place *both* the corner seams and the edge hems on the back. Turn under ¼" on all raw edges and insert pins to hold them in place.

8. Stitch the hems in place by hand or machine. Press to remove wrinkles.

Facings: Adding Fabric Strips to Finish Edges

A *facing* consists of a narrow strip of fabric (typically 2"–4" wide) cut to *exactly fit* the outer edge of a work, then sewn to it (*front* sides together) and folded to the back along the seam line (which then runs along the center of the folded edge). Because of the way they're made, facings are hidden on the back or inside of the work (unlike bindings, discussed below, which are visible on both sides).

Facings are relatively flat, add support and strength that help prevent curled edges, and create a smooth, neat edge. They are easy to cut and attach and are often used on curved garment edges such as necklines, armholes, lower edges of dresses, and the front and bottom edges of jackets and vests but can also be useful on the outer edges of patchwork, wall hangings, bags, and works with unusual exterior shapes.

Unlike hems, facings require only a minimal seam allowance (¼") on the work for attaching the strip, making this a good finishing method on works with limited excess fabric at the edges. Because the attachment seam holds the layers together at the edges, facings are especially useful on works composed of *multiple layers* of fabric, such as quilts, collages, and reverse-appliquéd images.

Facing Rectangles and Squares

Instructions for facing a rectangle or square:

1. Trim the work on all edges, leaving a ¼" or ½" seam allowance *outside* the finished boundaries of the composition. Then cut four strips of fabric for the facings, each strip 2"–3" wide and at least 2"–3" *longer* than each edge of the rectangle.

2. Lay the work front side *up*. Starting on one edge, lay the facing strip front side *down* along the edge. Pin the strip in place, inserting the last pin at each at the point where the two seam lines will eventually cross (the *match points*). Machine-stitch the facing strip to the edge, starting and stopping precisely at the match points.

3. Repeat step 2 to attach facing strips on the remaining three sides. Press the seams flat. Then, fold and press the facings to the back of the work so the fold runs precisely in the middle of the seam lines along each edge. Leave the *corners* of the facing strips open for now.

4. Working on the *back*, miter the four corners, using the "Instructions for simple mitering," pages 256–257. Trim off any excess fabric as necessary to create the 45° folds where the facings meet to construct 90° corners. Arrange the folds to lie flat at each corner. Press and pin each corner in place.

   Turn under a ¼" hem along the raw edge of the facing around the entire piece. Press and pin the folded hem in place.

   Hand- or machine-stitch the folded edge in place.

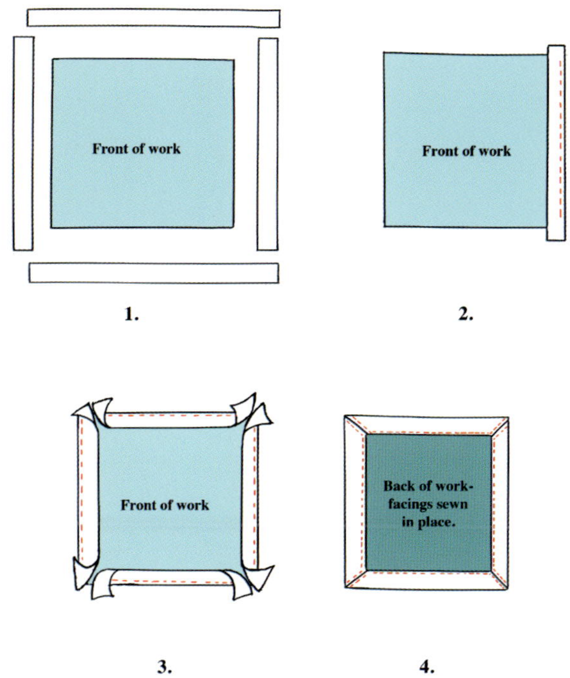

A-14 Construction diagram, facing a rectangle.

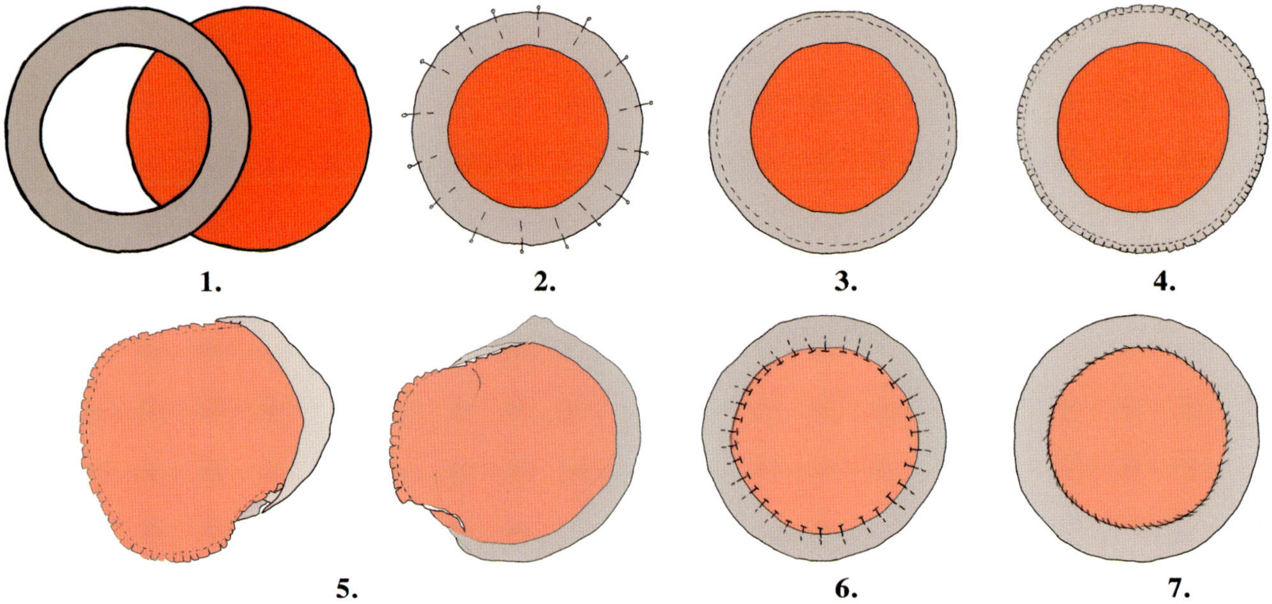

A-15 Construction diagram. Sequence of steps to attach a facing to a circular work with the front of work (*in red*), facing fabric (*in gray*), and back of work (*in pink*).

Facing Curved or Irregular Shapes

Instructions for facing curved or irregular shapes:

1. Prepare the facing: Choose a facing fabric of the same weight, or lighter than, the work to be faced. Place the facing fabric on a work surface, *front side down*. Lay the work *front side up* on top of the facing fabric. (The facing fabric and the work are now lying with their *backs* together.) Using a pencil, trace the exact contours of the work onto the back of the facing fabric (especially important for irregular shapes). For now, set aside the work while you finish drawing and cutting the facing. Working only on the facing fabric, use a pencil to draw a second line, parallel to but 3" *inside* the traced line. Cut the facing from the fabric along *both* drawn lines to produce a 3" wide facing strip that precisely fits the edges of your work. (In A-15, where the work itself is circular, this cutting likewise produces a "ring" of facing. The facing shape would differ for noncircular work.)

2. Placing *front* sides together, align the edges of the facing strip with the edges of the work. Pin the facing strip in place along the *outside* edge.

3. Use a machine straight stitch to attach the facing along all the edges of the work, removing the pins as you approach them, to prevent sewing across them. Press the seams flat.

4. Where necessary, use small, sharp scissors to make frequently spaced cuts halfway into the seam allowance along the edges. Clip straight perpendicular into the edges of *convex* curves. Cut out notches on *concave* curves. For complex serpentine contours, alternate clips and notches along the edge as needed to smooth the changing shape perimeter. If the shape is combined of curves, straight lines, *and* angles (such as the exterior shape of the letter *D*), clip and notch the curves, then clip diagonally into any angles.

5. Turn the facing to the *back* of the work. (Depending on the shape, this may resemble turning it inside out.) Press the fold that runs precisely in the middle of the seam line along the new finished edge of the work.

6. Working on the *back*, press and pin the folded facing in place.

7. Hand-stitch the facing to the back of the work. For a flatter finish, whipstitch the raw edge to the back. For a cleaner finish, turn under and press a ¼" hem along the raw edge and then hand-stitch the hem in place with a blind hem stitch.

Binding: Narrow Edge Finish on Multiple Layers of Fabric

Binding uses separate long, narrow strips of fabric to encase the edges of the work. Whether utilitarian or decorative, the added layers of fabric in the binding protect the edges (for example, on quilts or clothing) from wear during use or washing. Bindings can also be replaced or added at any time, to "freshen" or update a work. Whether cut on the bias or true to grain, attached by hand or machine, bindings produce a clean and precise aesthetic (A-01) and also offer opportunities to add a "pop" of new color or pattern at the edges. Bindings are particularly useful on multilayered works because they help hold together, in a single sewn seam, all the layers. They are commonly used on quilts, blankets, trousers, jackets, vests, and bags but are also useful for wall hangings.

Bias Strip Binding

This technique requires a separately constructed long, continuous binding strip, entirely *cut on the bias*, which is folded and pressed to encase raw edges and then stitched in place. You can buy bias-binding tapes at any fabric store or make your own from any fabric you have on hand. Because of their ability to *stretch* slightly, bias strip bindings are especially useful for finishing *irregular* edges, unusual shapes, curves, and circles. But cutting long strips from yardage on the bias also wastes fabric (for example, cutting a 45" binding strip on the bias might require an entire yard of fabric. Here's a method of constructing long bias strips from smaller fabric squares.

Instructions for making a bias strip:

1. Begin with a square piece of fabric. Mark or fold a diagonal across it and make marks at the center of two parallel sides (red marks in A-16, step 1). Then, cut the fabric in half on the diagonal (dashed line) to create two triangles.

2. Construct a parallelogram and mark the strips:

   - With the *front* sides of the fabric facing each other, and with the marked center points matched (red marks in A-16, step 2), sew the triangles together into a parallelogram.

   - Calculate the strip width: the strips (represented by the intervals between the marked lines in A-16, step 2) can be any width you need for your purposes. Use this formula to calculate the strip width: width on front + width on back + width of two hem allowances = total width. For example, for a ½" binding on *both* front and back (i.e., 1", and two ¼" hem allowances—i.e., ½"), you will need a 1½" wide bias strip.

   - Mark the strips on the fabric: working on the *back* of the fabric, use a marking tool and a ruler to mark parallel lines across the longest length of the joined triangles (A-16, step 2), at the width you have calculated (in the example above, this would be 1½").

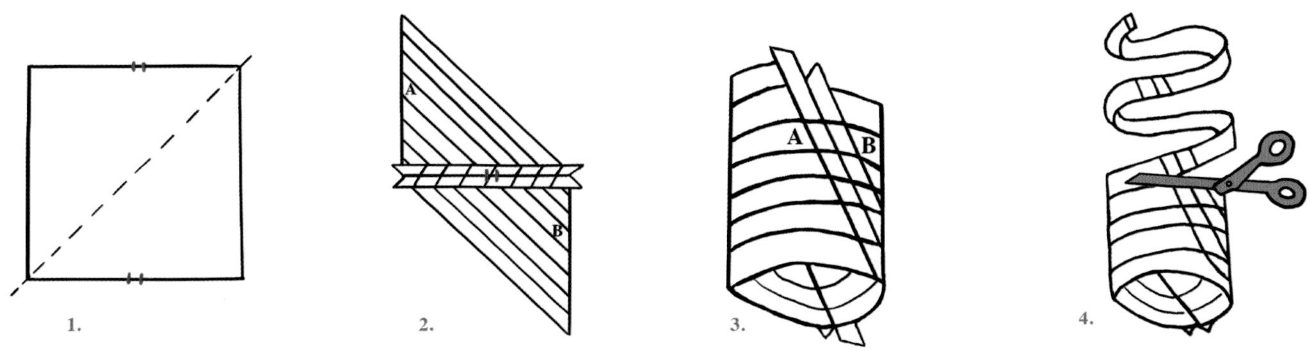

A-16 Construction diagram, creating a bias binding strip from a smaller square of fabric.

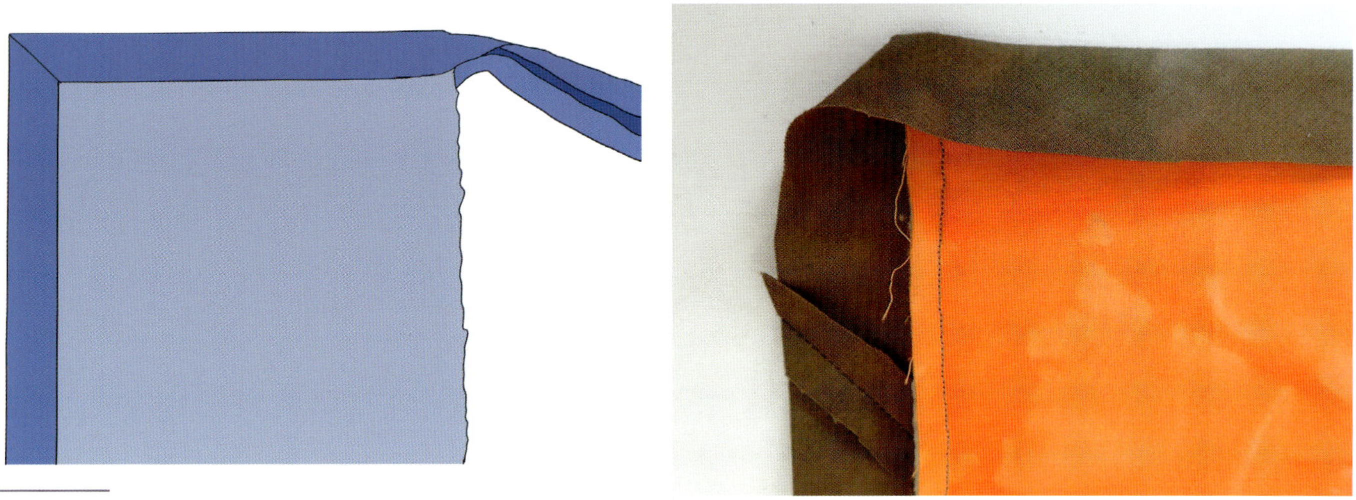

A-17 Method 1 for attaching a bias strip to the edge of the work.

3. With the *front* sides of this fabric *facing* each other, fold or roll it into a tube. Instead of matching the marked lines directly across the joined edges, offset one edge against the other by the width of one strip, to match up the line markings so they will run straight across the seam (A-16, step 3) to create a continuous strip (not separate ones). Pin the matched edges in place and make sure the raw edges of the *initial* seam are turned to the same side as the *new* seam. Stitch the two sides of the parallelogram together into a tube. Press seam and clip threads.

4. Following your marked lines, cut the fabric into one continuous bias strip.

A-18 Method 2 for attaching a bias strip to the edge of the work.

Attaching the bias strip to the edge of the work:

- Method 1 (A-17): Fold under and press hem allowances along *both* long edges of the bias strip. Then fold the strip in half and press it. Slip the folded strip over the edge of the fabric piece, aligning the center fold with the raw edge of the work. Pin the strip in place and stitch the edges in place by hand or machine, finger-pinching miters at the corners.

- Method 2 (A-18): Place the *front* side of the *flat* bias strip against the *front* side of the work, with edges aligned. Machine-stitch the strip to the work. Press the seam flat, then fold the strip over the seam toward the edge of the work. Press again. Turn under a hem allowance on the *unattached* raw edge of the bias strip, then fold the strip in half to enclose the edge of the work. On the back, arrange the folded edge of the strip so that it barely covers the machine-stitched seam line. Pin the bias strip in place, easing, folding, or mitering around the corners as needed. Blind-hem-stitch the folded edge to the *back*.

True-to-Grain Strip Binding

For quilts, kimonos, and other work constructed from rectangular pieces (which, unlike curve-edged work, do not require the stretch of a bias binding; a simple true-to-grain binding will suffice). When cut wider, this type of binding can serve double duty as a decorative border. Apply the strips by hand or machine.

Instructions for true-to-grain strip binding:

1. Determine the *width* of the binding strip. Choose the strip width that is appropriate for the work. As a rule of thumb, figure 2.5 to 4 times the finished width and be sure to include two hem allowances of at least ¼" each. For example, a binding strip of ½" on each side, with two added ¼" hem allowances, would require cutting a strip 1½" wide.

2. Determine the *length* of the binding strip. Measure the edges of your work, add them together, and add several more inches to ease mitering or folding around corners. For example, if your work is 10" × 20", the length of the binding strip would be 60" plus some surplus for corners, for a total of perhaps 65".

3. Cut the strips.

4. Fold and press *under* a hem allowance on *one* long edge of the binding strip.

5. Working on the *front*, place the *front* side of the remaining *raw* edge of the binding strip along the *raw* edge of the work. Insert pins perpendicular to the edges, easing, folding, or mitering around the corners.

6. Machine-stitch the binding strip to the edge of the work.

7. Press the seam flat. Then press the binding toward the outside edge of the work.

8. Fold the binding strip in half to encircle the edge of the work, then align the fold of the hem allowance to barely *overlap* the machine stitching on the back. Pin the folded edge in place.

9. Hand- or machine-stitch the folded edge onto the back:

   - To *hand*-stitch the hem, work on the *back* of the work and use a blind hem stitch that won't show on the front of the work.

   - To *machine*-stitch the hem (which will make the stitching visible from both sides), work on the *front* of the work. Machine-stitch ¹⁄₁₆"–⅛" outside the seam of the binding strip, removing the pins one by one as the fabric advances toward the needle, in order to prevent the machine stitching over them.

APPENDIX B: MATERIALS, TOOLS, AND EQUIPMENT

In my studio practice, I first determine the types of materials and tools best suited to a project, then use the highest quality I can afford. In general, I choose quality over quantity, because good beginnings are more likely to produce pleasurable creative experiences and successful aesthetic outcomes. And I generally use the same materials for "studies" as I expect to use in the project itself, because learning how materials can be "worked," and feeling what they "want" to do (or not do), is part of the creative process.

While the following overview provides some reliable brand names at the time this book was written, vendors come and go with the passage of time, product offerings change, or a particular product may not be readily available where you live, work, or shop.

Regardless of when you first encounter this book, you can use the following information to locate similar or alternative products.

General

Desirable Characteristics:

- High-quality art supplies of all kinds will inspire you with confidence and an attitude of serious commitment to your creative endeavors. Invest for the long term. I generally find that good tools are a pleasure to use: they fit the hand well, respond to your working motions, last longer, and clean up easily. On the other hand, cheap tools are often frustrating to use, feel clumsy in the hand, wear out faster, and are more apt to break.

- Paintbrushes should have strong wood or plastic handles and firmly attached ferrules. Good-quality brushes usually are expensive. Sets of brushes provide a variety of shapes (rounds, brights, fans, flats, filberts, etc.) and sizes. Natural-bristle brushes are generally preferable for dyes, pigments, and acrylic paints, but discharge chemicals (to remove color from dyed fabric) actually require brushes with *synthetic* bristles.

- For color references, I recommend Color Aid or Pantone chips/papers, color wheels, and value charts. In any case, choose easy-to-use formats and, concerning wheels and charts, choose products that contain as much printed color theory information as possible.

- Sketchbooks come in a variety of sizes (from 3" × 5" to 18" × 24"), paper types (Bristol, watercolor, drawing, ruled, graph), bindings (cloth bound, spiral), and formats (top opening, side opening). Choose the types that fit the way you draw, and the places where you're most likely to use the sketchbooks (in the studio, traveling, in the field).

My Stash Includes:

- tools for direct-application work: wide variety of natural-bristle and synthetic paintbrushes; lots of sponge brushes; line tools; old spoons, forks, knives, and rubber spatulas; rubber and plastic stamps; cotton swabs; netting bags and scrubbers; monoprint tools; plastic stencils; natural and synthetic sponges; squeeze bottles with metal tips

- drawing tools: pencils, colored pencils, watercolor pencils, fabric markers, charcoal, pastels, Speedball pen and points, ink stone

- sketchbooks of various sizes and types: a spiral-bound 9" × 12" book with thick, wet-media paper that opens flat for extensive studio work. When traveling, I carry a 5" × 7" Moleskine Two-Go journal with alternating blank (left side) and ruled (right side) pages so that I can make both sketches and written notes about the same observation, a 3" × 5" watercolor Moleskine in my purse or backpack, and a self-contained portable watercolor set with water receptacle brush handle (useful for quick watercolor sketches because it doesn't require using or carrying a separate water container).

- papers: inkjet transfer paper, Color Aid paper set, scrapbooking papers, tissue paper, origami papers, old postcards, archival mat board pieces, handmade papers, Saral transfer papers (assorted colors), graph paper, construction paper

Beads and Beading Threads

Desirable Characteristics:

- uniform bead size for each type
- evenly cut and drilled
- consistent color
- no chips, cracks, or blemishes
- no painted interiors or exteriors, which are apt to fade, chip, or wash away
- strong beading threads in a variety of colors and fiber types

My Stash Includes:

- a large assortment of glass seed beads and Delicas in a wide variety of colors, and sizes (#6, #8, #11, #13, #22)
- bugle beads in a small range of colors
- bone and wood rounds, bugles, and roundels
- sterling silver rounds, charms, and filigreed beads
- selected well-made plastic beads
- specialty beads in stone and unusual materials for specific projects
- Silamide, Nymo, and Fireline beading threads
- beading tools: needle-nose pliers, round pliers, bead reamer
- bead scoops (one wide, one narrow)

Whenever possible, I leave the beads in their plastic packages or containers with the label intact (including the color name or number) for future reference. I sort and organize the packages, by type and color, in a small plastic chest of drawers.

Dyes, Pigments, Textile Paints, and Chemicals

Desirable Characteristics:

- dyes (whether fiber reactive or acid) purchased in powdered form but later to be mixed and stored in liquid form
- easy-to-use plastic containers (dye powder in an actual jar is easier, and safer, to manage than powder in limp plastic bags)
- Product is accompanied by adequate and detailed written instructions for its use: good supporting online information, Materials Safety Data Sheet (MSDS), and telephone access to actual human beings (specifically dye chemistry staff) at the manufacturer.

My Stash Includes:

- dyes: MX Fiber Reactive Dyes from Pro-Chemical and Dye in about a dozen basic colors
- pigments: ProChemical and Dye Color Concentrates, and other textile pigments and paints (also typically a dozen or so)
- AquaBrite print base/extender (for pigments) from Standard Screen Supply or Pro-Chemical and Dye
- textile paints for cotton or silk (assorted manufacturers)
- weighing scales, measuring cups and spoons, stirring spoons, mixing containers with tight-fitting lids, dye buckets, rubber gloves, work shirts, and aprons

Fabrics

Desirable Characteristics:

- strong fibers and even weaves; solid construction
- free of flaws, shredded selvedges, dirt, grease, and evidence of careless manufacturing practices (unless you have *intentionally* purchased "seconds")
- for dyeing and printing (if you'll want to do your own): "ready to dye" cloth or clothing blanks *without* surface coatings or finishes (but even if not intended for dyeing or printing, uncoated fabrics feel better in the hand and more easily accept the threaded needle)
- Most fabric companies provide economies of scale (i.e., the unit cost decreases as the quantity purchased increases). If you will use a single type of cloth for many projects, consider buying it in quantity or by the roll.

My Stash Includes:

- *Undyed* natural-fiber fabrics from plant and animal sources. Cotton: broadcloth, print cloth, velveteen, sateen, sheeting, gauze, cheesecloth, heavy twill, and muslin; heirloom napkins and tablecloths, crocheted table covers. Rayon: satin and challis. Silk: noil, organza, organza mesh/netting, torpedo, dupioni, figured, and twills. Linen: softened, handkerchief, heirloom. Wool: flannel, felts.
- my own dyed fabrics left over from previous projects and saved for future use.
- Commercially printed fabrics when needed. My own patterned, printed, discharged, and handwoven fabrics left over from previous projects.
- nylon netting, metallics, and synthetic felts (suitable for very specific uses and therefore the main exceptions to my general preference for natural fibers)
- for digital printing: pretreated fabrics, precut and paper-backed, sized to fit my home studio printer
- interfacings (iron on and sew in), tear-away interfacings, fusible webs, Solvy dissolvable web, and synthetic nonwoven fabrics for making stencils and templates

Hoops and Frames

Desirable Characteristics:

- continuous contact between the inner and outer hoops
- durable wooden hoops with smooth edges (or use sandpaper to smooth them), which resist cracking or splitting under tension and hold the fabric stretched tightly
- or plastic hoops with *interlocking grooves*
- grooved screw heads (whether for plastic or wooden hoops), which can be tightened with a standard screwdriver (thumbscrews are acceptable but more difficult to tighten)

My Stash Contains:

- Edmunds hoops (both round and square, high quality), Hardwicke Manor quilting and embroidery hoops (very high quality and priced accordingly), a few heirloom hoops from family members, assorted grooved plastic hoops from various sources
- simple modular wooden scroll frame with interchangeable sizes of dowels
- handbuilt wooden slate frame

See the separate discussion of stands, below.

Needles

Desirable Characteristics:

- strong and straight, but flexible enough to bend repeatedly without breaking or remaining bent
- selection of types and sizes matching the fabrics you'll be using (the *larger* the needle size number, the *smaller* the needle diameter)
- needle eyes large enough to thread easily and allow the thread to move freely during stitching

My Stash Includes:

- Hand needles: variety of Bohin needles (a very fine brand made in France): embroidery, sharp, crewel, and millinery, in varying sizes and lengths, sharps, size 10 and 11, and an assorted package including tapestry, chenille, darners, sharps, betweens/quilting, and embroidery/crewel. Beading needles: long and short, usually in size 11 or 12. John James needles (an older generation still manufactured in the UK, which I consider superior to the current generation made in Asia). Blunt tapestry needles (size 16).
- machine needles: Bernina, 70/10, 80/12, 90/14; twin (2,0/80 narrow set, and 4,0/80 wide set); top stitching; and ballpoint
- telescoping magnetic wand for picking up dropped needles

I keep needles in various locations. The larger inventory is collected in a plastic basket in my sewing cabinet. A wool felt pincushion on my worktable provides a temporary home of whatever needles I'm using on a current project. Others may be stashed in my worktable caddy, my "art studio travel bag," beside my sewing machine, and probably in some other places I hope to remember eventually.

Scissors

Desirable Characteristics:

- sturdy stainless-steel construction
- comfortably shaped handles that fit your *dominant* hand
- continuous contact between the inner and outer blades to allow clean cutting out to the points

My Stash Includes:

- generally: shears for large fabric cuts, medium-sized "craft" scissors for small fabric cuts, embroidery scissors or snips for cutting threads
- Gingher: shears, embroidery scissors, and snips for the studio (high quality and dependable)
- Mundial: shears, craft scissors, and snips (adequate for workshops and travel where the chance of loss or damage to tools is greater)
- miscellaneous types: suture scissors, paper scissors
- Gingher sharpening stone

Screen Printing and Supplies

Desirable Characteristics:

- for hand printing: screens small enough and light enough to lift and move easily
- Commercially made frames are usually superior to handmade and cost about the same.
- frames straight (mesh side should be able to lie flat against the table), sturdy, free of cracks, splits, and other evidence of injury
- screen mesh tightly stretched, with grain straight and free of flaws, wrinkles, buckles, and rips

My Stash Includes:

- wooden waterproof frames from Mel-Ray (screen meshes 109, 200)
- small rubber squeegees with wooden or plastic handles

Sewing Machines

Desirable Characteristics:

- heavy-duty construction with metal parts, especially the internal cams (this may involve buying an older machine, made before the industry increased the number of plastic components)
- for ease of free-motion stitching, feed dogs that easily disengage with a simple lever, knob, or button
- attachments: Among other standard styles, at least one of the following feet: quilting, darning, open-front free motion
- freely moving dial or rheostat to control stitch width smoothly during stitching
- sturdy carrying case

My Stash Includes:

- Bernina 930 (manufactured in 1985 but still available used from online sources and occasionally from local Bernina dealers): heavy, all-metal, versatile, and ideal for free-motion work
- Juki TL-93E: an industrial-strength machine, powerful and fast (although with a governor for speed control). Straight-stitch only, which nevertheless makes it a good choice for extensive free-motion work through thick or multilayered fabrics.
- Singer Featherweight (manufactured in 1966): small, lightweight, and portable. Straight-stitch only. Throat plate cover for feed dogs facilitates free-motion work.

Stands for Stitching or Quilting

Desirable Characteristics:

- strong clamp that holds a hoop or frame to provide a "third hand" during stitching, grips the hoop or frame tightly, holds it firmly in place without loosening or slipping when stitching, and allows easy access to the *back* of the work during stitching *without* loosening a screw or knob
- smoothly finished, strong, and easily turned gears, screws, clamps, joins, levers, and knobs
- Well-balanced *metal* stands are more sturdy, durable, and dependable than most wooden stands. Modular stands can be disassembled for storage or travel.

My Stash Includes:

- For a permanent location in my studio, I use a K's Creations floor stand. It is heavy (stainless steel), durable, and well balanced—an industrial-looking "workhorse."
- For travel, when packing space is tight, I have a lighter-weight heavy-gauge aluminum Lowery Workstand (made in the UK), which disassembles easily to stow in carry-on luggage. As a bonus, its base slips easily beneath a lounge chair or sofa, enabling use in a more casual sitting position.
- For flexibility, portability, and light weight, I prefer the modular Needlework System 4, whose well-designed, sturdy, and cleanly finished clamp (described by the manufacturer as "space-age plastic") can alternately be attached with stainless-steel fittings to four different types of aluminum stands (floor, travel floor, table clamp, or laptop/tabletop) from the same manufacturer.

Threads and Yarns

Desirable Characteristics:

- strong enough to avoid breakage as threads rub through the eye of the needle
- sufficiently friction-resistant to resist shredding when pulled repeatedly through fabric
- sufficiently colorfast to avoid bleeding their own dye onto the fabric or adjacent threads when wet
- consistent and even thread weight (diameter), quality control (no weak spots, bumps, or knots), and dye lot accuracy (in case you need to buy more of that color)
- You can buy specific threads for each project or (my own approach) keep a broad inventory of threads on hand to allow spontaneous choices and interesting or unusual color mixes.
- inventory suggestions: Variety of natural and synthetic fiber types and weights in both tight and loose spins. Wide ranges of colors, from many areas of the color wheel, light to dark and bright to muted. Variegated threads in subtle, sophisticated, jarring, or high-contrast color mixes. An assortment of textures (e.g., shiny, matte, rough, smooth, wiry, stiff, soft, or furry).

My Stash Includes:

- DMC cotton embroidery floss in a wide variety of colors, variegations, and special twists; DMC rayon embroidery threads
- DMC 50 wt. cotton machine embroidery threads and Sulky 40 wt. machine rayon threads in a variety of colors
- Valdani threads: cotton floss, pearl, and 35 wt. machine thread. Silk floss. Wool threads. This company offers both solid and variegated thread colors; I find the variegated especially attractive.
- Assorted manufacturers: Pearl cottons in a variety of weights, color, and variegations. Silks in varying weights, plies, and colors. Specialty gimps, cords, narrow tapes, and ribbons. Wool threads and yarns, such as those spun for embroidery, tapestry, needlepoint, knitting, or crewel work. Bast fibers: various spins of linen, ramie, jute, and hemp. Leaf fibers: raffia (stripped length of palm). Metallics: synthetic flosses and real gold (gold purl, passing). Mixed-fiber-content yarns and novelty threads: wide assortment originally intended for weaving, crocheting, tatting, or knitting, in small amounts (silk threads and tapes, nylon, bamboo, paper, hemp, transparent fishing line, ramie, raffia, and human hair).
- hand-dyed threads from small specialty companies: Weeks Dye Works (North Carolina), Oliver Twists (UK), Stef Francis (UK), or individual dye artists fortuitously encountered at stitchery trade shows
- When I need very specific colors (color matching) or absolute color control, I buy *undyed* threads on large cones and dye the colors myself with chemical or natural dyes. In fact, whenever I dye fabric, I tend to throw in a few skeins of thread at the same time.

APPENDIX C: KEEPING SAMPLES: YOUR CUMULATIVE CLOTH "LIBRARY" AND "TOOLBOX"

Want to learn a new technique, test an idea, practice with new materials, try alternative compositions, or "break the rules"? Want the ability to repeat it if you like the results and need to remember "how I did it"? Include sample making as a regular part of your creative practice. For the best results, use the same quality of materials you'll use in your projects. Collected, documented, and organized, your saved samples can be a valuable future resource.

My own studio contains a "reference library" of my sample *notebooks* (an entire shelf of them, accumulated over years). As I explore new ideas, I still save more new samples. This valuable collection has not only supported my creative practice but provided many of the illustrations for this book.

Organizing and Storing Samples

Organize your samples into related topics (such as specific techniques, types of materials, color effects) that make access easy and logical. For each group of samples, choose a separate container in an appropriate format (such as a notebook, box, plastic bag, or bin). To identify the contents of each container at a glance, attach content labels to the outside.

C-01 Sample notebook pages: natural dye tests (*left*) and information sheet with samples (*right*).

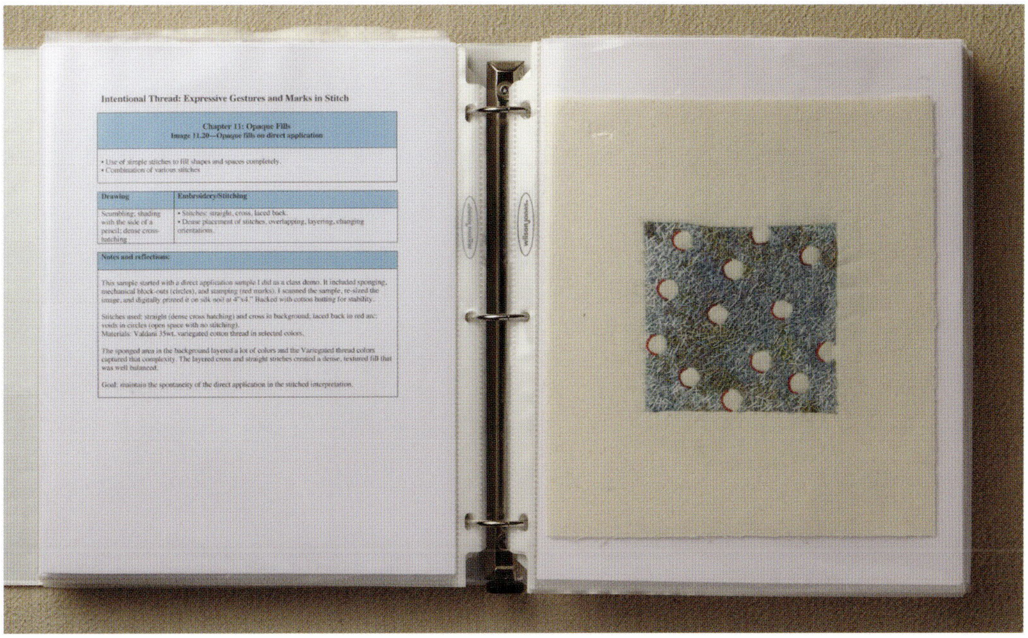

C-02 Sample notebook page: information sheet (*left*) and larger sample of shaded fill stitches.

Notebooks:

Three-ring binders are a convenient and flexible way to store flat samples. (I recommend 1.5" or 2" three-ring binders with clear plastic sleeves to hold labels on the front, back, and spine. And I prefer the binders themselves in neutral colors, i.e., black, white, or gray.) To provide maximum protection for each sample, support it on a piece of 8.5" × 11" card stock, then insert it into a top-loading protective plastic sheet in your notebook. You can update and rearrange the binder and insert new samples as frequently as you wish.

C-03 Sample container: miscellaneous large or bulky pieces.

Containers:

For larger or more three-dimensional samples, try archival storage boxes, clear plastic containers with tight-fitting lids, or zippered plastic bags with some air trapped inside. Inside a larger bin or container, you can still subdivide the samples into separate boxes, plastic bags, cloth envelopes, or rolls.

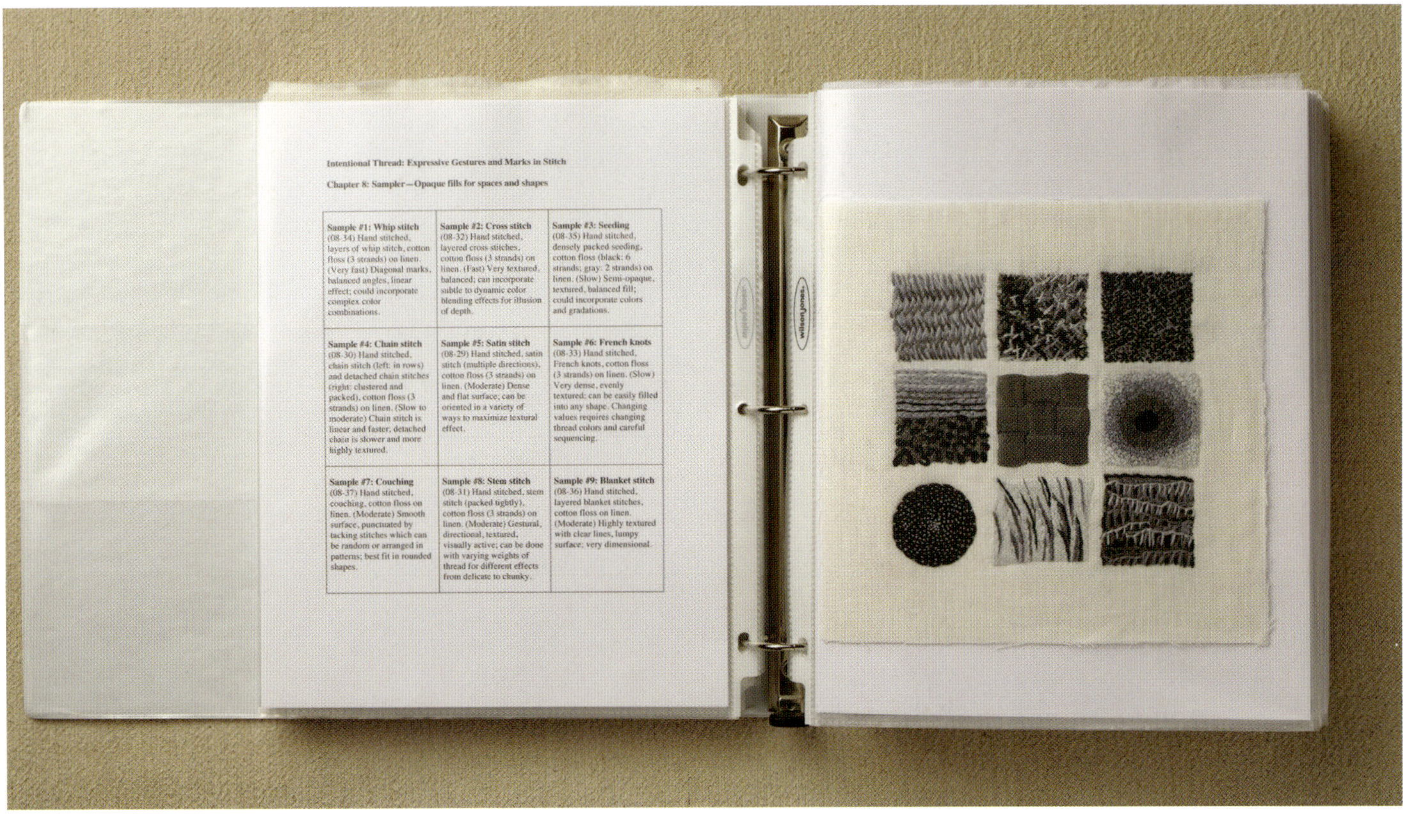

Documenting Your Samples

To make your entire collection of samples even more useful, write a few comments or reflections about each sample as you complete it. Then store the notes next to each sample in the notebook, box, or bin.

I use information sheets that include the details I might later want to know about a sample: the techniques or materials used, the idea being tested, notes and reflections about the making, problems (and solutions) encountered, and ideas sparked for other work. Your approach to documentation can be formal (computer-typed and printed on a form you designed) or casual (handwritten notes).

Some things you might want to document on sample information sheets:

- techniques used (dyeing, resist dyeing, piecing, appliqué, embellishment)
- fabrics and threads used (fiber type, content, structure, and sources)
- dyes or pigments used (type, manufacturer/vendor, color name/number)
- specific measurements (amounts of dye, amounts of fabric, etc.)
- unique notes about the sample (such as technical difficulties, observations on the material's appropriateness, things that went right or wrong, things to remember or try next time)
- general notes and reflections on what you learned by making the sample or insights to remember for the future reference

C-04 Sample notebook pages: charted information sheet (*left*) and sampler of different opaque fill stitches (*right*).

A Special Note about Dye Sample Notebooks

Over the years, I have found *dye sample notebooks* especially helpful references. Most dye companies post color charts online and sell dye swatches of their available "pure" colors, making your initial color choices simple and straightforward. However, for your own *custom* dye work, those charts and swatches are just starting points. No dye company can possibly provide swatches of the countless potential *combinations* of the pure colors.

Therefore, I highly recommend that you keep a detailed and systematic notebook of your dyed fabric samples. This saves you from later having to rely on your memory about what you did to achieve a certain color effect. Instead, you record, "in the moment," exactly what you do and exactly how you do it, and (afterward) can also make note of which dyeing choices produced the results you'd expected and which produced something different (which doesn't necessarily mean "worse"). Your sample notebook then links each individual dye sample to its accompanying written record. In effect, doing this, you're creating your own small-scale version of a manufacturer's *dye lot* identification (a number used to identify all yarns or fabrics present in the same dye vat and exposed to the same precise amount of dye, chemicals, water temperature, time, and processing), which can also be used to replicate the same color, on the same fabric, in the future.

Your assembled and annotated dye sample notebook will be the *only* resource that *precisely* documents your *applied* experience with the dyes you use (i.e., the colors you *actually* achieved on *your* specific goods, using *your* local water source [with its own mineral content and chemical idiosyncrasies], and *your* way of managing the dye processes).

C-05 Sample notebook pages: information sheet (*left*) and rainbow dye sample (*right*).

C-06 Sample notebook pages. Dye samples on two different cottons (print cloth in left column; broadcloth in right column) overlapped in clusters. Pages trimmed ½" to reveal color relationships with samples on following pages. Labeled with dye colors and depth of dye information.

Because this dye sample notebook might serve as a reference and guide for your current and future dye work, take the time and expense to make it durable and of good quality. Clean, press, and trim the fabric samples to make them wrinkle-free and tidy. Mount the samples in a logical order on heavy card stock pages. Fabric samples can be affixed with double-stick tape. Yarn samples can be looped through holes punched in the edges of the vertically folded pages of card stock, as in 01-35 and 01-38.

Glossary

achromatic: Without color or chroma. In color theory and practice: black, white, and grays.

acid dyes: Water-soluble dyes that work in an acid environment, typically useful for dyeing protein fibers such as silk, wool, and nylon.

activator: A catalyst compound that sets in motion the chemical reaction that makes dye permanent on cloth.

air pen: A compressor-driven stylus that can be loaded with ink or thinned textile pigment and used to draw or write on a surface. Similar to but more focused than an airbrush.

alchemy: An apparently magical process of transformation, creation, or combination.

alginates: Naturally occurring substances found only in brown seaweeds. Sodium alginate, dissolved in water, forms a viscous solution, which is commonly used as a thickening agent for painting or screen printing with dyes on fabric.

alum: A sulfate salt of aluminum or potassium, used as a mordant in dyeing cloth with natural dyes.

analogous colors: Those colors *adjacent* to each other on the color wheel.

bast fibers: Cellulose fibers that originate in the *stems* of plants.

blind hem stitch: A simple hand stitch that runs continuously through the fold of a hem, only occasionally catching a thread of the fabric to hold the hem in place, making it invisible on the front of a fabric.

block-out: Any material used on a screen mesh to form those parts of a stencil impervious to the printing medium.

cartoon: A full-scale sketch or drawing, sometimes in color, used as a guide to create a work (painting, tapestry, embroidery, etc.).

cellulose fibers: Fibers that come from the stems, leaves, seeds, or flowers of *plants*. Examples: cotton, linen, hemp, ramie, reed, Tencel, rayon, and bamboo.

collage: Combining and affixing mixed materials (particularly those that contrast real with implied tactile qualities) onto a two-dimensional surface. When expanded into the realm of digital composition, collage can include any combination of images from various sources.

colorfast: The characteristic of possessing dyed color that retains its original hue without fading or running.

color separations: The breakdown of multicolor printed images or pattern modules into separate parts, resulting in one separate stencil for each color in a design. When printed in succession, color separations fit together precisely to create seamless and visually precise results.

color story: A group of colors combined to create atmosphere or mood.

color wheel: An abstract circular arrangement of colors that illustrates their theoretical relationships. Standardized printed color wheels are commonly used as guides by artists, printers, dyers, craftsmen, designers, quilters, and other artists who use color in their work.

complementary colors: Those colors directly *opposite* each other on the color wheel.

composite color: Any color created by combining two or more different "pure" commercial dye colors.

composition: In visual art, the organization of *elements* (such as point, line, shape, plane, volume, texture, color), using guiding *principles* (such as balance, context, contrast, emphasis, gradation, pattern, placement, point of view, positive/negative space, proportion, repetition, rhythm, scale, variety, and illusion of space) to form a *coherent whole*. These elements and principles constitute a form of "visual language."

copyright: A type of intellectual property that conveys the exclusive right to make copies of a creative work (musical, artistic, educational, or literary). This right is automatically given to the creator of the work, though often for a limited duration; in the US, usually the life of the author plus 50 to 70 years. The work must be registered with the US Copyright Office to withstand and support protection against infringements.

de-intensified colors: Hues or colors that are lowered in intensity or dulled in effect.

dissolvable web: A gel-like substance (also referred to as "wash-away embroidery stabilizer") used to support fabric for stitching, but that subsequently dissolves when placed in hot water.

depth of dye: The ratio of a certain weight of dye to a given weight of fiber/fabric expressed as a percentage.

digital printing: Using a computer and inkjet printer to print images on paper-backed fabric.

direct application: An "umbrella" term that describes ways to apply color, marks, patterns, and images to cloth with hand tools (including, but not limited to, painting, spraying, drawing, sponging, stamping, stenciling, or monoprinting).

discharge: Using bleach or other chemicals to reduce, fade out, lighten, or completely remove dyed color from cloth.

drape: A fabric's relative stiffness or limpness of structure, as demonstrated by its response to gravity (i.e., what the fabric does when you place it over your extended hand).

dye (noun): A natural or synthetic compound or substance used to add or change the color of fabric by combining chemically with the fiber.

dye (verb): The process or act of adding or changing the color of a fabric by soaking it in a solution impregnated with a dye or dyestuff.

dye powder: A natural dyestuff or chemical dye that has been finely ground and prepared to render it immediately and easily usable as a component with water in a dyebath.

dye solution: A combination of dye powder and water in any ratio (*see also* stock solution).

dyebath: A solution composed of dye or dyestuff, water, and appropriate chemical assistants. The purpose of the dyebath is to submerge the fabric into the concoction, which over a prescribed period of time will activate the chemistry, allow the dye to enter the fibers, and set the color more or less permanently.

dye lot: In commercial production, a number attached to all yarns, threads, or fabrics present in the same dyebath or dye vat (and exposed to same precise amount of dye, chemicals, water temperature, time, and processing), which renders them identical in color.

dyestuff (noun): Any substance that yields a dye or can be used as a dye, particularly when placed in a water solution. This could include a variety of chemicals or natural plants, insects, minerals, or earths.

embroidery stand: A device with a clamp to hold an embroidery hoop, frame, or stretcher, to free up both hands for stitching. Stands in many styles, made from metal, wood, or fiberglass, can stand on the floor, sit on a tabletop, or clamp to a table edge.

extender: Paste used to reduce the color intensity of a dye or pigment paste.

fiber reactive dyes: Those dyes (example: Procion MX) that combine chemically with the fiber on fixation. Valued for their transparent brilliant color.

figure: A form or shape, determined by outlines or exterior surfaces. The major element(s) of a pattern or composition.

figure-ground reversal: A design or composition with roughly equal quantities of two contrasting colors, textures, or other elements, both of which may be perceived as either figure or ground.

flatbed scanner: A device resembling a small light table, with a glass surface, an underlying movable light, and a hinged lid, that captures and immediately deposits an image of anything placed on the glass onto an attached computer.

floss: A shorthand reference to *embroidery floss*, a type of loosely twisted cotton, rayon, or silk thread that is specifically made for embroidery.

four-color printing: Separation of the colors in an image into cyan, magenta, yellow, and black layers, which when printed sequentially reproduce the original color image with interspersed dots of only four component colored inks. Used throughout the graphic arts and commercial printing industry.

frame: The part of a screen, usually wood or aluminum, to which a polyester or nylon mesh is attached.

freezer paper: A paper, usually dispensed on a roll, waxed on one side and plain on the other side (also called *butcher paper*).

fusible web: A commercial heat-sensitive adhesive specifically made for use with textiles, sold temporarily mounted on a paper backing, and transferred to the fabric surface with ironing (after which, the paper is removed).

goods: Any textile material in any form—fabric samples or yardage; skeined threads, yarns, or cords; clothing, quilt tops, or accessories.

gradation: Gradual change across a surface in an orderly way. The characteristics of a gradation include the *way* that elements change across a surface (for example, changes of color, shape, or position), the *speed* of the change (rapid steps give the viewer visual jerks, slow steps a smooth transition), and the *direction* of the change (up, down, across, parallel, concentric, zigzag, or other).

grain (of the fabric): The grid of intersecting *warp* (lengthwise) and *weft* (crosswise) threads in a woven fabric.

graphics tablet: A device that allows direct drawing with a stylus on a digitally sensitive surface, mimicking the action of drawing with pen and ink on paper, and directly creating a digital file.

gray scale: A digital version of a value scale (black, grays, and white) found in computers and photocopiers.

grid: A regular network of lines used to correctly place a module or element on a surface.

ground (or background): The space existing around the major elements of a pattern or composition.

hand: The tactile qualities of a fabric perceived by touch (softness, firmness, elasticity, fineness, resilience, etc.).

head strikes: In digital printing, errors caused by the print heads physically contacting the fabric and leaving blotches or smears of ink.

hem: The folded edge of fabric, meant to hide and protect raw edges and finish a textile.

hue: The name of a color or its place on the color wheel.

immersion dyeing: Coloring cloth in a pot with water, dyestuff, and activating chemicals (synthetic dyes) or mordants (natural dyes).

inkjet printer: A type of digital printer that disperses tiny droplets of colored ink onto the paper, plastic, or fabric surface to reconstruct and produce an image from a computer.

intensity: The brightness or dullness of a color (also referred to as "saturation," or "chroma," or "purity").

invisible appliqué stitch: A simple stitch that occasionally catches a thread in the folded edge of an appliqué patch to hold that patch in place on the foundation cloth. The stitch is nearly invisible from the front but quite visible on the back.

lightfast: Dyed color that retains its original hue without fading when exposed to sun or artificial light.

low-immersion dyeing: Coloring cloth in a pot with dyestuff, chemical assistants, and *insufficient* water to produce *intentionally* irregular color distribution.

lozenge: A four-sided equilateral figure whose opposing angles are equal (such as a diamond).

masking tape: A common type of tape with a persistent rubber adhesive used by house painters to mask out areas to be protected from paint. Left in place on any surface, it commonly leaves a sticky residue. Its adhesive contains an acid that can eat away at natural fiber fabrics.

match points: Marks used to accurately align two pieces of fabric to be seamed, and to signal the precise start and stop points for the stitching.

Materials Safety Data Sheets (MSDS): Internationally standardized documents that list the ingredients and occupational safety information on substances or products, especially chemicals and chemical compounds (including instructions for safe use, potential hazards, and spill-handling procedures).

metaphos (sodium hexametaphosphate): Used as a water softener in preparing thickeners for fiber reactive dyes to make a smoother paste and modify its flow.

module: A basic unit or element. In repeat pattern, a cluster of motifs grouped to work as a unit in the pattern.

moiré pattern: A watery or wavy image created *unintentionally* by the misalignment of two grids (physical), or *intentionally* on fabric by calendaring (heat and pressure) treatment.

mola: The name for the reverse-appliquéd blouses made by the Cuna Indian women from the San Blas Islands off the coast of Panama in Central America. Panels in a clearly identifiable style, depicting local flora, fauna, or human activities, inset as decoration on front and back of blouses.

monochromatic: Tints, tones and shade of a single hue.

monogum: A modified starch gum used to thicken bleach for controlled direct application or screen printing.

mordant: A catalyst for setting natural dye colors, often metal salts.

motif: A theme, or dominant recurring visual element, form, or subject. In repeat pattern, a single repeated shape or element.

natural dyes: Dyes derived from plant or animal sources.

natural fibers: Fibers that come from living or natural organisms (plants or animals).

needle (verb, the action): Used by many needleworkers as a verb, *to needle* indicates the action of pushing a needle through cloth. The amount of resistance met depends on the type, twist, and density of the threads in the cloth's structure, in relation to the size of the needle. For example, a cloth that firmly resists any needle is said to be "hard to needle."

needle (noun, the object): A slender metal tool used for sewing, with a point on one end and a hole (called the "eye") for thread in the other. Needles are made in a variety of sizes and lengths suited for different uses. Some common types include straw (or milliner's), "betweens," sharps, tapestry, beading, and embroidery.

negative space: The background, ground, or space in a composition or field not occupied by the figure or major element(s).

network: The basic understructure of a repeat system.

neutrals: Surface characteristics without strong chroma (for example, tan, beige, brown, gray, cream, taupe, buff, fawn).

one-piece patchwork: A piecing method in which a single shape (such as a square, rectangle, or right triangle) in a single size is repeated, fitted, and sewn together with plain seams in a simple grid.

optical blending or optical mixing: The results of combining colored dots, marks, lines, or small bits of material. The *tiny scale* of the interactions among the bits aids the human eye (and brain) to combine the separate colors into "composite" colors.

overdyeing: Dyeing over previously dyed areas with another color.

overprinting: Printing over previously printed areas with another color, image, or pattern.

painter's tape: A common type of tape (similar to masking tape, but with a less sticky adhesive) used by house painters to mask out areas to be protected from paint. It does not adhere well to textiles or screens and peels off easily in contact with water.

pattern: The regular repetition of modules or elements on a surface or in space.

pieced construction (or piecing): Sewing together smaller bits of fabric to compose and assemble a larger cloth.

pH (potential of hydrogen): In chemistry, a scale numbered from 1 to 14 that defines the relative acidity or alkalinity of a liquid or solution (or dyebath). In the center of the scale, pH of 7 is neutral, and is the natural pH of pure water.

pigment: A material that colors fabric by coating the fiber. Pigments are held to the surface by means of a binder.

placement: The location or arrangement of the elements of a composition.

pliability: Refers to a fabric's responsiveness to folding and manipulation, limiting the types of three-dimensional forms the cloth can *naturally* assume.

pointillism: A technique of painting with small dots of color, applied in patterns to form shapes and images through the juxtaposition of colors and optical blending. The Pointillist art movement, an outgrowth of late-19th-century Impressionism, was spearheaded by the French painters Georges Seurat and Paul Signac.

positive space: The space in a composition occupied by the figure or major elements.

precision craft knife: A tiny cutting or carving tool with a handle that is fitted with triangular-shaped replaceable blades. The knife is held in the hand with an overhand or tripod grip and used to cut accurately through papers and lightweight plastics or boards.

primary colors: The basic colors from which all other colors are mixed. In pigments or dyes they are cyan, magenta, and yellow. In light they are red, blue, and green.

print base or emulsion: A white gelatinous substance visually resembling thick yogurt and containing a binder, meant to suspend and distribute pigment colors for even applications to fabric. The emulsion can be transparent or opaque in character.

print paste or dye paste: A combination of pigment or dissolved dye, a thickening agent, and the necessary fixative chemicals, meant for color printing or direct application on cloth.

protein fibers: Those that come from the hair or fur of animals (for example, wool, camel, llama, alpaca, nylon, and silk).

registration: Exact alignment of one pattern repeat with another in printing.

registration mark: Visible line or other indicator used as a guide to register pattern repeats in screen printing.

repeat: The basic unit of design in fabric pattern.

repeat pattern: A pattern composed of two or more identical elements or units.

repeat systems: Mathematically described movements and relationships of a module as it repeats in a pattern.

repetition: The act of repeating something, such as a line or shape, a sound or tone, a musical phrase, or an interval.

reproducibility: The ability to repeat a result (for example, to mix the same dye color and match it to a previously dyed cloth).

retardant: An additive for printing pigments that slows down their drying time.

saturation: *See* intensity.

scale: In composition, the *relative* size of elements that establishes a hierarchy of importance among them.

scale: In pattern, a tiling pattern network formed by overlapping circles.

screen: A wood or aluminum frame, covered with a tightly stretched, durable, porous, polyester or nylon mesh, which will hold a *stencil* firmly and flatly in place. The screen frame gives a printer a way to hold and move a stencil to different areas of the fabric.

screen degreaser: A commercial product that efficiently and effectively removes the dirt, oils, and greasy fingerprints on a screen that might resist the adherence of a block-out.

screen printing: Technique of decoration or image making in which color is forced onto the fabric through a stencil attached to a screen made of fabric mesh stretched on a frame.

seam allowance: Extra fabric left at the edges of pattern pieces to accommodate the space needed to stitch a seam (typically ¼" in quilts and ⅝" in clothing).

seam (noun): The line where two pieces of fabric are sewn together.

seam (verb): The act of sewing two pieces of fabric together.

secondary colors: Those colors about midway between a pair of primaries on the color wheel. In pigments and dyes: red, blue, and green; in light: cyan, magenta, and yellow.

selvedge: The dense edge produced on woven cloth during manufacture that prevents it from raveling.

sgraffito: Drawing or scratching into or through a surface covered with wet paint or textile pigment.

shade: A color to which black has been added, which darkens and de-intensifies the original hue color.

silk organza mesh: A material more transparent than silk organza, though woven with the same thread types, which allows underneath layers to show through. Stiffer, stronger, more opaque, and more substantial than nylon netting, its advantages include easy acceptance of dye and resistance to raveling.

simultaneous contrast: A visual phenomenon in which a single color is perceived differently when set against each new background color (for example, the same yellow will *appear* to be a different color when surrounded by blue than when surrounded by orange).

soda ash: *See* sodium carbonate.

sodium alginate: Pure dried and ground kelp (seaweed), commonly used to thicken food, but also an excellent *dye thickener* for direct-application and screen-printing purposes.

sodium carbonate (soda ash): An effective activator or catalyst for fiber reactive dyes.

split fountain: Screen printing with multiple colors in the screen.

squeegee: Tool with a wooden or plastic handle and a rubber blade used to force a print paste through a mesh in screen printing.

stamping: Means of transferring a design to fabric by pressing a wet color-coated object onto its surface.

steam heat setting: Exposing dyed or printed fabric to steam over a period of time to set dye permanently.

stencil: A material (paper, tape, plastic, etc.) from which certain areas have been removed, allowing colored paste to pass through the holes and transfer the cut out shapes to the surface below the stencil.

stock solution: Powdered dye dissolved in water at a specific chosen concentration and stored for future use.

straight of grain: Straight warp threads in a fabric aligned straight *and* squared with the weft threads perpendicularly. Straight of grain can also refer to aligning the fabric straight and squared with a frame, table edge, template, or other perfectly straight set of perpendicular lines.

string quilts: Another name for strip piecing, a way of making larger pieces of fabric by sewing long, thin strips of fabric together.

strip piecing: A way of making larger pieces of fabric by sewing long thin strips of fabric together. A thrifty way to use up fabric scraps.

studies: Smaller works, often done to scale, that provide a means for working out ideas.

surface qualities: The qualities of a fabric that can be either felt by touching it (such as softness, firmness, elasticity, fineness, resilience, scratchiness, stiffness, smoothness, flexibility) or seen by looking at it (such as density of weave or structure, twist of threads, patterning, decoration, color, drapability).

synthetic fibers: Man-made textile fibers extracted from a variety of both natural and chemical sources, including petroleum distillates and plastics.

Synthrapol: A specially formulated gentle detergent for washing out dyed or printed fabrics that helps keep the colorants from redepositing on preserved white areas of the cloth.

tacking iron: A long-handled electric implement with a small iron (about 3") attached to one end. The iron heats up as any clothing iron might, but is especially nimble for small jobs and tight corners.

temperature (of a color): The relative warmth or coolness of a color. Warm colors are associated with the sun or fire (red, yellow, orange), cool colors with ice, snow, water, or plants (blue, green, violet).

tetradic: Any four colors on the color wheel connected by a square imposed inside it.

thick F: Low-viscosity, high-solids *sodium alginate* thickener for all dyes. Primarily used on silk, wool, and synthetic fabrics when fine line definition is required.

thick SH: High-viscosity, low-solids *sodium alginate* thickener for all dyes. Primarily used for cotton. May be used for silk and synthetics when fine line definition is not required.

thickener: Substance made with gum or starch and added to dye paste to achieve the consistency needed for application to fabric.

tiling shapes: Geometric shapes (such as hexagons, diamonds, scales, and ogees) with complex contours (multiple sides, curves, or arcs) that fit together in repeat without leaving empty space or holes.

tint: A color of paint or pigment to which white has been added, yielding a lighter, chalky, opaque "pastel".

tone: A color to which gray or its complement has been added, resulting in slightly de-intensified mid-value colors.

triad: Any three colors on the color wheel connected by an equilateral triangle imposed inside it.

unit: The figure that is the basic element of a pattern or repeated in a composition.

urea: A synthetic nitrogen compound used to increase solubility and to preserve moisture in printing and painting with dyes.

value: The relative lightness or darkness of a color. High-value colors are light; low-value colors are dark.

value *contrast*: The relative positions of two or more colors on a value scale. Each color has a value that corresponds to a step on the value scale. The *closer* the values of two colors are on the scale, the *lower* the contrast between them. The *farther apart* the values of two colors are on the scale, the *higher* the contrast between them. The highest possible value contrast is between black and white, the two ends of the value scale.

value *scale*: An achromatic sequence from white at one end, through incremental steps of gradating grays, to black at the other end. Standardized value scales are commonly used by photographers, artists, printers, dyers, quilters, and other visual artists to establish the relative *lightness* or *darkness* of colors they are combining.

void: An empty unit in a pattern network or compositional space.

washfast: Resistant to fading with washing.

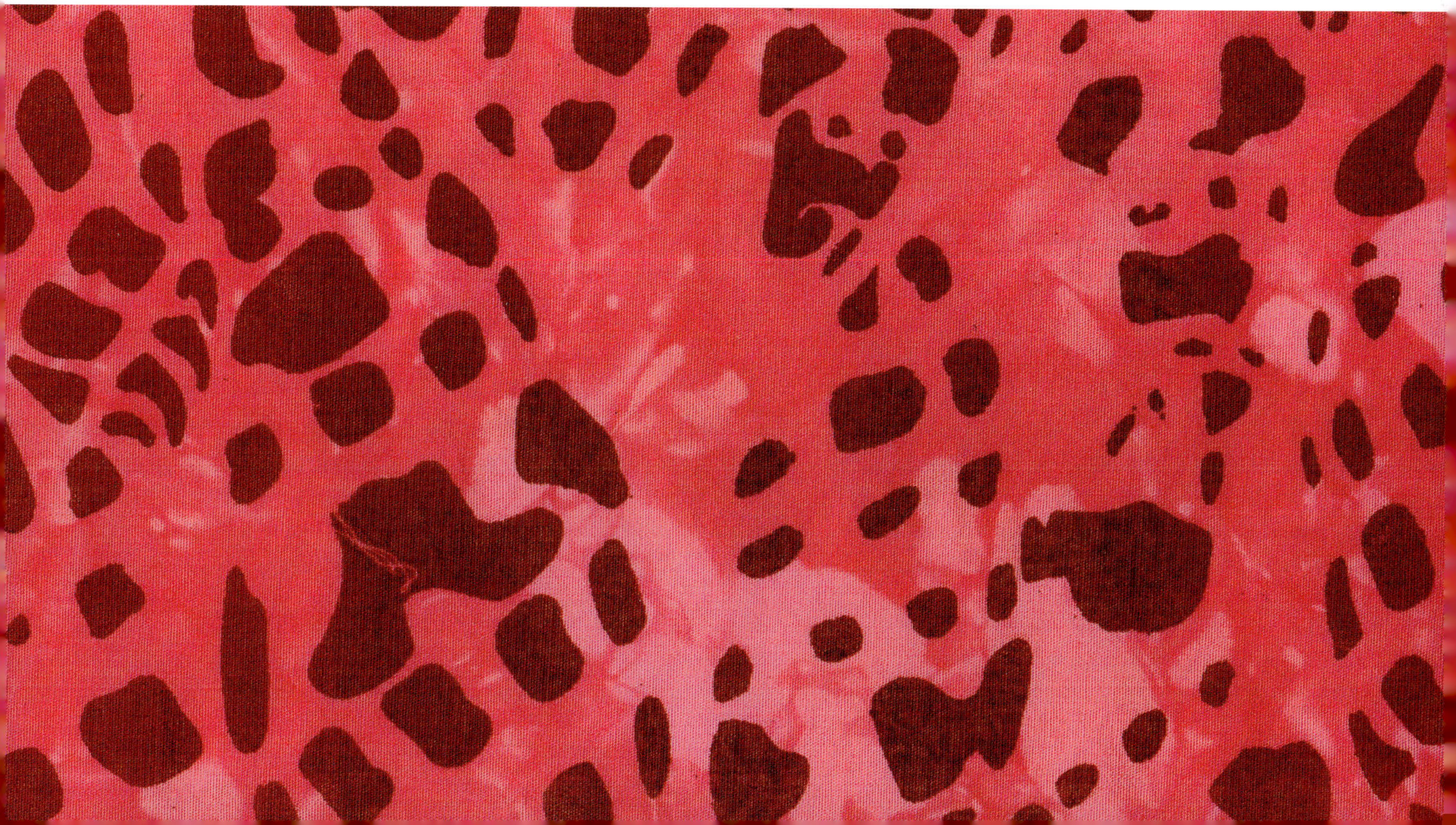

Bibliography

Chapter 1: Dyes and Dyeing

Blumenthal, Betsy, and Kathryn Kreider. *Hands On Dyeing*. Loveland, CO: Interweave, 1988.

Ellis, Catharine, and Joy Boutrup. *The Art and Science of Natural Dyes: Principles, Experiments, and Results*. Atglen, PA: Schiffer, 2019.

Finlay, Victoria. *Color: A Natural History of the Palette*. New York: Random House, 2002.

Flint, India. *Eco Color: Botanical Dyes for Beautiful Textiles*. Loveland, CO: Interweave, 2010.

Galli, Andrew, and Slow Fibers Studio. *Natural Dye Workshop with Michel Garcia: Colors of Provence Using Sustainable Methods*. Video. Berkeley, CA: Studio Galli Productions, 2011.

Johnston, Ann. *Color by Accident*. Lake Oswego, OR: Ann Johnston, 1997.

Johnston, Ann. *Color by Design*. Lake Oswego, OR: Ann Johnston, 2017.

Johnston, Meda Parker, and Glen Kaufman. *Design on Fabrics*. 2nd ed. New York: Van Nostrand Reinhold, 1981.

Kay-Williams, Susan. *The Story of Color in Textiles: Imperial Purple to Denim Blue*. London: Bloomsbury, 2013.

Kendall, Tracy. *The Fabric & Yarn Dyer's Handbook*. London: Collins & Brown, 2001.

Lambert, Patricia. *Controlling Color: A Practical Introduction for Designers and Artists*. New York: Design Press, 1991.

Lambert, Patricia, Barbara Staepelaere, and Mary G. Fry. *Color and Fiber*. West Chester, PA: Schiffer, 1986.

Menz, Deb. *Colorworks: The Crafter's Guide to Color*. Loveland, CO: Interweave, 2004.

Noble, Elin. *Dyes & Paints: Hands-On Guide to Coloring Fabric*. Bothell, WA: Fiber Studio Press, 1998.

St. Clair, Kassia. *The Secret Lives of Color*. New York: Penguin Books, 2016.

Vinroot, Sally, and Jennie Crowder. *The New Dyer*. Loveland, CO: Interweave, 1981.

Wells, Kate. *Fabric Dyeing and Printing*. Loveland, CO: Interweave, 1997.

Chapter 2: Resist Dyeing

Caldwell, Lynne. *Shibori: A Beginner's Guide to Creating Color and Texture on Fabric*. New York: Lark Books, 2006.

Ellis, Catharine. *Woven Shibori*. Loveland, CO: Interweave, 2005.

Larsen, Jack Lenor. *The Dyer's Art*. New York: Van Nostrand Reinhold, 1976.

Lawler, Mickey. *Skydyes: A Visual Guide to Fabric Painting*. Lafayette, CA: C&T, 1999.

Meilach, Dona. *Contemporary Batik and Tie-Dye: Methods, Inspirations, Dyes*. New York: Crown, 1973.

Wada, Yoshiko Iwamoto. *Memory on Cloth: Shibori Now*. Tokyo and New York: Kodansha International, 2002.

Wada, Yoshiko, Mary Kellogg Rice, and Jane Barton. *Shibori: The Inventive Art of Japanese Shaped Resist Dyeing*. Tokyo and New York: Kodansha International, 1982.

Zicafoose, Mary. *Ikat: The Essential Handbook to Weaving Resist-Dyed Cloth*. New York: Penguin / Random House, 2020.

Chapter 3: Direct Application

Aimone, Steven. *Expressive Drawing: A Practical Guide to Freeing the Artist Within*. New York and London: Lark Books, 2009.

Bautista, Traci. *Printmaking Unleashed: More Than 50 Techniques of Expressive Mark Making*. Blue Ash, OH: Northlight Books, 2014.

Borgeson, Bet. *The Colored Pencil*. Rev. ed. New York: Watson-Guptill, 1993.

Cambras, Josep. *Bookbinding Techniques and Projects*. Translated by Michael Brunelle and Beatriz Cortabarria. Hauppauge, NY: Barron's, 2007.

Clayton, Elaine. *Making Marks: Discover the Art of Intuitive Drawing*. New York: Simon & Schuster, Atria paperback, 2014.

Clayton, Ewan. *The Golden Thread: The Story of Writing*. Berkeley, CA: Counterpoint, 2013.

Dodson, Bert. *Keys to Drawing*. Cincinnati: North Light Books, 1985.

Edwards, Betty. *Drawing on the Right Side of the Brain: A Course in Enhancing Creativity and Artistic Confidence*. Los Angeles: J. P. Tarcher, 1979.

Engelbrecht, Lisa. *Modern Mark Making from Classic Calligraphy to Hip Hand-Lettering*. Beverly, MA: Quarry Books, 2008.

Hedley, Gwen. *Drawn to Stitch: Line, Drawing, and Mark-Making in Textile Art*. Loveland, CO: Interweave, 2010.

Impey, Sara. *Text in Textile Art*. London: Batsford, 2013.

Laliberté, Norman, and Alex Mogelon. *Drawing with Ink: History and Modern Techniques*. New York: Van Nostrand Reinhold, 1970.

Laliberté, Norman, and Alex Mogelon. *Drawing with Pencils: History and Modern Techniques*. New York: Van Nostrand Reinhold, 1969.

LaPlantz, Shereen. *Cover to Cover: Creative Techniques for Making Beautiful Books, Journals, and Albums*. New York: Lark Books, 2000.

Lohan, Frank J. *The Drawing Handbook: Comprehensive, Easy-to-Master Lessons on Composition and Techniques Using Pencil and Pen & Ink*. Chicago: Contemporary Books, 1993.

Martin, Judy. *Encyclopedia of Colored Pencil Techniques*. London: Quarto, 1992. Reprinted in 1997 (Philadelphia Running Press).

Moyer, Susan. *Silk Painting for Fashion and Fine Art*. New York: Watson-Guptill, 1995.

Nettles, Bea. *Cooking the Books: A Concise Guide to Bookbinding*. Urbana, IL: Inky Press Productions, 2010.

Nice, Claudia. *Sketching Your Favorite Subjects in Pen and Ink*. Cincinnati: North Light Books, 1993.

Rinehart, Benjamin D. *Creating Books and Boxes: Fun and Unique Approaches to Handmade Structures*. Beverly, MA: Quarry, 2007.

Simmons, Gary. *The Technical Pen: Techniques of Artists*. New York: Watson-Guptill, 1992.

Sussman, Pam. *Fabric Art Journals*. Gloucester, MA: Quarry, 2005.

Weston, Heather. *Bookcraft: Techniques for Binding, Folding, and Decorating to Create Books and More*. Beverly, MA: Quarry, 2008.

Chapter 4: Screen Printing (and Pattern)

Christie, Archibald H. *Pattern Design: An Introduction to the Study of Formal Ornament*. New York: Dover, 1969.

Cole, Drusilla, ed. *Design through the Centuries: 1000 Patterns*. San Francisco: Chronicle Books, 2003.

Cole, Drusilla, ed. *Patterns: New Surface Design*. London: Lawrence King, 2007.

Doczi, György. *The Power of Limits: Proportional Harmonies in Nature, Art, and Architecture*. Boston and London: Shambhala, 1994.

Dunnewold, Jane. *Complex Cloth: A Comprehensive Guide to Surface Design*. Bothell, WA: Fiber Studio Press, 1996.

Dunnewold, Jane. *Improvisational Screen Printing*. Bothell, WA: Jane Dunnewold, 2003 (reprinted 2020).

Elliott, Verda. "Pattern." *Shuttle, Spindle, and Dyepot* 26, no. 4 (Fall 1995): 42–45.

Elliott, Verda. "Pattern, Part Two: The First Twelve Symmetries." *Shuttle, Spindle, and Dyepot* 27, no. 1 (Winter 1995–96): 36–39.

Elliott, Verda. "Pattern, Part Three: The Five Hexagonal Symmetries." *Shuttle, Spindle, and Dyepot* 27, no. 2 (Spring 1996): 30–32.

Elliott, Verda. "Pattern, Part Four: Analysis of Patterns, Point and Border Pattern Types, and Other Ways of Covering a Plane with Pattern." *Shuttle, Spindle, and Dyepot* 27, no. 3 (Summer 1996): 55–59.

Gentille, Terry. *Printed Textiles*. Englewood Cliffs, NJ: Prentice-Hall, 1982.

Howard, Rob. *Gouache for Illustration*. New York: Watson-Guptill, 1993.

Jackson, Lesley. *Twentieth-Century Pattern Design: Textile and Wallpaper Pioneers*. New York: Princeton Architectural Press, 2002.

Jones, Owen. *The Grammar of Ornament: A Visual Reference of Form and Colour in Architecture and the Decorative Arts* (originally 1856). Princeton, NJ: Princeton University Press, 2016.

Joyce, Carol. *Designing for Printed Textiles: A Guide to Studio and Free-Lance Work*. Englewood Cliffs, NJ: Prentice-Hall, 1982.

Laury, Jean Ray. *Imagery on Fabric: A Complete Surface Design Handbook*. Lafayette, CA: C&T, 1997.

Meller, Susan, and Joost Elffers. *Textile Designs: Two Hundred Years of European and American Patterns for Printed Fabrics Organized by Motif, Style, Color, Layout, and Period*. New York: Harry N. Abrams, 1991.

Nakamura, Shegeki. *Pattern Sourcebook: Japanese Style 2*. Beverly, MA: Rockport, 2009.

Phillips, Peter, and Gillian Bunce. *Repeat Patterns: A Manual for Designers, Artists and Architects*. London: Thames and Hudson, 1993.

Proctor, Richard M. *The Principles of Pattern*. New York: Van Nostrand Reinhold, 1969.

Proctor, Richard M., and Jennifer F. Lew. *Surface Design for Fabric*. Seattle: University of Washington Press, 1984.

Stocksdale, Joy. *Polychromatic Screen Printing*. Berkeley, CA: Oregon Street, 1984.

Stroud, Marion Boulton, ed. *An Industrious Art: Innovation in Pattern and Print at the Fabric Workshop*. New York: W. W. Norton, 1991.

The Surface Designer's Art: Contemporary Fabric Printers, Painters and Dyers. Asheville, NC: Lark Books, 1993.

Terashima, Ayako. *Pattern Factory*. New York: HarperCollins, 2009.

Trilling, James. *The Language of Ornament*. New York: Thames & Hudson, 2001.

Valoma, Deborah. "The Impermanent Made Permanent—Textiles, Pattern, and the Migration of a Medium." *Fiberarts Magazine* 32, no. 3 (2005): 44–49.

Watermann, V. Ann. *Surface Pattern Design*. New York: Hastings House, 1984.

Chapter 5: Digital Printing

Bowles, Melanie. *Digital Textile Design*. London: Laurence King, 2009.

Carden, Susan. *Digital Textile Printing*. London and New York: Bloomsbury Academic, 2016.

Linford, Chris. *The Complete Guide to Digital Color: Creative Use of Color in the Digital Arts*. New York: Harper Design International, 2004.

Redmond, Wen. *Wen Redmond's Digital Fiber Art: Combine Photos & Fabric—Create Your Own Mixed-Media Masterpiece*. Concord, CA: C&T, 2017.

Schminke, Karin, Dorothy Simpson Krause, and Bonny Pierce Lhotka. *Digital Art Studio*. New York: Watson-Guptill, 2004.

Threinen-Pendarvis, Cher. *The Photoshop and Painter Artist Tablet Book: Creative Techniques in Digital Painting*. Berkeley, CA: Peachpit, 2005.

Chapter 6: Discharge

Laury, Jean Ray. *Imagery on Fabric: A Complete Surface Design Handbook*. Lafayette, CA: C&T, 1997.

Wells, Kate. *Fabric Dyeing and Printing*. Loveland, CO: Interweave, 1997.

Index

SUSAN BRANDEIS is Distinguished Professor Emerita at North Carolina State University's College of Design and is a member of the university's Academy of Outstanding Teachers. She holds graduate degrees in both art education and textile art and is a studio artist who has been making, exhibiting, teaching, and writing about textile art and design for over 40 years. She founded the Southeast Fibers Educators Association. Her work has been pictured in leading publications in the field and exhibited throughout the United States; in Canada, Great Britain, Japan, Finland, South Korea, Colombia, the Netherlands, and the Philippines; and at the Textile Museum in Washington, DC, and the International Biennial of Tapestry in Lausanne, Switzerland. She is represented in numerous private and public collections, including the Smithsonian Institution's Renwick Gallery. She is also the author of *The Intentional Thread: A Guide to Drawing, Gesture, and Color in Stitch*.

susanbrandeis.wordpress.ncsu.edu